CHILD ABUSE

A Multidisciplinary Survey

Series Editor

BYRGEN FINKELMAN, J.D.

A GARLAND SERIES

SERIES CONTENTS

VOLUME
6

TREATMENT
OF OFFENDERS
AND FAMILIES

Edited with introductions by

BYRGEN FINKELMAN, J.D.

GARLAND PUBLISHING, Inc.
New York & London
1995

Library of Congress Cataloging-in-Publication Data

Child abuse : a multidisciplinary survey / series editor, Byrgen
Finkelman.
    p.   cm.
    Includes bibliographical references and indexes.
    Contents: v. 1. Physical and emotional abuse and neglect
— v. 2. Sexual abuse — v. 3. Causes, prevention, and remedies
— v. 4. Short- and long-term effects — v. 5. Treatment of child
and adult survivors — v. 6. Treatment of offenders and
families
    ISBN 0-8153-1813-8 (v. 1 : acid-free paper). — ISBN
0-8153-1814-6 (v. 2 : acid-free paper). — ISBN 0-8153-1815-4
(v. 3 : acid-free paper). — ISBN 0-8153-1816-2 (v. 4 : acid-
free paper). — ISBN 0-8153-1817-0 (v. 5 : acid-free paper).
— ISBN 0-8153-1818-9 (v. 6 : acid-free paper)
    1. Child abuse—United States.   I. Finkelman, Byrgen.
HV6626.52.C54 1995
362.7'62'0973—dc20   95-753
                                  CIP

Printed on acid-free, 250-year-life paper
Manufactured in the United States of America

CONTENTS

SERIES INTRODUCTION

In 1960 Elizabeth Elmer said of child abuse "little is known about any facet of the problem and that methods for dealing with it are random and inadequate." She spoke of a "professional blind-spot" for abuse and of "the repugnance felt by most of our society for the entire subject of abused children."[1] Two years later, Dr. C. Henry Kempe and his colleagues brought national attention to the problem of child abuse with their article, "The Battered-Child Syndrome."[2] Prior to the publication of that landmark article, the literature on child abuse was almost non-existent. In the three decades since its publication, the research and literature on child abuse have become vast and daunting.

Social workers, psychologists, psychiatrists, counselors, and doctors have studied child abuse in great detail. As a result, we know that child abuse includes physical, emotional, and sexual abuse as well as neglect. Researchers have studied the causes of abuse from both the individual and societal perspectives. There are effective interventions for tertiary remediation of the problem, and there are many prevention models that hold out hope that child abuse can be stopped before it starts. Studies of the short- and long-term effects of child abuse show a range of maladies that include infant failure-to-thrive, learning disabilities, eating disorders, borderline personality disorders, violent behavior, delinquency, and even parricide. We now recognize the need for treatment of child victims, adult survivors, and adult perpetrators of all forms of abuse. Lawyers, legislators, and judges have grappled with the profusion of legal problems raised by protective services and proceedings, foster care, and the termination of parental rights to free abused children for placement in permanent homes. Legislatures have passed and amended statutes requiring various health, education and child care professionals to report suspected abuse, and they have dealt with the difficult problem of defining abuse and determining when the state should intervene to protect children from abusive parents. They have also struggled with the legal and psychological issues that arise when the child victim becomes a witness against his or her abuser. Even the Supreme Court has been called upon to sort out the constitutional rights of victims and criminal defendants and to determine the extent of government liability for failure to adequately protect children from abuse.

The articles in this series document our passage through five of the six stages that C. Henry Kempe identified in his 1978 commentary "Recent Developments in the Field of Child Abuse" as developmental stages in addressing the problem of child abuse:

> Stage One is denial that either physical or sexual abuse exists to a significant extent . . . Stage Two is paying attention to the more lurid abuse . . . Stage Three comes when physical abuse is better handled and attention is now beginning to be paid to the infant who fails to thrive . . . Stage Four comes in recognition of emotional abuse and neglect . . . and Stage Five is the paying attention to the serious plight of the sexually abused child, including the youngster involved in incest . . .

In spite of the voluminous research and writing on child abuse, the sixth and final of Kempe's stages, "that of guaranteeing each child that he or she is truly wanted, is provided with loving care, decent shelter and food, and first class preventive and curative health care," remains elusive.[3] There are many explanations for our inability to conquer the problem of child abuse. In reality, the explanation for our continued inability to defeat this contemptible social problem is as complex as the problem itself.

We continue to sanction the use of violence in the name of discipline. We put our societal stamp of approval on "punishment inflicted by way of correction and training" and call it discipline. But discipline also means "instruction and exercise designed to train to proper conduct or action."[4] It is not difficult to see the inherent conflict in these two definitions when applied to child-rearing. How can we "train to proper conduct or action" when we use physical punishment as a means of training, punishment that we would not inflict upon an adult under the same circumstances?

The courts and legislatures have been unable to find the correct balance between a family's right to privacy and self governance and the need of children for protection. We are unable or unwilling to commit sufficient revenue to programs that combat abuse.

There is also the tendency among many professionals working with abused children and abusive parents to view the problem and solution through specialized cognitive lenses. Doctors, social workers, lawyers, psychologists, psychiatrists, counselors, and educators are all striving to defeat child abuse. However, for the most part, these professionals focus on the problem of child abuse from the perspective of their own field of expertise. The literature on child abuse is spread throughout journals from these fields and in more specialized journals within these fields. It would be impossible for any single person to remain abreast of the developments in all other disciplines working toward a solution to child abuse. But it is also patently clear that the solution to the problem of child abuse is not going to come from any one individual or discipline. It is going to take professionals and lay people from all disciplines, working with knowledge from all disciplines.

An interdisciplinary examination is important in the fight against child abuse. The more professionals know about all aspects of the problem of child sexual abuse, the better equipped they will be to do work within their area of expertise. It is important, for example, for lawyers, working in the midst of the current backlash against child sexual abuse claims, to understand that there is a long history of discovery and repression of childhood sexual abuse. With a full understanding of why this backlash is occurring, lawyers and social service professionals can continue to effectively work against child sexual abuse.

Child abuse is a complex social problem. The issues confronted in these volumes are interconnected and overlapping. It is my hope that bringing together the articles in this series will aid in the fight against child abuse by facilitating a multidisciplinary search for a solution.[5]

NOTES

1. Elizabeth Elmer, M.S.S., "Abused Young Children Seen in Hospitals," *Social Work* 5(4), pp. 98–102 (October 1960).
2. C. Henry Kempe, M.D., F.N. Silverman, M.D., Brandt F. Steele, M.D. and others, "The Battered-Child Syndrome," *JAMA* 181, pp. 17–24 (1962).
3. C. Henry Kempe, M.D., "Recent Developments in the Field of Child Abuse," *Child Abuse & Neglect* 3(1), pp. ix–xv (1979).
4. *The Random House Dictionary of the English Language*, unabridged edition.
5. The articles in this collection may give the impression that child abuse and neglect and child sexual abuse are uniquely American

phenomena. They are not. There is a wealth of similar articles from almost every country imaginable. American sources have been used mainly because of the space limitations and because understanding the American child welfare system is vital to developing a cure for the problem.

VOLUME INTRODUCTION

The articles in this volume address the treatment of perpetrators of physical and sexual child abuse and neglect. Where sexual abuse is concerned, the focus of counselors and other professionals has traditionally been on the psychological and emotional well-being of the victim. Focus on treatment of the perpetrator of sexual abuse came much later in practice and in the literature. This is understandable since cases of sexual abuse are so unpalatable that our societal reaction is to punish the offender (and remove him or her from our midst).

Just the opposite is true in cases of physical abuse. As the articles in Volume 5 demonstrate, treatment of victims and survivors of physical abuse lagged far behind the treatment of sexual abuse victims and survivors. The initial focus in such cases was on stopping the abuse. This led to treatment programs for the perpetrators of physical abuse with belated emphasis on the psychological and emotional well-being of the victims.

John S. Wodarski (1981) explained five major approaches to the treatment of parents who abuse their children. The *psychopathological model* of treatment emphasizes "direct services," including "individual, group and lay treatment, volunteer companions, and self-help groups, all of which focus on the psychopathology of the parent and provide the parent with the necessary supports for maintaining the family intact." The *sociological model* emphasizes "the need for wide-ranging changes in social values and structures." Citing Parke and Collmer (1975), Wodarski noted that in the sociological model prevention of abuse "would require reconceptualization of childhood, of children's rights and of child-rearing." The third approach, the *social-situational model,* "is based upon the assumption that the cause of child abuse lies not in the individual, but in the social situation, which may, in turn, be maintaining abusive patterns of behavior. . . . This model focuses upon the modification of observable behavior in the home environment." Under the *family systems model* "treatment resembles that of the social-situational model in that it too emphasizes changing the family's pattern of interactions and behaviors. However, this model emphasizes that the underlying structure and organization of the family must change to prevent the recurrence of the same destructive patterns." The fifth model, the *social learning approach,* "involves the identification of behavioral goals and specific techniques for achieving these goals, and the use of social reinforcers to facilitate this process." Wodarski criticizes these five approaches for their focus on only certain elements contributing to child abuse. He believes a single focus limits the effectiveness of treatment. Wodarski, therefore, favors a treatment program which focuses on a variety of factors that operate to produce child abuse.[1]

Keith L. Kaufman and Leslie Rudy (1991) reported that "[p]hysical child abuse represents a devastating form of maltreatment which has continued to increase over the past 15 years (based on reported cases)." They noted that "intensive efforts to identify the most effective treatment approaches appear to have been abandoned in favor of prevention and early intervention initiatives." And while they do not question the importance of prevention and early intervention services, they do not believe it will be possible to ameliorate physical child abuse "unless identified abusers receive effective treatment that reduces their potential to reoffend and unless victims receive services which preclude them from becoming part of the intergenerational 'cycle of abuse.'"[2]

Sandra T. Azar and Beth R. Siegel (1990) warned the clinician to "adopt a broadened developmental perspective" of behavioral problems within abusive families. They believe that addressing abuse without confronting other dysfunctional behaviors "will only resolve the most 'visible' of the problems [in these families] and in the long run will not decrease the negative consequences to the child."[3] They reviewed the treatment literature and identified pressing issues facing the field: (1) "the lack of empirically demonstrated ways of dealing with the obstacles to working with this population (e.g., low cognitive functioning, high level of stresses competing with treatment requirements, resistance to engaging in interventions);" (2) "the lack of treatment outcome work with parents of infants and teenagers."

They also found that "behavioral and cognitive approaches to treating abuse . . . show real promise as effective means of changing interaction patterns within abusive families."[4]

Rand D. Conger and Benjamin B. Lahey (1982) discussed the variety of intervention strategies which have been employed to inhibit abusive behavior: "These include traditional psychotherapy as well as procedures specifically developed to decrease parental violence, e.g., parent groups, homemaker services, lay therapists, health visitors, crisis hotlines, parent education, crisis nurseries, and daycare centers. . . ."[5]

Some effective treatment has been as elementary as a mother's group that met weekly for six months. One such group successfully helped mothers overcome low self-esteem, social isolation, relationship problems, and unrealistic expectations of their child. This treatment setting also provided a group for the children who had been damaged by abuse to enable them to begin to overcome some developmental and behavioral problems following abuse. This children's group also proved quite successful.[6]

Vincent J. Fontana and Esther Robison (1976) described a multidisciplinary team of professionals providing medical, psychiatric, and social services in a therapeutic program that provided residential care for the mother and child, behavior modification through corrective child care experiences, and personality changes through individual and group therapy.[7]

Arthur H. Green (1976) also discussed the need for a therapeutic focus on the abused child, which "must be approached gradually and with caution, as the parents feel threatened by a change in their special relationship with this child. They feel a great deal of jealousy and competitiveness with adults who would preempt their parental role."[8]

A therapeutic focus on the child is especially important because of the dynamics of the dysfunctional family. Marvin L. Blumberg noted that the victimized child, "though logically not a prime or causal factor of the hostility that is directed against him, may be a reciprocal stimulus for the continued brutality that he receives. Conscious and subconscious mechanisms provoked him to poor feeding (which usually distresses the mothers), excessive crying, overaggression, lying, stealing, and demanding more attention." An abused school-aged child may also exhibit these reciprocal stimuli. He or she may "develop behavior problems in class, be a fighter, and may seek to be a scapegoat. These actions add further reason and, in the parent's mind, justification for excessive physical punishment."[9]

When reviewing the literature on treatment of physical child abuse, one is struck by the focus of treatment on women. Group treatment is for women, often with a separate group for their children. Residential programs are for women and their children and often exclude the male entirely or allow only visitation. Judith A. Martin (1984) assessed 66 studies of child abuse during a five year period and documented the lack of attention to abusive fathers. This is true despite the fact that "approximately half of. . . physically abusive adults are fathers."[10] Martin attributed the lack of attention to males as physical child abusers to "the impact of powerful cultural expectations concerning the relative roles and responsibilities of men and women in child rearing." He found that "despite many changes in attitudes towards parenting in recent years, the developmental literature points out that women are still considered the child's most important parent, while the role of the father is undervalued. . . ."[11]

Despite advances in treatment of perpetrators and dysfunctional families, studies have shown that the repetition of child abuse is all too common. In a follow-up study of 328 families who received services for physical abuse, sexual abuse, emotional abuse, or neglect over the ten year period 1967–1976 Roy C. Herrenkohl and his colleagues (1979) found that "more than one perpetrator was identified in 44.2% of the validly cited families, and in 45.3% of these families more than one child was abused." Where there was only one type of abuse, they found "the percentage of recurrence is 51.9%, while in families where there are two or three types, the percentages are 66.3% and 85.0%, respectively."[12]

Similarly, Anne Harris Cohn and Deborah Daro (1987) gave a grim view of the success of treatment programs: "One-third or more of the parents served by these intensive demonstration efforts maltreated their children while in treatment, and over one-half of the families served continued to be judged by staff as likely to mistreat their children following termination." While Cohn and Daro admit that these figures are susceptible to a glass half full or half empty type analysis, one cannot dispute their conclusion that we must continue our efforts at prevention of child abuse.[13]

We can see from the articles on physical child abuse in this volume the evolution of the model of maltreating parents discussed by David A. Wolfe (1993):

> Psychological interventions with reported maltreating parents have developed gradually from an individually based pathology model to an all-encompassing ecological model, with an evolving emphasis on the importance of the parent-child relationship and its context. Simultaneously, the orientation toward the treatment issue, . . . has shifted gradually away from a parent-focused, deviance viewpoint and more toward one that accounts for the vast number of stress factors that impinge on the developing parent-child relationship.

The shift Wolfe described "toward a more process-oriented, contextual theory of maltreatment" has placed "greater emphasis on the importance of promoting parental competence and reducing the burden of stress on families."

In spite of what Wolfe considers theoretical advances, he too reports that treatment efforts do not appear to be very effective. This may be because "our child welfare system functions on the basis of reaction to crises and conflicts, and consequently little effort is directed toward the 'front-end' of the child welfare system." Wolfe considers how we might develop an "alternative service delivery for abusive and neglectful families, and provides an overview of the more promising programs that have emerged in recent years based on a family support model of prevention and early intervention."[14]

Much less has been written about treatment of neglectful parents despite the fact that every year "there are more incidents of child neglect than child abuse . . ." and that "child neglect may be as psychologically and physically harmful as child abuse." Indeed, neglected children "lack self-esteem, are unhappy, and have inadequate coping skills. Further, they may suffer physical harm as a result of inadequate nourishment and health care. . . . Finally, children who have been neglected are likely to become neglectful parents, because they lack models for healthy developmental caretaking."

Treatment of child neglect is, however, problematic because "parents investigated by child protective services for child neglect may have far greater difficulty recognizing their deficiencies than parents investigated for and accused of abuse." Parents accused of neglect often lack an "understanding of any public agency's right to intervene in their home when no acts of commission have occurred. Also, they may come from subcultures in which their neglectful child-rearing practices may fairly be the norm."[15]

Professionals disagree about whether or not treatment of adult perpetrators of child sexual abuse is effective. Judith V. Becker and John A. Hunter (1992) reviewed therapy outcome studies on adult sexual perpetrators and were optimistic about treatment outcomes. They believe that treatment "works for some in the short-run and for others in the long-run." They found that further empirical inquiry is needed to determine which therapeutic approaches are most efficacious given various client characteristics and conditions of treatment. They feel that "children in our society will be best served if those individuals who have a proclivity to molest children are identified and treated. Data are now available and should be presented to legislators to inform them that not only is it efficacious to provide treatment to men who molest children, but it is also cost effective."[16]

Jane F. Gilgun (1988) discussed self-centeredness in the adult male perpetrator of child sexual abuse and treatment and prevention methods which target self-centered behavior. Gilgun noted that the "notion of the self-centered and divided self suggests the need for methods which would foster self-acceptance and integration." She felt that treatment should include "remedial nonsexist socialization and sex education."

Additionally, "the sexual perpetrator may be oblivious to the needs of others because of the imperviousness of his or her own sensory deprivation." This might necessitate "long-term exposure to sensory stimulation. . . . Learning to appreciate expression of adult sexuality and sensuality might be an integral part of sensory education." Perpetrators must understand that acting out sexually "was harmful to children, themselves, and many others," and that it "also appears to make the perpetrator feel worse." Therefore, a successful treatment modality must "explore ways of helping perpetrators develop coping strategies which help them feel better and which also are not harmful."[17]

Robert D. Card (1991) discussed the failure of criminal penalties to deter sex offenders and the need to treat sexual offenders independently from punitive measures. He found that "sentencing the offender to a treatment program which mixes punishment with treatment tends to drive sexual problems underground." When this occurs, "we release 'treated' individuals back into society with a high probability that the problem is only partly solved and children may still be at risk."

Card believes that "only treatment segregated from punishment is likely to result in complete confessions and genuine personality changes where further child victimization becomes less likely."[18] Card's observations may be especially important where the adult perpetrator of child sexual abuse is himself a survivor of childhood sexual abuse. It is perhaps unlikely that a perpetrator receiving treatment in a punitive setting will feel the sympathy and support to work through his own childhood trauma and come to see his abusive conduct as a product of his own unhealthy upbringing.

The articles in this volume provide many insights into the treatment of perpetrators of child maltreatment. And while we still have much to learn about treating offenders, many programs offer hope that prevention through treatment can be effective at stopping child abuse—one perpetrator at a time.

NOTES

1. John S. Wodarski, "Comprehensive Treatment of Parents Who Abuse Their Children," *Adolescence* 16(64), pp. 959–72, 959–60 (1981).

2. Keith L. Kaufman, and Leslie Rudy, "Future Directions in the Treatment of Physical Child Abuse," *Criminal Justice and Behavior* 18(1), pp. 82–97 (1991).

3. Sandra T. Azar, and Beth R. Siegel, "Behavioral Treatment of Child Abuse: A Developmental Perspective," *Behavior Modification* 14(3), pp. 279–300, 280 (July 1990).

4. Id. at 295–96.

5. Rand D. Conger, and Benjamin B. Lahey, "Behavioral Intervention for Child Abuse," *Behavior Therapists* 5(2), pp. 49–53 (April 1982).

6. Jacqueline Roberts, Keith Beswick, Bridget Leverton, Margaret A. Lynch, "Prevention of Child Abuse: Group Therapy for Mothers and Children," *Practitioner* 219(1309), pp. 111–15 (July 1977).

7. Vincent J. Fontana, and Esther Robison, "A Multidisciplinary Approach to the Treatment of Child Abuse," *Pediatrics* 57(5), pp. 760–64 (May 1976).

8. Arthur H. Green, "A Psychodynamic Approach to the Study and Treatment of Child-Abusing Parents," *Journal of the American Academy of Child Psychiatry* 15(3), pp. 414–29, 426 (1976).

9. Marvin L. Blumberg, "Psychopathology of the Abusing Parent," *American Journal of Psychotherapy* 28(1), pp. 21–29 (1974).

10. Judith A. Martin, "Neglected Fathers: Limitations in Diagnostic and Treatment Resources for Violent Men," *Child Abuse & Neglect* 8(4), pp. 387–92, 387 (1984).

11. Id. at 391.

12. Roy C. Herrenkohl, Ellen C. Herrenkohl, Brenda Egolf, and Monica Seech, "The Repetition of Child Abuse: How Frequently Does It Occur?" *Child Abuse & Neglect* 3(1), pp. 67–72, 72 (1979).

13. Anne Harris Cohn, and Deborah Daro, "Is Treatment Too Late: What Ten Years of Evaluative Research Tell Us," *Child Abuse & Neglect* 11(3), pp. 433–42, 440 (1987).

14. David A. Wolfe, "Prevention of Child Neglect: Emerging Issues," *Criminal Justice and Behavior* 20(1), pp. 90–111, 91 (1993).

15. John R. Lutzker, "Behavioral Treatment of Child Neglect," *Behavior Modification* 14(3), pp. 301–315, 301–302 (1990).

16. Judith V. Becker, and John A. Hunter, "Evaluation of Treatment Outcomes for Adult Perpetrators of Child Sexual Abuse," *Criminal Justice and Behavior* 19(1), pp. 74–92, 89–90 (1992).

17. Jane F. Gilgun, "Self-Centeredness and the Adult Male Perpetrator of Child Sexual Abuse," *Contemporary Family Therapy—An International Journal* 10(4), pp. 216–234 (1988). Gilgun also advocates non-sexist childrearing (which teaches children to recognize and express their feelings) as a form of primary prevention. It is also designed to be gender-blind: "Boys and girls are encouraged to express their feelings while at the same time they are educated to be respectful of the feelings and rights of others." Gilgun also believes that sex education should be "an integral part of a primary prevention program. Although the connections are not yet clear, the sex abuser's sex education and socialization are likely to contain the explanation as to why sex with children is chosen as a means of stabilizing the self."

18. Robert D. Card, "Sexual Abusers: The Case for Treatment," *Annals of Sex Research* 4(1), pp. 7–21 (1991).

FURTHER READING

Aderman, Joan, and Tom Russell. "A Constructivist Approach to Working with Abusive and Neglectful Parents." *Family Systems Medicine* 8(3), pp. 241–50 (1990).

Card, Robert D. "Sexual Abusers: The Case for Treatment." *Annals of Sex Research* 4(1), pp. 7–21 (1991).

Dougherty, Nora. "The Holding Environment: Breaking the Cycle of Abuse." *Social Casework* 64(5), pp. 283–90 (May 1983).

Gilgun, Jane F. "Self-Centeredness and the Adult Male Perpetrator of Child Sexual Abuse." *Contemporary Family Therapy-An International Journal* 10(4), pp. 216–34 (1988).

Hall, Gordon C. Nagayama, and Richard Hirschman. "Sexual Aggression Against Children." *Criminal Justice and Behavior* 19(1), pp. 8–23 (March 1992).

Herrenkohl, R.C., et al. "The Repetition of Child Abuse: How Frequently Does It Occur?" *Child Abuse & Neglect* 3(1), pp. 67–72 (1979).

Isaacs, Christine D. "Treatment of Child Abuse: A Review of the Behavioral Interventions." *Journal of Applied Behavior Analysis* 15(2), pp. 273–94 (1982).

McGrath, Robert J. "Sex-Offender Risk Assessment and Disposition Planning: A Review of Empirical and Clinical Findings." *International Journal of Offender Therapy and Comparative Criminology* 35(4), pp. 328–50 (Win 1991).

Milner, Joel S. "Physical Child Abuse Perpetrator Screening and Evaluation." *Criminal Justice and Behavior* 18(1), pp. 47–63 (March 1991).

Prentky, Robert A., ed. *Criminal Justice and Behavior* 21(1) (March 1994).

Tuszynski, Ann. "Group Treatment that Helps Abusive or Neglectful Parents." *Social Casework* 66(9), pp. 556–62 (1985).

Watson, Mark J. "Legal and Social Alternatives in Treating Older Child Sexual Offenders." *Journal of Offender Counseling, Services & Rehabilitation* 13(2), pp. 141–47 (1989).

Treatment of Offenders and Families

A PRACTICAL APPROACH TO THE PROTECTION OF THE ABUSED CHILD AND REHABILITATION OF THE ABUSING PARENT

C. Henry Kempe, M.D.

Professor and Chairman, Department of Pediatrics, University of Colorado School of Medicine, Denver, Colorado; Editor, The Battered Child

MANY judges and social workers feel that anyone can turn on to mothering. The fact is that some parents frankly do not like their children. They hate them. We don't find it socially acceptable to let them say so. It is tragic that we don't.

We have faced the problem of parents not getting along and we call that divorce.

We must acknowledge as a socially acceptable situation that a parent can admit she cannot mother her child for one reason or another. Allowing a mother or father to say in a socially acceptable way that try as they may, they cannot tolerate this child, will help us on the way to giving protection to all children.

I would like to now propose the thought that the quality of mothering is a continuum of from none of it to a lot of it. By mothering, I mean not only the female term but a quality of caring for a defenseless young child, giving without limit if you please, to a tiny child, which fathers have in great abundance as well. This quality saves many lives and can be had by maiden aunts and spinsters and people who have never had a baby. For practical purposes we have to face the fact that very few of us, fathers or mothers, have it in us to be "that kind of a mother" 24 hours a day, seven days a week, all year long.

If we have money we can arrange to supplement mothering for pay. If we need respite, we can for money get relief by going off skiing in Aspen, Colorado. If you don't have money, but you have a skill, say you are a physician or nurse or social worker, then we say to you, "Isn't it marvelous that Mrs. Smith went right back to work so soon?" We say this, though we know that she makes very little money compared to the expense of providing for reasonable care for her child. Such a mother has titrated herself properly and has said, "I can be a marvelous mother 16 hours in the day but not 24." We find it socially highly acceptable.

It is the poor, the people who have no money skills, who are expected to be perfect mothers seven days a week. This is very unfair. Judge Kelley does not see middle-class and well-to-do people. She doesn't, and that's not her fault, because the rich have ways of managing their problems very well.

A number of speakers have talked about intervening on behalf of the child. They really mean that it looks like we are intervening on behalf of the child but that we are really intervening on behalf of the family as a whole.

Everything we do' is done on behalf of the family as a whole. When you intervene in the private life of a family which has its right to privacy, you do it on behalf of the family.

Parents do not mean willfully to kill their child. It is a rare family, in more than 750 that we have carefully studied, who means to kill a child. The vast majority of our families, both rich and poor, are people caught in a terrible problem of their own past, each other, the baby, and the crisis.

If this was not the case, there would be many more battered children, because the impulse for battering children is universal. In this city, and I think in mine as well, work on behalf of child abuse has been work in crisis. Either we have a disaster and the child is killed after the court returns it, and then there is a great hue and cry to place all children in care, or the receiving facilities are found to be deficient and then no child is placed in care because

PEDIATRICS, Vol. 51, No. 4, Part II, April 1973

then there is the great feeling that they must all be kept at home.

I would plead with you to develop a different philosophy and get away from crisis planning, to what seems to me a more rational approach.

In Queens or Manhattan in New York City the population is about that of greater Denver, 1,700,000. Looking at populations alone, there are some things that we have tried in Denver that might work very well here. In any case you should learn from our mistakes.

We have made progress in diagnosis. We have made some progress in understanding, in prediction, and in prevention. We've not yet made sufficient progress in disposition, as is your case in New York as well.

The clinical approach to the child abuse problem starts with prediction. Could we predict the risk family? In a book that will be out soon,* we have some evidence that we can predict the families at risk with pretty high certainty. Given a predisposed mother, and finding that she married someone just like her, the odds of that family having a failure-to-thrive child or a child that will be abused, is much higher than in a control case.

What are some of the factors? We have developed questionnaires that we use prenatally. Mothers who are waiting for obstetrical work-up in the prenatal clinic take this test.

We have also developed some techniques at the time that the baby is born. In the very first 48 hours of the child's life, it tells us something about attachment by the mother to a child. You all know this. Physicians just don't want to hear of it. Our nurse says to the doctor: "Mrs. Jones doesn't want to name her baby. She says he's ugly and she doesn't want him." Our intern says, "She'll love him in time." That is the standard answer. Happily she does. Sometimes she doesn't. The mother might cry and cry after this baby is born, even

* Kempe, C. H., and Helfer, R. E.: Helping the Battered Child and His Family. Philadelphia: J. B. Lippincott Co., 1972.

though she wanted just that baby. There are many, many leads in the very earliest contact with the mother and child that we resolutely fail to face. We make every effort not to listen.

We recently had a mother who finally named her child Barnabus. Barnabus, for those of you who don't have children who look at television, is a vampire in a current television series. Our intern not only didn't know this, but insisted that the mother breast-feed. This child was subsequently battered, happily not badly. This was a technical mistake on the part of the physician who should have known better.

What about postpartum prediction? We are doing a very interesting study in Aberdeen, Scotland. Aberdeen is a unique city in many ways. To my knowledge, it has the only child advocate system in the world. Aberdeen has about 3,000 deliveries a year. There are 65 health visitors in Aberdeen. All are very able nurses who go to every house, rich, poor, middle class, knock on the door and say, "How are you, Mrs. Jones?" They are always courteous to the mother. Eventually they have some tea in the kitchen and eventually they see the child and they then do what amounts to an advocacy job for the child. These are highly trained people, but in fact, a good neighbor could do it. In Aberdeen, we do a study at 8 weeks of life, when there is a routine visit. There are some set questions asked. They are:

1. Does your baby cry excessively and does it make you feel like crying?
2. Do you dislike having somebody watch you feed the baby or take care of this baby?

Battering parents are very defensive about being criticized. They have always been criticized. It has been the story of their lives. Their parents criticized them. All people criticized them. They don't like people watching.

3. Does your older child know when you're upset and does she take care of you at that time?

3

This is the reversal of roles that Dr. Helfer discussed earlier. There are no more than six such questions which take no more than five minutes to answer.

We then study every child in Aberdeen that has an accident or fails to thrive. Since Aberdeen has only one hospital for children, they all come to one emergency room and one hospital ward, or if they die, to one morgue. It is a totally closed population in that people don't either move into or leave Aberdeen. I can tell you now that people who are going to have children who have accidents, inflicted or otherwise, answer these questions very differently from matched controls who enter the study because they had a child born the same day who had not had an accident.

Once you identify a family that is at risk, you can successfully intervene.

What is next? If you fail to predict, and the child has a minor injury (not yet a five-star fracture, a periostitis, or subdural hematoma, but just a few bite marks or a few bruises that aren't explained) this is the first chance for the hospital to intervene. In our hospital if there is a discrepancy between the history and the physical findings, the child is admitted. This is very much along the lines that were suggested by Dr. Joyner. We have a team that has been operating very successfully for 16 years, which then makes an effort to find out what is going on.

This includes one or more home visits. That is where the action is, in the home. We find out essentially what Dr. Helfer mentioned this morning: (1) How were the parents raised? (2) How do they see this child? (3) Was there a crisis? (4) Was there no rescue or lifeline during the crisis?

If the clinical findings were suspicious, and if these four points are suspicious, the gray area of diagnosis comes to be very narrow. By and large, we can persuade our courts that the gray area in the civil case of a filing of dependency is not a difficult one. Very rarely is there a substantive question.

When we have lost the first chance of prevention and have lost the second chance of minor injury, we come to the third chance which is major injury. When major injury occurs all reported cases should lead to court filing. Many of you feel specifically that the children's codes in the states mandate them to keep children out of court. It is my own view that the Children's Court in fact mandates them to bring the child to society at large; and to me, society happens to be the judge, fallible though she sometimes may be.

The fact is that society has said the judge shall represent us. I believe that in the final analysis the child must have his day with society and that is the Juvenile Court.

Case work in the orthodox sense, that is a visit once a week for an hour, is insufficient to manage the problem of the family with an abused child. Early on you need a very careful diagnosis of family abnormality. About 80% of our cases are dependent, inadequate, yearning people, such as described by Dr. Helfer earlier.

Another 10% are, frankly, mentally ill. These are paranoid schizophrenics, psychopathic personalities, aggressive psychopaths who don't communicate except through bashing. They in effect don't talk, they bash their friends, their neighbors, and their children indiscriminately. With this group case work can only go on when the child is out of the home. I am not opposed to them getting all kinds of help but the child may not stay in the home.

Over 20 years, we have had tragedy after tragedy with the constant attempt to throw these children at these sick people. It does not work. The risk to the child in terms of specific survival is too great.

There should be accurate psychiatric diagnosis of family abnormality made in every child abuse case.

Psychiatrists or psychiatric social workers can make such a diagnosis. I do not think it is fair to take a general medical social worker and put her in the situation where she must make a major psychiatric diagnosis alone. This should be best done by an interdisciplinary approach in which a psychiatrist, pediatrician, a social worker, and somebody from the court can discuss the case together.

While a lot of skill is required in diagnosis, much less skill is required in treatment if skill is defined in terms of organized, educated, learned kinds of professions. We have given up having anyone get psychiatric treatment or case work treatment in the social work sense in our unit.

Psychiatrists, Dr. Steele and Dr. Pollack who are analysts, have had in analysis a number of people who are rich and motivated and battered their children. They did no better at $35 an hour than we have done with our mothering aides, family aides, who have training in two different ways. They have had the training of having had a loving mother and father. Then they have been a loving father or mother. They have not gone to any courses. They have not had any indoctrination. We pay them $1.35 an hour. I suppose it would be $2 in New York, but even that's cheap; and they do well.

The concept of a child advocate is built into what Dr. Joyner presented. In a sense, his hospital becomes the child's advocate. We've come to feel that there is nothing worse than our own situation in Denver, where a social worker for Child Welfare gets the case from the Hospital social worker who turns it over to the court social worker who works for the probation department who turns it over to the social worker concerned with foster home care. So far that is just four social workers.

You see how this must look from the patient's point of view. She is bounced around from place to place. We call this intake that does not take in.

Protective Services do not protect. What works? I suggest that you try some of the methods that we have tried. Not any one of them is magical. In any case, work out your own salvations.

Dr. Helfer mentioned Parents Anonymous; that is the help, the lifeline help in moments of crisis, that parents give each other who are on the battering circle. This works.

A hot line of some kind, as the one in Santa Barbara and some other places, works. This consists of a telephone that will reliably answer and say, "Tell me more about it, I will come and help you, or bring the child here."

We have two "Crisis Nurseries." These are places where any mother, any time of day or night, seven days a week, can bring a child on her own authority, without calling a social worker or calling the Welfare Department or calling anybody. The child can stay there one hour, one week, a month or year.

You say, if you had that in New York you might have 12,000 children deposited on the doors of the crisis nursery. There are that many people you feel that would want to get rid of their children. The attitude of our society is essentially this. We say to the parents, "You've had your fun, now take care of it."

Now let's think about that a minute from the child's point of view. He didn't ask to be conceived. We don't license people for parenthood. If we did we wouldn't be having all this trouble. We are, in fact, having to face the fact that these people do not want these children terribly much. If they mean to give them up, we should take them. The children deserve better.

The idea that blood is thicker than water and people must take care of their own, is destructive to everyone. Face the reality that mothering will not occur, parenting will not occur, and the child should have another chance. There are thousands of people now, with the abortion laws going as they are, trying to adopt children who would be willing to give such children a chance.

It makes more sense to go that way. We have the use of homemakers who are therapeutic and do not just help with the dishes, but in fact, provide mothering.

Finally, we have mother surrogates who are, to my mind, the most useful therapeutic tool. These are men and women, of all ages, whom we got to use through the Foster Grandparent Program, which is a program of the Office of Economic Opportunity. We have 25 foster grandmothers in our ward who do nothing but rock one child each. These are children who come from long distances in Colorado, whose parents cannot come in to mother them. These same foster grandparents had taken hold of these battering parents and a good number of them, perhaps a third, were found to be highly useful to us. They were not only holding one baby on one arm but they were holding this battering mother virtually on the other. They began to make house calls. This worked into a program which we tried in England and here, and which is very able to do what amounts to a very sufficient job, at very little cost.

How much time does it take early on to do this surrogate mothering? The average number of hours spent in the home the first week is 15. That is not homemaking but just holding hands, being on the phone, coming back, helping with minor problems of getting through life, and being very sympathetic.

The second week the average time is ten hours. The third week it is about four. After that it stays about four hours a week for six to eight months.

It is a lot of time. The surrogate mother has to be available by phone, day and night. She is the recognized lifeline for that family. She tries to give these people, who are damaged, suspicious, unfriendly, and hurt, their first experience in mothering because these people, for better or worse, missed out with their parents. Later on they missed out with teachers and then friends. They never had loving mistresses or lovers and they didn't marry someone very competent to mother them either. They married each other.

We are giving these people one more run through in caring and loving. No social worker in our society has the time to do that. If you carry more than two cases, you are not carrying any in these terms. Therefore, a social worker working for a city institution, that carries 15 or 20 or 30 such cases, is not doing it.

The time involvement is enormous. It is possible to have the case aide supervised and consulting with social workers who are able to keep track of things. I think that is the way to go.

In addition to the crisis nursery, we have day care centers, where mothers can see each other and their children in more positive terms. We do use foster homes as a socially acceptable and highly valued activity. Around the country foster care is not highly regarded. We have not managed in this country to make foster placement a socially attractive and well-paid profession. People that could be working at foster home care for children are working in industry instead.

Obviously, welfare departments could turn this around by paying foster parents enough so it is in fact possible financially to be a foster parent.

Foster home therapy in interim is a very useful approach. If you combine all of these: the crisis nursery, day care facilities, foster home therapy, homemakers, lay therapists, Parents Anonymous and hot line, you can get 80% of the children back home in about eight months' time. Ten percent won't go back for longer. Ten percent will never go back.

We terminate parental rights if we are substantively able to persuade the court that this is a situation where parenting will never occur. We have been able to persuade our courts, based on the best evidence that we can provide them, that this is the case.

In closing, let me say where some problems still are. If a child is wanted by both parents, who love each other and who mother each other, which a good family and a good marriage does, the child is safe. In fact, even a battering kind of parent marrying a different one doesn't batter their child. We must teach in our schools, early on, something about mothering. We teach about mother crafting: how to feed babies and change the babies because we are obsessed with physical care of babies, which couldn't matter less.

What we must talk about is love and mothering. We must accept the fact that some people shouldn't have children and that it isn't necessary for everybody to have a child. We must then recognize that where mothering is inadequate, that we must supplement. In our society it should be possible to titrate mothering quite well, and to supplement it where it is required.

The future is quite bright. We understand the problem much better. We know, I think, what to do. We will be able to predict quite well who is at risk and intervene before anything goes wrong. Medically speaking, we are about there. We have a long way to go yet to coordinate the professions of social work, law, and medicine but I think a start is being made.

PANEL DISCUSSION

DR. FONTANA: Dr. Kempe, could your surrogate mother program be successful in New York?

DR. KEMPE: Absolutely. I will tell you what they do. They go to the home. They generally start out having some coffee in the kitchen. Then they go shopping, help along, listen. They concentrate on the parents, not on the child. They will take them out for a meal. They will do what a good neighbor will do. If they ask for a $50 loan, since they don't have $50 either, that is impossible. If they want a dime, they will lend a dime like a good neighbor would. They send Christmas cards, birthday cards. They do all the things that some social workers were told in school is unprofessional. They do what the social worker in past generations did, which was care. They hand out their telephone number. My bedside telephone number, my wife's, and Dr. Steele's are in the telephone book. We get calls at 2 AM. We think that is a good thing.

In this connection, when do you know that the child is safe to go home? We now have gone through this several hundred times and not had a child rebattered. We used to have a 30% rate. The child is safe to go home:

1. When the parents' self-image has improved. When they think better of themselves. We can sense this by the way they dress and when they have any kind of social life.
2. When they see the child in more positive terms.
3. When they prove to us that they can use lifelines in moments of stress and

they can use the telephone to call one of these three telephone numbers I mentioned.
4. When on weekend visits they have shown that they can handle the child emotionally.

When these four things are done, the child is ready to go home. That will be between three months and eight months. When it isn't done by eight months, it is likely to be quite a long time.

DR. FONTANA: Dr. Kempe, do you suggest physical punishment in reasonable degrees for children, or is "spare the rod, spoil the child" out?

DR. KEMPE: It depends on the mores of our society. I think it will soon be out. Before long, assault and battery will be just that even between parent and child.

DR. FONTANA: Judge Kelley, what services are available to the Family Court in making decisions with regard to an abused or neglected child? Is there any follow-up on a family after the child is returned?

JUDGE KELLEY: The services available are those obtainable through the Probation Department of our own court and also through investigation by the Bureau of Child Welfare. If it is an SPCC case, there has usually been a good and thorough investigation before the petition is filed. This information is available to the judge. The judge can ask for more investigation at that point. As an example, if the judge desires additional information before deciding on placement, the judge can ask for a reevaluation of the home.

Finally, after the judge has gotten all the

information that either public or private agencies can provide, then the decision will have to be the judge's. If the judge wants a follow-up, that can be done very simply by returning a child, but putting the respondents, which would be the parents on probation, with a requirement for report from time to time.

DR. FONTANA: Dr. Joyner, what do you see as the role of the nurse in prevention of child abuse and aid to the parents?

DR. JOYNER: The nurse on the ward can be invaluable in supplying information as to the responsiveness of the child, how the child acts with parents, how often parents visit.

Public health nurses could get involved in the team effort of both the investigative phase and even (if they had time enough, which I have never seen a public health nurse yet have) take over as surrogate mother. I hope we will be able to get a coterie of surrogate mothers. There are certain home conditions in New York where a surrogate mother would not work. In our last case the family had already been in and out of jail. We rarely could see them since every time somebody came to visit them, they thought it was the police, so they went down the fire escape. They were all drug pushers as well as users. This included having forcibly injected an 11-year-old with heroin.

Such cases are fortunately rare. Most of what Dr. Kempe proposed would work in the majority of our cases, but not all of them.

DR. FONTANA: Mr. Cameron, how do you reconcile a statutory obligation to provide for abused and neglected children and for follow-through care as you discussed, with the lack of resources presently available?

MR. CAMERON: How do we reconcile anything today in light of the realities of budget slashes? I think it is about time that we reestablished some of our priorities.

There is a lack of effective training for those asked to do the job. There is also inadequate support both within their own agency and within the community. Dearth of resources is part of the problem.

DR. FONTANA: Dr. Kempe, would you like to give us your feelings on this question?

DR. KEMPE: I disagree to some extent. If we wait for the money, we will wait forever. I am satisfied that the resources in this country have never been gathered together in any reasonable way to excite people to do a proper job. I mean the old and the very young.

Among the old are people who are vegetating away in front of television sets who could be used as resources for these families. We are doing this. We are putting babies that need fostering into homes for the aged, where four or five elderly ladies take four-hour shifts nursing babies and give more mothering than most babies can stand as a matter of fact. The only problem we've had is that some babies don't get enough sleep.

We haven't begun to really get at people who are able to give time. This is what this is about. They have time, and they have love. All you need are those two items.

We haven't been willing as social workers, as physicians, to hand over our sacred skills and our stethoscopes to lay people because we are afraid that somehow or other it is going to devalue our money, our skill. It think it is all wrong. These human skills people gave us because we had the lucky break of having a loving mother and father. We should put them to work. We have done that in reading programs around the country. You have a very elegant program in parts of New York for remedial reading. That same model would serve very well in the area of child abuse.

In this country, churches are standing absolutely empty except for three or four hours a week. They could all be used as day care centers as some of them are. They could be used as crisis nurseries. The manpower really is here.

DR. FONTANA: It may be a little early to make a judgment, but would anyone care to predict whether the incidence of abuse will change if abortion continues to rise? In terms of cases reported there hasn't been any change yet. The incidence of abandonment appears to be down at least 30%.

DR. KEMPE: I think you would not be able to show a great difference yet because abortion is still a middle- and upper-class phenomenon. It is the poor who don't get aborted, who appear in court for child abuse.

DR. FONTANA: Dr. Kempe, what do you see as the most effective role for the visiting public health nurse in attempting prevention and perhaps management of child abuse in a suspicious home?

DR. KEMPE: They do very well with us. We use them extensively. They are most ideal to go into homes, because the public accepts the visiting nurse. She has an entree that very few physicians, social workers, or the police ever have. We also often use them as the parent surrogate if she can take on a few.

You cannot take on more than one or two of these, not just because of time, because of emotional wear and tear. These people wear you out. My wife, who is a very long-suffering, able adult and child psychiatrist, tells me that in her practice, she cannot tolerate more than one or two such clients. That is also true for Dr. Steele and the rest of us. In terms of emotional wear and tear you are better off with just one client at a time. You are going to have to use other people to do the work.

I would add that nobody should ever think that we will ever make these people whole. I think it is naive for any of us, social workers, psychiatrists, pediatricians, to believe so. It is ludicrous. The most you can hope for is that they will get one experience in trusting an adult, and that they will begin to behave differently around their children. If you have modest goals using those criteria you will do very well. If you are aiming for mental health, you can forget that. They are too damaged.

JUDGE KELLEY: Dr. Kempe, I understand that you are saying, you don't make the adult person whole, but do they finally get a glimmer of a feeling of affection?

DR. KEMPE: Very often they do. And that is how you make the decision as to when to return the child to their full custody. When they begin to talk about the child in positive terms, with some pleasure and some joy as their own, and have a better image of themselves, and when they have used lifelines successfully, it is quite safe to send the child home.

Conversely, some never do, and you have got to simply face that. Social workers by and large cannot face the concept that they could fail, that there is no salvation. One of the deep religious parts of social work is that there is salvation.

DR. FONTANA: Judge Kelley, are there any inservice educational programs concerning child abuse and neglect that the judges of the Family Court can be exposed to?

JUDGE KELLEY: We have judicial conferences fairly frequently and we have had conferences on child abuse. Dr. Joyner has joined us at one at the Bar Association last spring. Mr. Isaacs, who is a consultant to the Judicial Conference on the Family Court, has set up several conferences. Dr. Helfer came to the court and spoke about what he and Dr. Kempe have been doing. We have been trying to keep the judges up to date.

DR. KEMPE: Judge Kelley, in Colorado at least, one of our basic problems is that the Welfare Department of some counties essentially prejudges the cases. They decide which case will stand up in court, if I can use that in terms of physical evidence. They figure out what judge will do what.

They have arranged it so they can't lose a case because they bring to the judge only one case in 20. The other 19 they try to handle in-house, and among them we have had some terrible disasters.

I wonder whether there isn't something to be said for a child having his minute in court, even if it is just to the point that the judge says, "I think it is all right, all of you agreeing to leave the child home." I just don't like the idea that there is another judge before you come on the picture who is a 22-year-old social worker who has never had a case.

JUDGE KELLEY: We have done away with trying to pick your own judge. We haven't, however, been able to do anything to get a person to bring a case to court if indeed the social worker thinks it won't stand in court. And it would seem to me that the social worker should somehow, if there is any doubt, leave the decision as to whether there is a case or not to the court.

DR. KEMPE: If the court uses only physical evidence and will not use psychiatric and psychiatric social workers' evidence and if the social worker isn't treated well in court, as they are not sometimes, then I could see the social worker's reluctance to go.

My bias has been that the court is society. The child should have his minute in court. Every case that a physician feels is serious enough to report should come to court in some setting or other, if only to discuss that there is nothing to worry about.

WORKING WITH ABUSIVE PARENTS

A Social Worker's View

by Elizabeth Davoren

Working with the problem of abused and neglected children means being a witness to the effects of violence and—sometimes—death. It means being involved in "parents' rights," "children's rights" and a diversity of views on how to bring up children. These loaded subjects stir the feelings of everyone involved. Reactions range from disgust ("How can anyone hurt a helpless little child?") to identification ("I've often felt like hurting my own child—I don't know what kept me from doing it").

People who identify strongly with parents have found one way or another to ignore child abuse: "It's none of my business," "It really didn't happen," "The child deserved it," "I don't know what to do about it" or "What good would it do to call someone?" People who feel strongly identified with children have also tended to ignore child abuse: "I can't stand to think about it," "It's really none of my business," "I don't know what to do" or "It won't do any good to interfere—it will only make the parents more angry."

The child abuse reporting laws passed during the 1960s are modifying some but not all of that resistance. When parents seriously hurt their children they arouse feelings of anger and a desire for revenge. Yet the fear that punitive action will be taken against parents—by calling the police, for instance—prevents large segments of the child population from being offered possible protection. The reason for this is that most people do not wish to subject parents—whom they see as just like themselves—to police, court or other authoritarian action.

This is why working with parents is becoming increasingly important. It is a proven way of protecting children

---

Elizabeth Davoren is a psychiatric social worker who has worked in the field of child abuse since 1960. A consultant to the Extended Family Center in San Francisco and the San Francisco Child Abuse Council, she is the author of The Battered Child in California—A Survey, *produced under a grant from the Rosenberg Foundation in 1973, and a contributor to* The Battered Child *(edited by Ray E. Helfer and C. Henry Kempe).*

while, at the same time, encouraging recognition of the child abuse problem. When parent and child are treated as a unit in need of help, rather than as wrongdoer and victim, there can be positive results from the recognition and report of child abuse. If reporting child abuse results in treatment, it is no longer perceived as a terrible action taken against the parent.

The child is also safer in every way when he or she is not made the adversary of the parent. The reality of court trials or hearings is such that their outcome may not result in child protection when needed. A child may be returned to a home where he has been abused and where the situation remains essentially unchanged. This doesn't mean that law enforcement is an unnecessary or undesirable tool in solving the child abuse problem. The problem could not be tackled as it has been without the backing of child abuse reporting laws and the use of the court system to enforce them. The police—in some cases the first outsiders to encounter child abuse and neglect—are extremely valuable allies in casefinding, and police help is needed to protect children in some families. However, no matter who the first contact person is, offering abusive parents help and understanding makes more sense than punishing them for what they usually consider to be the proper way to raise children—the way they were raised by their parents.

Why Child Abuse?

Parenting is learned, and battering parents have usually been taught some very potent lessons by their own parents.

• They learned that their survival depended on their ability to conform to their parents' wishes and to perform feats abnormal for their respective stages of development. For example, during infancy they may have had to learn not to cry, not to move while being diapered and not to reach for the spoon while being fed.

• They learned that not only would they *not* be nurtured or cuddled or handled lovingly, but that they were also expected to reassure and comfort their own parents—role reversal as it is called.

• They learned that no matter how well they behaved,

(Continued on page 38)

2

A Social Worker's View—*(Continued from page 2)*

or how much care they were able to provide their parents in this turn-about process, it was never enough. *They were no good and they deserved to be hit.*

• They learned that their parents could not see what they were like, how they functioned, or what their needs were.

• They learned that having children was a way for *parents* to be taken care of and loved.

• They learned that children must be punished to achieve desired results.

• They learned that the day would come when they could release stored up hostility without fear of reprisal.

All they had to do was to survive, grow up, and have children.

This destructive childrearing method, passed on from generation to generation, produces adults who, first of all, have an understandable stake in having children. They want children to provide for them what they tried to provide for their parents. They believe their babies will love them and make them feel better. Since they do not see babies as helpless, taking care of them is not an anticipated problem. The babies will behave, because they know how to make them behave. This misunderstanding of what a child's capabilities are, combined with a willingness to punish as severely as necessary to meet extremely high expectations, often leads to serious physical injury of their children.

Reporting the Parents

If reported for child abuse, these parents—who normally avoid contact with other people—are suddenly brought in touch with a lot of people with whom they have an extremely difficult time in relating. Their incredibly poor opinion of themselves, and their distrust of all others, make it hard for these parents to like or to be liked. They are also frightened and deal with their fright by either acquiescence or threats.

Their acquiescence, based on childhood experiences of being forced to meet parental expectations, is backed by extraordinary sensitivity to the expectations of others. They can be so skillful at saying what they are expected to say that it is often difficult to know when words have been put in their mouths. The parents' ways of meeting expectations result in differing opinions about what "abusive parents are really like," and it also makes workers feel they know or understand the parent better than they really do. This "trying to please" also leads to wrong impressions of the parents' improved child caring capability. One purpose of parents' acquiescence is to get people off their backs, so to speak, so they can live their lives without interference by others, bringing up their children in the only way they know how—by making harsh demands.

So much for acquiescence. Parents can also be very threatening, particularly when told they are being reported for child abuse. They feel blamed, picked on, and interfered with in an area that they regard as no one's business but their own—how to raise their children. Often workers can't help but feel accusatory or vengeful for what the parents have done to their child. They also feel uneasy about interfering in the time-honored sanctity of the parent-child relationship. This all adds up to a situation in which workers may find themselves confronted by people who don't like them, who are threatening them, and whom they find it hard to like.

Workers need to realize that in most cases threatening parents appear to be far more in control of the situation than they really are. Understanding and empathy go a long way toward reducing the parents' fright and, in turn, their anger. Questions like: "What did your child do that upset you?", "Is your youngster hard to handle?" and "Does your baby need too much attention?" can show parents that their feelings count. At the same time, questions like these help workers find clues to both parent-child interaction and the parents' need for help.

Another way of relieving tension around abuse reporting procedures is to make sure the parents have an accurate picture of what is going to happen to them. If there are specific people who can help them, such as a public defender, they should be told who is available. Offering practical and specific help in contacting family members, finding child care for other children in the family and obtaining transportation—or simply thinking through with parents how they can do these things—will help them be more open to treatment.

Treatment

The kind of help abusive parents have responded to involves relationships that are more intense and more personal than the usual professional therapeutic relationships. Some call it "reparenting" or nurturing. What it means in practice is fulfilling parents' needs in the following areas:

• Parents need help to feel good about themselves, to make up for the devastating belittling they've experienced in their own lives.

• Parents need to be comforted when they are hurt, supported when they feel weak and liked for their likeable qualities—even when these are hard to find.

• Parents need someone they can trust and lean on, and someone who will put up with their crankiness and complaining. They also need someone who will not be tricked into accepting their low sense of self-worth.

• Parents need someone who will not be exhausted with them when they find no pleasure in life and defeat all attempts to help them seek it.

• Parents need someone who will be there in times of crisis and who can help them with their practical needs, by leading them to resources that they can use or by giving more direct help.

• Parents need someone who understands how hard it is for them to have dependents when they have never been allowed to be dependent themselves.

• Parents need someone who will not criticize them, even when they ask for it, and who will not tell them what to do or how to manage their lives. They also need someone who does not need to use them in any way.

• Parents need someone who will help them understand their children without making them feel either imposed upon by having to understand what they cannot, or stupid for not having understood in the first place.

• Parents need someone who can give to them without making them feel of lesser value because of their needs. Parents need to feel valuable, and eventually they need to be able to help themselves and to have some role in helping others.

Worker Characteristics

Working with abusive parents is as demanding a job as the list of parents' needs implies. It requires workers who are themselves exceptionally sensitive to other human beings, who can accept hostility and rejection without being devastated by it and without feeling the need to retaliate. It requires workers who will not be critical of the parents' behavior and who can feel at ease with parents' criticisms. It also requires workers who can share themselves without sharing their problems and who can befriend while maintaining awareness of their helping role. Workers must also be able to think first about the parents' needs and not their own, and they should have a sense of self-worth and achievement that will sustain them through work that is demanding and brings few immediate rewards.

Even when workers feel strong within themselves, and have reasonably fulfilling lives of their own apart from their work, the nurturing of abusive parents can be quite exhausting. The parents' needs are extensive—at times like bottomless pits. Workers calling on their own emotional resources are constantly aware of themselves, their own upbringing and the way they are raising their own children, if they have any. This awareness can be wearing. But the most draining part of caring for these parents is knowing that a child may be seriously injured or neglected, or even die, if the worker misjudges the parents' capacity to care for the child.

15

Workers' unreal estimates of how much parents have been helped and how well they are doing have sometimes proved fatal for children. Moving abuse cases from one worker to another, or one agency to another, has resulted in losing track of the cases—and in fatalities, too.

Some communities are using interagency committees or multidisciplinary teams to keep track of abuse cases, and to provide workers with a support system in making decisions on diagnosis, treatment and final disposition. The composition of such a team depends upon who deals with child abuse problems in the community, but in general the fields of medicine, law enforcement, education and social service are represented. Involving consumers—abusive parents who have had treatment—adds an important dimension to the team.

The teams provide interdisciplinary education for their members and can serve to educate the community as well. But most of all the use of such teams means that the workers who handle child abuse cases, and the agencies they represent, are no longer making what can be life and death decisions without others to help and share responsibility.

Workers need on-the-job support, too. Ways of providing such support vary from conventional supervision and staff meetings—where workers describe their cases, discuss their feelings about them and seek advice—to staff get-togethers where newer techniques of role-playing, validation exercises and facilitating are used to raise levels of consciousness and to allow group support for each worker who needs it. Some agencies also limit the number of child abuse families each worker may carry to one, two or three, with less demanding cases rounding out their loads.

Supportive Services

Supportive services now in use include homemaking services, emergency funds, emergency shelter care, 24-hour telephone hotlines, child day care, 24-hour crisis nurseries, parents' groups and visits by public health nurses. These help families directly and prevent the worker from having to shoulder all the burdens. Supportive services also bring more people into the lives of the families. This diminishes the need of the family to gain so much from one worker and, at the same time, enriches the family's life by providing new contacts and experiences.

Homemakers are ideal if they can cuddle the young and make them comfortable without freezing out the parent. Their role amounts to demonstration parenting. Done well, it gives the parents a feeling of being cared for, too.

Public health nurses, trained and given supervisory support, can be the primary workers in child abuse cases. A public health nurse can also function as the person responsible for keeping a very close watch over the children so that the family's worker can focus on concern for the parents. Health services are usually easy for the parents to accept.

A hotline, available 24 hours a day, 7 days a week, is a necessary adjunct of treatment.

Day care is one useful way of relieving the parent from too close contact with his or her child while at the same time providing more nurturing for the child. The day care staff can be strong allies of the parent's worker, if they have the time, capacity and know-how to help parents better understand their children. A staff that can also recognize the parents' capabilities is invaluable. Day care staff members, however, almost always identify so strongly with the children that being able to understand the parents' needs, and then to help meet them, is very difficult. Perhaps the most that can be expected of the staff is that it *not* compete with the parents for the child's loyalty, and that it *not* let the inevitable parent complaints about how staff members deal with the child threaten them.

Crisis nurseries can relieve parents by their immediate availability in times of unresolvable parent-child tension. They safeguard the child and allow parents distance and time to discover more about the source of their tension, be it the child or something else. A positive attitude of nursery staff members toward the parent helps, of course. Their concern is with the child, and asking them to do much for the parent in the temporary crisis situation is out of place. But alliances for abusive parents develop in unexpected ways, and with each exposure to a person who might want to help comes the possibility of the parents finding the kind of support that is right for them.

Emergency shelter care deals with parent-child crises without separating parent and child, since a shelter will have a full time staff to care for the child if necessary. Rarely available, emergency shelter care is ideal. It can allow the parent to separate from the child for part or all of the day, whichever seems best, but it does not make complete separation necessary as a part of relief and treatment. A shelter staffed by treatment people can observe crisis behavior and either intervene when necessary, at an especially meaningful time or, in less threatening situations, allow the crisis to run its course.

Parents groups provide the opportunity for parents to get together to share their frustrations and to support each other, usually under the guidance of trained leaders. Most groups are mothers' groups. Some mothers are experimenting with including older children in their groups. Fathers are often overlooked. They tend to be less available because they work and because childrearing is traditionally thought to be woman's work. Many fathers will not involve themselves in therapy, which they see as a put-down. If there is some way they can be involved as decision makers, their participation is more likely.

Emergency loans "put one's money where one's mouth is." This is an extremely important attitude in our culture. Being able to give money can mean handling stress situations which have no other solution. It establishes the worker as a person who is sensitive to the "real" needs of the parent and it can also reinforce the parent's feeling of being nurtured in ways no other service can.

These are a few of the supportive services that can help both parent and worker. Others, not listed here, can be adapted to the needs of abused children and their families. By sharing the know-how of child abuse treatment with staff members of various community services through seminars, training programs or written material, we can expand the growing list of facilities that can help the abused child and his or her parents.

40

Meeting the Parents

When the parent's first contact is with hospital trauma workers or protective service workers who are trained to understand abuse and neglect, intervention has a more useful beginning. Offering help to people who don't believe there is such a thing, or don't believe they need it, requires more than an average amount of skill. If the worker who does the reporting or takes the complaint to the parents is also to treat the parent, he or she will need even more skill and much more self-assurance.

Being able to stay with the parent throughout the reporting process, and going to court with them when that is necessary, can strengthen a relationship, provided this is done well and with sensitivity to the potential for parental acquiescence. Having one worker report and a different worker treat has the advantage of giving parental resentment a focus outside of the treatment relationship. But parents who are forced to see many people in the course of referral for child abuse, and to go through their

Foster Placement of Abused Children

by Elizabeth Davoren

Foster placement has often been the only resource available to protect children who are at risk. However, while foster placement at its best can be a very important treatment resource, it has its disadvantages.

For a child who is old enough to be aware of his surroundings, removal from home and placement with a stranger can be very frightening, more frightening often than the unstable or threatening home he or she knew. In addition, a family whose relationships are already very troubled is more traumatized by enforced separations than most families would be. Later, when children are returned to their home after the separation, they may be scolded or punished for behavior which the parents then see as caused by the foster parent. If the children have identified with the different values of the foster home they are rebuked for that, too. In fact, when foster parents are underpaid and overworked, what help they can give to a child, short of prevention of severe physical and nutritional injury, may not be enough to make up for the damage caused by the separation.

One problem arises because foster parents usually pride themselves on taking better care of a child than the child's natural parents. This concept, understandably gratifying for the foster parents (sometimes making up for poor pay and long hours), can be very disruptive to the natural parent-child relationship. It reinforces the parents' poor image of themselves in the very area where better self-concept and performance are essential: namely, child care. There is every reason, however, to believe that foster parents can take just as much pride in helping the child and parent get on better with each other. Instead of being cast in the role of a separating person who nurtures the child and regards the parent as an intruder, the foster parent can be nurturer for parent and child and a model for good parenting.

Another problem is that foster parents are often especially curious about the details of physical abuse and natural parents are—understandably— unhappy to have such information shared. The more severe the abuse, the harder it is for the parent to admit his role and talk about it. By providing information about the parent and his personal hardships, the protective service worker can redirect the foster parents' curiosity to the source of the trouble and enlist their help. Getting the natural parents to share some of their personal problems with the foster parents can also bridge a large gap. The story of Erica and her daughter Jennifer illustrates how, at its best, foster family care placement can help both parent and child.

Throughout the court hearing and all the interviews such intervention entails, Erica had maintained that the cause of her 5-month-old daughter's severe injuries was unknown to her. She considered the psychiatrist and social workers assigned to "help" her unfair, unfeeling and useless, and she was not able to benefit from the contacts. In the meantime, Jennifer was placed in a foster home. At first, Erica avoided the home because she was ashamed and afraid of what the foster mother would think of her. Her husband George did not visit either, feeling little attachment to the baby and no responsibility for her care. But Erica began to worry that she would be thought an unfit mother for not visiting and so she did. To her surprise, the foster mother was a sympathetic person, who talked with her about the baby's behavior, not about what Erica "had done." The foster mother, who liked to sew, made a kerchief for Erica and she invited Erica and George for meals from time to time. Soon her parents began to give Jennifer her baths and to do other things for her. These activities not only helped them feel closer to Jennifer but also relieved the foster mother of much of Jennifer's care. As soon as possible, Jennifer went home for visits. Gradually, the home visits lengthened until she was able to be home for good.

Jennifer's return to a safe home was expedited by the protective service worker's ability to support the foster parents in doing what she could not herself do to help parents and child and by the relationship that developed between the foster parents and Jennifer's family. The active and close contact maintained between parents and child during placement and the generous spirit of the foster parents, which led them to share the warmth of their home, their skills and, most of all, the care of Jennifer with the parents, was a crucial factor in returning Jennifer to her home. ∎

17

story over and over again, are likely to be much harder to reach with an offer of help. To take an extreme situation—but one that actually happens—parents may be seen first by an emergency room physician, who has seen the injured child, then a medical social worker, who prepares them for the fact that the injury must be reported, by a policeman who responds to the report that has been made, and then by a juvenile police officer, a probation worker and a protective service intake worker—all before being assigned to the protective service worker who will continue seeing them. Even if all people interviewing the parents are understanding, it takes a lot more strength than most people have to go through all those explanations and interviews. Such "institutional abuse" of abusive parents is a poor way to get started.

Beginning Treatment

Being able to reach out to parents is an essential part of treatment. In many situations the first thing parents need is someone who is willing and able to go to a lot of effort just to see them. Home visits are not only useful in themselves, but may be the only way workers will get to see the parents at all—at least in the beginning. With parents who avoid involvement by disappearing when the worker is expected, or by hiding and not answering the door, or by focusing their attention on television during the worker's presence, patience and persistence are important. Going back again and again, insisting upon contact of some sort, is often necessary with these parents. Being able to offer the specific practical help already mentioned under supportive services is a meaningful way to start, but such help may not be available.

Sympathetic, responsive, non-judgmental listening is an extremely valuable service. People who have never been listened to before will find it hard at first to believe that anyone is interested in what they have to say. Convincing parents that talk is useful is a tough way to have to begin a treatment that uses talking as its main tool, but it can be done. Friendly chatting is an icebreaker.

Workers need to find their own ways of relating to parents because genuine, honest, forthright behavior is the only kind that means anything to them. Such parents quickly spot pretense. When a parent feels threatened or angry or distrustful, or all three, the reaction may be hostile silence. A sincere worker may be genuinely ill at ease and find it hard to think of what to say. But it doesn't matter if the words seem silly or not right because wanting to do right is what comes across. The important point is that parents matter: they are a necessary part of the program and will determine what happens in treatment and its outcome.

Showing honest respect for the parents and their capabilities helps put parents at ease and parents need to feel at ease if they are to engage in a useful dialogue. Information given by parents early in the contact is often unreliable. For one thing, these parents have been wrongly perceived so often by their own parents that they are confused about themselves. They "misperceive" themselves, so to speak. Furthermore, when they don't trust their workers—and they usually don't—incorrect information may serve as a camouflage and a protection from feared punishment. Or they may simply be trying to say what they think they are supposed to say. When two workers are seeing the same parents they are often astonished by the different impression each gets of the parents—based on the completely different stories parents tell them. As parents feel more trusting, talk becomes more useful to both parent and worker and what is said is usually more realistic.

There is no orderly progression to treatment. Much needs to be worked on simultaneously. For instance, exploring what parents want for themselves can be done more successfully after parents feel more trust. However, exploring what parents want shows them that their opinions matter, which in turn helps them develop trust.

In the beginning abusive parents are less likely to know what they want to accomplish for themselves because they don't believe they are capable of doing anything. They usually wish passively, but without much hope, to have things done for them. They will say that they want their children back—if the children have been placed—no matter how they feel about placement. They will wish for a better place to live or new clothing or a vacation. But beneath these layers of wants or desires lie others. For example:

• A mother of two repeatedly injured, poorly cared for children had been raped by her father when she was 10. Years of promiscuity followed, then prostitution, then procuring, then prison. Actually, she wants a kind of respectability that will allow her to approve of herself. She wants her marriage to be monogamous and her family to be respected in the community.

• A mother of four was adopted when she was young by parents who later totally rejected her. She wants to be able to give up one of her children, toward whom she alternately feels murderous rages, apathy and guilt because the child continuously reminds her of her inability to cope with certain aspects of her life. She has to know that her child will not be rejected by adoptive parents.

• A brain-damaged mother of two children, abused by her own mother and father, wants to be able to function as a reasonable, competent adult. Among other things, she wants to learn to read.

• A father of two, brought up in an orphanage and beaten there, wants to feel more comfortable with others. He needs relationships with people who will understand his need to depend on others.

• A mother of three, who has been brain damaged by child abuse herself, causes her own child to have a fractured skull. She wants to learn how to mother well and to bring up her child herself.

• A mother of two children finds comfort in a life without children and would like to place them permanently, something she can only seek to do after she is able to accept her desire without feeling guilty about it and without being fearful of social ostracism for not wanting to raise her children.

• A mother brought up by a grandmother, because her own mother beat and neglected her as a child, loses her

42

first baby. Child abuse is suspected. A second baby is injured shortly after birth. Now, the mother wants no children under age five to care for. She wants to be alone with her husband and she wants her mother to care for the baby.

Parents who are beginning to take their own needs seriously can begin to think of their children's needs. But before they reach that point they will need some special care.

A Declaration of Dependence

Encouraging parents to depend on the worker is a key part of the reparenting process. Dependence sometimes frightens workers. They see themselves being used up, or they fear they will have to take care of the parent's overwhelming needs forever. Some treatment approaches have even emphasized the importance of self-reliance. However, abusive parents usually have a lifetime of unsuccessful self-reliance behind them. As children they were used to taking care of the adults in their lives, as well as having to take care of themselves. If not helped out of old habits, they can neither care for children nor seek worthwhile self gratification. Dependence allows parents the nurturing that permits them to grow.

The more people involved in nurturing parents the better. Parents who are together in groups can do a great deal for each other. They feel more comfortable with each other and they are more readily available to each other. When groups exist and parents can use them, they provide a tremendously important adjunct to therapy, or therapy itself. The most devastated parents, however, need help before they can join a group and almost all parents need individual attention in addition to group help.

Services come in handy when meeting dependency needs. Tender Loving Care = TLC = Transportation, Lending money, Child care. If services are not available elsewhere and workers are able to give some of these services themselves, it can be well worth the time. Chauffeuring, for instance, is considered nuisance work by many, but some of the best interviews take place in the casual giving atmosphere such service creates.

Parents' self-esteem is increased by the caring process. Having their needs met says to them that they are important. If there is no way to give services, or they are not required, there are other ways to communicate care. Being on time for appointments, for instance, even with parents who forget appointments or are not on time themselves, tells them they matter in a way that no words can.

The Next Step

As parents begin to feel worthwhile, as they begin to trust and depend on their workers, they tend to be more honest about their feelings. They also feel more friendly toward their workers and others. This is a good time to find ways of helping them include more people in their lives—if they haven't already done so on their own. They may be able to do more for their children, though they may complain more about the children at the same time. Complaining is one way to release angry aggression—usually a much better way than has been used in the past.

Questioning parents about their children—what they expect of and want for them, what changes they notice in them, what they enjoy most about them and when they feel most stumped about knowing what to do with them—will give the worker many clues. Parents who are ready to explore these questions are often at a stage when they can allow their children to be more dependent, while at the same time demanding less from them. They are also ready for their children to have more people in their lives. In other words, the children can have something for themselves, without the parents feeling excluded or put down. Giving parents specific information about child development and what they can realistically expect of their children is useful at this stage. Telling them how to take care of their children is another matter. Respecting parents' ways of dealing with their children is not always easy. This does not imply that workers should ignore or accept abusive behavior. Although the feelings that cause a parent to abuse a child are accepted and understood from the beginning, their acting on those feelings is clearly not acceptable.

With support and acceptance, parents' threshold of anger may be lowered appreciably. This can result in their being less angry with their children. If at the same time aggression can be funneled into productive, even pleasurable, activity that is even better. Workers, of course, cannot do this for parents, although they can let parents know what resources are available to them. As all other people, abusive parents have ups and downs, some of which are totally dependent on events over which they have no control. Although poverty is no direct cause of child abuse, money crises—as other crises that make parents feel helpless and powerless—can result in child abuse. At times of severe crisis, a drop-in nursery, a shelter home, or an emergency foster home may be the only way to prevent child abuse.

Conclusion

Although the success of treatment will be judged by what happens ultimately to the abused child, the protection of that child will depend upon the well-being of the parents or caretakers. This is why the treatment efforts described here have focused on the parents and their need for support and understanding.

The desire to punish parents who have abused their children, particularly when the abuse is severe, dominates those who do not understand the causes of child abuse. Understanding is necessary not only of the parents, but of the workers as well. The capacity of workers to deal with the difficult problem of child abuse will depend on their individual strengths and the support of their efforts by a system and people in the social service and other systems who are not consumed by the pressure of power struggles. As Desmond Morris points out in *The Human Zoo*:

"The viciousness with which . . . children . . . are subjected to persecution is a measure of the weight of dominant pressures imposed on their persecutors." * ∎

* *The Human Zoo* by Desmond Morris, Dell Publishing Co., 1971.

WORKING WITH ABUSIVE PARENTS

A Psychiatrist's View

by Brandt F. Steele

The following article is excerpted from the forthcoming OCD booklet, Working with Abusive Parents from a Psychiatric Point of View *by Brandt F. Steele, M.D. The booklet is one of a series of six being published by the National Center on Child Abuse and Neglect for use by professionals, community leaders, national organizations and others concerned with child abuse and neglect.*

The actions of parents or other caretakers which result in abuse of infants and children do not fall into any standard diagnostic category of psychiatric disorder, nor should they be considered a separate specific psychiatric disorder themselves. Yet to consider child abuse as a derailed pattern of childrearing rather than as a psychiatric disorder does not mean that abusing or neglecting parents are free of emotional problems or mental illness. They may have many psychiatric disorders, much the same as the general population.

Abusing or neglecting parents have about the normal incidence and distribution of neuroses, psychoses and character disorders which exist rather independently and separately from the behavioral patterns expressed in abuse of their offspring. Such psychiatric conditions may warrant appropriate treatment in their own right regardless of the coexistence of patterns of abuse.

There is a small group of abusive parents (less than 10 percent of the total) who suffer from such serious psychiatric disorder that they may be either temporarily or permanently unavailable for treatment of the more subtle problems of abuse. Among such conditions are schizophrenia, serious postpartum or other types of depression and incapacitating compulsive neuroses, with or without phobias. Ideally, such persons should be screened out of the regular treatment program and given inpatient or outpatient care as necessary. Also in this group are those parents who suffer from severe alcoholism, abuse of narcotic and non-narcotic drugs or from significant sexual perversion, and those who have been involved repeatedly in serious antisocial violent or criminal behavior. Such troubled persons need much more intensive, prolonged psychiatric care and social rehabilitation than can be provided in the usual child protective program. Until such measures have been accomplished, it is futile to try to alter the pattern of abuse.

It is obvious, then, that psychiatric consultation should be available in all situations where workers are dealing with the problem of child abuse and neglect. Proper psychiatric screening procedures ensure that the most troubled parents will receive the appropriate type of care and also protect workers from spending enormous amounts of time and energy on problems which require other special kinds of intervention. Working with such disturbed parents should never be delegated to the usual worker in child protective agencies. It is unfair to child, parent and worker, and the results are usually unhappy for all concerned.

A few words must be said about the socioeconomic status and racial background of abusing families. Unfortunately, because so many of the early reports and descriptions of child abuse came through welfare agencies and municipal hospitals it became a common belief that abuse and neglect of infants were associated with racial minorities and poverty-stricken groups of people. Such ideas still persist in many quarters, despite the increasing knowledge that child abuse and neglect occur among families from all socioeconomic levels, religious groups, races and nationalities. These facts should not be interpreted to deny the profound effect which social and economic deprivation, housing problems, unemployment, and subcultural and racial pressures have on the lives and behavior of the caretakers who abuse and neglect their children. Any stress can make life more difficult, and the ramifications of poverty can make anything worse than it would otherwise be. Such factors may be, and often are, involved in one way or another or in varying degree in many cases of abuse. They must be considered in every program of treatment of the families in which abuse occurs and appropriate actions and remedial measures undertaken through social case work, psychotherapy, counseling, vocational rehabilitation, financial aid, or any other method available to the agencies involved with the family.

21

A word of caution is appropriate, however: no matter how necessary and useful it might be to improve the socio-economic status of parents, this should not in any way be confused with treating the more deeply seated personal character traits which are involved in abusive behavior. It is well recognized that individual acts of abuse may occur when the parents are faced with a crisis in relation to finances, employment, illness and so forth, but such crises cannot be considered adequate causes for abuse. Crises of this kind are equally common in the lives of many people who never display abusive behavior and, on the contrary, abuse can occur in families who are wealthy, well educated and well housed. The role of crisis as a precipitating factor in abusive behavior is an important one, however.

Working With The Parents

The first task faced by all those who try to work in the area of child abuse, regardless of professional background or lack of it, is that of coming to peace with one's own attitudes toward the problem of abuse and neglect of infants and small children. It is very emotionally disturbing to see a seriously injured or neglected baby, and we usually respond in either of two ways when confronted with the situation. We may disbelieve that such a thing could actually be true. We deny that parents could really have attacked their own offspring and that some other explanation for the situation must be found. Alternatively, if we do believe actual facts of what has happened we tend to have a surge of righteous anger and feel disposed to scold and punish the parents. Obviously, neither of these attitudes is useful in trying to do something to better the situation and help the parent improve his method of child care. Denial precludes any chance of dealing with the problem, and long experience of many people has indicated over and over again that criticism and punitive attack of the parents have adverse effect and no real therapeutic value.

Most useful in eliminating to the highest degree possible an attitude of anger toward the parents is a knowledge of how the parent's own life and difficulties help in understanding why he happened to become an abusive parent. Probably the thing which is most helpful in producing an understanding non-punitive stance in the one who is working with the abusive parent is to realize that one is not working with an abusive parent as much as one is working with a grownup person who was in his own early life a neglected or abused child himself. This one basic premise is probably the most important thing to keep as an organizing principle in the back of one's mind as one is trying to understand and work with abusive parents, regardless of one's own professional training or type of approach.

Characteristics and Problems of Abusive Parents

For most abusive parents their immaturity and dependency is essentially functional in nature and related to the emotional deprivation endured in early life. Hence it can be remedied to a significant degree by more rewarding and more satisfying experiences in adult life, especially those occurring during carefully managed therapeutic working relationships. However, it is necessary to keep in mind

another cause for the inadequacy and inept parenting behavior. A small but significant number of children who were abused or neglected in their earliest years suffered organic brain damage due either to head trauma or to malnutrition during critical growth periods. As a result they had perceptual defects, diminished IQ and significant delay in language development. These deficits may produce in later adult life a condition characterized by significant lack of basic knowledge and attitudes of helplessness, immaturity and dependency.

If such organic causes of difficulty are suspected by the worker, careful evaluation by appropriate psychological testing and psychiatric examination should be undertaken. Such parents who are organically impaired will not respond easily, if at all, to the usual methods of working with abusing parents, whereas those whose immaturity and dependency are essentially functional in origin are much more responsive to interventions. If parental dysfunction due to brain damage is documented, therapeutic goals can be appropriately revised and limited, thereby preventing the expenditure of much unproductive effort by the worker.

The Constellation of Psychological Characteristics

No two abusive parents are exactly alike, of course, but in general all of them share certain characteristics to some degree in a variety of combinations. The main components of this constellation of factors involved in abuse may be summarized as follows: the special form of immaturity and the associated dependency in its various manifestations; the tragically low self-esteem and sense of incompetence; the difficulty in seeking pleasure and finding satisfaction in the adult world; the social isolation with its lack of lifelines and reluctance to seek help; the significant misperceptions of the infant, especially as manifested in role reversal; the fear of spoiling infants and the strong belief in the value of punishment; and the serious lack of ability to be empathically aware of the infant's condition and needs, and to respond appropriately to them.

The cumulative effect and dynamic interactions of these various factors make it extremely difficult for the parent to maintain equanimity and be successful as he or she tries to meet the demanding tasks of child care. The daily care of infants and small children requires large amounts of time, physical energy and emotional resources. The caretaker needs to have much patience, ingenuity, empathic understanding and self-sacrificing endurance—the very things which we see tragically lacking in abusive parents.

These parents have never had their own needs satisfied well enough to provide the surplus which would enable them to give to the infants under their care. With good reason they often doubt their own ability to do even a minimally acceptable job and they do not know where or how to seek help. In contrast to averagely successful parents, they do not have an adequate support system of spouse and extended family, or helpful neighbors, friends, pediatricians and so forth. Probably most important of all, they do not have a background of life experience which has enabled them to get pleasure out of life and to trust other people. They have no storehouse of spare emotional

4

energy but live a precarious hand-to-mouth emotional life, without a built-in cushion of hope, or available contacts to tide them over tight spots and crises. It is because of this that crises are crucially important in the lives of abusive parents and are often the precipitating factor in single events of abuse.

Treatment Modalities

The matching up of parent, worker and treatment modality is difficult and usually managed on a less than ideal scientific basis. Abusive parents are unique individuals, often with great reluctance to become involved in any form of treatment. Hence the type of treatment may be selected under great influence of what the parent will go along with at the given moment, rather than because of any theoretical preference for a specific method. It is equally true that the selection of a worker or a mode of treatment will be influenced by availability rather than theoretical principles. There is at present no data derived from thorough comparative studies which indicate how or why any one modality of treatment is more effective than another for particular kinds of parents. It is known, on the other hand, that even in the face of rather haphazard selective mechanisms, remarkably good results have come for parents who have been treated by many different methods.

By far the greater part of the burden of caring for abusive parents is carried by public and private social agencies. Although the traditional values and methods of social case work are maintained in such agencies, there is also an increasing use of other techniques and of paraprofessional workers under supervision. Social workers in health-based child protective services have also been active in developing innovative techniques of working with abusive families and social workers in many different kinds of programs have been active in developing services and training people in the areas of lay therapy, parent aides and homemakers.

Many different modes of psychotherapy have been used in the care of abusive parents and their families. A few parents have been successfully treated by classical psychoanalysis, but the general character structure and lifestyle of most abusive parents make this procedure quite impractical and probably unsuccessful. Psychoanalytically oriented dynamic psychotherapy in the hands of skilled experienced therapists has been extremely successful in many cases. With most abusive parents, the therapist must be more willing to adapt to patient needs and to allow more dependency than is ordinarily considered appropriate. Intensive psychotherapy which skillfully utilizes the transference, with avoidance of the development of a full transference neurosis, can stimulate great growth and deep structural change in these patients despite their severe immaturity and developmental arrest. In general, abusive parents respond best when psychotherapy is accompanied by supportive adjuncts associated with a cooperative child protective service or provided by individual social workers, lay therapists or group therapy. Skilled and experienced psychologists can also work successfully as counselors and therapists in both individual and group situations.

There is increasing use of group therapy as a mode of working with abusive parents, but as yet there is a dearth of published reports describing fully either techniques or long-term results. Groups may be composed of the single parent who has done the actual abusing or of mothers or of couples. Most groups are formed and led by professionally trained group therapists such as psychologists, psychiatrists or other mental health workers, although social workers in protective agencies have also taken up this pattern of treatment. It is thought by some that it is always wise to have at least two leaders, preferably a man and a woman, and especially if there is an attempt to develop a couples group the leaders must be male and female. A rapidly growing and extremely important movement is the development of self-help groups formed under the titles of Parents Anonymous and Families Anonymous. Organized on a voluntary basis by abusive parents themselves, with sponsorship and guidance from a professional worker, these groups provide a haven of safety and help for people who might otherwise be unable—out of fear and anxiety—to relate to any other kind of treatment program. After some time of working in such self-help groups the participants may be able to enter into other more extensive programs.

For those parents who have the courage and ego strength to enter into group programs, the process helps them express their emotions more openly, and also to become desensitized to criticism. They find out they are not alone in their troubles and their self-esteem is improved. As an especially important benefit the group provides channels for developing contacts into the wider community, first with group members and later with others, a kind of relationship in which the abusive parent has been woefully lacking. Experience suggests that even though group therapy may be the chief mode of treatment involved in caring for abusive parents, it may not be sufficient by itself. Contacts outside the group, either with group leaders on an individual basis or with other workers from other agencies or disciplines, are often necessary for the patient's best development and improvement.

Couples groups can help solve the common difficulty of getting both spouses involved in treatment. Husbands are notoriously reluctant to get help, but the presence of male workers leads some of them to accept either group or individual treatment programs. It is important for both partners in the marriage to be involved in rehabilitative efforts if at all possible, regardless of which one was the actual abuser. Abuse is always, in part, a family problem with one parent actively abetting or condoning the abusive behavior of the other, even though not actually participating in the abusive acts.

Behavior modification techniques have been used to obtain changes in the attitudes and actions of abusive parents in a relatively short time. Whether this technique has validity for long-term rehabilitation is not yet clear.

Other modes of dealing with abusive parents have used "role modeling" and techniques derived from learning theory. These modes are at least partly based on the assumption that the parent is in difficulty because he has not been given proper opportunity and material to develop adequate parental attitudes and actions. To some extent

(Continued on page 44)

23

A Psychiatrist's View—*(Continued from page 5)*

this is true, but these modes are based essentially upon the provision of material for cognitive learning whereas the deepest deficit in abusive parents is in the emotional or affective sphere. There is apparently a small group of parents who are neglectful or only mildly abusing, who can profit by the chance for cognitive learning of good parental techniques. However, the fallacy of believing this can be a standard method is demonstrated most clearly by the fact that in many cases, even those of serious abuse of a child, the parents are able to take care of other children in the family perfectly well. It is evident in such situations that it is not lack of factual knowledge which hampers the parents but the emotional difficulties involved with specific attitudes and misperceptions of the parent toward an individual child.

Psychiatric understanding of the tragic long-term troubles of abusive parents can provide a perspective on the place which child abuse takes in their lives, and their attempts to adapt to their world. It offers a rational framework which enables workers from many disciplines—and who use various modalities of treatment—to help parents grow and to develop new and better patterns of childrearing. The most valuable ingredients, over and beyond intellectual insight, which enable parents to grow and develop are the time, attention, tolerance and recognition of the worth of an individual human being which the worker can provide. ■

Brandt F. Steele, M.D., is professor of psychiatry at the University of Colorado Medical Center and chief psychiatrist at the National Center for the Prevention and Treatment of Child Abuse and Neglect, Denver, Colorado.

44

WORKING WITH ABUSIVE PARENTS

A Parent's View

An interview with Jolly K. by Judith Reed

hat I can tell you is what you won't get from the other speakers—the guts of a person going through child abuse. Being there doesn't automatically make you an expert on child abuse but it tells what it's like . . .

"Child abusers are going through hell. We have a vision of how powerful our anger can be, a concept of where this anger will take us if we are pushed too far, and the constant dread that we will be pushed that far. For abuse is usually not a singular incident but part of a consistent pattern . . .

"We don't like being child abusers any more than society likes the problem of abuse. If a positive approach is offered abusers, they will usually respond . . .

"I'm convinced that parents are aware of their feelings and let others know. But we don't know how to listen. Too many of our parents have told society time and time again: 'Help me! I'm at my wit's end. Help me before I bring my kid there too!' How can we learn to listen and respond? Too many parents are afraid to go to agencies because they fear that their child will be taken away . . .

"Our defense mechanisms may make it difficult to read us but look to see what went into our lives to make us this way . . . It's true that we're socially alienated, most of us with good reason. Ninety percent of us were abused as children. I can remember not being loved when I was a child. But I just thought I was a rotten little kid and that's why I was being tossed from foster home to foster home. Since most of us grew up viewing others as part of negative, hurtful relationships, why should we form more relationships now? . . .

"The feeling parents most often talk about in P.A. is fear—fear of what they're doing, fear of what will happen if they don't get help and fear of what will happen if they do. And, of course, their fears are reality-based.

"Many of us in P.A. also have a constant dread that our behavior is indicative of insanity, that we are losing our minds. We think: 'I had no control over a lot of things in my life and now I have no control over even my mind!' Many times we also work in symptoms that we have read about—game-playing, attention-getting. Then comes fear that we really are that psychopathic . . .

"I've abused my child physically and emotionally. Now

I can talk in retrospect. I live in bits and pieces of those feelings now, but not the hell!"

* * *

The speaker is Jolly K., graduate of 35 foster homes, former abusive parent and founder of Parents Anonymous, Inc. of Los Angeles, California, a private organization of self-help groups that now has 1,500 members in 150 chapters in the United States and Canada.

Jolly is speaking to one of the many professional and lay citizen groups she addresses across the country each year in her role as director of programs for the organization—workers in state departments of social services and other agencies involved in the problems of child abuse and neglect, delegates to child welfare conferences, researchers and advisory groups.

Jolly founded her organization, first known as Mothers Anonymous, in 1970. It happened, as she tells it, in response to her bitter complaints to her therapist that there was no place for fearful abusers—and potential abusers— to turn for services. "Well, why don't you start one?" was his answer.

In 1974 Parents Anonymous received a grant from the Children's Bureau, OCD, to help establish additional chapters—by preparing and distributing materials on the organization and by providing technical assistance to communities wishing to form such groups, including the training of regional coordinators and local group leaders.

How is a P.A. chapter formed? Who are the parents who join such groups? Who leads them and what do they do in their meetings? To find out, CHILDREN TODAY discussed the following questions with Jolly K.

CT: *How do your members learn about Parents Anonymous?*

Jolly K.: Surprisingly, over 80 percent of our members come by themselves after hearing about us on television or radio programs or through newspaper stories and other published materials. The remaining 20 percent are referred through agency contacts, the courts, mental health practitioners and friends, neighbors or relatives.

CT: *How does a new chapter get started and where may a chapter meet?*

Jolly K.: New chapters are the direct result of someone's dedicated interest coupled with his or her willing-

6

ness to work in developing the chapter. Chapters may be started by a parent with an abuse problem or a professional or a service agency wishing to help such parents. More specific information on starting a chapter is contained in our new *Chapter Development Manual.**

A chapter may meet in any non-threatening environment, such as a YMCA or YWCA, church, school or community center. We definitely must not meet in a city, county, state or Federal agency such as a Department of Public Welfare, Bureau of Adoptions or police department. Because feelings like "I have to have a clean house" and "Those kids better behave" can lead to potential pressure situations, we do not recommend that chapter meetings be held in private homes.

CT: *Are most of your members parents who have abused their children or are a good proportion mothers or fathers who fear they may? What percentage of members have had a child removed from their home?*

Jolly K.: The majority of P.A. parents have already experienced the anguish of having an active problem, but we are beginning to see more and more parents become involved prior to actual abusive behavior. By the end of 1976 we expect to have more concrete information on this. We also will be gathering data on the percentage of parents who have children in placement.

CT: *Who, besides parents, are involved in the chapters?*

Jolly K.: All chapters have a Sponsor and Chairperson. The sponsor should be a professional who has a profound respect for the self-help concept and understands group dynamics. Our sponsors include psychiatrists, psychologists, marriage and family counselors, social workers, ministers and others. If a sponsor is already employed by an agency that has an authoritative position in regard to parents with abuse problems, such as a protective service agency, he or she must work with P.A. autonomously, not as a representative of the agency.

The chairperson is always a parent. He or she may be the parent who helped start the group, or one of several who worked to form the chapter and who was later chosen informally to serve as chairperson by the other parents.

Many of our chapters also have various volunteers working with and for the chapter. Babysitters who care for the children during meeting times constitute the largest number of volunteers. We also have volunteers who help by providing transportation, hanging P.A. posters, circulating P.A. literature, making public contacts on our behalf and raising funds.

CT: *What is the relationship between a P.A. chapter and the national organization?*

Jolly K.: The National Office is committed to provide chapters with the support necessary to start and maintain a P.A. chapter. This is accomplished primarily by providing literature, public exposure, technical assistance and con-

sultation. An individual chapter is autonomous in most things; however, each is part of an overall national movement and receives support from the National Office. The main benefit, of course, is that there is strength, encouragement and unity in numbers, so that no one chapter is left with the overwhelming sense of responsibility, of "having to do it all by themselves."

CT: *Can you tell us something about what happens at a meeting?*

Jolly K.: Meetings begin and take shape in many different ways. Sometimes they start by someone saying, in response to the body language of a member, "Hey, what's happening?" Other times it begins by picking up on a problem a member was discussing at the last meeting or by asking for follow-up on a phone crisis call.

If I were at a meeting of a new group I might say, "Look, we're meeting here for a purpose—we're here to talk about what's churning inside us. Let's do something now to stop this behavior." We'd exchange telephone numbers and addresses and begin to form a lot of support contact.

I remember one meeting when a member, Lenny, was sitting on the couch, sharing with us how "down" she felt. Questioned many times as to the whys and wherefores, Lenny answered by saying, "I don't know," "I'm so confused" and "Stop badgering me." All the while she was quietly crying. She appeared so vulnerable, so young at that moment and most of all, so very needy.

I reached out, put my arms around her, practically putting her into my lap as if she were a lonely, lost child. At this, Lenny cried openly, much in the same way that a hurt, pained child cries. We as a group then knew, and verbally discussed the fact, that there are times when our need for nurturing exceeds our need to know the whys and wherefores. We also found out that when this overwhelming need is fulfilled—for Lenny it was within a half an hour's time—we can then turn our attention and response to the realities of our daily situations. Most of all, we learned that we can ask for inner fulfillment, that some others will respond with positive methods to help, and that we are not bad, unloveable people.

Another typical moment came at a meeting when Joel told other members: "I did it! Last week," she said, "I got so teed off at my son!" (He is five). "But instead of abusing him I squashed the milk carton I was holding until the milk went all over the place . . . I released my anger in a more positive way and it worked. Now I know I can do other things besides being abusive when I'm uptight."

Sure, the members laughed, but most important, we learned. Joel had shown us that a potential abusive situation can be averted, that we can be non-abusive regardless of how uptight we are! Call these heavy times or light times in a meeting. More than anything else, we in P.A. call the meetings "our time." The times with Lenny and Joel were very real moments in Parents Anonymous.

8

CT: *How do members support one another between meetings and in emergencies?*

Jolly K.: My last answer illustrated support but also a lot of caring. Suppose Joel had not squashed the milk carton. Alternate ways to release angry feelings include calling another member and releasing the feelings over the phone. Joel could also have asked another member to care for her boy until she "pulled it together," or she could have asked to have someone care for her (meaning stay with her) for a while.

CT: *Is P.A. the sole source of help for most of the parents involved, or are some also receiving treatment or therapy through another source? And is therapy suggested and/or provided with the guidance of P.A.? For example, do some chapters use the services of professionals, such as psychiatrists, etc?*

Jolly K.: Many of our members are receiving services other than P.A. and, yes, P.A. supports and suggests other therapy alternatives. On an as-needed basis we utilize the advice and input of professionals other than our chapter sponsor.

CT: *Do many parents drop out of the program? And if so, for what reasons?*

Jolly K.: Some members drop out after realizing that a group situation isn't their cup of tea. Others find P.A. uncomfortable for them. Also, some drop out by choosing to use other treatment resources.

CT: *Have you found that there are certain kinds of parents with whom P.A. cannot work successfully? Are you able to guide them to other help?*

Jolly K.: We've not found "certain kinds" of parents that we're not able to work with. We have found that some people find our program to be less successful for them. Again, we're not the "cup of tea" that they find comforting. When we are made aware of this, yes, we usually are able to guide them to other helping resources.

We have also found that persons who are acutely mentally ill and who come to a P.A. meeting may find that the group can't offer them the comprehensive services they need. It may also be that the group feels it is not prepared to deal with the behavior that may arise from their illness. In such cases the group, with the assistance of the sponsor, is able to refer the person to a more appropriate source.

CT: *What is the rate of recidivism for those who attend meetings? Do you follow up former members?*

Jolly K.: Recidivism has been very, very low. In the five years of the program's existence, we know of only two incidents which resulted in a child's hospitalization. That's not to say all is sweetness and roses and that our members have become "instant Pollyannas." It is to say that life- or limb-threatening abuse has been vastly reduced.

No, we do not do a formal follow-up on former members.

CT: *Do you feel that members of P.A., who have voluntarily sought help, are typical of most abusive parents?*

Jolly K.: Yes . . . emphatically, yes. We are seeing much the same, and then some, of the parents so often described in the available literature and research studies. We are seeing the very withdrawn, the very aggressive, the isolationist, the uptight, the psychotic . . . in short, we are seeing human beings displaying a lot of different "typical human traits."

CT: *How many members meet in an average group and how long do most parents remain members?*

Jolly K.: Average group size is between six to 10 members, with most members staying in for one or more years.

CT: *What is the percentage of men to women in your groups?*

Jolly K.: Too small a percentage. The average among the groups would probably be 25 to 30 percent men. Confirmed percentages are not currently available.

CT: *Do both parents in an abusive family usually attend meetings? And what have you found the role of the non-abusing (passive) parent to be?*

Jolly K.: No. Again, this is not one of our most successfully realized objectives. Incidentally, we've found the passive parent to be not so darn passive as people think. We know that a whole lot of "behind the scenes setting of the stage" is going on and contributing to the activeness of the active abusing parent.

CT: *Is dependency on the P.A. group a problem for members who must leave for one or another reason? Is any follow-up provided for those who do move away?*

Jolly K.: Dependency can be and is a problem when a member leaves the group. But then the P.A. program is based on the premise that we, as members, will work towards resolving our problems, including how to handle relationships that are broken. The only follow-up provided is whatever is asked for or through the suggestion that a departing parent get involved with a chapter in the city he or she is moving to. If none exists, parents are encouraged to start one.

CT: *What action is taken if the group learns that a member has committed an abusive act or fears that he will?*

Jolly K.: Group peer pressure, group commitment to work extra hard with the parent and, as an extreme last resort, if P.A. doesn't work and the parent doesn't stop, then with or without the parent's agreement other people will be asked to intervene and provide services that will guarantee the safety of the child or children and the parent. ∎

* A copy of *Chapter Development Manual* and other material produced by Parents Anonymous, including a general information flyer on child abuse, are available from Parents Anonymous, 2930 W. Imperial Highway, Suite 332, Inglewood, California 90303.

29

A Multidisciplinary Approach to the Treatment of Child Abuse

Vincent J. Fontana, M.D., and Esther Robison, M.A.

From the New York Foundling Hospital Center for Parent and Child Development, New York, New York

ABSTRACT. A multidisciplinary team of professionals and paraprofessionals provides an innovative therapeutic approach for the treatment of child abuse and neglect among a deprived and disadvantaged population of abusing mothers. The therapeutic approach stresses residential care for mother and child, behavior modification through corrective child care experiences, personality modifications through individual and group therapy, and environmental and social changes through staff assistance and education. *Pediatrics,* 57:760-764, 1976, MALTREATMENT SYNDROME, CHILD ABUSE, CHILD NEGLECT, BATTERED CHILD.

The problem of child maltreatment has in the last decade been receiving an increasing amount of attention by physicians.[1-6] The need to develop treatment programs for maltreated children and their families has become clearly evident in the continuously increasing number of child abuse cases being reported to child protection units throughout the country. The problem of child maltreatment, in some localities, has reached epidemic proportions and statistics strongly suggest that the neglect and abuse of children may well be the leading cause of death in young children.[7,8] The Children's Division of the American Humane Association has estimated that there are between 30,000 and 40,000 cases of "truly battered children," but suggests that there are at least 100,000 who are being sexually abused and probably 200,000 to 300,000 children who are psychologically abused each year.

In 1962, Kempe *et al.*[9] coined the term "battered child syndrome." In 1963, one of the authors[10] reported observations on a large number of children who presented with no obvious signs of being battered but who had multiple minor physical evidences of parental neglect and abuse. The term "maltreatment syndrome" was applied to describe an all-encompassing picture of child abuse ranging from the simple undernourished infant reported as "failure to thrive" to the "battered child syndrome" which is often the last phase of the spectrum of child maltreatment.

In the past decade, the physician's prime responsibility was caring for the maltreated child's injuries and arranging for his immediate protection. Treatment for the parents was lacking because of difficulties in diagnosing the maltreatment syndrome of children and the absence of cooperation on the part of the parents who were abusing the child. Recognizing the essence of parental abusive behavior as a deficit in parenting wherein there is a deficiency or inappropriateness in the area of emotional interaction with the child, intervention programs have been devel-

(Received May 14; revision accepted for publication August 20, 1975).
ADDRESS FOR REPRINTS: (V.J.F.) New York Foundling Hospital Center for Parent and Child Development, 1175 Third Avenue, New York, New York 10021.

30

oped which not only protect the child but also demonstrate therapeutic approaches directed towards breaking the cycle of parental abuse. Kempe et al.[2] were the first to recognize that providing a therapeutic approach must encompass an attempt to provide "mothering" to the deprived adults who were maltreating their children. The concept of a "mother surrogate" came into being and Kempe et al. reported successes in treating parents leading to the safe return of a majority of battered children to their homes. Encompassing the concept of the mother surrogate, a program was established in 1973 at the New York Foundling Hospital to treat and prevent child abuse and neglect within the family unit. At the onset, it was theorized that the abusing mother should have an intervention plan developed which could improve her capacity to mother, namely, one which would (1) eliminate or diminish the environmental stresses precipitating abuse, (2) reduce the demands on the mother to a level which is within her capacity to handle, (3) provide emotional support, encouragement, sympathy, and empathy, (4) teach appropriate responses to her child through "role modeling," and (5) develop for the mother within her community a human network of support that could be available during times of crisis.

In 1973, the New York Foundling Hospital Center for Parent and Child Development began a demonstration program utilizing a multidisciplinary treatment approach to the prevention of child maltreatment. The main goal of the program was to provide services to maltreating mothers in an effort to maintain the family unit and prevent separation of mother and child; a secondary goal was to effect a separation where necessary while providing supportive services for the family.

The therapeutic approach involved a multidisciplinary team of professionals providing medical, psychiatric, and social services. Psychiatrists and psychiatric social workers, a pediatric nurse, five social work assistants, and eight group mothers work with the parents toward improving parental responsibilities and lessening the social and environmental stresses that oftentimes lead to child abuse. A hot-line or life-line is provided between patient and the paraprofessional surrogate mother. On a wider scale, a hot-line at the Center, manned by treatment personnel, is available on a daily 24-hour basis. Anyone can call directly on behalf of a potential patient. The Program has enjoyed a particularly close working relationship with the New York City Bureau of Child Welfare, since most of the cases referred to the Program

come from that agency. All calls coming through the Center hot-line are carefully monitored by staff in order to provide instant crisis intervention and coordination with the Bureau of Child Welfare, so that, if appropriate, an intake interview for admission to the Program can be expedited.

There are two components to the Program: a residence inpatient portion and an outpatient "I Care" program. The inpatient component provides a residence that accomodates eight mothers and eight to ten children. In the case of families with more children, if the mother is willing to enter the program, the child who is abused remains with the mother while the other children are admitted to the nurseries in the Center where facilities are available. Provisions are made for these children to spend time and to interact with the mother during the day. If a father or paramour is involved, although he does not enter the residence, he participates in all treatment services. Although the experience of child abuse is not limited to mothers alone, it is the mother who has primary care-taking responsibilities for the child. In response to a community need and priority in terms of etiology, our principle target of treatment has been the mother.

During the course of a year, the program is equipped to care for approximately 35 inpatients. The mothers live in for a three- to four-month period and then return to the community where they are followed in "after-care," with continued supervision and supportive services, for up to one year. On admission to the program, all patients are given a complete battery of psychological tests. Through use of interviews and on-going daily observations of mother and child during the first three weeks in the program, individual treatment plans are formulated utilizing the professional and paraprofessional services in achieving the treatment goals. Each mother is assigned a social worker assistant (lay therapist) who serves as a companion, friend, supporter, and advocate. This individual is the primary link between the mother and the community. She acts as liaison and aids in the parents' negotiations with other agencies in securing housing, a job or job training, education, or day care for the child. In addition, another paraprofessional, called the group mother, assists the mother in the development of homemaker skills by developing a daily routine around housekeeping, shopping, and cooking. She is also involved in teaching the mother how to discipline and train her child by demonstrating appropriate mothering techniques.

A nursery is provided for structured therapeutic approaches to the child through play activities. Mother-child sessions are scheduled twice each week when each mother and child participate in a stimulation session with the psychologist. A variety of toys oriented to stimulate the child's visual, auditory, and tactile senses are available. The purpose is to encourage the mother to relate more positively towards her child. These sessions also serve to pinpoint particular behavior deviations that trigger the mother's negative responses.

The treatment principle involved in our program emphasizes the notion of role-modeling based on the premise that abusing and neglectful mothers have been recipients of inadequate mothering themselves and hence continue the pattern of violence, abuse, or neglect that they themselves experienced in early childhood. The group mother and social service assistant provide corrective experiences through "model" demonstration and through supportive interaction with the mother. The importance of the paraprofessionals' operation in the context of a multidisciplinary team backed up by competent professional expertise cannot be overemphasized. A psychiatrist is of great importance in diagnosis and screening and in providing of individual and group therapy for mothers. The psychiatrist is also an active participant in formulating treatment plans and in consultation to staff for staff development.

The mothers participate in a variety of other educational experiences including sessions in self-improvement, child care, family planning, family health, arts and crafts, sewing, and dance instruction.

A behavior modification technique utilizing videotape feedback around two situations (feeding and free play) provides another therapeutic approach. These tapes are usually reviewed by the psychiatrist and psychologist who rate and codify salient positive and negative features. After each session, the tape is played back to the mother by the psychiatrist who discusses it with her.

The development of this videotape feedback technique for behavior modification has proved most helpful as an adjunct in the therapeutic approach and has also proven a useful tool in the teaching and demonstration of the problems encountered by an abusing parent when interacting with the child. It has also been useful to us in the program as a means of evaluating progress and in determining assessment criteria for final disposition.

Mothers and children who are discharged from the shelter to "after-care" are visited weekly by a visiting nurse, are seen in group therapy once each week, and are visited by a social service assistant at least twice each week. In after-care, the parents are assured a continuation of a long-term program providing medical and social services as well as emotional support.

The presence of at least 25,000 reported cases of child abuse and neglect in New York City in 1975 and the large unknown existing number of undetected and unreported cases highlighted an urgent need for expansion of our therapeutic efforts to a larger number of parents in need of these services. In March 1975, the outpatient "I Care" program was opened to the community. The services offered were identical to the inpatient services with the exception that patients would live in their own homes and receive therapeutic assistance at home, reporting to the Center for services on a "day hop" basis.

RESULTS

In two years the program served 62 families. Intervention was successful in preventing separation of mother and child in 40 (65%) families of the cases that have been treated. In the remaining cases, long-term separation has been necessary with the exception of two cases where children were voluntarily surrendered for adoption. The staff has continued to work with mothers who temporarily relinquished custody of their children in order to help them adjust to the separation and to work towards eventual reunion.

The mothers range in age from 17 to 28 years; the average age is 22 years. Fifty percent of the mothers were black; 35% were Spanish in origin; the remainder were white. One quarter of the mothers had two children, one had three, and all the others had one. Four of the mothers had one child who died prior to contact with our program. In three cases, the cause of death was suspected neglect. In one case, the child died while in placement.

Only one of the mothers had completed high school. Their IQs ranged from 66 to 120 with the majority testing somewhere in the dull normal range. Reading levels averaged the level of fourth grade. Two of the mothers were former drug addicts enrolled in detoxification programs while some of the others had experimented with drugs to varying degrees from time to time. All of the mothers were unwed except one. The available data on early family history indicated that all of the mothers in the treatment program came from multi-troubled and disorganized families. The majority of the mothers reported being severely abused and neglected during their early childhood. All of the mothers themselves experienced a life-style similar to the one they have recreated and used in rearing their own children, namely one involving violence. Child abuse in our patient population has not infrequently been traced back three or four generations.

All of the mothers had received prenatal care. The pregnancies were full-term except for the birth of one premature infant.

The mothers in our therapeutic program fell into a wide psychiatric diagnostic spectrum. The mothers ranged from the clinically immature, neglectful type of parent who tends to abandon her responsibilities towards her child to the overwhelmed mother whose lashing out at her child during a "crisis" situation will result in a serious physical injury. The majority of the mothers suffered from unsatisfied dependency needs and depressive attitudes, oftentimes leading to a sense of frustration, vulnerability, and self-hatred.

Psychiatric consultations revealed that 47 mothers fell into the following four categories: dependency-depression, 18; passive-aggressive, 16; sociopathic, 6; and schizophrenic, 7.

An effort was made to evaluate what type of mother was most amenable to the treatment offered in the program based on psychiatric diagnosis. It was found that 15 (88%) of the mothers diagnosed as dependent-depressive retained custody of their child while three (12%) in this category did not. In the category of passive-aggressive nine (53%) were able to return home with their children and seven (47%) did not. In the sociopathic group, three (50%) of the mothers retained their children and the other half did not. The sociopathic and schizophrenic mothers in the program did more poorly than expected on the basis of chance. It would appear that mothers whose needs can be satisfied by a supportive relationship and who can form dependent ties with other individuals are more amenable to our type of therapeutic intervention.

Interviews conducted in the home of the mother after discharge to evaluate program effectiveness included questioning the mother, observing mother-child interaction, observing the condition of the household, and interviewing day care and school officers where appropriate. Fifty-six of the 62 mothers completing the program were interviewed. Two were no longer living in New York and four could not be located. Forty-four of the mothers indicated that they were considerably helped by the program. Of this group, 30 retained custody of their children and 14 surrendered their children for temporary placement in foster homes. Of the 12 mothers claiming not to be helped, seven lost custody of their children. Although the number of mothers interviewed is small, there appears to be a relationship between the disposition of the child and the mother's perception of the program's helpfulness.

When the mothers were questioned concerning the components of the program which were most helpful to them in solving their problems, instructions in child care and learning patience and self-control were most frequently noted. The establishment of a relationship with the paraprofessionals in the program was the most frequently cited component as being most helpful in enabling the acquisition of specific skills for greater internal control and self-direction. It would appear from these observations that establishing a trusting relationship with the staff is necessary before internal controls and mothering skills can be successfully developed.

In our study we were able to identify by history five of the more common factors contributing to the crisis situations leading to child maltreatment. The stress factors included drugs, alcohol, marital problems, unemployment or financial problems, and mental illness.

The majority of the mothers showed a decrease in stress factors after discharge. As a direct result of the program, 20 of the mothers moved into new and improved apartments; 16 moved into new neighborhoods; 7 secured employment; and 9 mothers reported an improved relationship with their paramours or other family members.

Observations of the maltreated children in the program suggested that a mixture of abuse and neglect are often seen together. The children reported as abused on entering the program were usually found to be isolated, withdrawn, sullen, and apprehensive. They showed no warmth or attachment to their mothers. Role reversals were noted, with children often comforting the mother during stressful situations. In the physically abused category, 16 children, 11 boys and 5 girls, ranging in age from 6 months to 5 years were tested for motor, adaptive, and language development. Three of the children showed moderately delayed behavior development; three were in the low average range; and ten were fully average in their growth and development testing. Developmental testing of 14 neglected children, all boys, ranging in age from 3 months to 4 years, revealed 3 children in the low average or delayed and 11 in the average or above average category. These children appear to do better in perceptual motor functioning than with tasks that involve language skills.

All the children in the program showed growth and development gains a few weeks after admission. Their weight, height, motor, and speech development showed marked improvement and in many cases paralleled the mother's improved emotional stability.

REFERENCES

1. Helfer RE, Kempe CH (eds): The Battered Child. Chicago, University of Chicago Press, 1968.
2. Kempe CH, Helfer RE (eds): Helping the Battered Child and His Family. Philadelphia, Lippincott, 1972.
3. Fontana VJ: The Maltreated Child, ed 2. Springfield, Illinois, Charles C Thomas, 1971.
4. Fontana VJ: Somewhere a Child Is Crying. New York, Macmillan, 1973.
5. Fontana VJ: The neglect and abuse of children. NY State J Med 215:64, 1964.
6. DeFrancis V: Child Abuse—Preview of a Nationwide Survey. Denver, Colorado, Children's Division, American Humane Association, 1963.
7. Family physician, editorial. JAMA 176:942, 1961.
8. Battered child syndrome, editorial. JAMA 181:42, 1962.
9. Kempe CH, Silverman FN, Steele BF, et al: The battered child syndrome. JAMA 181:17, 1962.
10. Fontana VJ, Donovan D, Wong RJ: The maltreatment syndrome in children. N Engl J Med 269:1389, 1963.

A Psychodynamic Approach to the Study and Treatment of Child-Abusing Parents

Arthur H. Green, M.D.

Abstract. The author presents the psychodynamics of the distorted patterns of family interaction encountered in a study of 60 cases of child abuse. Sixty nonabusing subjects served as controls. Child abuse is regarded as a dysfunction of parenting in which the parent misperceives the child due to his own frustrating childhood experiences. The beating represents the parent's attempt to master trauma passively experienced as a child. The child abuse syndrome is conceptualized as the product of three factors: the parent's abuse-prone personality, the child's abuse-provoking characteristics, and environmental stress. The techniques, aims, and pitfalls of psychotherapeutic intervention with abusing parents are described.

The age-old phenomenon of child abuse, a severe dysfunction of parenting, has only recently attracted the attention of mental health professionals. Psychiatric and psychological exploration of child battering has lagged two decades behind the pioneering efforts of pediatricians and radiologists in establishing medical diagnostic criteria for physical abuse in children. Kempe et al.'s (1962) classic description of "the battered child syndrome" stimulated widespread interest in child abuse, which soon became recognized as a major pediatric problem. Between 1963 and 1965, all 50 states passed laws requiring medical reporting of child abuse, ultimately subjected the abusing parents to legal process, and catalyzed the formation of child protective services throughout the nation. The first psychological studies of abusing parents were carried out during this period.

The child abuse law in New York State became effective on July 1, 1964. During the first 12-month period, 313 cases were reported in New York City, with 16 deaths. The latest New York City statis-

Dr. Green is Clinical Associate Professor of Psychiatry, Downstate Medical Center, and Director, Comprehensive Treatment Center for Abused Children and Their Parents, Kings County Hospital Center.

This paper is a revision of a presentation at the American Medical Association Annual Meeting in New York, June 26, 1973. This investigation was supported by Public Health Service Grant MH 18897 from the National Institute of Mental Health, Center for Studies of Suicide Prevention.

Reprints may be requested from the author, Division of Child and Adolescent Psychiatry, Box 32, Downstate Medical Center, Brooklyn, N.Y. 11203.

414

tics indicate that 3,134 cases were reported in 1973, with 89 deaths.[1] The tenfold increase in reported abuse over an 8-year period undoubtedly reflects an improvement in reporting procedures as well as an absolute increase in the incidence of child abuse. The proliferation of child abuse might bear some relationship to the alarming general increase of violence in our society, demonstrated by the rising incidence of violent crimes, delinquency, suicide, and lethal accidents. Child abuse is considered a leading cause of injury and death in infants and young children, yet we know very little about its etiology and dynamics. In addition, the amenability of abusing parents to psychotherapeutic techniques has not been fully assessed.

PREVIOUS OBSERVATIONS OF ABUSING PARENTS

A multitude of behavioral characteristics and psychopathology has been attributed to parents and other adults who engage in child abuse. They have been described as impulsive (Elmer, 1965), immature (Cohen et al., 1966), rigid and domineering (Merrill, 1962), dependent and narcissistic (Pollock and Steele, 1972), chronically aggressive (Merrill, 1962), isolated from family and friends (Steele and Pollock, 1968), and experiencing marital difficulties (Kempe et al., 1962). The diversity of these psychological observations might be explained by the nature of contact effected with many abusing adults. Their personality characteristics have often been inferred from superficial interviews divorced from the parent-child interaction. The lack of controlled studies raises further questions regarding the reliability and specificity of these observations.

More penetrating impressions of the personalities and underlying psychopathology of abusing parents have been elicited during their psychiatric treatment and while interacting with their children. Steele (1970) described specific key psychodynamics contributing to the parental dysfunction encountered in child abuse. He stressed the importance of the parent's closely linked identifications with a harsh, rejecting mother and with a "bad" childhood self-image, which are perpetuated in the current relationship with the abused child. The abusive parents submit their children to traumatic experiences similar to those they had endured during childhood. Steele observed the use of such defense mechanisms as denial, projection, identification with the aggressor, and role reversal. The last, a maneuver by which the abusing parent turns toward

1. New York City Central Registry for Child Abuse.

the child for an inordinate amount of dependency gratification, has been noted by other investigators (Morris and Gould, 1963) as well. Galdston (1971) studied the parents of abused preschool children who attended a therapeutic day care center. He emphasized the importance of unresolved sexual guilt associated with the conception of the child who is subsequently abused. Feinstein et al. (1964) explored the behavior of women with infanticidal impulses in group therapy. These women displayed deep resentment toward their parents for failing to satisfy their dependency needs. They frequently demonstrated a hatred of men which could be traced to intense sibling rivalry with their brothers. Many of these women had witnessed or been subjected to excessive parental violence. They manifested phobic and depressive symptoms in addition to fears about harming their children.

The influence of socioeconomic factors on the incidence of child abuse has also been a subject of controversy. Some observers (Johnson and Morse, 1968; Simons et al., 1966) have considered child abuse a syndrome indigenous to the poor, while others (Elmer, 1965; Helfer and Pollock, 1968) have cited its occurrence in the middle and upper classes. The latter authors suggest that child abuse is psychodynamically determined and independent of education, race, and socioeconomic level. Some abused children appear to be physically neglected, while others seem to receive adequate material and physical care.

The wide variety of behavior and personality traits observed in abusing parents suggests that a specific "abusive" personality does not exist; rather, individuals with a certain psychological makeup, operating in combination with the burden of a painfully perceived childhood and immediate environmental stress, might be likely to abuse the offspring who most readily elicits the unhappy childhood imagery of the past.

The greatest area of agreement in the field of child abuse has pertained to the history and background of abusive parents themselves. These individuals have usually experienced abuse, deprivation, rejection, and inadequate mothering during childhood (Steele, 1970; Steele and Pollock, 1968).

Study of Abusing, Neglecting, and Normal Control Parents

Based on this frame of reference, a study of mothers of abused children was carried out at the Downstate Medical Center. Its purpose was (a) to identify the personality traits of the abusing parents; (b) to explore the contributions of the child toward his abuse; (c) to determine the more immediate environmental factors precipitating episodes of child abuse; (d) to document the patterns of parent-child interaction in which abuse typically occurs; (e) to attain an understanding of the key psychodynamics underlying the phenomenon of child abuse; and (f) to suggest a rationale for the treatment of abusing parents based on the preceding observations. The exploration of specific facets of child abuse was facilitated by comparing the abusive mothers and their families with those of "neglected" and "normal" children who had no history of abuse.

This was the first study of abusing parents to utilize nonabusing controls: 60 mothers of abused children were compared with 30 neglecting mothers, and 30 normal controls. The children, who served as subjects in additional studies (Green et al., 1974a, 1974b; Sandgrund et al., 1974), were between 5 and 13 years old. The mothers of the abused children had been referred by the Bureau of Child Welfare and the Family Court of New York City, where

Table 1

Ethnic Composition of the Study Sample

Sample		Abused Group	Neglected Group	Normal Group	Total
Black	N	39	16	20	75
White	N	8	5	2	15
Hispanic	N	13	9	8	30
Total	N	60	30	30	120

they were currently under supervision. Almost all of the abuse families resided in inner-city ghetto areas and represented a lower-class socioeconomic group, with a majority receiving public assistance. Criteria for abuse specified that it be of an ongoing or recurrent nature and confirmed by investigation.

The mothers of the neglected children were referred by the Family Court. The criteria for "neglect" specified a legal finding by the Court pertaining to the failure of the parents to provide adequate physical care—food, clothing, medical attention—and supervision. The neglect families were socioeconomically comparable to the abuse families. The "normal" control mothers were obtained from the Pediatric Outpatient Clinic at Kings County Hospital. They were chosen from families typically receiving supplementary assistance, and they also resided in the inner-city slums. The majority of the 120 mothers or maternal caretakers were black or Hispanic, which reflected the racial composition of the ghetto areas from which the sample was drawn (see table 1).

A structured interview was conducted with each mother (or female caretaker) by a staff member in order to obtain the following information: family background and early experience; quality of child rearing and punishment experienced during childhood interaction with parents, siblings, and peers; dating, courtship, and marital history, and current relationships with men: obstetrical, birth, and perinatal history; mother's behavioral assessment of the child, including symptoms, school performance and behavior, peer and family relationships; maternal attitudes toward child rearing and punishment; presence of outstanding maternal psychopathology, including psychoses, addiction, and alcoholism.

The average time allotted to each interview was 1½ hours. The interview data were augmented by agency records, which contained reports by protective caseworkers and probation officers. Additional information bearing on family psychodynamics and patterns of interaction was obtained from follow-up interviews with approximately 20 percent of the abusing mothers (and children) who were interested in outpatient psychiatric treatment. Over half of this group participated in the psychotherapy program, which became a valuable source of information regarding the psychodynamics underlying the abusive parent-child interaction.

From the original interview, 58 items were selected in the likelihood that they could differentiate the abused from the nonabused control groups. Each item was tested separately by a chi square.

FINDINGS

As can be seen in table 2, the mothers of the abused sample most frequently reported their children to be problems at home and in school. They also were more likely to see themselves as having problems with their families and mates. In contrast, the mothers of the control group reported that their study children required less attention than their siblings.

The mothers of the neglected children reported the highest percentage of unplanned pregnancies and the absence of a husband or male companion at home. The neglecting mothers also exhibited the highest incidence of alcoholism, psychosis, and chronic physical illness. In addition, significant differences between the mothers of the abused children and the neglecting mothers were obtained for school behavior problems, child's self-destructive behavior, child requiring most attention, and current marital difficulty.

The manner in which the abused children were characteristically perceived by their mothers seems to be closely related to the way these women were regarded by their parents. The interview data confirmed some of the observations of previous investigators and provided a basis for understanding the psychology of child abuse. The mother's perception of the abused child as the most aggressive, difficult, and demanding of her offspring made this child vulnerable to scapegoating. The rejection, criticism, and punishment experienced by these mothers at the hands of their own parents reinforced their feelings of having been burdensome children, and facilitated their identification with a hostile, rejecting parental figure. The emotional unavailability of the families and spouses of

Table 2

History Items Differentiating Abused, Neglected,
and Control Groups
(N = 120)

| Item | Percentage of Mothers Answering Affirmatively | | | |
	Abused	Neglected	Control	X^2
Self-destructive	40.6	17.2	6.7	8.18 *
Poor school behavior	66.2	22.3	10.0	31.13 ‡
Aggressive behavior	61.1	48.3	10.0	21.21 ‡
Child required most attention	50.0	27.6	17.2	9.94 †
Child required least attention	12.7	10.7	53.5	20.73 ‡
Lack of help with children	38.1	27.6	10.3	7.26 *
Mother experienced poor relationship with parents	54.5	37.9	24.1	7.52 *
Current marital difficulty	34.6	7.7	21.4	6.98 *
Mother beaten by husband or boyfriend	50.9	34.5	27.6	13.23 †
Male in the home	61.7	30.0	90.0	22.79 ‡
Unplanned pregnancy	83.6	89.3	55.2	11.77 †

* $P < .05$;   † $P < .01$;   ‡ $P < .001$.

these women explained their turning toward their children for dependency gratification (role reversal).

The information derived from the interviews was augmented by an in-depth exploration of the personality structure of the mothers and their abused children during psychotherapy. Direct observations and reports of the interactions between the abusing mothers and their children, spouses, and families provided a clearer understanding of etiology and psychodynamics of the child abuse syndrome. Although numerous patterns of family interaction were associated with child abuse, several basic ingredients were shared by most abusing families: (a) environmental stress consisting of a child-rearing crisis, caused by a discrepancy between an increased burden of child care and a limited or reduced nurturing capacity of the parents; (b) specific "abuse-prone" personality characteristics of the parents; and (c) behavior of the child which increases his susceptibility to abuse.

Environmental Stress

A child-rearing crisis occurs when the equilibrium between the capacity for parenting and the child-rearing pressures is disrupted. Decreased parental capacity might be due to (a) a loss or diminution of support from a spouse or key family member previously involved in sharing parental functions; (b) a breakdown of external arrangements for child care, such as the sudden unavailability of babysitters or day care facilities; (c) physical or emotional illness of the parent; (d) pregnancy.

> *Case 1.* Calvin, age 10, appeared in school with bruises, scars. and cuts sustained during repeated beatings by his alcoholic father, Mr. A. The father began to beat Calvin and two younger children with a knotted ironing cord two years ago when he assumed full-time responsibility for their care after his wife had suffered a stroke. Mr. A. left his job in order to stay at home with the children, and subsisted on public assistance. The pressures of full-time child care caused Mr. A. to increase his drinking, which exacerbated his progressive loss of impulse control.

The pressures of child rearing might be increased by the birth of another child, illness or deviancy of the children, or assuming the care of children of friends or relatives. The final impact of the environmental stress widens the discrepancy between the limited parental capacity and the increased burdens of child care.

Personality Characteristics of Abuse-Prone Parents

The parents demonstrate impaired impulse control as a result of early childhood exposure to harsh punishment and of identification with violent adult models. They suffer from a poor self-concept, and feel worthless and devalued as a consequence of the rejection and hostility accorded them by their parents during childhood.

They manifest disturbances in identity. Identifications are shifting and unstable, and are dominated by hostile introjects of "bad" self and object representations of early childhood. They exhibit heightened narcissism and ambivalence. Because of their need to maintain a positive façade, they are unable to integrate the negatively perceived aspects of themselves with the more acceptable elements of their personality. These undesirable traits are then projected or externalized onto others. The projection of these negative parental attributes onto the child causes him to be misperceived and scapegoated, and permits the parents to rationalize their assaultiveness toward him. The parents turn to the child for the satisfaction of dependency needs which are unmet by their spouses and families. This represents the phenomenon of role reversal. The child's inability to gratify these demands elicits memories of earlier rejection experienced during the parent's own childhood, and further facilitates scapegoating.

Case 2. Sonia, a 6-year-old Puerto Rican girl, suffered a fractured femur as a result of a severe beating by her mother when she was 4. Sonia was the daughter by Mrs. G.'s first husband, who left her when Sonia was a year old, after frequent quarreling, drinking, and "running around."

Mrs. G. married in order to escape from her brutal godparents, who had raised her since the age of 18 months after she had been abandoned by her mother. They had been extremely punitive and restrictive. Mrs. G. remembered one occasion in which her stepfather had broken a flowerpot over her head. Mrs. G.'s marriage, which was arranged by the godparents, deteriorated rapidly. She went to work in a factory and was ignored by her husband. She soon became pregnant, but did not want the child, as her husband spent so little time with her. He deserted when she was 6 weeks pregnant, and Mrs. G. moved in with her sister-in-law to have the baby. She hoped for a boy, stating, "I don't like girls, boys are more interesting."

In addition to displacing her rage toward her ex-husband and godparents onto Sonia, Mrs. G. identifies with her little girl and brutalizes her in the same fashion that she had experienced at the hands of her godparents. She described the following feelings about Sonia. "Since she was born, I let out all the anger and frustration that I had in myself on her. Whenever she came to me for something, I sent her away with a beating."

Mrs. G. subsequently entered into a common-law relationship with a man who fathered her two young boys. It is significant that she describes them in warm and affectionate terms, and does not subject them to physical punishment.

Contributions of the Child to His Being a Target for Abuse

In general, these consist of attributes of the child which impose a greater than average burden on parental functioning. The period of infancy and early childhood during which the child is most helpless, demanding, and dependent on the continuous presence of a parental figure may be experienced as a particularly stressful time by parents. The majority of reported child abuse cases occur in the first two years of life.

Physically or psychologically deviant children are especially vulnerable to abuse. Children with prominent physical defects and congenital anomalies, brain damage, mental retardation, or atypical development are extremely burdensome and provoke anger, guilt, and frustration in most parents. The narcissistic parents view them as current symbols of their own defective self-image.

> *Case 3.* Ira, an 8-year-old black youngster, was hospitalized at the age of 4 for multiple welts and bruises after a beating administered by his father. His mother complained about his provocative and disruptive behavior, which consisted of soiling, wetting, and failure to do what he was told. Ira has four younger siblings aged 6, 5, 4 years, and 9 months. His mother claims that he demands more attention than the infant. The father continued to beat Ira until he left home. Both the mother and her current boyfriend continue to hit the child when he becomes provocative, as they attribute his deviancy to willful disobedience.
>
> Ira's developmental history indicated that he was born prematurely during the 7th month of gestation. He weighed 2 pounds at birth, and exhibited a marked delay in his speech and motor development, Ira's speech was often incoherent during the interview, and at times he failed to comprehend what was said to him. His Full-Scale IQ on the WISC was 54, and the neurological examination yielded signs of unequivocal cerebral dysfunction. The impression was that Ira's receptive and expressive language impairment represented an aphasic disorder.

Children who respond poorly to nurturing by virtue of their extreme irritability or sluggishness are readily scapegoated. The mothers perceive their unresponsiveness as a rejection reminiscent of similar experiences with their own parents, reinforcing their feelings of inadequacy.

School-age children exhibiting behavior problems and poor impulse control are at risk for abuse. They are often disruptive in the classroom, and manifest assaultive and delinquent conduct. They relate to others in a provocative, sadomasochistic fashion, and seem to derive pleasure from the ensuing punishment. In addition, the "stepchild," who is often regarded as an unwelcome burden, is often beaten by the stepparent. This child is usually viewed as a sibling rival who threatens the stepparent's dependency on the mate. The stepparent's hostility toward his spouse is often displaced and redirected toward the stepchild.

Case 4. Don, an 11-year-old black child, had been subjected to chronic physical abuse at the hands of Mr. P., his stepfather, since the age of 7. At that time Don left his maternal grandparents in the South to live with his mother and Mr. P. His mother had placed Don with her parents when she came to New York to find a job.

Don has been a source of friction between his mother and stepfather ever since he joined them. Mr. P. accuses his wife of spoiling Don and catering to his "meanness," and often refuses to provide for his financial support. When Don's mother intervenes on his behalf, Mr. P. threatens to leave if the child is not returned to the grandparents. During the last beating, Don suffered multiple contusions and lacerations and had to be hospitalized.

PSYCHODYNAMIC CONSIDERATIONS

The psychodynamics in a given case of child abuse are largely determined by the "abuse-prone" personality traits of the parent. The relationship between the abusing parent and his child is distorted by the cumulative impact of the parent's own traumatic experiences as a child reared in a punitive, unloving environment. Individuals who abuse their children cannot envision any parent-child relationship as a mutually gratifying experience. The task of parenting mobilizes identifications with the parent-aggressor child-victim dyad of the past. The key psychodynamic elements in child abuse are role reversal, excessive use of denial and projection as defenses, rapidly shifting identifications, and displacement of aggression from extraneous sources onto the child.

Role reversal occurs when the unfulfilled abusing parent primarily identifies with the unloved "child victim" and seeks parental gratification from his own child. Frustration of these demands intensifies the parent's feeling of rejection and unworthiness which threaten his narcissistic equilibrium. These painful feelings are then subject to denial and are projected onto the child, who then becomes the recipient of the parent's self-directed aggression. This is accomplished by a shift toward identification with the aggressive parent, terminating the role reversal. By beating the child, the abuser assuages his punitive superego and attempts to master actively the traumatic experiences passively endured as a child.

The scapegoating process continues as the child becomes the additional target for aggression displaced from various despised and frustrating objects in the parent's current and past life, such as a rejecting mate or lover, a hated sibling rival, or a depriving parent substitute. These objects are unconsciously linked to the original "parent aggressor." The choice of the particular child for scape-goating might depend upon accidental factors, such as time of birth, physical appearance, temperament, sex, in addition to actual physical or psychological deviancy.

Nonabusive mothers whose children have been battered by hus-bands or boyfriends exhibit a slight variation in the psychodynamic pattern. The interaction between mother and child begins in a sim-ilar fashion as the mother endows the child with the attributes of her own rejecting mother. However, the resulting "bad" childhood self-image derived from her mother is partly maintained and partly transferred to the child, while the internalized "bad mother" is projected onto the abusive mate. The mother identifies primarily with the "child victim" rather than with the "mother aggressor."

These women submit to the physical cruelty of their mates as a masochistic repetition of their childhood victimization by rejecting, aggressive parents. The pain-dependent attachment to the spouse serves as a defense against their hostility toward the child. This is confirmed by the tenacity with which these women cling to brutal and humiliating relationships, and by their tendency to assume the abusive role if the spouse leaves.

Case 5. Andy N., a 7-year-old black youngster, had been re-peatedly beaten by his father, Mr. N., with a belt buckle and pool stick for the past three years. The case was finally referred to the Bureau of Child Welfare when welts and scars on Andy's back and stomach were noticed in school. Andy's mother, Miss J., had also been subjected to violent assaults by Mr. N., who is her common-law husband. On the morning of the interview, Miss J., suffered broken ribs after being struck with an iron bar by Mr. N. He had also stabbed her in the leg several months pre-viously.

Miss J. was also a victim of violence during her childhood. Her father, an alcoholic, beat up her mother and left home when Miss J. was 10 years old. Her mother was depicted as an angry woman who whipped her with a belt. Her mother and stepfather forced her to leave home when she became pregnant with Andy at the age of 16. When Andy was one month old, he was placed with his maternal aunt while his mother found a job and moved in with her grandmother. Miss J. currently complains about Andy's lying and stealing, and admits to beating him with a belt.

Treatment of Abusing Parents

Any logical plan for the treatment of child-abusing parents must be designed to modify the major components of the child abuse syndrome: the personality traits of the parents that contribute to "abuse proneness," the characteristics of the child that enhance his scapegoating, and the environmental stresses which increase the burden of child care. A multidisciplinary approach to the problem is required in order to provide the parents and children with a wide variety of home-based, comprehensive services. Such innovative techniques as homemaking assistance, regular home visiting by nurses or parent surrogates, and a 24-hour hotline for emergencies will help neutralize environmental pressures and provide direct child-rearing support. The availability of day care facilities for infants and preschool children, and outpatient psychiatric treatment for school-age youngsters will relieve child care burden and facilitate the identification of pathological or deviant traits which would increase a child's likelihood of being abused. Child-rearing advice, based on an understanding of the child's physical and psychological development, will counter inappropriate parental expectations for precocious or unrealistic performance.

The crucial ingredient of this type of comprehensive treatment program is the involvement of the parent in a corrective emotional experience with an accepting, gratifying, and uncritical adult. The helping person need not be a psychiatrist or physician. Social workers, nurses, and mature volunteers who have mothered successfully may be trained to help-abusing parents.

The treatment of child-abusing parents poses special difficulties beyond those usually associated with an impoverished, often poorly motivated, and psychologically unsophisticated multiproblem population. Those difficulties impinge on the treatment team as well as on the family of the abused child. The following problems are superimposed on the treatment situation by the characteristics of the abusing parents.

1. The effects of ongoing investigative and punitive procedures inhibit the establishment of a confidential and supportive relationship with the therapist. The problem of confidentiality may be met by divorcing the child protective services and court-related activities from the therapeutic team. Psychiatric evaluations required by the agencies or the court should be performed independently by their own personnel.

2. The suspiciousness and basic mistrust of authority exhibited by these parents also interfere with the formation of a trusting relationship with the treatment staff. This is a result of their life-long experience of humiliation and criticism at the hands of their own parents and others in positions of authority and control, and is intensified by their dealings with investigating caseworkers and probation officers.

3. The fragile self-esteem of these parents makes it difficult for them to accept advice and help from the therapeutic team. Crucial advice concerning child rearing and home management might be rebuffed if it is construed as criticism. The parents require continual reassurance and support, especially during the initial stages of treatment. Their own basic dependency needs must be gratified before "demands" can be placed on them.

4. Therapeutic focus on the abused child must be approached gradually and with caution, as the parents feel threatened by a change in their special relationship with this child. They feel a great deal of jealousy and competitiveness with adults who would preempt their parental role. This has been observed in cases in which the abused child has been treated simultaneously with the parent. The parent often attempts to interrupt treatment as soon as the child develops a warm attachment to his therapist.

5. The abusive parents are masochistic and provocative, possessing a strong unconscious need to turn the treatment situation into a repetition of their frustrating and humiliating interaction with their parents and spouses. The treatment staff must be trained to handle such provocative behavior without counterreacting.

The next group of treatment obstacles is primarily determined by those personal attitudes and feelings elicited in therapists by abusive parents and the act of child abuse itself.

1. The phenomenon of negative countertransference is such an obstacle. This involves the instinctive tendency of the therapist to condemn and dislike a parent who would cruelly subject an innocent infant or child to physical abuse. The primary therapist of the abusive parent, as well as the whole treatment staff, must learn to control feelings of anger and self-righteous indignation toward the guilty parent. Such expressed attitudes are, of course, incompatible with a therapeutic program.

2. The therapist tends to overidentify with a "good" parent, by rescuing the child from a threatening situation. These rescue fantasies are often accompanied by an attempt to "reform" the abusive parent by transforming him or her into a model parent. The abusive parent is obviously unable to tolerate such zealous competitiveness on the part of the therapist.

3. The infantile, demanding qualities of the abusing parent are often threatening to the therapist, especially when they are accompanied by hostility and a lack of cooperation and commitment to the treatment process. These parents frequently arrive late or miss their appointments, seemingly unappreciative of the therapist's investment of time and energy. Their behavior is certainly a threat to the narcissistic gratification of the therapist.

In view of these formidable obstacles to treatment, many have questioned the value of involving the abusing parents in a therapeutic program. Some workers in the field consider the parents untreatable, and recommend that abused children be taken routinely from their parents and referred for placement in foster homes or institutions. This solution, however, is not without its limitations and disadvantages. Abused children usually manifest serious psychiatric impairment and may adjust poorly to placement. In addition, the quality of children's shelters and institutions leaves much to be desired and, in fact, might be even more damaging to the child. Foster parents vary immensely as to their child-rearing capabilities, and it is not uncommon for abused children to receive additional abuse at the hands of foster parents. Another consideration is the cost of foster and institutional care which constitutes an enormous economic burden for the city.[2]

Others familiar with child-abusing parents feel that many of them can be rehabilitated. Pollock and Steele (1972) estimate that 80 percent of these parents can be treated with satisfactory results under optimal conditions. Our own treatment program at the Downstate Medical Center, operating with limited resources, has helped the majority of the families involved. The Downstate Program supplies psychiatric treatment to both abusing parents and the abused children. The basic goals and techniques of the therapeutic intervention with the parents are as follows: helping the parent establish a trusting, supportive, and gratifying relationship with the therapist and with other adults. This is accomplished by an initially noncritical, need-satisfying therapeutic posture. The parent is "indulged" and permitted to regress and enjoy the type of dependency gratification he or she was previously unable to obtain. "Giving" to the parent may appear in the form of child-rearing advice, being available on an emergency basis, making home visits, securing medical services for the family, and establishing liaison with the schools and numerous social agencies as an advocate of the parent.

The parent is helped to improve his chronically devalued self-

[2] The annual cost to maintain a child in a foster home or institutional setting in New York City ranges between $4,000 and $13,000 (Bureau of Child Welfare, 1973).

image by the mobilization of his assets with eventual educational and vocational assistance. The therapist or a visiting nurse dispenses information about normal child development, and provides the parent with a model for child rearing. The parent is encouraged to develop friendships with peers and participate in community activities. Group therapy has been extremely helpful as a bridge to social involvement as a means of ventilation and support. As the parents begin to experience gratification and support from the treatment staff and strengthen relationships with family and peers, they will no longer require their children to fulfill a disproportionate share of their dependency needs. The ultimate goal of treatment is to enable the parent to derive pleasure from his child and to increase his capacity for successful nurturing.

Once the parent is able to establish trust and rapport with the therapist, he can begin to explore and understand the relationship between the painful experiences of his own childhood and the current misperception and mistreatment of the child. At this point, the parent is amenable to interpretations and suggestions. He is provided with alternatives to scapegoating and the use of physical punishment as a principal child-rearing device. He is encouraged to ventilate his long-standing rage and frustration resulting from the chronic frustration of his dependency needs. The knowledge that others have similar difficulties in raising their children and harbor identical destructive feelings toward their offspring eases guilt, which in the past served to perpetuate excessive use of denial and projection.

It is obvious that the traditional psychiatric treatment process must be greatly modified if these goals are to be attained. The therapist must be active, supportive, and flexible. Overcoming the numerous obstacles to successful treatment and the attainment of therapeutic goals require imaginative deployment of the many services and techniques available to those whose professional concern is the welfare of children and families.

REFERENCES

Bureau of Child Welfare (1973), Schedule of rates paid to voluntary child and maternity care agencies (Form M-283c). New York City: Special Services for Children.

Cohen, M., Raphling, D., & Green, P. (1966), Psychological aspects of the maltreatment syndrome of childhood. *J. Pediat.*, 69:279–284.

Elmer, E. (1965), The fifty families study: summary of phase 1. Neglected and Abused Children and Their Families. Pittsburgh, Pa.: Children's Hospital of Pittsburgh.

Feinstein, H., Paul, N., & Pettison, E. (1964), Group therapy for mothers with infanticidal impulses. *Amer. J. Psychiat.*, 120:882–886.

GALDSTON, R. (1971), Violence begins at home. *This Journal*, 10:336–350.

GREEN, A., GAINES, R., & SANDGRUND, A. (1974a), Child abuse: pathological syndrome of family interaction. *Amer. J. Psychiat.*, 13:882–886.

———— ———— ———— & HABERFELD, H. (1974b), Psychological sequelae of child abuse & neglect. Abstr. in: *Proc. Amer. Psychiat. Assn. Annu. Meet.*, p. 191.

HELFER, R. & POLLOCK, C. (1968), The battered child syndrome. *Adv. Pediat.*, 15:9–27.

JOHNSON, B. & MORSE, H. (1968), Injured children and their parents. *Children*, 15:147–152.

KEMPE, C., SILVERMAN, F., STEELE, B., DROEGMUELLER, W., & SILVER, H. (1962), The battered child syndrome. *J. Amer. Med. Assn.*, 181:17–24.

MERRILL, E. (1962), Physical abuse of children. In: *Protecting the Battered Child*, ed. V. DeFrancis. Denver: American Humane Association, pp. 1–15.

MORRIS, M. & GOULD, R. (1963), Role reversal: a necessary concept in dealing with the battered-child syndrome. *Amer. J. Orthopsychiat.*, 33:298–299.

POLLOCK, C. & STEELE, B. (1972), A therapeutic approach to parents. In: *Helping the Battered Child and His Family*, ed. C. Kempe & R. Helfer. Philadelphia: Lippincott, pp. 3–21.

SANDGRUND, A., GAINES, R., & GREEN, A. (1974), Child abuse and mental retardation: a problem of cause and effect. *Amer. J. Ment. Defic.*, 79:327–330.

SIMONS, B., DOWNS, E., HURSTER, M., & ARCHER, M. (1966), Child abuse. *N.Y. State J. Med.*, 66:2783–2788.

STEELE, B. (1970), Parental abuse of infants and small children. In: *Parenthood*, ed. E. Anthony & T. Benedek. Boston: Little, Brown, pp. 449–477.

———— & POLLOCK, C. (1968), A psychiatric study of parents who abuse infants and small children. In: *The Battered Child*, ed. R. Helfer & C. Kempe. Chicago: University of Chicago Press, pp. 103–147.

Treatment of the Abused Child and the Child Abuser*

MARVIN L. BLUMBERG, M.D.† | *Jamaica, N.Y.*

Abusing parents are not always criminals. Deficient rearing during childhood deprived them of ego controls that could prevent them from injuring their children as projections of their own anger. Psychoanalytic therapy and ancillary measures can rehabilitate the crisis family. Methods are under study to identify and check potential abusing parents.

It is difficult to conceive, let alone to comprehend, the anguish of the child-abusing parent that impels her into the crisis of cruelly injuring her child and that torments her after the deed. Tangled in a web of her own childhood, the demands of her child and the pressures of marital discord or of other ambient problems, she is often a pitiable creature in need of help rather than of retributive punishment. There is no implication in the use of the feminine pronouns beyond the fact that most child abuse is attributable to the victims' mothers. While fathers, consorts, or other adults in the household may be the abusers, mothers, who spend most of the day coping alone with their young children, are most often the ones that are challenged and provoked to violence.

Child Abuse: A Family in Crisis

The vicious act of inflicting harm upon a defenseless child is not to be belittled nor condoned. Serious injuring is a criminal act and murder is a capital crime. In such cases, the law must impose punishment upon the offender. Concomitantly, however, there is the human side, the emotionally distraught individual. Child abuse is a family crisis or, a fact not always appreciated, child abuse is a symptom of a family in crisis. The emphasis should be on treatment, including psychotherapy, for the abuser and the abused. The aim should be rehabilitation of the individual and the family group. Before psychotherapy can be discussed, the questions must be considered why does an adult batter a child, what personality defects exist in her or him and what were the factors in the past or present that produced these defects. The following quotation from an article written by a mother (1) who murdered her infant son,

*Presented at the Twelfth National Scientific Meeting of the Association for the Advancement of Psychotherapy, May 9, 1976, in Miami Beach, Fla.

†Chairman, Department of Pediatrics, The Jamaica Hospital, 89th Ave. & Van Wyck Expressway, Jamaica, N.Y. 11418

204

portrays the main elements that contribute to the psychopathology of the abusing parent.

I am a child abuser. That is difficult enough to admit, even harder to accept. Even more incredible to me is that my son's life ended as a result of a beating I gave him. Although this happened over seventeen months ago, time has not eased my pain.

Where did it all go wrong, or was it ever right? As a result of being emotionally and physically abused as a child, I grew up with many emotional handicaps. When I got married at eighteen, I thought I'd be "happy" for the first time in my life. But along with my problems, my husband had emotional problems, too. We were a breeding ground for disaster.

Thirteen months after our marriage I gave birth to premature twins. Johnny weighed four pounds. Bobby three and one half. Along with the low birth weight, Bobby had a congenital birth defect, and I blamed myself for both the premature birth and the defect.

Almost immediately pressures began building up inside of me. The first incident of child abuse occurred when I spanked Johnny, he was three weeks old. I was terrified and told my husband about it. But he had little understanding and told me that if I ever did that again he would take the boys and leave. When the public health nurse came to our home, I told her that I was afraid of hurting my children. She was of no help; she told me I just had the new mother jitters.

I controlled my frustrations for the next couple of months. Each day that I did not slap or yell at Johnny and Bobby became some sort of achievement for me. I tried to find help for my problems and went to a mental health center near our home. I was so full of fear of harming the babies. I was told that perhaps I should get a divorce, or get a full time job so that I could get away from my children. That was not the answer and I never went back. Finally I gave up trying to get help because no one seemed to understand how I felt.

The second serious incident of child abuse occurred when Johnny was three months old. I was overcome with frustration because he wouldn't stop crying. Almost before I knew it I had twisted his arm until it broke. I can't begin to describe how I felt at that moment. I took him to the doctor and as he was resetting the arm, he asked me for an explanation. I lied to him and, although he was suspicious, he let me go.

From then on things kept going downhill. I was overcome with guilt and the fear that I would end up taking my frustrations out on the kids. I tried temporary jobs to get away from them, but that did not ease the strain at all. Then, when Johnny and Bobby got on my nerves, I tried leaving the house. Sometimes I stayed away from them twenty minutes or more, trying to regain control of myself. Nothing helped, and soon very few days went by that I didn't abuse them, either physically or emotionally.

Another crisis entered the picture. My marriage was falling apart, and I did the only thing I knew I could do—get pregnant. My husband wanted me to have an abortion but I refused, saying that I didn't want to kill it.

My husband got a part time job. He was seldom home except to sleep. Life was hell. I began sleeping all day because I just couldn't cope anymore. The house was filthy, my children were filthy, and I couldn't find the strength to do anything about it.

I was extremely depressed on the night of May 31, 1974. I had been crying for hours because I did not know what to do or where to go for help. My husband called at 10:30 p.m. and told me he wouldn't be home until 1:00 a.m. I became almost hysterical, pleading with him to come home.

After the phone call, I became even more depressed. Around 11:30 p.m. I took Bobby out of the crib where he was sleeping. Because I had just awakened him, he did not respond to my attempts to love him, and he began crying. I tried to feed him and he spit it all over himself and me. Something in me seemed to snap and I began slapping his face—hard, crying all the time. When I regained some sort of control, I got some ice and tried to bring the swelling down; but it was too late. The bruises were very noticeable, and I was filled with fear. I tried to show him love, but he was terrified. Soon, I tried to feed him and again he spit it all over. I started to bang his head against the floor—all control gone. I knew what was going on but it was as if my mind were above it all, watching. I couldn't seem to stop. I don't know how many minutes passed. As I realized what I had done, I felt absolute horror. I tried to convince myself that Bobby was all right. He appeared to be stunned. I sat there on the floor rocking him, tears streaming down my face, trying to tell him I was sorry.

After awhile, I took him into the bathroom to give him a bath because he was covered with cereal. I was filled with the fear that I would hurt him again; so I left him in the bathtub with the water running. I wasn't gone long when I realized he could drown and I rushed back. He was under the water and unconscious. Time stood still. I don't know how long it took me to revive him. I was almost hysterical, pleading for Bobby to live. After he regained consciousness, I called my husband and asked him to please come home. By the time he got home, I had convinced myself that Bobby was fine. I lied to my husband, saying that I had bruised Bobby's face when I tried to revive him from the bath water. He seemed to accept my explanation.

By the next afternoon it was apparent that Bobby was not fine. I was standing beside his crib when that realization struck me. I grabbed him by the throat and began shaking him. He had lapsed into a coma from which he never recovered. At 6:50 p.m., June 1, 1974, Bobby was pronounced dead as the result of a blood clot on the brain.

The woman was sentenced to prison for five years to life. This was subsequently reduced to five years. She wrote, "When I am released, it is my goal to help other child abusers like me so that what happened to my family does not happen to theirs." "I have come to realize just how precious life and children really are. I'm only sorry it had to take this experience to find out." She paid dearly indeed for her insight.

Maternal instinct is a delusional societal concept. In a previous paper (2), I stated that the biologic parent is not endowed with automatic cathexis toward her infant that guarantees the child constant protecting mother love. Nor is it true that violence and aggression are biologic instincts. Their overt manifestations are rooted in culturally determined practices, the constant exposure to brutality in the public media, environmental pressures of poverty, unemployment and racism, and the inadequate ego of the miscreants. Furthermore, violence and particularly the battering of children are rarely the consequence of psychosis. Alcohol and narcotic habits have contributed to child abuse. These agents, however, like the ferocity that they may abet are symptoms of the psychopathology of the abuser rather than the causes of the act.

Psychopathology and Psychodynamics of the Abuser

It has been frequently said that every mother is potentially a child abuser who only needs the right provocation to trigger her reaction. This is an extravagantly false generalization arising from the failure to distinguish between discipline and punishment on the one hand and abuse on the other. The difference is qualitative rather than quantitative for the former may be justified or at least rationalized as beneficial for the child whereas the latter is completely indefensible (2). Flynn (3) noted that there are occasions in every parent-child relationship when there is a temptation to strike an irritating child. This fantasy is a trial action that makes the person realize the nature of the conjured deed and helps her to discharge some of her anger. The potential act of violence is checked by the normal ego mechanisms of reality testing and memory. The sociopathic parent, on the other hand, brings into play the ego defense mechanisms of repression, denial, and projection that prevent the realization of the consequences of the violence about to be committed. Thus, the abusing parent projects her anger over other matters onto the child while denying it in herself.

Whatever school of psychology or psychiatric doctrine one follows, it is an accepted fact that the basic pattern of an individual's character is set in the early years of his childhood as a result of the influences of the parents and the environment. In psychoanalytic terms, the proper development of the ego and subsequently the superego depends upon a satisfactory early parent-child relationship. The majority of abusing parents were abused or neglected themselves as children. They may have been beaten physically, harrassed emotionally, neglected in their nutritional or social needs, or even pampered materialistically while being deprived of attention by busy, selfish parents. Having never been adequately nurtured or parented, the children never learned how to love or to nurture others and they grow up with this deficit. In the absence of proper gratification for the frustrations of infancy and childhood, the individuals lack ego strength and have a poor self-image. As they grow into adolescence and adulthood they develop subconscious self-defeating mechanisms as support for their weak egos, in the form of repression, denial, and projection. Their poor self-image and mistrust of others, usually identified as parent figures, afford them low frustration tolerance. The yearning to be loved renders them vulnerable, especially the young women, for a poor sexual, not always a marital, union with weak characters like themselves or with domineering psychopaths.

The Victimized Child

It is this type of union that often sets the stage for child abuse. Frequently it results in a passive-aggressive or dominant-submissive relationship, as indicated by Terr (4), with the man being the dominant aggressor. The marriage or relationship is thus unsatisfying and stormy, occasionally with either or both partners having other sexual affairs and further arousing mutual resentment. The passive-submissive woman is often dependent, moody, and ineffective as a wife or mother. The child born of this marriage is at a perilous disadvantage for several reasons. His mother does not know how to be a mother. She is immature, isolated, and lonely, and has a low frustration tolerance. Frequently lacking emotional support from an often absent and abusive husband, she seeks love and support from the infant. In a state that has been described by Morris and Gould (5) and others as role reversal, the mother identifies herself with her child and the child with his own mother. In failing to receive love and gratification from the child, the mother may project her hatred of her parents onto him and consequently beat him. Under other circumstances, she might project her resentment of her mate onto the child at a moment when her low tolerance is exceeded, with unfortunate consequences to the child. The father may develop intense jealousy over his wife's attention to the child and express his hatred of him in violence. There is another element in this bizarre psychopathic give-and-take situation. The infant responding to abuse with irritability and demands for attention or the older child responding with a neurotic behavior disorder invites more abuse by his behavior, thereby perpetuating a vicious cycle. Thus, it is apparent that the child in the unstable psychopathic family is a scapegoat.

While the family exists in a state of repeated crises, there is rarely intervention or help from outside until the child is so severely harmed that he is brought to a hospital emergency room—almost always by his own mother who inflicted his injuries. The fact is that she does "love" her child in her own warped fashion and does regret her deed that her sick ego did not prevent.   Most children involved in parental abuse are under three years of age and many of them are less than one year old when they first come to attention.   It is almost as if the older ones either learn to comply more or can escape serious injury because they are bigger and more mobile.

Some children may be victimized for another reason.   An unwanted child may be the butt of a rigid, compulsive, unreasonable parent either as the product of an unwanted pregnancy or as the child of the other parent by a previous marriage.   This child may be emotionally destroyed rather than physically beaten.   He or she may grow up more bitter and hateful than immature and may become a rigid unyielding adult like the parent.

There have been reports that low-birth-weight babies are at high risk for battering. Klaus and Kennell (6) and Klein and Stern (7) consider the reason to be failure of bonding or attachment due to separation of the mother from her infant during the neonatal period.   Smith and Hanson (8), however, explain the fact that many abusing mothers have low-birth-weight babies as being caused by those maternal factors that ordinarily predispose to delivery of low-birth-weight infants and incidentally to child abuse, namely, low social class, youthful and single status, and rejecting attitude toward the pregnancy.   This brings to mind the fact that physically or mentally abnormal children are not necessarily at increased risk for battering unless the parent has fantasied guilt feelings about her own misdeeds as the reason or has poor ego control for other reasons, as noted before.

Psychiatrists are rarely exposed to infants and their problems.   As a rule it is the developmental psychologist or the knowledgeable pediatrician who handles the behavior problems of the infant and toddler.   It is, however, within the purview of this paper to discuss the effect of physical and emotional trauma on the young child's psyche and his immature ego.   The battered infant reacts with fright to the approach of any adult.   He will cry out and paradoxically cling to the very mother who has been abusing him.   He is fretful and demanding of her attention in a confused, "unbelieving" fashion.   When left alone, he is often lethargic and does not smile or play.   His appetite fails and his sleeping habits become very restless.   At about one year or older, he may have distressing dreams and wake screaming.   Another young child may exhibit a different picture that Ounsted et al. (9) have described as the behavioral syndrome of "frozen watchfulness."   This child makes no sounds, not even crying when his wounds are dressed.   He stares with fixed gaze and does not smile.   The authors attribute this state to "an adaptation to situations in which the loving and loved parent unpredictably and without provocation becomes transformed into an aggressor, and then immediately reverts to good parental behaviour." This child has been unable to establish trust in anyone in his erratic existence.

Therapeutic Considerations

Therapeutic considerations are not simple and must be conceptualized as a multidisciplinary approach with psychotherapy tactfully and timely applied. There are three persons involved, the abusing parent, the nonabusing parent and the abused child. Treatment must be directed not only at each one's problems but to their interaction as a family group which is the situation that created the crisis in the first place.

When a maltreated child is brought to attention, the first procedure that is dictated by conscience and mandated by law is to separate the child from the guilty parent. Then official investigation takes place. All of this serves as a threat to the abuser and enhances her basic fear and mistrust of the authority figure whom she identifies with her own hated parent. At this time, her negativistic attitude might thwart any direct attempt at individual psychotherapy and prevent any positive transference with a therapist. It is here that an intermediary procedure may prove expedient. A number of treatment centers have instituted living-in arrangements for the mother and child where she is nurtured and parented by trained lay persons while the child is also properly mothered. Both are thus gradually freed from their fear and distrust. The mother, in experiencing nurturing that she never received herself as a child, learns how to react to her own child.

As idyllic as this appears and as valuable as it is, this is only a preliminary step and by no means the entire answer. As in the case of other psychopaths, like the chronic alcoholic and the narcotic addict or even the psychotic, the initial rehabilitation within the shelter of a protecting institution may not last in the outside threatening world. Further long-term therapy and follow-up are necessary; it is to be hoped that the now trusting, ex-abusing parent may be in a better condition to relate to a psychotherapist.

Psychotherapy for the Adults

There are some caveats for the psychiatrist. The subject of child abuse is highly charged with emotions even for the beholder or the listener. The psychiatrist must be objective enough to avoid feelings of disapproval and developing a negative countertransference toward his patient. He must focus primarily on the intrapsychic conflicts within the parent and not on the parent-child interactions. If he stresses the latter too strongly, the infantile, narcissistic parent will feel threatened by the child's competition for the therapist's attention.   This could lead to role reversal on the patient's part and hostility toward the psychiatrist.

The psychopathology of the abusing parent, originating in the individual's own early childhood as a result of interaction with his or her own parents, is best treated with psychoanalytically oriented psychotherapy. The parent-patient usually has a poor self-image, lacks ego strength and is, therefore, immature and a loner.   Adversity and criticism are unacceptable and usually provoke impulsive violence.   She lives with fantasies relevant to herself and her child.   In her role-reversal episodes she fantasizes a change in position with the child.   Often enough, early in her motherhood, she had felt that she was on the verge of beating the child, or perhaps she had on occasion beaten him.   Actually loving the child and fearing her own lack of self-control, she may have sought help in her own inadequate fashion just as the mother did in the account in her letter at the beginning of this article.   Her veiled pleas had gone unrecognized and unheeded until the final terrible disaster occurred.

The psychotherapist must use skill and considerable tact in helping the patient to abreact.   It is a difficult process for the abuser to gain insight into her own pathologic mechanisms and the reasons for her actions.   Her subconscious may resist strongly the traumatic admission of her hatred for her parents.   Through understanding her own background and its relation to her present attitudes and life style, she can build up her own self-esteem and ego strength.   As important as therapy and catharsis for the abusing parent is the therapeutic involvement of the nonabusing parent.   He may be a dominant, aggressive husband who has been driving his wife to despair and to seeking a scapegoat.   He may be a weak character who, lacking ego strength himself, has not afforded her the moral or other support for which she has begged.   Perhaps, his employment or an alcoholic habit keeps him away from home much of the time or at odd hours.   The two of them, husband and wife, must be helped to understand each other and their problems, to seek treatment, and to learn to accept each other.   If this can be accomplished, and if the parents can learn proper child-rearing practices, the family will no longer be in crisis and the child or children will be reabsorbed into the rehabilitated group.

There are many cases where the abusing parent feels so threatened by the authority figure or so hostile towards anyone identified in a parent role that a one-to-one therapeutic relationship is an impossibility. This type of patient might more readily accept participating in a group of Parents Anonymous.   There the troubled man or woman can share experiences with other child abusers.   Mutual confessions, exchange of expressions of emotions and attitudes, and criticisms of self and others in the group, may afford the individual considerable catharsis. Such groups may serve as adjuncts, or even as preparation to individual psychotherapy.

One must not underestimate the role of the well-trained social worker as an integral part of the scene. The abuser, the family, the abused child are all part of society. There are legal, social, and financial matters involved. There are relations with the family court or, at times, the criminal court. The matter of employment of one or both parents and financial support of the family are important. These and other factors must be handled and the patient must be helped to cope with them. This must be managed if psychotherapy is to be successful to any degree.

Psychotherapy for the Child

In the process of furnishing all of this attention and therapy for the parents, the child, the innocent victim or pawn, must not be overlooked. His psyche as well as his soma have been traumatized. The person who furnishes his creature comforts and upon whom he is dependent for his very existence alternately cuddles him and harms him. He is confused. Often his crying from distress or for attention brings more punishment. Some children are grossly and continually neglected even though they are not beaten. The abused or neglected child is sad. He has learned to mistrust even before he could develop the trust that grows from gratified dependence. It is small wonder that he is fretful, fearful, withdrawn, or even exhibits "frozen watchfulness" as described previously. For the infant and toddler cuddling and nurturing are the only therapy, first by a trained surrogate and then by the reeducated mother. For the older preschool child psychiatrically directed play therapy, parenting, preparation for and then attendance at nursery school go a long way toward mending the parent-child relationship.

There are some adjuncts that are quite necessary in the total rehabilitative therapy plan for the family. Both parents must learn how to relate to friends, neighbors, and their extended families for moral support and to overcome their depressing isolated loneliness. Day-care centers for infants and toddlers may be an answer for the mother who would be emotionally better off with some form of employment. The same function would be served by nursery school for the preschool child in addition to the psychosocial value that this would have for him. Parenthood service twenty-four hours a day can put a strain on any person and the proportion is inversely related to levels of frustration and tension tolerance. The best mother, the most well adjusted mother, does sometimes become exasperated by constant exposure to the demands and foibles of a young child. How much more vulnerable is the neurotic, immature mother with a problem life of her own and with a limited frustration tolerance.

When a child is found to be badly injured by the intent or neglect of the parent, the ambient populace, in righteous indignation, demands not only punishment for the offender but also wresting the child from him or her. Unfortunately, not one of the righteous will accept the care and responsibility for the child nor are there anywhere near enough foster homes or other facilities to care for the large number of children that are abused. Furthermore, with proper psychotherapy and the ancillary measures already described, a majority of families in crisis can be rehabilitated. It is well to note that often the damage to a child's psyche from being separated from his family can be more permanently harmful than the reparable damage to his body.

Preventive Measures

In the field of medicine, when a disease is delineated, first a treatment is sought, then a cure if possible, and ultimately prevention. In general, prophylaxis is always preferable to having a disease expand to the epidemic proportion that child abuse has reached. There are suggestions for prevention of child abuse ranging from the utopian proposals for coping with the problems of poverty, unemployment, and racism that are certainly aggravators for the abuse-bound parent, to more practical measures. There are areas that have established publicized daily, twenty-four-hour "hot lines" manned by trained personnel to talk down and cool off any telephoning parent who feels on the verge of battering a child. Parents-anonymous groups have prophylactic as well as therapeutic value. Nursery schools and day-care centers have already been mentioned for their value in offering temporal relief to a tense and overburdened mother.

For the past eight years Helfer (10) and his associates have been developing and revising a child-rearing questionnaire for the purpose of screening and early identification of parents who might have trouble interacting with their children and, consequently, be risks to become abusing parents. These questionnaires are usually administered early in the child's life to the parents in the physician's office, in the clinic, or even in the home. The author further describes detailed observations of mothers and babies in the delivery room, in studies carried on in Denver, Colorado and in Lansing, Michigan. Verbal and nonverbal clues in the types of behavior in the delivery room were found to correlate with potential problems in mother-child interaction. Fathers react to newborns in the same fashions as mothers do. Observation of infant-feeding behavior by either parent may be helpful in assessing potential problems (6).

In the school systems, from elementary through high school, children and youths are taught many things including cognitive subjects, homemaking, athletics, religion in sectarian school, and now even sex. A most useful addition would be courses in family relations, parenting, and mutual respect and trust.

Child abuse is a multifaceted problem that requires multiple approaches towards a solution.

SUMMARY

An abusing parent is not necessarily a criminal. He or she is usually an immature, lonely person with low self-esteem and lacking ego strength as a result of neglectful or cruel parenting during his or her early childhood. Lacking normal ego mechanisms of reality testing and memory, the potential abuser employs self-defeating defense mechanisms of repression, denial, and projection. These prevent the realization of the consequence of her violence and permit the parent to vent her anger on an inappropriate object in the person of the child. Fantasies and the mechanism of role reversal make the ego-deficient parent more vulnerable to inimical environmental factors. Again the child may be the scapegoat.

Therapeutic considerations require a multidisciplinary approach involving the psychotherapist, the social worker, the court, and child placement, temporary if possible. The maltreated child is traumatized emotionally as well as physically and often like the abusing parent, needs psychotherapy.

Preventive measures under study are identifying questionnaires and various means of professional help for high-risk families.

REFERENCES

1. Dabney, J. E. Bobby is Dead. (Reprinted by permission of the publisher, National Committee for Prevention of Child Abuse, Chicago, Illinois.) *Caring*, 2:1, 1976
2. Blumberg, M. L. Psychopathology of the Abusing Parent. *Am. J. Psychother.*, 28:21, 1974
3. Flynn, W. R. Frontier Justice: A Contribution to the Theory of Child Battery. *Am. J. Psychiatry*, 127:375, 1970
4. Terr, L. C. A Family Study of Child Abuse. *Am. J. Psychiatry*, 127:125, 1970
5. Morris, M. G. and Gould, R. W. Role Reversal: A Concept in Dealing With the Neglected/Battered Child Syndrome. In *The Neglected-Battered Child Syndrome*. Child Welfare League of America, New York, 1963, pp. 29–49
6. Klaus, M. H. and Kennell, J. H., Mothers Separated from Their Newborn Infants. *Pediatr. Clin. North Am.*, 17:1015, 1970
7. Klein, M. and Stern, L., Low Birth Weight & the Battered Child Syndrome. *Am. J. Dis. Child.*, 122:15, 1971
8. Smith, S. M. and Hanson R. 134 Battered Children: A Medical and Psychological Study. *Br. Med. J.*, 3:666, 1974

9. Ounsted, C., Oppenheimer, R. and Lindsay, J. Aspects of Bonding Failure: The Psychopathology and Psychotherapeutic Treatment of Families of Battered Children. *Dev. Med. Child Neurol.*, 16:447, 1974

10. Helfer, R. E. Early Identification and Prevention of Unusual Child Rearing Practices. *Pediatr. Annals.*, 5:3:91, March 1976

PREVENTION OF CHILD ABUSE:
GROUP THERAPY FOR MOTHERS AND CHILDREN

JACQUELINE ROBERTS, M.A., M.SC.
Research Social Worker, Park Hospital for Children, Oxford

KEITH BESWICK, M.B., F.F.A.R.C.S., M.R.C.G.P.
General Practitioner, Didcot Health Centre

BRIDGET LEVERTON, M.B.A.O.T., S.R.O.T.
Occupational Therapist

MARGARET A. LYNCH, M.B., M.R.C.P., D.C.H.
Research Paediatrician
Park Hospital for Children, Oxford

INFLICTED INJURY to children can be a considerable problem in general practice. In one practice, between January 1973 and February 1976, 12 cases of actual abuse were recognized; in February 1976 there were 22 families on the 'at risk' register of the practice. There has been an increased awareness in the community about the early warning signals of child abuse and this has led to dissatisfaction with the inadequate treatment facilities available.

This paper describes a joint project set up by the practice and a child abuse research team from the Park Hospital for Children. The aim of the project was to provide help for families with child-rearing problems that could lead to abuse (Lynch, 1976). Two groups were organized on a weekly basis: one for the mothers, the other for their children. This project is part of a wider preventive management plan (Beswick *et al.*, 1976).

PLANNING

Uncertainty was expressed about the value of changing the traditional doctor and social worker approach and there was a real fear that the project would only increase the work load. There were particular difficulties in visualizing the general practitioner as combining the role of personal doctor with that of group therapist. These attitudes led to a prolonged planning stage with frequent meetings and discussions between workers. In the long term this has had a beneficial effect on the management of cases of child abuse.

The groups met once a week for six months from October 1975 to the end of April 1976. We had two adjacent rooms, the larger of which had already been fitted out as a playroom. A grant of £100 from the local Round Table bought extra equipment for the children's group. Time was spent in careful selection of toys that were suitable for helping the children to learn to play, both individually and in a group. The toys could also be used to assess the children's development and allow them to express their emotional needs.

Previous experience at the Park Hospital had indicated that two therapists would be required for the mothers' group. A doctor and a social worker
acted as co-therapists; an occupational therapist skilled in play therapy ran
the children's group, and she was assisted by two volunteers and two senior
pupils from the local comprehensive school.

SELECTION OF PATIENTS

Only mothers with at least one pre-school age child were considered.
Previous experience in preventive work by Park Hospital staff (Ounsted
et al., 1974) has indicated that the following problems can be treated successfully in such a group:

(1) Mothers with difficulties in coping with their child; the child's eating, sleeping
or behaviour problems are often the presenting complaint
(2) Cases of child neglect or failure to thrive
(3) Children considered, either by the parents themselves or by the primary
health care team, to be at risk of abuse
(4) Some cases of actual abuse and cases of emotional deprivation.

Mothers with handicapped children were not necessarily considered
unsuitable.

The groups were not intended to be the primary treatment of severely
damaged parents who had already inflicted serious injuries on their child.
Such parents and their children initially need more intensive help. We
excluded mothers with psychotic behaviour and also those with considerable
psychiatric group experience. The aim was to protect the group from their,
possibly, disruptive influence. The actual selection of patients was carried
out at a meeting of group therapists, social workers, health visitors and
Park Hospital staff.

The following mothers were finally selected as likely to benefit from
participation in the groups:

(1) A young army wife, who requested help in the ante-natal clinic during her
second pregnancy, complaining about the exploratory behaviour of her toddler
(2) A mother who threatened to abuse her two-year-old son, the product of a
second unhappy marriage
(3) A deprived, immature army wife with totally unrealistic ideas of child behaviour and development; the child exhibited 'frozen' behaviour
(4) A young woman who was resenting motherhood and almost driven to the
abuse of her difficult second child by social stress and the child's recurrent illnesses
(5) An emotionally disturbed couple seeking a medical diagnosis for their child's
persistent failure to thrive; intensive clinical investigations were negative and
gross family disturbance was revealed
(6) A family who had acquired the label 'typical problem family' because child
neglect and marital violence had continued intermittently for years
(7) An isolated young family rehoused in this practice area following the abuse
of their child elsewhere.

Four of the mothers directly asked for help, because of fear of harming
their child, and gratefully accepted the idea of the group. The others
needed more encouragement to attend. Six attended regularly but case 7
attended only once in spite of many approaches. All prospective members
were visited by the group general practitioner. Following this an independent social worker visited both husband and wife in order to take a compre-

hensive social history and record both parents' views of the main problem and what they hoped to gain from the group. A second visit was planned to make an assessment at the end of the six months.

THE MOTHERS' GROUP

The mothers' group met together for an hour and a quarter each week. Coffee was provided and the mothers quickly organized their own provision of biscuits and milk.

The aim was to use group interaction to increase the mothers' self-esteem and confidence, especially in the area of child-rearing. We hoped that the mothers would learn to help each other and extend their contacts to outside the group. In order to achieve this we had a few simple management principles. We set out to avoid any one-to-one discussions between mothers and therapists and between group members. The co-therapists never sat together.

As the group did not have the anonymity of the more conventional therapy group we decided to let the mothers proceed at their own pace and not to challenge them with reality too soon. Group continuity was made possible because no mother joined after the fourth week. Direct links were kept with the children's group because of the mother/child difficulties. Strict time keeping was observed to establish a predictable routine for the children. Every week all the therapists met together after the group had finished to review each case.

The mothers showed many of the characteristics typically associated with child abusers. These were lack of self-respect, social isolation, relationship problems and unrealistic expectations of child and family (Kempe, 1971). Participation in the group helped in several ways.

They developed greater self-esteem by learning that they were not the only mothers with problems and by discovering their own areas of competence. They also lost the sense of uselessnesss by learning to help others. Social isolation was alleviated by regular contact with group members. Mothers often went home with another member of the group; at a later stage they took over the visiting of any member who did not attend. They learnt to trust all the therapists and began to form real friendships with each other. Some mothers changed remarkably in their ability to get on with other people. Also very important, they acquired greater knowledge of child-rearing and learnt more realistic standards of child development.

The independent interviewer, revisiting the families after the termination of the group, noted a reduction of tension in all the homes. The mothers all felt they had derived some benefit from attending, but some found it difficult to define how and why changes had occurred.

CHILDREN'S GROUP

Children who have been subjected to the abnormal child-rearing patterns that precede abuse are very likely to have developmental and behavioural problems (Baher et al., 1976; Martin et al., 1974; Martin, 1976). Our children's group was therefore designed to be a therapeutic rather than a caretaking group.

Observation of the children revealed a disturbed group needing considerable help in their own right. There were separation problems, inhibited behaviour (i.e. suspicious watchfulness and lack of motivation to move, speak or play), aggressive and attention-seeking behaviour and delayed maturation.

After the first session it was necessary to have clear, consistent policies for dealing with all these problems. Their progress was monitored throughout the six months. Clinging, over-attachment was replaced by increased independence through careful handling of both mother and child on separation. Also, inhibitions disappeared as the children established regular trusting relationships with adults. They learnt constructive play and developed enjoyment in play.

Social skills were learnt through greater contact with other children and adults and rapid physical and emotional developmental progress was made. For example, one child gained two kilograms in weight in two months and a whining baby developed into a chattering, extrovert toddler. Children with specific areas of developmental delay received special attention and teaching and, when required, were referred to specialist services.

The mothers were invited to bring the children 15 minutes before their group started and time was available at the end of each session for mothers to talk to the play-therapist and join in the child's play. The project therefore provided an opportunity to evaluate and treat both mother and child as individuals and to help them together with their relationship problems.

DISCUSSION

Careful preparation, selection and clear aims all contributed to the success of this project (Whitaker, 1975). However, it must be acknowledged that some cases cannot be helped by groups such as ours. Pressure to accept unsuitable cases is an inevitable consequence of the development of such a project. It is difficult for the community worker to withstand such pressure without the support of a specialist service. For example, the family doctor alone would have found it very difficult to refuse many requests to include a schizophrenic mother who could not be helped by the group and could disrupt the group for others. The mother's subsequent psychotic breakdown demonstrated this to have been the right decision.

The availability of experienced medical, social work and play therapy staff for consultation and discussion increased the confidence of the group therapists in dealing with difficult family problems. The back-up support of specialist services is essential for the success of such a project. A second group is now running with all community workers and the Park Hospital for Children continues in a consultative capacity.

It was important for the mothers' group to have close links with the children's group. This enabled them to adapt to changes in the children's behaviour and development. The interaction between the two groups provided opportunity for direct help with mother/child relationship problems.

Fathers were not included, mainly because of their work commitments. However, all were seen at the initial assessment and their support and approval were obtained. As the group progressed, they began to make the occasional appearance at the beginning or end of the groups; one father actually attended a group. Ideally, both parents deserve equal attention in trying to resolve the family's problems. This has been realized by the fathers who are now asking for their own group in the evenings.

At the project's outset there were anxieties about the likelihood of gossip and that the mothers' group would become known as the local baby batterers' group. The mothers openly discussed this problem from the beginning. It became clear that as they confided in each other more their fear of gossip diminished. The group general practitioner found it possible to keep surgery consultations separate from group discussions. This removed the mothers' fear of breach of confidentiality. Some group members brought along to the doctor other women in similar difficulties, which meant that they had openly acknowledged their own problems to comparative strangers.

After about three months the demands these families made on the local services were reduced. Health visitors and social workers found work with the families more easy and less anxiety-provoking. When crises did arise the families were able to accept help and use it more constructively; thus more time was available for other families not attending the group.

One of the most gratifying results of the project is that morale has been raised throughout health and social services teams. Staff are no longer reluctant to identify cases of potential abuse but rather seek out mothers likely to benefit from the help offered. Consequently, the problem of child abuse is now faced with greater confidence and optimism.

Jacqueline Roberts and Margaret Lynch are funded by a research grant from Action Research for the Crippled Child. We thank Kate Beswick and her helpers, St Birinus' School for Boys, Didcot, and Didcot Girls' School for their help and cooperation, Didcot Round Table for their financial support, and all members of the local social services and primary health care teams for their support and encouragement. The independent social work assessments were carried out by Hilary Paul. Invaluable advice was given by Dr J. Lindsay. We also thank the Park Hospital occupational therapy department for their kind cooperation.

References

Baher, E., et al. (1976): 'At Risk. The NSPCC Battered Child Research Team', Routledge and Kegan Paul, London.
Beswick, K., Lynch, M. A., and Roberts, J. (1976): Brit. med. J., ii, 800.
Kempe, C. H. (1971): Arch. Dis. Childh, 46, 28.
Lynch, M. A. (1976): in 'The Abused Child', edited by H. P. Martin, Ballinger, Cambridge, Mass.
Martin, H. P. (1976): Ibid.
—— et al. (1974): Advanc. Pediat., 21, 25.
Ounsted, C., Oppenheimer, R., and Lindsay, J. (1974): Develop. Med. Child Neurol., 16, 447.
Whitaker, D. S. (1975): Brit. J. soc. Work, 5, 423.

COMPREHENSIVE TREATMENT OF PARENTS
WHO ABUSE THEIR CHILDREN

John S. Wodarski, Ph.D.*

ABSTRACT

This article reviews the scope and current treatment approaches to child abuse. It elucidates the rationale for a comprehensive program consisting of child management, marital enrichment, vocational skills enrichment, and interpersonal enrichment components. Each of these four components of the program is briefly reviewed. The article concludes with a discussion of the implementation and evaluation of the program.

INTRODUCTION

Currently such various approaches as psychopathological, sociological, social-situational, social learning, and family systems are used in the treatment of parents who abuse their children.

The *psychopathological model* of child abuse emphasizes direct services (Grodner, 1977). The services provided may consist of individual, group and lay treatment, volunteer companions, and self-help groups, all of which focus on the psychopathology of the parent and provide the parent with the necessary supports for maintaining the family intact. Treatment goals for these parents include helping them establish trusting, gratifying relationships with the therapist and with other adults, improving the parent's chronically low self-esteem, enabling the parent to derive pleasure from the child and from his/her own accomplishments, and helping the parent to understand the relationship between his/her own painful childhood and current actions and attitudes toward the child (Green, 1978 a & b).

The *sociological model's* approach to intervention in child abuse emphasizes the need for wide-ranging changes in social values and structures. Parke and Collmer (1975) state that prevention of child abuse, according to this model, would require reconceptualization of childhood, of children's rights and of child-rearing. Major sources of stress and frustration, which are felt to trigger child abuse episodes, would

*Director, Research Institute, School of Social Work, University of Georgia, Athens, Georgia 30602

Preparation of this manuscript was supported in part by University of Maryland and University of Georgia Graduate School Faculty Research Awards.

ADOLESCENCE, Vol. XVI No. 64, Winter 1981
Libra Publishers, Inc., 391 Willets Rd., Roslyn Hts., N.Y. 11577

need to be eliminated. Some of the general suggestions offered by proponents of this model include:

> providing adequate income through employment and/or guaranteed income maintenance
> comprehensive health care and social services
> decent and adequate housing
> comprehensive educational opportunities geared toward the realization of each person's potential
> cultural and recreational facilities

Other proposals that are more specific to child abuse involve comprehensive family planning programs, family life education programs, and support services such as day-care and homemaker services.

The *social-situational model*'s approach to treatment is based upon the assumption that the cause of child abuse lies not in the individual, but in the social situation, which may, in turn, be maintaining abusive patterns of behavior (Parke and Collmer, 1975). This model focuses upon the modification of observable behavior in the home environment. It emphasizes that there is a high degree of interdependence between the abusing parent and the child and, therefore, both must be involved in treatment. This model advocates the use of techniques to modify the child's behavior such as reinforcement, time out, and verbal reasoning. Programs for parent education and retraining are suggested as a means of modifying the parent's disciplinary methods.

The *family systems model*'s approach to treatment resembles that of the social-situational model in that it too emphasizes changing the family's patterns of interactions and behaviors. However, this model emphasizes that the underlying structure and organization of the family must change to prevent the recurrence of the same destructive patterns (Levitt, 1977). The therapist must work with the family to find new, more attractive roles for all members of the family. The role of the therapist is collaborative and the parents are respected as the source of control in the family.

Finally, the *social learning approach* to treatment involves the identification of behavioral goals and specific techniques for achieving these goals, and the use of social reinforcers to facilitate this process (Tracy and Clark, 1974). This approach recommends the use of treatment personnel who are of similar socioeconomic and racial backgrounds as the abusive parents as it is felt that the parents are more likely to respond to these workers.

These approaches are characterized by their focus on only certain elements contributing to child abuse. This singular focus limits the

960

effectiveness of the various treatment regimens. This article addresses the scope of the problem of abuse and provides the empirical rationale for the comprehensive treatment program consisting of child management, marital enrichment, vocational skills enrichment, and interpersonal enrichment components. The article concludes with a discussion of the implications of implementing such an approach.

Scope of the Problem of Child Abuse

Assessing the seriousness and complexity of this social problem presents a difficult task. Three basic criteria were suggested by Manis (1974) to determine the seriousness of social problems: the extent or the frequency of the problem, the severity or level of harmfulness of the problem, and the primacy of the problem (its causal impact on other problems).

If we were to apply this set of criteria in analyzing the problem of child abuse, we would begin by looking at the incidence of the problem. Information regarding incidence, however, is confounded by several factors: differences in definitions between states and varied reporting mechanisms; the combining of abuse and neglect in the reporting statutes and statistics of some states; problems in determining whether reports of abuse have been substantiated; and, perhaps most importantly, the unavailability of data on the number of cases of abuse that take place within the private confines of a family and are never reported (Green, 1978 a & b).

Webb and Friedman (1976) proposed to employ randomized response techniques with a probability sample drawn from the entire United States in an effort to determine actual incidences of abuse. However, most estimates of the incidence of abuse use only reported cases as their starting point while failing to address the issue of unreported cases. Nagi (1975) arrived at an estimated annual incidence of approximately 260,000 cases while Cohen and Sussman (1975) have estimated 41,104 annual cases of abuse. Nagi based his estimate on the number of cases reported to a sample of county agencies and applied a correction factor for the number of cases typically substantiated. Cohen and Sussman applied the same technique but based their estimates on a sample of data from different states. Helfer and Kempe (1976) indicate that there were approximately 550,000 incidences of suspected child abuse in the United States in 1975. Newberger (1977) combined the estimates of incidence of abuse and neglect and arrived at a figure in excess of one million. These estimates, though widely diverse, illustrate the severity of this social problem.

The second criterion, the severity of the consequences of abuse, is probably a more valid indicator of the seriousness of the problem, even

961

though Cohen and Sussman (1975) suggest that estimates of deaths resulting from child abuse are about as variable as total incidence estimates. Blumberg (1974) estimated that 25% of all fractures diagnosed in children under five result from abuse. Even more frightening is the evidence that child abuse is currently regarded as the leading cause of death in children and as a significant public health problem (Green, 1978 a & b). Data on the frequency of irreversible but non-fatal physical injuries resulting from abuse are very important for a total evaluation of the seriousness of the problem of abuse but these data are frequently confounded.

The third criterion, the causal impact of the problem on other problems, is difficult to apply in the area of abuse, mainly due to the lack of follow-up studies. The long-term effects of abuse may be determined by the general conditions under which the abused child is raised (Elmer, 1967, 1975; Friedman and Morse, 1974; Martin, 1972; Martin, Beezley, Conway, and Kempe, 1974; Morse, Sahler, and Friedman, 1970; Rolston, 1971). Abused children raised outside of their own homes had fewer long-term deficits than those raised within their homes (Elmer, 1967; Morse et al., 1970), and children raised in homes characterized as stable suffered fewer long-term effects than did those raised in less stable homes (Martin et al., 1974). That the influence of the overall living conditions is greater than the influence of the actual abuse itself is supported further by Rolston (1971) who looked at formerly abused children living in foster care, and Friedman and Morse (1974) and Elmer (1975) who compared abused children with accident victims.

It appears that the behavioral and psychological effects of abuse may be reversible, but unless the environment is improved either through an effective treatment program or removal of the child to a new home, the abused child will likely develop severe mental and physical health problems. Thus the effects of child abuse are not only immediately evident, but unfortunately consequences endure.

Rationale for Comprehensive Treatment Program

Data indicate that parents who abuse their children face multiple social and psychological difficulties. The clearest empirical finding with regard to child abuse seems to be the lack of consistency by the parent or parents in the handling of their children and the consequent lack of effectiveness in managing the child's behavior (Elmer, 1967; Derdeyn, 1977; Young, 1964; Tracy and Clark, 1974). It has also been pointed out that another common feature of relationships between abusive parents and their children is unrealistic expectations by the parents about what constitutes appropriate behavior at each devel-

962

opmental stage, such as when the child can respond to reasonable requests, length of attention span, ability to entertain themselves, and so forth (Green, 1978 a & b; Laury, 1970; Steele, 1970; Steele and Pollock, 1968; Pollock and Steele, 1972; Spinetta and Rigler, 1972). Their data provide support for the position that abusive parents would stand to benefit from specific training in what to expect from their children, in procedures for teaching social skills and tasks to their children, and the appropriate application of child management procedures.

Another empirical finding of substance has been the high degree of marital strain evident in abusive families (and the interpersonal strain between unmarried adult parents) (Blumberg, 1974; Elmer, 1967; Green, 1978b; Johnson and Morse, 1968; Kempe and Kempe, 1978; Lukianowicz, 1971, 1972; Melnick and Hurley, 1969; Nurse, 1964; Smith, 1975; Smith, Hanson, and Noble, 1974; Thomson, Paget, Bates, Mesch, and Putnam, 1971; and Young, 1964). In view of this finding, a comprehensive treatment approach should include appropriate interventions that teach communications skills, problem solving, conflict resolution, and so forth, to marital or unwed partners.

Recent evidence suggests that many parents who abuse their children are dissatisfied with their vocational occupations and their interpersonal relationships with others, i.e., have poor self-concepts, feelings of worthlessness, and so forth (Brown and Daniels, 1968; Elmer, 1977; Gelles, 1973; Gil, 1975; Galdston, 1965; Green, 1978 a & b; Lystad, 1975; Holter and Friedman, 1969).

Data from these four different foci indicate that a comprehensive treatment program would involve provision of services in all four areas. The lack of effectiveness of traditional programs stems largely from their providing only one service (Gaines, Sandgrund, Green, and Power, 1978; Gil, 1975; Grodner, 1977; Kempe and Helfer, 1972; Selig, 1976; Tracy, 1974). It is logical that a treatment approach to abuse must view the problem as multi-determined and services should be structured in such a manner. Thus, the comprehensive treatment program should consist of the following:

1. Child Management Program
2. Marital Enrichment Program
3. Vocational Skills Enrichment Program
4. Interpersonal Enrichment Program

Programs to accomplish the acquisition of requisite skills in each area are chosen from the technology of applied behavioral analysis. Recent reviews of parent training programs (Berkowitz and Graziano,

963

1972; Graziano, 1977; O'Dell, 1974), marital enrichment (Jacobson and Martin, 1976; Bagarozzi and Wodarski, 1977, 1978), and interpersonal skills training (Lange and Jakubowski, 1976; Rich and Schroeder, 1976; Schinke and Rose, 1976) have shown that their effectiveness is substantial as compared to other treatment programs. Data supporting vocational enrichment programs from the behavioral perspective is accumulating (Azrin, 1978; Azrin, Flores, and Kaplan, 1975; Jones and Azrin, 1973; Kelly, Laughlin, Claiborne, and Patterson, 1979).

Behavioral Group Work Approach

Even though we have witnessed a growing emphasis on group treatment in recent years, relatively few clients who abuse their children are treated in this manner as compared to those treated individually. The provision of services in groups offers the following positive aspects: The group interactional situation more frequently typifies many kinds of daily interactions. Services that facilitate the development of behaviors which enable people to interact in groups are likely to better prepare them for participation in larger society; that is, will help them learn social skills necessary to secure reinforcement (Feldman and Wodarski, 1975). From a social learning theory perspective, it is posited that if a behavior is learned in a group context, it is likely to come under the control of a greater number of discriminative stimuli; therefore, greater generalization of the behavior can occur for a broader variety of interactional contexts. There are additional substantiated rationales for working with individuals in groups. Groups provide a context where new behaviors can be tested in a realistic atmosphere. Clients can get immediate peer feedback and support regarding their problem-solving behaviors. They are provided with role models to facilitate the acquisition of necessary and requisite social behavior. Groups provide a more valid locus for accurate diagnosis and a more potent means for changing client behavior (Holmes, 1978; Meyer and Smith, 1977; Rose, 1977). Additionally many parents who abuse their children feel guilt, emptiness, social isolation, and a sense of failure and could benefit from the support derived from the group (Galdston, 1971; Walters, 1975). Lastly, the provision of services through groups greatly increases the number of clients that can be served by an effective treatment program (Wodarski and Bagarozzi, 1979, Chapter Nine).

It has been suggested that the reason why treatment programs have not produced significant results in treating parents who abuse their children is that they focus on only one of the factors that operate to produce child abuse, i.e., lack of child management skills, marital dissatisfaction, vocational, or interpersonal dissatisfaction. Previous re-

964

search conducted by the author and a number of others suggests that treatment programs which focus on a variety of difficulties would be beneficial in reducing abuse.

Treatment Packages[1]

A. Child Management Program:

The child management program is based on Patterson's (1971, 1975), Patterson's and Fleischman's (1979), and Jensen's (1976) work with families. The general components that are emphasized include:

1. General introduction to the behaviors that are appropriate for children at different developmental stages.
2. General introduction to how the provision of certain consequences and stimuli can control behavior.
3. How to isolate and define a behavior to be changed.
4. The use of appropriate consequences to either increase or decrease a behavior.
5. Use of stimulus control techniques to influence rates of behavior.
6. Use of simple graphs and tables to chart behavioral change.

B. Marital Enrichment Program:

The Marital Enrichment Program is based on Bagarozzi's and Wodarski's (1977, 1978) and Wodarski's and Bagarozzi's (1979, Chapter 7) work on behavioral treatment of marital discord. The general components emphasized include:

1. Problem identification, assessment and determination of treatment procedures.
2. Formalizing the treatment process.
3. Preliminary training in communication skills, problem solving and conflict resolution strategies, and so forth.
4. Locating relationship, reward inequities.
5. Formulation of exchange contracts.
6. Phasing out of concrete reinforcers and building in natural reinforcers to insure behavioral change.
7. Follow-up evaluation.

C. Vocational Enrichment Program:

The vocational program is based on the work of Jones and Azrin (1973); Azrin, Flores, and Kaplan (1975); and Azrin (1978). The general components emphasized are:

[1]Manuals for implementation of each package are available from the author upon request.

965

1. Group discussions involving strong motivation for vocational enrichment. These discussions involve mutual assistance among job seekers, development of a supportive buddy system, family support, sharing of job leads, and widening the variety of positions considered.
2. Employment-securing aids such as searching want ads, role playing interview situations, instructions in telephoning for appointments, procedures for motivating the job seeker, developing appropriate conversational competencies, ability to emphasize strong personal attributes in terms of dress and grooming, and securing transportation for job interviews.

D. The Social Enrichment Program:

This program is based on the work of Lange and Jakubowski (1976) involving interpersonal skills training and development of assertive behavior for appropriate situations. Specific elements that are emphasized include:

1. Skills on how to introduce oneself.
2. Skills in how to initiate conversations and continue them.
3. Skills in giving and receiving compliments.
4. Enhancing appearance.
5. Skills in making and refusing requests.
6. Spontaneous expression of feelings.
7. Appropriate use of nonverbal behavior such as posture, gestures, eye contact, touching, interpersonal distance, body language, face, hands, and foot movement and smiling.

PROGRAM IMPLEMENTATION AND EVALUATION

Selection Criteria

Parents are referred by a network of agencies including the Department of Human Resources, Family Services, and community mental health centers.

Parents are administered a battery of self inventories assessing the following:

1. Parental attitudes toward child
2. Marital satisfaction
3. Vocational satisfaction
4. Social satisfaction

966

TABLE 1

MAJOR ASPECTS OF TREATMENT

Baseline	Child Management* Program	Marital Enrichment* Program	Vocational and Social Enrichment Program*	First Follow-Up	Second Follow-Up	Third Follow-Up
	8-Weeks Duration	8-Weeks Duration	8-Weeks Duration	8-Weeks after Conclusion	6-Months Later	1-Year Later

*Measurement occurs during baseline, at the conclusion of each 8-week program, and at the conclusion of the first, second, and third follow-up periods.

967

79

Previous research by Hudson indicates that a score of 30 or above on the Parental Attitude Toward Child Scale, Marital Satisfaction Scale and Social Satisfaction Scale provides criteria for selecting those who should benefit from the service program (Hudson, 1977; Hudson and Glisson, 1976; Hudson and Proctor, 1976). A similar criterion is being established for vocational satisfaction. Parents who score above the necessary criteria on three of these measures are asked to participate in the program. If the requirement were imposed that parents had to score above the necessary criteria on all four measures, the procedural difficulties involved in securing participants for the program might be too costly. However, the data are secured on all four measures to assess whether such stringent criteria can be imposed and how they relate to treatment outcome.

A behavioral observation scale is administered to assess the following parental behaviors directed toward their children: directions and commands, physical contact, praise, positive attention, holding, criticisms, threats, negative attention, and so forth, and the incidence of pro-social, non-social, and anti-social behavior exhibited by the children.

The major aspects of the comprehensive program are illustrated in Table 1.

DISCUSSION

Despite the recent attention the problem of child abuse has received, there is total lack of well developed and evaluated treatment programs that can offer concrete assistance to mental health and protective service workers.

To reduce or prevent child abuse, it will be necessary to offer new ways of developing behaviors that will bring parents reinforcement. The proposed program combines several means of effectively changing behavior for parents who abuse their children. Each aspect is chosen for the strong empirical base upon which it rests.

The manuscript elucidates the relationship between conceptual knowledge, research evaluation, and possible subsequent alteration of services provided. It has been illustrated how conceptual knowledge can be used in the foundation of a treatment program. Currently we are implementing a program based on this model. Our data will enable the determination of those aspects of the program which are relevant and essential to the ability of the comprehensive program to reduce child abuse.

968

REFERENCES

Azrin, N.H. *A learning approach to job finding*. Paper presented at Association for Advancement of Behavior Therapy, Chicago, November 1978.

Azrin, N.H., Flores, H. and Kaplan, S.J. "Job-finding Club: A Group-assisted Program for Obtaining Employment," *Behavior Research and Therapy*, 1975, *13*, 17-27.

Bagarozzi, D.A. and Wodarski, J.S. "A Social Exchange Typology of Conjugal Relationships and Conflict Development: Some Implications for Clinical Practice, Assessment, and Future Research, *Journal of Marriage and Family*, 1977, *39*, 53-60.

Bagarozzi, D.A. and Wodarski, J.S. "Behavioral Treatment of Marital Discord," *Clinical Social Work Journal*, 1978, 6, 2, 135-154.

Berkowitz, B.P. and Graziano, A.M. "Training Parents as Behavior Therapists: A Review," *Behavior Research and Therapy*, 1972, *10*, 297-317.

Blumberg, M.L. "Psychopathology of the Abusing Parent," *American Journal of Psychotherapy*, 1974, *28*, 21-29.

Brown, J. and Daniels, R. "Some Observations of Abusive Parents," *Child Welfare*, 1968, *47*, 89-94.

Cohen, S.J. and Sussman, A. "The Incidence of Child Abuse in the United States," *Child Welfare*, 1975, *54*, 432-444.

Derdeyn, A.P. "Child Abuse and Neglect: The Rights of Parents and the Needs of Their Children," *American Journal of Orthopsychiatry*, 1977, *43*, 377-387.

Elmer, E. *Children in Jeopardy*. Pittsburgh: University of Pittsburgh Press, 1967.

Elmer, E. *Fragile Families, Troubled Children*. Pittsburgh: University of Pittsburgh Press, 1977.

Elmer, E. Personal communication, 1975.

Feldman, R.A. and Wodarski, J.S. *Contemporary Approaches to Group Treatment*. San Francisco: Jossey-Bass Publishers, 1975.

Friedman, S.B. and Morse, C.W. "Child Abuse: A Five-year Follow-up of Early Case Findings in the Emergency Department," *Pediatrics*, 1974, *54*, 404-410.

Gaines, R., Sandgrund, A., Green, A.H. and Power, E. "Etiological Factors in Child Maltreatment: A Multivariate Study of Abusing, Neglecting, and Normal Mothers," *Journal of Abnormal Psychology*, 1978, 87, 531-540.

Galdston, R. "Observations on Children Who Have Been Physically Abused and Their parents," *American Journal of Psychiatry*, 1965, *122*, 439-540.

Galdston, R. "Violence Begins at Home: The Parents Center Project for the Study and Prevention of Child Abuse," *Journal of the American Academy of Child Psychiatry*, 1971, *10*, 2, 336-350.

Gelles, R. "Child Abuse and Psychopathology: A Sociological Critique and Reformulation," *American Journal of Orthopsychiatry*, 1973, *43*, 611-621.

Gil, D.G. "Unraveling Child Abuse," *American Journal of Orthopsychiatry*, 1975, *45*, 346-356.

Graziano, A.M. "Parents as Behavior Therapists," in M. Hersen, R. M. Eisler and P.M. Miller (Eds.), *Progress in Behavior Modification* (Vol. 4). New York: Academic Press, 1977.

Green, A. "Psychopathology of Abused Children," *American Journal of Psychiatry*, 1978a, *17*, 1, 92-103.

969

Green, A.J. "Child Abuse," in B.B. Wolman, J. Egan and A. Ross (Eds.), *Handbook of Treatment of Mental disorders in Childhood and Adolescence.* Englewood Cliffs, New Jersey: Prentice-Hall, Inc., 1978b.

Grodner, B. "A Family Systems Approach to Treatment of Child Abuse: Etiology and Intervention," in *Child Abuse and Neglect: Issues on Intervention and Implementation* (Vol. II). Symposium presented at 2nd Annual Conference on Child Abuse and Neglect, 1977.

Helfer, R.E., Kempe, C.H. (Eds.). *Child Abuse and Neglect: The Family and the Community.* Cambridge, Massachusetts: Ballinger Publishing Company, 1976.

Holmes, S. "Parents Anonymous: A Treatment Method for Child Abuse," *Social Work*, 1978, *23,* 3, 245-247.

Holter, J. and Friedman, S. "Etiology and Management of Severely Burned Children: Psychosocial Considerations," *American Journal Disturbed Child,* 1969, *118,* 680-686.

Hudson, W.W. *A measurement package for clinical workers.* Paper presented at the 23rd Annual Program Meeting of the Council on Social Work Education, Phoenix, February 1977.

Hudson, W.W. and Glisson, D.H. "Assessment of Marital Discord in Social Work Practice," *Social Service Review,* 1976, *50,* 293-311.

Hudson, W.W. and Proctor, E.K. A short-form scale for measuring self-esteem. St. Louis: Washington University Georgia Warren Brown School of Social Work, 1976, (mimeo).

Jacobson, N.S. and Martin, B. "Behavior Marriage Therapy: Current Status," *Psychological Bulletin,* 1976, *83,* 540-556.

Jensen, R.E. "A Behavior Modification Program to Remediate Child Abuse," *Journal of Clinical Child Psychology,* 1976, *5,* 1, 30-32.

Johnson, B. and Morse, N. "Injured Children and Their Parents," *Children,* 1968, 15, 147-152.

Jones, R.J. and Azrin, N.H. "An Experimental Application of a Social Reinforcement Approach to the Problem of Job Finding," *Journal of Applied Behavior Analysis,* 1973, *6,* 345-353.

Kelly, J.A., Laughlin, C., Claiborne, M. and Patterson, J. "A Group Procedure for Teaching Job Interviewing Skills to Formerly Hospitalized Psychiatric Patients," *Behavior Therapy,* 1979, *10,* 299-310.

Kempe, C.H. and Helfer, R.E. *Helping the Battered Child and His Family.* Philadelphia: J.B. Lippincott, 1972.

Kempe, R.S. and Kempe, C.H. *Child Abuse.* Cambridge, Massachusetts: Harvard University Press, 1978.

Lange, A.J. and Jakubowski, P. *Responsible Assertive Behavior.* Champaign, Illinois: Research Press, 1976.

Laury, G. "The Battered-Child Syndrome: Parental Motivation, Clinical Aspects," *Bulletin New York Academy Medicine,* 1970, *46,* 676-685.

Levitt, J.M. "A Family Systems Approach to Treatment of Child Abuse," in *Child Abuse and Neglect: Issues on Innovation and Implementation, 2.* Proceedings of the Second National Conference on Child Abuse and Neglect, 1977.

Lukianowicz, N. "Attempted Infanticide," *Psychiatria Clinica,* 1972, *5,* 1-16.

Lukianowicz, N. "Battered Children," *Psychiatria Clinica,* 1971, *4,* 257-280.

Lystad, M.H. "Violence at Home: A Review of the Literature," *American Journal of Orthopsychiatry,* 1975, *45,* 328-345.

970

Manis, J.G. "Assessing the Seriousness of Social Problems," *Social Problems,* 1974, *22*, 1-15.

Martin, H. "The Child and His Development," in C.H. Kempe and R.E. Helfer (Eds.), *Helping the Battered Child and His Family.* Philadelphia: J.B. Lippincott, 1972.

Martin, H.P., Beezley, P., Conway, E.F. and Kempe, C.H. "The Development of Abused Children," *Advances in Pediatrics,* 1974, *21*, 25-73.

Melnick, B., and Hurley, J.R. "Distinctive Personality Attributes of Child-abusing Mothers," *Journal of Consulting and Clinical Psychology,* 1969, *33*, 746-749.

Meyer, R.G. and Smith, S.S. "A Crisis in Group Therapy," *American Psychologist,* 1977, *32*, 638-643.

Morse, C.W., Sahler, O.J., and Friedman, S.B. A Three-year Follow-up Study of Abused and Neglected Children," *American Journal of Diseases of Children,* 1970, *120*, 439-446.

Nagi, S.Z. "Child Abuse and Neglect Programs: A National Overview," *Children Today,* 1975, *4*, 13-17.

Newberger, E.H. "Child Abuse and Neglect: Toward a Firmer Foundation for Practice and Policy," *American Journal of Orthopsychiatry,* 1977, *47*, 374-376.

Nurse, S.M. "Familial Patterns of Parents Who Abuse Their Children," *Smith College Studies of Social Work,* 1964, *34*, 11-25.

O'Dell, S. "Training Parents in Behavior Modification: A Review," *Psychological Bulletin,* 1974, *81*, 418-433.

Parke, R.D., Collmer, W. "Child Abuse: An Interdisciplinary Analysis," in E.M. Heatherington, Ed., Child Development Research, No. 5, 1975.

Patterson, G.R. *Families.* Eugene. Oregon: Castalia, 1975.

Patterson, G.R. *Families: Application of Social Learning to Family Life.* Champaign, Illinois: Research Press, 1971.

Patterson, G.R. and Fleischman, M.J. "Maintenance of Treatment Effects: Some Considerations Concerning Family Systems and Follow-up Data," *Behavior Therapy,* 1979, *10*, 168-185.

Pollock, C. and Steele, B. "A Therapeutic Approach to the Parents," in C.G. Kempe and R.E. Helfer (Eds.), *Helping the Battered Child and His Family.* Philadelphia: J.B. Lippincott, 1972.

Rich, A.H. and Schroeder, H.E. "Research Issues in Assertiveness Training," *Psychological Bulletin,* 1976, *83*, 1081-1096.

Rolston, R.G. "The Effect of Prior Physical Abuse on the Expression of Overt and Fantasy Aggressive Behavior in Children," *Dissertation Abstracts International,* Ann Arbor, Michigan: University Microfilms, Number 71-29389, 1971.

Rose, S.D. *Group Therapy: A Behavioral Approach.* Englewood Cliffs: Prentice-Hall, 1977.

Schinke, S.P. and Rose, S.O. "Interpersonal Skill Training in Groups," *Journal of Counseling Psychology,* 1976, *23*, 442-448.

Selig, A.L. "The Myths of the Multi-problem Family," *American Journal of Orthopsychiatry,* 1976, *46*, 526-532.

Smith, S.M. *The Battered Child Syndrome.* London & Boston: Butterworth's, 1975.

Smith, S.M., Hanson, R. and Noble, S. "Social Aspects of the Battered Baby Syndrome," *British Journal of Psychiatry,* 1974, *125*, 568-582.

971

Spinetta, J. and Rigler, D. "The Child-abusing Parent: A Psychological Review," *Psychological Bulletin,* 1972, *77,* 296-304.

Steele, B.F. "Parental Abuse of Infants and Small Children," in E.J. Anthony and T. Benedek (Eds.), *Parenthood.* Boston: Little, Brown and Co., 1970.

Steele, B.F. and Pollock, C.B. "A Psychiatric Study of Parents Who Abuse Infants and Small Children," in R.E. Helfer and C.J. Kempe (Eds.), *The Battered Child.* Chicago: University of Chicago Press, 1968.

Thomson, E.M., Paget, N.W., Bates, D.W., Mesch, M. and Putnam, T.I. *Child Abuse: A Community Challenge.* New York: Henry Steward, Inc., 1971.

Tracy, J.J. and Clark, E.H. "Treatment for Child Abusers," *Social Work,* 1974, *19,* 338-343.

Walters, D.R. *Physical and Sexual Abuse of Children.* Bloomington & London: Indiana University Press, 1975.

Webb, K.W. and Friedman, F.G.A. *Child Abuse and Neglect: Methods for Determining Incidence.* Paper presented at Annual Meeting of Council on Social Work Education, Philadelphia, March 1976.

Wodarski, J.S. and Bagarozzi, D. *Behavioral Social Work.* New York: Human Sciences Press, 1979.

Young, L. *Wednesday's Children.* New York: McGraw-Hill, 1964.

SEPARATION AND TREATMENT
OF CHILD-ABUSING FAMILIES

Patricia Ross Shelton

ABSTRACT

The effect of removing physically or sexually abused or neglected children from their families is examined. Working with the family and abused child(ren) throughout separation and the court process is discussed, including keeping a divided family in therapy, treatment contracts, cross-cultural therapy requirements, and inter-system coordination.

SEPARATION AND TREATMENT OF CHILD-ABUSING FAMILIES

The Effect of separating Child from Family

When a child or adolescent reports to someone that he or she has been physically abused, sexually molested, or severely neglected (or it appears so from behavior or physical evidence), the unwitting child is setting off repercussions that often include complete disruption of the family and immediate removal from home. The extent and severity of that separation and upheaval usually will be completely out of the child's control.

In many communities, children who must for the sake of safety be separated from their families are placed in an emergency shelter (or foster home) for boys or girls. Before being brought there by a social worker, they receive thorough physical examinations to determine the degree of physical or sexual damage. This evidence is necessary to bring the case to trial. Though examining physicians move cautiously and patiently, the process is a further invasion and stripping, especially for the sexually abused child.

A very frightened child walks through the door of the shelter, and despite the social worker's reassurance, does not know what to expect or even when he or she will see family again.

Generally, the child's most urgent fear about the shelter is relieved as soon as the child meets other residents. He or she may receive calls from family members and, under the watchful eyes of staff, is allowed parent visitation.

The author is Program Director of Charila Foundation (for abused girls 6-18) in San Francisco, CA and is a Ph.D. candidate in marital and family therapy.

Reprint requests to Patricia Ross Shelton, 42 Azalea, Fairfax, California 94930.

FAMILY THERAPY, Volume IX, Number 1, 1982
Libra Publishers, Inc., 391 Willets Rd., Roslyn Hts., N.Y. 11577

Meanwhile, the abusing or neglectful parent (unless mentally ill and requiring hospitalization) begins another kind of stripping process to determine adequacy and guilt. Many parents deny abuse, so the child's word and any other verification must be pitted against theirs. These are the battles that can mean the child languishes in shelter for six months or more—especially in the case of sexual molestation or pathologically enmeshed families. "Permanency planning" cannot begin until custody (with the parent or by the state) is determined.

Child abuse, whether physical or sexual, observes no socioeconomic boundary. It is well known that a high proportion of abusive parents were themselves abused (Martin, 1976). Women who were sexually abused as children seem to marry men and create families similar to their own.

Many of the sexually abused girls entering shelter have been molested by a stepfather, foster father, or mother's boyfriend. In these cases, as well as with biological fathers, denial of abuse means the girl cannot go back home until the man is out. Dependent, passive, needy women may be reluctant to lose a man who has been good to them, and may attempt to convince the daughter she is wrong. This triples the pain, guilt, and pressure the abandoned girl already feels.

Physically abusive families may likewise pull together to face a common enemy—the child and the social service system—and pressure the child to turn against self in order to save the parent(s) from further harm and responsibility. Some of these children then explode psychologically and act out sexually or against other children, as their parents have done to them.

As the days, weeks and months roll by, and the child remains in shelter, the impact on his or her life escalates. An emergency clothing allowance must be requisitioned just to obtain gym clothes (if the child has been allowed to remain in the neighborhood school) but that takes paperwork, coordination among several agencies, and perhaps two or three weeks wait. Even with proper clothing, sexually abused children tend to cut physical education class because the locker room situation is frightening.

If the child in shelter is well-behaved and polite, angrier residents may begin emotionally and physically to attack the child's conformity, identifying with the aggressor (introjected parent) to achieve a feeling of control.

Meals, snacks, outings, bedtime, passes, visits, phone calls and guests are institutionally prescribed to meet the needs of the understaffed shelter as a whole and for the protection of the child. Staff may be loving, competent and even therapeutic, but at times are severely tested by the children's pain and hopeless rage and the defenses used in order not to feel them.

54

Many of the children abused by their families have had to put self aside for years—parentifying mother, pacifying father, developing false selves that help to avoid abuse which may erupt unpredictably at any time.

These children generally do not separate psychologically from their mothers. Splitting occurs between the good, nurturing, idealized mother and the bad, abandoning, hated mother. The child clings emotionally to the former (or her substitute), and each time separation threatens, experiences raw survival fear. Many children harden themselves so as never to be hurt again.

In the present state of the social service delivery system, separation from family is typical in child abuse cases. Many children grow up in out-of-home placement such as foster or group homes because the system is funded that way. State and federal money has not been allocated for in-home family therapy as a preventive measure or following reunification.

In San Francisco, a consortium of private agencies is being formed to demonstrate the economic and social feasibility of preventing family separation by starting in-home treatment early. One hopes that a demonstration project will be funded. Family reunification is a trend, fortunately, and many agencies and therapists now orient themselves to this goal.

Family Therapy: Alternative to Total Family Disruption
A. Helping families through initial stages

Therapists in private practice and in agencies serving abused children attempt to maintain close working contact with parents. Private therapists usually encounter difficulty keeping an abusive family in treatment due to the hostility engendered if the therapist must report abuse or neglect to the police or child welfare department. This problem might be ameliorated by the following procedures:

1. Thoroughly explain to the family what the therapist is required to do, and when.

2. Prepare the family as to what will happen next and further in the future.

3. Help the family identify the specific problems in child- and self-management and marital functioning that contributed to abuse or neglect.

4. Educate the family as to what they can gain by successfully dealing with these problems, including possible return of the child.

5. Draw up and have parents sign a contract that delineates specific improvements required of them for eventual reunification with the child, and what they can expect from the therapist in this regard.

55

6. Be at the family home when authorities arrive to pick up the child(ren), and work with the family's anger and loss.

7. Foster family/agency contact, advocacy, and contain acting-out that leads to lengthy legal battles; get to know the social worker with primary responsibility for the case; mutual goals are imperative.

8. Have family members consult with groups concerned with abuse and related problems, such as Parents United (for child sexual abuse); Parents Anonymous (child physical abuse); Children Anonymous; Alcoholics Anonymous, Alanon and Alateen (families with an alcoholic member). These national groups are very effective and provide free service to families. Many local groups have also been established.

9. Retain one's therapeutic objectivity and a systems point of view.

B. Helping children through the court process

Abused and neglected children generally have to testify in court against a parent or parent-surrogate. Particularly if a child has been placed out-of-home during the proceedings, and consequently lacks family support, testifying against the loved (as well as hurtful) parent is a weighty and torturous prospect. Very often no one takes the time to prepare the child for the court process and probable outcome (e.g., parent placed on probation; child remanded to custody of the court; a six-month time period before next reassessment).

Many children are placed under excruciating pressure from family members to recant. This, combined with guilt from already "hurting the parents by telling on them," can produce an emotional breakdown and capitulation. The child returns home alone to face the family's wrath.

Children and teenagers who must testify against a parent therefore require good preparation, coupled with a strong and oft-repeated statement that they are not to blame for what has happened: "Parents are supposed to be responsible for children, and not vice versa. No matter how badly a child acts, abuse is never the right punishment. Children and adolescents never 'ask for' sexual molestation because it is the adult's responsibility to maintain proper boundaries."

Sometimes an abusive parent may be taken to jail even before the trial or serve a short sentence afterward. These results are traumatic for children, who fear the parent will never forgive them. A positive reframing of the situation may be helpful to the child: "The court has mandated that the parent get some help because he or she has serious problems that led to hurting a child. Parents can get help in jail. A parent doesn't change without help. Was the parent abused as a child? The child needs help too, in order not to harden and maybe even abuse her (his) own children. It is not the child's fault that the parent is in jail. She or he did the right thing to protect her/himself and other

56

siblings from further abuse. Parents who learn how to take responsibility for being abusive forgive their child for telling because the child *had* to tell."

C. Family treatment

Since rigid family patterns and low levels of ego differentiation rule out self-initiated system change in disturbed families when pressure is off, abusing systems will revert as quickly as possible to previous functioning. These families do not know how to correct the situation. Therefore, therapists working with them (under *either* voluntary or court-ordered circumstances) must maintain the pressure to change, and can do so through the use of a written contract (Saeger and Grandin, 1981) that specifies in detail the improvements that must be shown in such areas as:

1. Impulse and anger control.
2. Empathy with the child's feelings and needs.
3. Child management techniques, e.g., time-outs; clear limits and follow-through; reward versus punishment.
4. Ability to plan and spend constructive time with the child (e.g., in a family play-therapy format).
5. Time and home management techniques, including promptness and reliability in session attendance; maintaining a clean, orderly home.
6. Improvement in marital subsystem functioning and meeting of intimacy needs.
7. Ability to work as a team, with adequate parent-child role division; not triangulating a child or grandparent into marital or family discord.
8. Willingness to ask for help by turning to friends and/or others for support.
9. Regular attendance in individual therapy or with previously mentioned groups to further the separation-individuation process.
10. Taking complete responsibility for the abuse that has occurred and for protecting children from a potentially abusive spouse or other person.

When several therapists, groups or agencies are involved with family members, it is vital to coordinate their activities and maintain metacommunication. Since disturbed families tend to catch a number of agencies in their net, the coordinator must maintain a systems perspective inclusive of all involved parties. Uncommunicated goals, different views and approaches to individual or family dynamics, and cross-cultural misunderstanding by family workers can be disastrous.

57

In working with poor or cross-cultural families, two points must be observed: 1) the need for clear-cut goals; 2) the need to obtain consultation regarding unfamiliar cultural patterns. For instance, a teenager born in Vietnam of a Vietnamese mother and Mexican-American soldier-father, who later moved to the U.S. with her mother and her new Greek stepfather, then was neglected/rejected by them, has probably faced certain types of problems all her life. For example, she may have been ostracised or ridiculed in Vietnam once her biological father left because she looked like him; her mother also would have been embarrassed by the girl's differentness. In working with this girl's family, therapists would encounter the extreme secrecy of the Vietnamese culture, which prohibits sharing of problems with outsiders.

A girl of Central American descent who has been raped by her stepfather will be considered "spoiled goods" by many in her culture. She will merit neither respect nor empathy and her value as marriage material will be nil. She and her family may need a great deal of assistance for them to regain self-esteem and to counter her tendency to prove her family correct, i.e., to gain a feeling of control over her life by becoming promiscuous.

Family workers must also keep in mind the developmental stages of children, their age-related tasks, and the family's life phase.

Older adolescents may be candidates for early emancipation—enforced separation can speed up the normal process of leaving home. Sometimes family reunification is not possible before the age of majority.

Very disturbed younger children may need to live in a therapeutic milieu for several years, or in a group home, and require individual therapy, special school- and day-treatment programs, before they can unite with their own or substitute families. Emotionally or behaviorally disturbed children placed in foster homes will almost certainly fail—i.e., be rejected, return to shelter, be re-placed—thus compounding their fear, distrust, emotional chaos, and expectation of loss of love.

All professionals working with abused or neglected children must be able to understand and work with negative transference.

Whether or not a child and family are able to reunite, all members involved have to work through the crisis of the breakup of the family, mourn, and continue to develop. If family members are unable to re-stabilize relationships in functional ways, chances are the next generation will suffer a similar fate.

REFERENCES

1. Anthony, E.J., & Benedek, T. (Eds.). *Parenthood: Its psychology and psychopathology*. Boston: Little Brown and Company, 1970.
2. Blumberg, M. Psychopathology of the abusing parent. *American Journal of Psychotherapy*, 1974, *21*.
3. Bowlby, J. *Attachment and loss. Volume 2: Separation: Anxiety and anger*. London: Penquin Books, 1973.
4. Chase, N.F. *A child is being beaten*. New York: Holt, Rinehart and Winston, 1975.
5. Cohn, A.H., Ridge, S.S., & Collignon, F.C. Evaluating innovative treatment programs in child abuse and neglect. *Children Today*, 1975, *4*(3), 10-12.
6. Ebeling, N.B., & Hill, D.A. *Child abuse: Intervention and treatment*. Acton, Mass.: Publishing Sciences Group, 1975.
7. Gil, D.G. Unraveling child abuse. *American Journal of Orthopsychiatry*, 1975, *45*, 346-356.
8. Green, R.J., Visual imagery and behavior prescription in the treatment of parent-child conflict. In A.S. Gurman (Ed.), *Questions and answers in the practice of family therapy*. New York: Brunner/Mazel, 1981.
9. Brunebaum, H., Weiss, J.L., Cohler, B.J., Hartman, C.P., & Gallant, D.H., *Mentally ill mothers and their children*. Chicago: University of Chicago Press, 1975.
10. Helfer, R.E., & Kempe, C.H. (Eds.). *Child abuse and neglect—The family and the community*. Cambridge, Mass.: Bollinger Publishing Company, 1976.
11. Kempe, C.H., & Helfer, R. (Eds.). *The battered child*. Chicago: University of Chicago Press, 1974.
12. Kempe, C.H. and Helfer, R.E. (Eds.). *Helping the battered child and his family*. Philadelphia: J.B. Lippincott, 1972.
13. Lynch, M. *A place of safety: An in-patient facility for abusive families*. Paper presented at the Ad Hoc International Conference on Child Abuse, Bellagio, Italy, October, 1975.
14. Lystad, M.H. Violence at home: A review of the literature. *American Journal of Orthopsychiatry*, 1975, *45*, 328-345.
15. Martin, H.P. (Ed.). *The abused child: A multidisciplinary approach to developmental issues and treatment*. Cambridge, Mass.: Bollinger Publishing Company, 1976.
16. Morris, M.L., & Gould, R.W. Role reversal: A necessary concept in dealing with the "Battered Child Syndrome." *American Journal of Orthopsychiatry*, 1963, *33*, 298-299.
17. Ounsted, C., Oppenheimer, R., & Lindsay, J. Aspects of bonding failure: The psychopathology and psychotherapeutic treatment of families of battered children. *Developmental Medicine and Child Neurology*, 1974, *16*, 447-456.
18. Pardeck, J.T. Family policy: An ecological approach supporting family therapy treatment. In publication, *Family Therapy*, 1982.
19. Polansky, N.A., DeSaix, C., & Sharin, S.A. *Child neglect: Understanding and reaching the parent*. New York: Child Welfare League Publication 618, 1972.
20. Rutter, M. *The qualities of mothering:, Maternal deprivation reassessed*. New York: Jason Aronson, 1974.

59

21. Saeger, K.E., & Grandin, L.A. *Treatment agreement.* Unpublished document. Berkeley, California, 1981.
22. Schneider, C., Helfer, R.E., & Pollack, C. The predictive questionnaire in helping the battered child and his family. In Kempe and Helfer (Eds.), *Helping the battered child and his family.* Philadelphia: J.B. Lippincott, 1972.
23. Sherman, E.H., Neuman, R., & Shyne, A.W. *Children adrift in foster care: A study of alternative approaches.* New York: Child Welfare League Publication F46, 1973.
24. Smith, S.M., Hansen, R., & Noble, S. Parents of battered children: A controlled study. In A.W. Franklin (Ed.), *Concerning child abuse.* New York: Churchill-Livingston, 1975.
25. Spinetta, J.J. and Rigler, D., The child-abusing parent: A psychological review. *Psychological Bulletin,* 1972, 77, 296-304.
26. Stone, H.D. (Ed.). *Foster care in question.* New York: Child Welfare League, 1972.
27. Terr, L. A family study of child abuse. *American Journal of Psychiatry,* 1970, *127,* 125-131.
28. Winnicott, D.W. *The family in individual development.* London: Tavistock Publications, 1965.

This is the final article in Rand D. Conger's Contributing Topic Editor series on child abuse and neglect.

Editor

Behavioral Intervention for Child Abuse

Rand D. Conger, University of Illinois and *Benjamin B. Lahey*, University of Georgia

According to the best evidence that is presently available, there are an estimated one-half to two million acts of physical child abuse committed by parents in the United States each year (Light, 1973; Straus, Gelles & Steinmetz, 1980). In addition to the immediate physical and psychological trauma produced by these attacks, parental violence may have a multitude of adverse consequences for the later social, cognitive, and physical development of children (Conger, 1976; Kempe & Kempe, 1978; Martin, 1975; Rollins & Thomas, 1979). Thus, because of its frequent occurrence, the suffering it inflicts in its victims and the costs it imposes on the community in attempts to cope with the medical and behavioral problems it promotes, the physical abuse of children is now recognized as an important social problem (cf. Zigler, 1979). As such, it is an issue of consequence for behavior therapists (Wolf, 1978).

A variety of intervention strategies have been employed to inhibit abusive behavior. These include traditional psychotherapy as well as procedures specifically developed to decrease parental violence, e.g., parent groups, homemaker services, lay therapists, health visitors, crisis hotlines, parent education, crisis nurseries, and daycare centers (Kempe & Kempe, 1978). Unfortunately, the outcomes produced by these various treatment approaches have not been studied in a fashion that permits valid inferences concerning their effectiveness (Parke & Collmer, 1975; Williams, 1980). For example, none of the above treatment techniques has been evaluated using any type of experimental design nor any assessment procedure other than clinicians' ratings of change. Moreover, even reports based on clinicians' judgments suggest that one-half or fewer of the families served by the above programs improve to the extent that parent-child relationships are significantly altered (Berkeley Planning Associates, 1977; Kempe & Kempe, 1978, see pp. 108–109).

From this brief review it is clear that behavior analysts can make several important contributions to the development of more effective intervention programs for abusive parents. First, they can introduce the use of a variety of valid experimental designs and objective assessment procedures to the field so that various approaches to treatment can be adequately evaluated. Next, they can develop therapeutic techniques for abuse that are based on previous research with other types of family problems and on a body of relevant behavioral theory. Finally, they can determine the extent to which behavioral procedures influence treatment outcomes with these families when used either apart from or in combination with the treatment modalities which are typically employed.

The application of behavioral principles to the treatment of child abuse requires more than a simple extension of routine clinical practice to a new client group, however. By and large, abusive parents do not request help nor do they view their behavior as unusual or harmful. In the discussion that follows, we will first consider the difficult task that the therapist faces in working with this refractive population. Next, several areas of personal and family functioning will be noted that, according to etiological studies of child abuse, should be appropriate targets for behavioral intervention. Finally, a short review will be presented of current attempts to apply behavioral principles in the treatment of parental violence.

Special Difficulties in Child Abuse Intervention

Child abuse may be thought of as one extreme end of a continuum of corporal punishment used by parents to control the behavior of their children (Belsky, 1980). Although the majority of parents condone and at times actually use physical discipline with their offspring (Straus et al., 1980), there are community standards that impose limits on the frequency and intensity of parental violence (Parke & Collmer, 1975). Except for the most obvious cases of severe battering, however, it is not always clear when parents have violated either the formal or informal norms pertaining to the use of punishment. In most cases parents who are referred for treatment have been identified by a protective services caseworker as having exceeded the bounds for the appropriate use of physical discipline – but parents are unlikely to agree with that judgment. Indeed, parents usually will consider the efforts of public agencies to be a violation of their privacy and rights as caretakers.

The seriousness of this conflict between public concern and the traditional immunity of parental actions from outside scrutiny cannot be overemphasized. For example, Wolfe, Aragona, Kaufman, and Sandler (1980) found from their experience with abusive families that only 68% of their referrals

Preparation of this manuscript was supported by a grant from the National Institute of Mental Health (MH32143). Copies of this paper are available from Rand Conger, Department of Human Development and Family Ecology, University of Illinois, 1105 W. Nevada, Urbana, Illinois 61801.

completed treatment even though ordered to do so by the juvenile court. On the other hand, when parents were not coerced by the court but simply recommended for treatment by a child protection agency, only 13% completed the behavior therapy program. A first challenge for behavior analysts, then, will be to develop a technology capable of attracting abusive parents to and motivating them to remain in treatment until significant change occurs. Because judges are unlikely to order families to participate in a service program except in the most extreme cases of abuse, and since such a coercive tactic may have undesirable side effects, e.g., creating parental hostility toward the therapist, other means for increasing interest in treatment will be necessary.

Although describing the details of such a technology is beyond the scope of the present paper, a number of possible avenues for future study should be mentioned. In some cases the behavior therapist might contract with the parent to act as his or her advocate with a protective service agency or with the court if certain treatment objectives are met (Doctor & Singer, 1978). In addition, parents might actually be paid for the improvements they make in interacting with their children (Fleischman, 1979). In their work with abusive parents, the authors have found that assisting caretakers in their attempts to meet important objectives in their lives, e.g., the completion of a technical degree program, can increase cooperation with training in child management skills. Another tactic for making behavioral programs attractive might be to create a social event. For example, Embry (personal communication) has found that dropout rates substantially decrease when treatment is offered in a group rather than individual setting. Whichever procedures prove most worthwhile, it is clear that intervention efforts will not have an impact on a large proportion of officially documented cases of child abuse unless effective techniques are developed for increasing parental acceptance of such programs.

A second complication that mitigates against the successful inhibition of abusive behavior is the fact that parent violence, whether self-reported or officially determined, is most likely to occur in poorer families that are relatively isolated in terms of outside social relationships (Belsky, 1980; Straus et al., 1980). In a number of recent reports, Wahler and his associates have demonstrated that a combination of social isolation, or "insularity," and socioeconomic disadvantage reduces the probability that parent-child interaction will improve with treatment and, when change does occur, also limits the generalizabity of treatment outcomes over time (e.g., Dumas & Wahler, Note 1; Wahler, 1980). In sum, both the involuntary nature of intervention and the social characteristics of the majority of abusive families create a very difficult situation for the clinician. Unless the therapist is working in a setting that provides the time and professional support necessary for dealing with the above issues, the likelihood of producing lasting change in these families probably is not very great. Assuming that these conditions are met, however, the next question of interest concerns those aspects of personal and family functioning that might guide an intervention program.

Targets for Child Abuse Intervention

A number of explanatory frameworks have recently been proposed to account for abusive behavior (e.g., Belsky, 1980; Burgess, 1979; Conger, 1980; Garbarino, 1979; Parke & Collmer, 1975). A common feature of all these perspectives is their incorporation of multiple levels of analysis within each model. For example, there is general agreement that some combination of parental and/or child characteristics, family structure and process, and family relationships with the larger community serves to promote parental violence. In many cases the behavior therapist may need to intervene at all of these levels to have the desired impact on the family. Before enumerating possible targets for change, however, it will be useful to consider a general perspective for conceptualizing the problem of child abuse.

– For the most part, attempts to understand family violence have searched for events that might prompt a physical attack by a family member. The emphasis has been on factors that elicit, motivate, or maintain abusive behavior (Conger, 1980). In a sense, though, the use of physical force with children is nonproblematic. It is an easily learned, commonly used, and well accepted child-rearing technique. As noted earlier, most parents physically punish their children at least on occasion and also consider the practice an appropriate method for correcting a child (Straus et al., 1980). Indeed, given the disparity in size between parents and young children, the traditional privacy of the home environment, the conflicts and stresses typical of family life, and the effectiveness of severe punishment as a means for producing compliance, it is almost surprising that more parents are not abusive.

In fact, however, the overwhelming majority of parents restrict their use of physical discipline to activities that do not risk serious injury to a child (Straus et al., 1980). Despite financial and other environmental pressures, and despite the provocations they experience within the family unit, most parents show restraint in their use of punishment. From both a theoretical and a practical standpoint, then, it is as important to view the correlates of abuse in terms of the *restraints* they place on the behaviors of nonabusers as in terms of the role they may play in *eliciting* violence. Such a perspective suggests that the primary goal of the therapist is to help create in the lives of abusive parents the same personal and social controls that inhibit violence in other families.

In the following discussion we will pursue the above ideas as they apply to specific targets for child abuse intervention and to the behavioral procedures relevant to each target. Before proceeding, however, it should be mentioned that perhaps as many as 10% to 20% of all abusive parents are so behaviorally deviant or resistant to change that no amount of assistance from an outside consultant will make the home safe for an abused child. In these cases, the victim should be removed from the home to prevent additional, possibly permanent, injuries or even death (Kempe & Kempe, 1978; Williams, 1980). For the remaining families, improving the home environment for an abused youngster is often preferable to a succession of placements in foster homes (Kent, 1976).

Parental Characteristics

Abusive parents, compared to nonabusive parents, are (1) more likely to have been abused or emotionally deprived during their own childhood, (2) more aversive and less positive in their interactions with their children, (3) less consistent in their use of discipline and (4) more unreasonable in their expectations of their children (Isaacs, in press). It is important to note that the maltreatment abusive parents suffered during their own childhood may not have included severe physical punishment (Belsky, 1980). That is, the major difference between the childhood of abusers and nonabusers appears to be the positive modeling and nurturance experienced by the latter parents. Quite likely these differences in childhood histories help to account for the deficits in parenting skills and empathy toward children that characterize child abusers (Garbarino, 1979; Isaacs, in press).

At the individual level, then, the behavior therapist must attempt to provide parents with behavioral practices and cognitions that will help to inhibit violence. To begin with, parents can be taught child management procedures that emphasize nonphysical methods of punishment, e.g., time out, and also the reinforcement of desired behaviors (e.g., Patterson, 1976). Once these techniques become an effective part of the parent's behavioral repertoire, they should be less reliant on physical discipline as a control strategy. In addition, parents must also be taught to decrease their generally negative mode of interacting with their children and to increase positive contacts in order to create a general climate in the home that is less conducive to violence (Burgess & Conger, 1978; Garbarino, 1979; Straus et al., 1980).

Through direct instruction and modeling, the above techniques should have an impact on the behaviors of abusive parents. However, it is likely that the effectiveness of these procedures will be enhanced if the therapist also attempts to influence directly the beliefs of parents. For example, cognitive restructuring (Beck, 1976; Meichenbaum, 1977) may be employed to alter the unreasonable expectations that abusers often have of their children. In addition, relaxation training (e.g., Benson, 1975) may help to reduce the heightened level of physiological arousal often experienced by child abusers in response to the normal activities of their youngsters (Frodi & Lamb, 1980).

Family Process and Structure

Abusive families, like many other families experiencing difficulties, are often locked into system-wide patterns of interaction that promote hostility and violence (Conger, in press). Because there may be difficulties with more than just the parent-child relationship, the therapist may need to attend to other problems within the family system using appropriate behavioral techniques, e.g., marital conflict (Jacobson, 1978). Children may also need to learn less coercive approaches to interacting with their parents, and youngsters with special handicaps or difficulties may need to be referred for appropriate services. In addition, special help may be needed for especially large or single-parent families wherein childcare responsibilities are particularly burdensome. In these cases the behavior therapist may need to work with the family to locate affordable day care or other outside supports that might facilitate the modifications in parental behavior and beliefs that are desired.

Community Relationships

There is little doubt that socioeconomic status and social activity are inversely related to child abuse (Belsky, 1980; Conger, 1980; Garbarino, 1979). Social isolation, or the lack of attachments to others outside the home may be part of a syndrome of difficulties that results to a large extent from the poor social training provided by the abuser's own parents. Violent parents may lack the social skills necessary to cultivate friendships and other social ties. Importantly, such relationships tend to inhibit the noxious behaviors of parents toward their children (Wahler, 1980). An important role the therapist might play in the lives of these families, then, is to provide both instruction and modeling regarding behaviors necessary for cultivating social relationships. A first step in this direction might be to conduct treatment sessions in group rather than individual settings.

Finally, the therapist may need to assist the parent in alleviating environmental stress by finding appropriate community services, e.g., emergency financial aid to families. Short-term assistance for immediate crises may be followed by the implementation of a program for meeting long-range goals. For example, the therapist may help a parent find the resources needed for special training that would lead to a marketable job skill. Some parents may profit from assertiveness training to increase their ability to take advantage of available educational or employment opportunities. Research by sociologists suggests that increasing both an individual's level of attachment to others and also his or her payoffs from conventional activities should decrease the tendency to engage in a wide range of deviant activities (Hirschi, 1978). The assumption here is that behavioral procedures aimed at producing these outcomes will also serve to inhibit parental violence.

Treatment Outcome Studies

Isaacs (Note 2) has recently completed a very thorough review of the behavioral literature on child abuse. As she notes in her paper, work in the area tends to fall in one of three categories: (a) suggestions for applying behavioral procedures to the problem of parental violence, (b) descriptions of behavioral work in progress prior to the availability of outcome data, or (c) findings from single subject or single group studies employing A–B research designs. One can conclude from Isaacs' discussion of the findings to date that, in spite of the several methodological shortcomings that hamper present research, behavior therapists appear to have had some degree of success in decreasing the hostile or aversive behaviors between parents and children in abusive families. In addition, there is some evidence that behavioral techniques may be effective in promoting positive exchanges in abusive families and also in improving the child management skills of abusive parents.

As noted, though, most studies have employed a research design (A–B) that involves several threats to internal validity (Cook & Campbell, 1979). However, there currently are several studies in progress that will soon overcome this present limitation in the available data (e.g., Luzker, Frame, & Rice, Note 3; Reid, Patterson, & Loeber, Note 4). Moreover, two recent reports have evaluated treatment outcomes using control group designs that attenuate some of the methodological problems of earlier research in the area (Conger, Lahey, & Smith, Note 5; Wolfe, Sandler & Kaufman, in press).

In their study of 16 abusive families, Wolfe and his associates (in press) assigned the first eight referrals from a local child welfare agency to the treatment group and used the next eight referrals as waiting list controls. Most of the referrals were low income white females with children ranging from 2 to 10 years of age. The two groups did not differ on relevant demographic variables. The control sample in the study remained on a waiting list for 8 weeks while the first group of families received treatment. Several outcome measures were taken in both groups prior to (pretest) and immediately following (posttest) this time period. The intervention program consisted of a weekly parent training group that involved instruction in human development and child management, problem solving of particular child management difficulties, and impulse control procedure. In addition, a clinical psychology graduate student visited the home each week to help parents apply the procedures they learned in the classroom to their interactions with their own children. The use of particular skills progressed in order of difficulty, i.e., from the simplest to the most complex.

Using systematic, in-home observations, Wolfe and his colleagues found that parents in the treatment group significantly increased their level of child management skills from pre- to posttest while controls did not. In addition, parents in the treatment group were less likely than controls to be seen as needing services by agency caseworkers and were also less likely to report child behavior problems at the end of the intervention period. Follow-up assessments at 10 weeks suggested that these improvements were maintained over time.

In a second control group study, Conger et al. (Note 5) compared five single-parent lower SES abusive families who were referred by a local child protection agency with five matched-control families. The two groups did not differ significantly on relevant demographic characteristics. Behavioral assessments were made prior to treatment (pretest) and immediately following intervention (posttest) along the following dimensions: (a) parental physical contacts with children that were negative, e.g., spankings, (b) parental physical contacts with children that were positive, e.g., hugging, (c) the rate of compliant behaviors by children divided by the rate of commands or requests by mothers (a measure of parental control), and (d) a measure of maternal depression. The intervention program lasted about 3 months per family. Control families were assessed at about the same time intervals as those in the treated group but there was no contact with the project between assessments. Intervention was carried out in the home by graduate students in clinical psychology. All families received instruction in child management skills, and in addition, the therapists attempted to form friendly, supportive relationships with each family. As needed, these mothers were also taught stress management techniques, behavioral procedures for relaxation, or received assistance in their couple relationships.

By the end of treatment the abusive mothers in this study became significantly less negative and significantly more positive toward their children while the control mothers did not. Abusive mothers also demonstrated significant decreases in their reported levels of depression and, in four out of five cases, were more effective in producing compliant responses from their children by the end of treatment. This latter outcome suggests that behavior therapy may decrease the occurrence of an important elicitor of abuse – child noncompliance – while at the same time decreasing reliance on physical punishment (negative physical behaviors).

Although the two studies just reviewed represent a needed addition to research involving single cases, it is worth noting that they were still quasi-experimental in nature (Cook & Campbell, 1979). Neither study reported adequate follow-up, and the results from both studies are open to alternative interpretations on several counts, including nonspecific effects of treatment and selection bias. To be sure, both studies employed practical alternatives to classical experimental design; however, to produce real confidence in the effectiveness of behavioral treatment for child abuse, humane and ethical procedures will need to be developed for random assignment of abusive parents to treatment and control conditions.

Summary

This paper began by noting that the physical abuse of children is an important social problem worthy of attention by behavior therapists who can contribute to current therapeutic efforts in terms of behavioral theory, experience treating family problems, and methods for assessing intervention programs. Some caution was expressed, however, because this population usually involves parents who are not interested in receiving assistance from outside agents. Indeed, a major contribution of behavioral technology would be to make intervention more attractive to these individuals. In terms of targets for intervention, our discussion emphasized the need to create in the lives of abusive parents the restraints that normally inhibit violence in other families. The brief review of behavioral programs suggested that some progress in this direction has been made but that more rigorous evaluation research is needed. Finally, although we have not addressed the issue of prevention in this paper, the most dramatic progress in protecting children from physical violence will likely come from early education in childrearing. One of the most important contributions behavior therapists can make in their work with abusive parents, then, is to help create educational techniques that will make effective prevention possible.

REFERENCES NOTES

1. Dumas, J. E., & Wahler, R. G. Predictors of treatment outcome in parent training: Mother insularity and socioeconomic disadvantage. Unpublished manuscript, Child Behavior Institute, University of Tennessee, Knoxville, TN, 1981.

2. Isaacs, C. D. Treatment of child abuse: A review of empirical and nonempirical approaches. Unpublished manuscript, Department of Human Development and Family Life, University of Kansas, Lawrence, KS, 1981.

3. Lutzker, J. R., Frame, R. E., & Rice, J. M. Project 12-ways: An ecobehavioral approach to the treatment and prevention of child abuse and neglect. Unpublished manuscript, Southern Illinois University, Carbondale, IL, 1981.

4. Reid, J. B., Patterson, G. R., & Loeber, R. The abused child: Victim, instigator, or innocent bystander? A paper presented at the Nebraska Symposium on Motivation, University of Nebraska; Lincoln, NE, November, 1980.

5. Conger, R. D., Lahey, B. B., & Smith, S. S. An intervention program for child abuse: Modifying maternal depression and behavior. A paper presented at the Family Violence Research Conference, University of New Hampshire, Durham, NC, July, 1981.

REFERENCES

Beck, A. T. *Cognitive behavior therapy and the emotional disorders.* New York: International Universities Press, 1976.

Belsky, J. Child maltreatment: An ecological integration. *American Psychologist,* 1980, *35,* 320-335.

Benson, H. *The relaxation response.* New York: Avon Books, 1975.

Berkeley Planning Associates. *Evaluation of child abuse and neglect demonstration projects 1974-1977: Vol. II. Final Report.* Berkeley, CA: Author, 1977.

Burgess, R. L. Child abuse: A behavioral analysis. In B. B. Lahey & A. E. Kazdin (Eds.), *Advances in child clinical psychology.* New York: Plenum, 1979.

Burgess, R. L., & Conger, R. D. Family interaction in abusive, neglectful and normal families. *Child Development,* 1978, *49,* 1163-1173.

Conger, R. D. Social control and social learning models of delinquent behavior: A synthesis. *Criminology,* 1974, *14,* 17-40.

Conger, R. D. The child as victim: The emerging issue of child abuse. *Journal of Crime and Justice,* 1980, *3,* 35-63.

Conger, R. D. The Assessment of dysfunctional family systems. In B. Lahey & A. Kazdin (Eds.), *Advances in child clinical psychology,* Vol. III. New York: Plenum, in press.

Cook, T. D., & Campbell, D. T. *Quasi-experimentation: Design and analysis issues for field settings.* Chicago: Rand MacNally, 1979.

Doctor, R. M., & Singer, E. M. Behavioral intervention strategies with child abusive parents: A home intervention program. *Child Abuse and Neglect,* 1978, *2,* 57-68.

Fleischman, M. J. Using parenting salaries to control attrition and cooperation in therapy. *Behavior Therapy,* 1979, *10,* 111-116.

Frodi, A. M., & Lamb, M. E. Child abusers' responses to infant smiles and cries. *Child Development,* 1980, *51,* 238-241.

Garbarino, J. An ecological approach to child maltreatment. In L. Pelton (Ed.), *The social context of child abuse and neglect.* New York: Human Sciences Press, 1979.

Hirschi, T. Causes and prevention of juvenile delinquency. In H. M. Johnson (Ed.), *Social systems and legal process.* San Francisco: Jossey-Bass, 1978.

Isaacs, C. A brief review of the characteristics of abuse-prone parents. *the Behavior Therapist,* 1981, *4*(5), 5-8.

Jacobson, N. S. Specific and nonspecific factors in the effectiveness of a behavioral approach to the treatment of marital discord. *Journal of Consulting and Clinical Psychology,* 1978, *46,* 442-452.

Kempe, R. S., & Kempe, C. H. *Child abuse.* Cambridge, MA: Harvard University Press, 1978.

Kent, J. T. A follow-up study of abused children. *Journal of Pediatric Psychology,* 1976, *1,* 25-31.

Light, R. Abused and neglected children in America: A study of alternative policies. *Harvard Educational Review,* 1973, *43,* 556-598.

Martin, B. Parent-child relations. In F. D. Horowitz (Ed.), *Review of child development research.* Vol. IV. Chicago: University of Chicago Press, 1975.

Meichenbaum, D. H. *Cognitive behavior modification.* New York: Plenum, 1977.

Parke, R. D. & Collmer, C. W. Child Abuse: An interdisciplinary analysis. In B. M. Caldwell & H. N. Ricciuti (Eds.), *Review of child development research.* Vol. V. Chicago: University of Chicago Press, 1975.

Patterson, G. R. The aggressive child: Victim and architect of a coercive system. In E. J. Mash, L. A. Hamerlynck, & L. C. Handy (Eds.), *Behavior modification and families.* New York: Brunner/Mazel, 1976.

Rollins, B. C., & Thomas, D. L. Parental support, power, and control techniques in the socialization of children. In W. R. Burr, R. Hill, F. I. Nye, & I. L. Reiss (Eds.), *Contemporary theories about the family: Research-based theories.* Vol. I. New York: The Free Press, 1979.

Straus, M. A., Gelles, R. J., & Steinmetz, S. K. *Behind closed doors: Violence in the American family.* New York: Anchor Press, 1980.

Wahler, K. G. The insular mother: Her problems in parent-child treatment. *Journal of Applied Behavior Analysis,* 1980, *13,* 207-219.

Williams, G. J. Management and treatment of parental abuse and neglect of children: An overview. In G. J. Williams & J. Money (Eds.), *Traumatic abuse and neglect of children at home.* Baltimore: Johns Hopkins University Press, 1980.

Wolf, M. M. Social validity: The case for subjective measurement or how applied behavior analysis is finding its heart. *Journal of Applied Behavior Analysis,* 1978, *11,* 203-214.

Wolfe, D. A., Aragona, J., Kaufman, K., & Sandler, J. The importance of adjudication in the treatment of child abusers: Some preliminary findings. *Child Abuse and Neglect,* 1980, *4,* 127-135.

Wolfe, D. A., Sandler, J., & Kaufman, K. A competency-based parent training program for child abusers. *Journal of Consulting and Clinical Psychology,* in press.

Zigler, E. Controlling child abuse in America: An effort doomed to failure? In R. Bourne & E. Newberger (Eds.), *Critical perspectives on child abuse.* Lexington, MA: D. C. Heath, 1979.

97

Child Abuse & Neglect, Vol. 8, pp. 387–392, 1984
Printed in the U.S.A. All rights reserved.

NEGLECTED FATHERS: LIMITATIONS IN DIAGNOSTIC AND TREATMENT RESOURCES FOR VIOLENT MEN

JUDITH A. MARTIN, PH.D.

University of Pittsburgh, School of Social Work, Pittsburgh, PA 15260

Abstract—In its examination of violent activity within the family, current literature assumes a "pecking order" exists: Larger and stronger family members attack those who are smaller and weaker. Adult males are usually studied as primary maltreaters of spouses, while females are considered mainly responsible for physically abusive behavior with children. Use of this perspective has led to neglect of male abusers, who injure half of the mistreated children in the United States. Through assessment of 66 studies of child abuse published during a 5-year period, this paper documents the lack of attention abusive fathers have received. Twenty-eight of these studies included only mothers, while two dealt exclusively with fathers. Most of the 36 remaining two-parent studies did not discuss sex differences. No diagnostic categories consistently differentiated male from female abusers. No study discussed specialized treatment needs of women and men. This survey suggests that the therapeutic field considers the child's mother the primary responsible parent, even though she may not be the perpetrator of violence in the family. As a result, inadequate treatment resources have been made available to maltreating fathers. The survey points to the need for much more comprehensive research comparing male and female maltreaters.

Résumé—La littérature actuelle, consacrée au comportement violent intra-familial, assure qu'il existe une espèce d'ordre naturel à l'intérieur de ces familles. Les plus forts attaquent les plus petits et les plus faibles. Les adultes du sexe mâle maltraitent les épouses, et les femmes maltraitent physiquement les enfants. Cette conception a conduit à négliger un certain nombre de personnes violentes du sexe mâle qui, en fait, sont responsables de la moitié des sévices chez les enfants, aux Etats-Unis en particulier. L'auteur a revu 66 études sur la maltraitance d'enfants, publiées ces 5 dernières années. Il est évident d'après cette revue, que les pères violents n'ont pas reçu l'attention qu'ils méritaient. Vingt-huit études ne concernaient que les mères, alors que 2 seulement étaient consacrées aux pères. La plupart des 36 autres articles ne faisaient pas de différence entre les deux parents. Les besoins thérapeutiques spécifiques aux hommes et aux femmes n'étaient pas dissociés. L'auteur conclut qu'en général, on ne considère que la mère dans la problématique de la maltraitance, alors même qu'elle peut être innocente. Le résultat est qu'on n'a pas, jusqu'à présent, offert grand chose en guise de traitement aux pères violents.

INTRODUCTION

PHYSICAL MALTREATMENT OF CHILDREN is considered a major contemporary problem of parenting. In the U.S. alone, it is estimated that some .5 million to 1.5 million children are abused annually [1, 2]. Only a small number of abusers receive assistance in altering their behavior. As a result of increasing unemployment and resulting family stress, the number of these parents is, once again, increasing. In Pennsylvania, suspected abuse reports grew from 12,845 in 1979 to 13,703 in 1981, a rise of 7% [3].

Approximately half of these physically abusive adults are fathers. In the first nationwide survey of such activities, David Gil reported that mothers were perpetrators in 47.6% of the cases and fathers in 39.2% [4, p. 116]. When single parent homes were excluded from the analysis, the proportion of fathers rose to two-thirds. Subsequent annual studies conducted by the American Humane Association confirm the major involvement of male parents in

---

Presented at the Fourth International Congress on Child Abuse and Neglect, Paris, September 1982.

A list of works reviewed is available upon request from the author.

maltreatment cases. The Association's 1978 report noted they were perpetrators in 55% of these incidents [5].

Fathers and mothers are equally likely to mistreat young children, but there is some evidence to suggest fathers are more deeply involved in cases of adolescent abuse. In a survey of 830 abuse reports submitted during a two-year period in Wisconsin, Kadushin and Martin [6] found fathers abused 51% of the preschoolers and infants, 53% of the latency-age children and 71% of the teenagers in the sample.

Despite overwhelming evidence to the contrary, the popular image of the child abuser continues to depict a young, single and frequently poor woman who seriously harms her infant. A recent article in the *Wall Street Journal* [7] reflects this bias:

Judson Stone, a mental health worker in Elk Grove, Ill., describes a typical case. It involves a man who worked in an auto-related industry, and his wife, who worked in a department store. Both lost their jobs, ran through their savings, gave up their house, moved into a trailer and took money from their parents. The couple began fighting, and the woman began turning on their 2-year-old daughter, violently shoving and slapping her.

Fathers are almost never used to exemplify typical incidents of maltreatment.

This paper examines the current state of our knowledge concerning male abusers and explores the similarities and differences between them and females. It assesses current research on gender differences in the etiology of such actions as well as differences in responses to treatment.

PROCEDURES

Studies of abusive parents published between 1976 and 1980 were identified through a computer search of the literature, from a review of recent research [8] and from other available sources. Multiple publications growing out of one research effort were omitted unless each contained substantially different data analyses. No attempt was made to omit studies because of inadequacies in design, sampling or measures.

Sixty-six different works were reviewed. Dissertations and published studies in book form are underrepresented because of difficulties in gaining access to them. However, this review does reflect findings of most published researchers working in the field in recent years. In order to facilitate comparisons, their efforts were classified as *father-only, mother-only,* and *two-parent* studies.

STUDIES OF ABUSIVE FATHERS

One of the most startling outcomes of this literature review involved comparison of the relative number of published studies focusing only on abusive mothers or fathers. We fully expected the proportion of mother-only studies would be substantially larger. However, we discovered that exclusive examination of these men almost never occurs. Only two such reports were available during the entire 5-year period. One of these described use of systematic desensitization techniques with one father, while the second work, titled "Aggression against Cats, Dogs and People," [9] discussed the early background of violent male psychiatric patients. Twenty-eight studies (42%) conducted research only with mothers, while the remaining 36 (55%) included parents of both genders.

Mother-only and two-parent samples tended to be drawn from different sources. Mother-only researchers were twice as likely to use outpatient treatment populations and small samples (20 or fewer cases), while two-parent efforts were twice as often drawn from investigative agency files and to use large samples [10]. As a result, there were consistent differences in the amount and type of data available describing male and female perpetrators. While the picture of abusive mothers was more often developed through review of voluminous materials contained in clinical treatment files or through interviews with clinicians, information on males was more often based on use of less detailed, less clinically oriented protective service agency files. Data on males are more frequently representative of all males reported to public agencies, while samples of females are more restricted, reflecting qualities of women who seek treatment, frequently in mental health settings.

Several of the two-parent studies did not provide comparative data for male and female abusers. More than half (53%) of the 36 two-parent reports discussed no such differences. As a result, only 17 of the entire group of 66 studies provided any information on fathers and/or compared their characteristics with those of abusive mothers.

The unique qualities of male abusers were explored through assessment of these 17 studies. Because discovery of male/female differences was not a primary research objective in any of these reports, it is difficult to determine how thorough an evaluation of sex differences was undertaken. As a result, these findings should be considered suggestive, pending more direct examination of gender effects. Contrasting characteristics of mothers and fathers were then compared with the picture of women that emerged from the mother-only works.

DIAGNOSTIC DIFFERENCES

Significant aspects of abuse are usually reported in three major areas: intrapsychic, interpersonal and environmental [11]. In the intrapsychic realm, differences in the psychological makeup of abusers and nonabusers are of particular concern; interpersonal assessments focus on abusers' relations with family members, neighbors and friends, and others in the community; an environmental evaluation describes the impact of economic conditions and sociocultural factors on the lives of these individuals. Most contemporary research attempts to examine parental functioning in all three of these areas.

On the individual level, abusers have been depicted as more aggressive, angry and impulsive than nonabusive individuals. They are also characterized as anxious and defensive, as more dependent and less self-confident than other parents. Two-parent comparison studies reported gender-related differences in these characteristics. Moore and Day [12] found fathers tend to be especially passive individuals, while Baher et al. [13], Hyman [14] and Paulson et al. [15] described mothers as more anxious and impulsive.

However, a clear picture of male/female differences does not emerge from this literature. Some of the qualities repeatedly used to describe women in mother-only studies (easily angered, low self-esteem, emotionally needy) were found to typify both males and females in two-parent research. Moreover, there were inconsistencies in results, even within the small number of studies that compared men and women. In contrast to Moore and Day [12], Kertzman [16] found dependency a typical trait of both male and female maltreaters.

Lack of clarity in this area reflects, in part, our general inability to discover intrapsychic factors that consistently differentiate abusers from their nonabusive counterparts. Maltreatment results from a complex combination of variables. It can occur when an emotionally vulnerable individual finds himself or herself in an unstable interpersonal situation at a time when environmental stress is severe. Although psychological factors, by themselves, do not cause abuse, they do influence development of such events. Further work to discover similarities and differences between men and women who mistreat children is, therefore, essential.

Research examining interpersonal qualities of abusers has described them as rigid and punitive parents, as unhappy spouses, and as individuals isolated from their broader social support networks. When one attempts to explore male/female differences in the child-rearing

101

arena, conflicting evidence abounds. A few examples will indicate the difficulties. Clark [17] interviewed 21 women attending Parents Anonymous meetings and found them highly coercive and punitive in their parenting practices. Dibble and Straus [18] noted further that males and females reinforced each other in their attitudes supportive of the use of slapping children in families where such practices were utilized. Burgess [19] and Oates et al. [20] reported that maltreating mothers were more punitive than fathers in their sample, while Bavolek et al. [21] reported the opposite results. In a study of attitudes towards parenting of some 3,000 adolescents in Utah, they found both abused and nonabused teenage males expressed more punitive views.

Results discussing general preparedness for parenthood are equally in need of clarification. These studies evaluated abusers' knowledge about parenthood and child development and their skill in basic caretaking tasks. In studies of mothers, Egeland [22] found them generally unprepared; Elmer [23], in contrast, found them no less prepared than control group mothers in similar economic circumstances. Burgess [19] described both mothers and fathers as unready to assume their child care responsibilities, while both Baher et al. [13] and Neufelt [24] indicated there were no differences between these parents and nonabusers using the PARI research instrument. The need for more detailed comparisons between families in which mothers or fathers abuse children and for comparisons between parental practices within abusive families are indicated by these results.

In other interpersonal areas, there is greater consistency in findings across studies. They indicate the importance of including both male and female maltreaters in future research efforts. While the mother-only research has described these women as individuals in conflict with their spouses and their own parents and isolated from other sources of community support, two-parent studies clearly indicate these qualities typify both male and female abusers. Straus [25] discovered that abusive men and women express less satisfaction with their marriages; Oates et al. [20] found that parents in such families participated in less shared decision-making and reported more disagreements with their spouses.

Research examining the general environmental context in which abuse occurs reports similar findings. Characteristics ascribed to mothers in women-only studies actually apply to both men and women. In general, these individuals find themselves in poverty situations [26], dealing with an unusually high degree of life stress [27, 28], with fewer supports to help them cope than other individuals [29].

This review indicates the need for more intensive examination of personal qualities and parental practices of male and female abusers. Such study must be accompanied by ongoing sensitivity to the generally difficult life circumstances of individuals who physically maltreat their children.

TREATMENT DIFFERENCES

Of the 66 studies we reviewed, 16 examined results of treatment efforts on behalf of abusive parents. Treatment provided ranged from provision of broadly based social services to use of highly structured behaviorally oriented programs. Ten of these projects included parents of both genders; five worked exclusively with mothers; and one dealt with an abusive father. None of these studies described differences in programing or outcome for male and female participants.

Failure to examine these factors is particularly worrisome, since the therapeutic field has been aware of gender-related differences in client responses to treatment and of difficulties clinicians face in encouraging men to enter and continue in therapy [30–32]. Problems have also existed for male clients in obtaining equal access to treatment. Some programs are specifically structured only for women, while others, operating only during daytime hours, prevent most working males from attending. Lack of understanding of special treatment needs of male perpetrators results in provision of services ill-equipped to help them overcome their child-rearing deficits and, therefore, unnecessarily endangers the welfare of children in their care.

IMPLICATIONS

This review has documented the essential need for greater attention to delineation of significant characteristics of abusive studies comparing mothers and fathers who maltreat children. We can only speculate about the reasons why fathers have been so persistently neglected in this research field. Baher et al. [13], in an intensive study of 25 abusive families, found that he was able to clearly identify one parent as the abuser in only twelve instances. The inability to determine which parent was the perpetrator may lead some investigators to focus their efforts on the adult considered the child's primary parent, the mother.

Of probably greater significance than missing information is the impact of powerful cultural expectations concerning the relative roles and responsibilities of men and women in child rearing. Despite many changes in attitudes towards parenting in recent years, the developmental literature points out that women are still considered the child's most important parent, while the role of the father is undervalued [33, 34]. Fowler and Stockford [35] point out the impact of this perspective:

There is an underlying assumption in much of the literature on non-accidental injury that the person who is responsible for the child's injuries, even if she has not actually inflicted them, is the child's mother. This assumption is often disguised by apparently neutral references to "the battering parent" or "the family," but careful reading will usually reveal the underlying assumption that the person who is actually responsible, and in the particular the one for whom therapeutic techniques are designed, is female.

Interpretation of results in several recent studies reflect this assumption [12, 29, 36].

Because the outcome of child rearing is such a significant concern of any culture, attitudes concerning appropriate and inappropriate approaches to this task will always be strongly supported and deeply ingrained. When these views are uncritically applied to analysis of data in re-search studies, however, they act as sources of bias that distort knowledge and unnecessarily restrict therapeutic efforts. Based on this review, it is clear that more attention must be paid to frequently unstated, untested assumptions concerning the role and responsibilities of mothers and fathers in families where abuse occurs. Adoption of these assumptions may well have led to institutionalized neglect of treatment needs of abusive fathers.

REFERENCES

1. LIGHT, R. Abused and neglected in America: A study of alternative policies. *Harvard Educational Review* 43:556–598 (1973).
2. FONTANA, V. *The Maltreated Child.* MacMillan, New York (1973).
3. COMMONWEALTH OF PENNSYLVANIA. *1981 Child Abuse Report.* Department of Public Welfare, Harrisburg (1982).
4. GIL, D. *Violence Against Children: Physical Child Abuse in the United States.* Harvard University Press, Cambridge, MA (1970).
5. AMERICAN HUMANE ASSOCIATION. *National Analysis of Official Child Neglect and Abuse Reporting.* Author, Denver (1978).
6. KADUSHIN, A. and MARTIN, J. *Child Abuse: An Interactional Event.* Columbia University Press, New York (1981).
7. WALDHOLZ, M. Child abuse seems to be increasing in areas with unemployment. *Wall Street Journal* Section 2, 1 (August 6, 1982).
8. KALISCH, B. *Child Abuse and Neglect: An Annotated Bibliography.* Greenwood Press, Westport, CT (1978).

9. FELTHOUS, A. Aggression against cats, dogs and people. *Child Psychiatry Human Development* **10**:169–177 (1980).
10. MARTIN, J. Maternal and paternal abuse of children: Theoretical and research perspectives. In: *The Dark Side of Families,* M. Finkelhor (Ed.), pp. 293–304. Sage, Beverly Hills, CA (1983).
11. PARKE, R. D. and COLLMER, C. W. Child abuse: An interdisciplinary review. In: *Review of Child Development Research,* E. M. Hetherington (Ed.). University of Chicago Press, Chicago (1975).
12. MOORE, J. and DAY, B. Family interaction associated with abuse of children over five years of age. *Child Abuse & Neglect* 3:391–399 (1979).
13. BAHER, E. and CASTLE, R. *At Risk: An Account of the Work of the Battered Child Research Department, NSPCC* Routledge and K. Paul, Boston (1976).
14. HYMAN, C. Report on the psychological test results of battering parents. *British Journal of Social and Clinical Psychology* **16**:221–224 (1977).
15. PAULSON, M., SCHWEMER, G. and BENDEL, R. Clinical application of the PD, MA and OH experimental MMPI scales to further understanding of abusive parents. *Journal of Clinical Psychology* **32**:558–564 (1976).
16. KERTZMAN, D. *Dependency, Frustration Tolerance, and Impulse Control in Child Abusers.* Century Twenty-One, Saratoga, CA (1980).
17. CLARK, K. Knowledge of child development and behavior interaction patterns of mothers who abuse their children. *Dissertation Abstracts International* **36b**:5784 (1976).
18. DIBBLE, U. and STRAUS, M. Some social structure determinants of inconsistency between attitudes and behavior: The case of family violence. *Journal of Marriage and the Family* **42**:71–80 (1980).
19. BURGESS, R. Project Interact: A study of patterns of interaction in abusive, neglectful, and control families. *Child Abuse & Neglect* 3:781–789 (1979).
20. OATES, R. K., DAVIS, A. A., RYAN, M. G. and STEWART, L. F. Risk factors associated with child abuse. *Child Abuse & Neglect* 3:547–553 (1979).
21. BAVOLEK, S., KLINE, D. F., MCLAUGHLIN, J. A. and PUBLICOVER, P. R. Primary prevention of child abuse and neglect: Identification of high-risk adolescents. *Child Abuse & Neglect* 3:1071–1080 (1979).
22. EGELAND, B. Preliminary results of a prospective study of the antecedents of child abuse. *Child Abuse & Neglect* 3:269–278 (1979).
23. ELMER, E. *Fragile Families, Troubled Children.* University of Pittsburgh Press, Pittsburgh (1977).
24. NEUFELD, K. Child rearing, religion and abusive parents. *Religious Education* 74:234–244 (1979).
25. STRAUS, M. Stress and child abuse. In: *The Battered Child,* (3rd ed.), C. H. Kempe and R. E. Helfer (Eds.), pp. 86–103. University of Chicago Press, Chicago (1980).
26. GELLES, R. A profile of violence toward children in the United States. Paper presented at Annenberg School of Communications Conference on *Child Abuse: Cultural Roots and Policy Options.* Philadelphia (1978).
27. CONGER, R. D., BURGESS, R. and BARRETT, C. Child abuse related to life change and perceptions of illness: Some preliminary findings. *The Family Coordinator* **28**:73–78 (1979).
28. SHAPIRO, D. *Parents and Protectors* Child Welfare League of America, New York (1979).
29. GARBARINO, J. and SHERMAN, D. High-risk neighborhoods and high-risk families: The human ecology of child maltreatment. *Child Development* **51**:188–198 (1980).
30. CHESLER, P. Patient and patriarch: Women in the psychotherapeutic relationship. In: *Women in Sexist Society: Studies in Power and Powerlessness,* V. Gornick and B. K. Moran (Eds.) Basic Books, New York (1971).
31. EHRENREICH, and ENGLISH, D. *For her own Good: 150 Years of the Experts' Advice to Women.* Anchor, Garden City, NY (1978).
32. PATTEE, C. Population characteristics and sex-role patterns in a youth-run crisis center. *Journal of Youth and Adolescents* 3:231–246 (1974).
33. LAMB, M. *Role of the Father in Child Development.* Wiley, New York (1976).
34. RAPOPORT, R., RAPOPORT, R. and STRELITZ, Z. *Fathers, Mothers and Society: Toward New Alliances.* Basic Books, New York (1977).
35. FOWLER, J. and STOCKFORD, D. Leaving it to the wife: A study of abused children and their parents in Norfolk. *Child Abuse & Neglect* 3:851–856 (1979).
36. ROBERTSON, B. and JURITZ, J. Characteristics of the families of abused families. *Child Abuse & Neglect* 3:857–861 (1979).

A BIRD'S EYE VIEW OF THE CHILD MOLESTER*

The child molester's physical appearance and intellectual abilities are the same as yours or your neighbor's. Child
molesters do not appear to be monsters, ugly, or stupid. Some
are married with families and most have good steady jobs. They
live in communities of all sizes and descriptions. They are
people.

Child molesters in our program range from 10 to 72 years
of age. The majority of them were sexually abused as children.
All of them were abused in some manner: physically, emotionally, or witnessed abuse on someone else. Several of the molesters in our program are females. We have found that the female
offender comes to us as a result of dealing with her own victimization. They want to stop abusing children on their own,
rather than through the court system.

The statistics regarding the number of sexual abuse
victims are frightening. It is estimated that one out of
four female children, and one out of six male children
will be sexually victimized in some way before the age of
18. Yet, from our work with the child molester this is not
hard to believe. About 50% began their acts of abuse during
childhood or during their teen years. The molester has frequent and easy access to a victim because he is usually
known to the child. Thus, the molester may be you, a family
member, neighbor, babysitter, teacher, pastor or friend. He
may be a parent, step-parent, relative or family friend. He
is rarely a stranger.

Most of the sex offenders in our program are on probation. This means they have been convicted but did not receive a jail term. Some are on parole, having served time in
prison. Others are mandated by Children's and Youth Services,
Juvenile Court, and a few come voluntarily, outside of the
legal system. We view agency and court involvement as critical, as it provides the "clout" essential to the treatment
process. The act of victimizing a child or many children
usually occurs over many years. Contrary to popular belief,
the acts do not cease forever at the time of disclosure. Yes,
the offender is "sorry;" he is sorry he got caught. The act
of abusing a child is an obsession-compulsion and changing
that behavior pattern requires primarily the commitment of
the offender, but also the "clout" necessary to keep him in
treatment.

In our work with offenders, we have developed some idea
of what may occur in the person who molests a child:

1) The Learned Process - The child is abused or observes
   others being abused. The child learns what it is like
   to feel helpless and learns the method by which another
   made him or her feel this way. The child has learned
   about "power."

* If we refer to the molester as "he," please bear in mind
that both males and females molest children.

105

2) <u>Low Self Esteem</u> - Being a victim is experienced as being an object, a "nothing." The person desires to get away from these intensely negative feelings about the self. The desire is experienced as a *need for release*. Two routes are available: the "power-over" position of the offender or the "powerless" position of the victim.

3) <u>Out of Control</u> - The person is out of control, arguing, drinking, taking drugs, being bossy, lashing out to control the emotions and behavior of others.

4) <u>Opportunity</u> - The offender has access to a child. Child molesters relate very well to children. He begins to relate to a child as an object: someone to make do what he wants. Sex is only a means. He has no regard for the child's feelings and rarely recognizes the psychological damage being done to the child.

5) <u>Conditioning his Method of Operation</u> - The offender allows an inappropriate arousal system to develop. He experiences this as his being sexually attracted to children. Because the goal is to have "power-over," the child is not important. Next, deviant fantasies develop. His behavior is felt to be beyond his control and he acts on his desires, as the compulsion pattern unfolds. Mind, body, and behavior are activated and the sexual abuse is committed. He has completed a psychological process that we call obsession-compulsion.

6) <u>Blocking and Denial</u> - The offender is able to perform the acts over and over by making them "OK" in his mind, i.e., the child liked it, she wanted it, I was teaching about sex.

For the treatment of the sex offender to be effective, he must make a commitment to quit sexually abusing children. The treatment is a long process, usually much longer than two years. Since the compulsion becomes a lifestyle, the offender must be helped to develop an alternative lifestyle. There is no cure for child molesting; however, there is control.

Our program often uses a teaching format. We teach the offenders that they are totally responsible for their acts of sexual abuse and, because other options exist, they can change. The offenders learn to be aware of self, thoughts and actions. Assignments, designed to keep them thinking and working when they are away from the group, are given. Some of the learning focuses on:
- low self esteem and how to gain self confidence
- when they were victims
- how they committed their acts, i.e., their method of operation: their feelings, thoughts, and actions
- what is going on in their lives now (past-present)
- power and powerlessness
- obsession and compulsion
- blocks and denial

We also want them to understand the concept of the "struggle" that occurs within them. They must become familiar with the self (who they really are), and the forces within (that lead them towards loss of control). This allows the offenders to direct themselves towards appropriate and responsible behavior.

The following rules pertain to our program. When followed, they assist the offenders in achieving their goal, never to sexually abuse a child again. They are:
- No drugs or alcohol
- Never to be alone with a child
- Never to touch a child
- To keep individual counseling appointments
- To do all assignments
- To attend all group therapy sessions
- To keep the confidentiality of the group
- To receive help from and give support to others in the group
- To treat others as you want to be treated by them
- Not to choose an alternative "power" process

We also do marital counseling, family counseling and have groups for victims

Caroline M. Russell, Director
Barbara Bowlus,Ph. D. Therapist
"Together We Can"
P. O. Box 1523
Pittsburgh, PA 15230

Legal Issues Raised in Treating Sex Offenders

Barbara A. Weiner, J.D.

For the past 50 years the criminal justice system has distinguished sex offenders from other criminals. This has resulted in their differential treatment, with the goal being to eliminate their inappropriate behavior. This article discusses the history and status of mentally disordered sex offender (MDSO) statutes. A review of the legal issues which arise when treating a sex offender without statutory authorization is provided. A discussion of problems raised in treating the offender on both an inpatient and outpatient setting is presented. The article concludes with an analysis of the legal problems confronting the treatment provider in working with this group of individuals.

INTRODUCTION

For almost 50 years persons who committed crimes of a sexual nature have been viewed differently than other criminals. This has been reflected in the criminal law, as well as in attempts by mental health professionals to design treatment programs to cure these criminals of their inappropriate sexual propensities. This article will review the history and status of laws designed for mentally disordered sex offenders (MDSO). There will then be a review of the general legal issues which arise when attempting to treat sex offenders while incarcerated and on an outpatient basis. Finally, the article will close with a discussion of the legal problems presented for the treatment provider by undertaking treatment of the identified sex offender.

Barbara A. Weiner, J.D., is Assistant Professor of Psychiatry in Law, Rush Medical College.
Correspondence and reprint requests should be addressed to: Barbara A. Weiner, J.D. Administrator and Counsel, Section on Psychiatry and the Law, Rush-Presbyterian-St. Luke's Medical Center, 1725 W. Harrison St., Suite 344, Chicago, IL 60612.

Behavioral Sciences & the Law, Vol. 3, No. 4, pp. 325–340 (1985)
© 1985 John Wiley & Sons, Inc.   CCC 0735–3936/85/040325–16$04.00

MENTALLY DISORDERED SEX OFFENDER STATUTES

In 1937, Michigan adopted the first so-called sexual psychopath law.[1] This marked the beginning of a trend that peaked in the mid-1960s, by which time more than half the states had adopted laws providing special legal and medical treatment, including in some instances, special facilities, for persons with abnormal sexual propensities manifested through criminal behavior. These laws were viewed as alternatives to criminal processing and imprisonment for this group of offenders. Referred to by various names including "sexual psychopath laws," "sexually dangerous persons acts," and "mentally disordered sex offenders acts," these laws had the dual goals of removing the sex offender from the community and treating him.[2]

More recently, a contrary trend has taken hold: since 1976, 13 states have repealed their laws[3] and another 12 have greatly modified them.[4] The primary modification has been to make treatment voluntary to the prisoner. For example, Maryland now provides that an offender must volunteer and consent to treatment to be part of a treatment program while in prison.[5] California makes a similar provision allowing the offender to participate in treatment during the year prior to his scheduled release from prison.[6] The MDSO laws today only exist in 16 states and the District of Columbia.[7] Of these jurisdictions, only six actually enforce the laws in more than an isolated case.[8]

Each statute defines the MDSO somewhat differently. Most provide that the defendant has been convicted of, or pleaded guilty to a sex crime and in addition has a history of sexual acting out behavior, usually of a threatening or violent nature. The majority of these statutes are aimed at persons who engage in sexual activity with children. Most specify a standard to the effect that the person be mentally ill and/or dangerous. Generally, the statutes come into play only at the time of sentencing, when a finding of being an MDSO and the resultant need of treatment may be an alternative to the standard prison sentence.

In some states a person may be committed under a MDSO law without having been convicted of a crime.[9] Nonetheless, there is usually a criminal charge in the

---

1. Michigan Public Act, 1937 No. 196 at 35.
2. Psychiatry and Sexual Psychopath Legislation: The 30's to the 80's Group for the Advancement of Psychiatry, Report No. 98, at 842 (1977), hereinafter cited as the GAP report.
3. Alabama, Florida, Indiana, Iowa, Mississippi, Minnesota, Missouri, Oklahoma, Pennsylvania, Rhode Island, Vermont, Virginia, and Wisconsin.
4. These laws have been modified in California, Connecticut, Kansas, Maryland, Nebraska, New Hampshire, New Jersey, Oregon, Tennessee, Utah, Washington, and Wyoming.
5. Md. Ann. Code. Art. 31 B. Sec. 8-13.
6. Cal. Welf. & Inst. Code. Sec. 6300-6330.
7. California, Colorado, Connecticut, District of Columbia, Florida, Illinois, Massachusetts, Minnesota, Nebraska, New Hampshire, New Jersey, Oregon, Tennessee, Utah, Virginia, Washington, Wyoming.
8. Based on an informal survey by the author, it was found that they were only being used on a regular basis in Massachusetts, Nebraska, New Jersey, Oregon and Washington. Florida has a large treatment program, but it is a voluntary one. The other states which have such laws, rarely, if ever, invoke them.
9. The District of Columbia, Illinois, and Minnesota.

background, or at least an arrest, and it is the prosecution who must initiate the MDSO proceedings. In the past, commitment under both these "preconviction" statutes and the "post-conviction" schemes was typically for an indeterminate period. However, today, only five states still permit indefinite confinement and of these only one uses its law with any frequency.[10] Commitment absent a criminal conviction can only be to a mental institution. But imprisonment limited to the statutory maximum for the crime or for an indeterminate period continues to be an option under some of the post-conviction statutes. The standard for release is a medical finding that the person is "fully recovered" or improved sufficiently so that he "no longer presents a danger to others."

Profile of the Person Committed under Sexual Psychopath Laws

There have been a number of studies examining the effects of MDSO laws. Four studies have analyzed aspects of the California program (the nation's largest) providing a rough profile of the typical committee.[11] One study found that the majority of subjects were sentenced following a plea bargain.[12] The other studies showed that the determination and treatment of the defendant as an MDSO was based primarily on his social history related in a presentence report, rather than on clinical observations.[13] Involvement in sexual activity with a child or a previous history of being charged with sex offenses proved to be the key factors correlated with a defendant's being determined to be a MDSO.[14]

Two other studies have compared persons committed under MDSO laws with those sent to prison after being convicted of sex offenses.[15] Analyzing data from California and Wisconsin, these studies found that persons committed under the MDSO laws were usually older, more likely to be white than other prisoners, and they had been involved in sexual offenses against children. In 1978, a national

10. Colorado, District of Columbia, Illinois, Massachusetts, and Minnesota. Mass. is the only one of the states which uses the law on a regular basis.
11. See, e.g., V. Konecni, E. Mulcahy, & Ebbesen, Prison or mental hospital: Factors affecting the processing of persons subjected of being "mentally disordered sex offenders," in P. Lipsitt & B. Sales (Eds.), *New Directions in Psychological Research* (1980); Sturgeon & Taylor, Report of a Five-Year Follow up Study of Mentally Disordered Sex Offenders Released from Atascadero State Hospital in 1973, 4 Criminal Justice J. of Western State Univ. 31 (1980); M. Forst, Civil Commitment and Social Control, (Lexington, Massachusetts: Lexington Books, 1978); Dix, Differential Processing of Anormal Sex Offenders; Utilization of California's Mentally Disordered Sex Offender Program, 67 J. of Criminal Law & Criminology 233 (1976).
12. See Forst, note 11 supra at 121.
13. See Dix, supra note 11 at 236.
14. See J. Monahan & S. Davis, Mentally disordered sex offenders, in J. Monahan & H. Steadman (Eds.), *Mentally Disordered Offenders*, Chap. 6 (New York: Plenum Press, 1983), which provides a brief review of each of the studies discussed in this section.
15. See Sturgeon & Taylor, supra note 11, which compated 260 MDSO in California with a group of 122 persons convicted of sexual crimes. See also Pacht & Cowden, An Exploratory Study of Five Hundred Sex Offenders, I Criminal Justice and Behavior 13 (1974) which compared 380 persons committed under the Wisconsin sexual psychopath law with 121 persons given prison sentences who had been evaluated under that law.

study of persons in public mental institutions revealed that 6% were there due to MDSO laws.[16]

Without further study it is impossible to know if the information revealed by these studies would be applicable to persons convicted under MDSO laws in states other than California or Wisconsin. However, with the widespread repeal and modification of these laws, there has been and will continue to be, a dramatic decrease in the number of persons committed as mentally disordered sex offenders.

Procedural Challenges to MDSO Laws

When first enacted, MDSO laws were viewed as civil in nature. This meant that statutory definitions of the applicable procedural rights were not as rigorous as those required in criminal proceedings. Early challenges to the laws alleged that they were unconstitutionally vague and that the difference in treatment between mentally disordered sex offenders and other offenders violated equal protection. These contentions were brushed aside by the United States Supreme Court in the 1940 case of *Minnesota ex. rel Pearson v. Probate Court.*[17] Twenty-seven years later, however, the Court in *Specht v. Patterson,*[18] took a far more critical line: while MDSO proceedings may be ostensibly civil in nature, the reality that they could lead to indeterminate institutionalization entitled persons subject to these proceedings to certain fundamental protections, including the right to "be present with counsel, have an opportunity to be heard, be confronted with witnesses against him, have the right to cross-examination and offer evidence of his own." Furthermore, "there must be findings adequate to make meaningful any appeal that is allowed."[19]

Specht did not go so far as to specify the standard of proof applicable in MDSO proceedings. The United States Court of Appeals for the Seventh Circuit, however, following the Supreme Court's reasoning in *In Re Winship,*[20] which applied the beyond a reasonable doubt standard of proof to juvenile proceedings, which is the same standard used in criminal cases, held that standard applicable to the Illinois Sexually Dangerous Persons Act.[21] Other courts have followed with identical holdings.[22] In addition to the equal protection and due process reasoning in *Specht* and other cases to upgrade the procedural safeguards for the alleged mentally disordered sex offender, one court accepted the contention that the laws, at least as

---

16. Steadman, Monahan, Hartstone, Davis & Robbins, Mentally disordered offenders: A national survey of patients and facilities, 6 Law & Human Behav 31, 34 (1982).
17. 309 U.S. 270 (1940).
18. 386 U.S. 605 (1967).
19. *Id.* at 610.
20. 397 U.S. 358, 364 (1970).
21. U.S. ex. rel. Stachulak v. Coughlin, 502 F.2d 971 (7th Cir., 1975).
22. People v. Burnick, 535 P.2d 352 (Cal., 1975); People v. Pembrock, 342 N.E.2d 28 (Ill., 1976). For commentary on these cases see Comment, Due Process Requires Proof Beyond Doubt for Sex Offenders, 1975 Wash. U.L. Q. 1092 (1975); Comment, Dangerousness, Reasonable Doubt and Preconviction Psychopath Legislation, 1 S. ILL. U.L. J. 218 (1970).

administered in Oregon, violated the cruel and unusual punishment clause of the Eighth Amendment.[23] The declining use of the MDSO statutes may in part reflect the view that the laws are too vulnerable to legal attack or at least that they are not worth the continuing litigation that they have generated.

Challenges Based on Lack of Treatment

One of the original goals of MDSO statutes was to provide treatment. At the time of their enactment, it was believed that mental health professionals could identify a specific mental disability called sexual psychopathy that made persons suffering from this disability more likely to commit dangerous sex offenses and that through treatment, improvement and cure were possible. The literature of the past decade has pointed out, however, that these laws were enacted with little or no data to support the premise that there is a broad category of people known as "sexual psychopaths" who can be treated successfully.[24] The Group for the Advancement of Psychiatry has stated that the category lacks clinical validity and that sexual psychopathy is not a psychiatric diagnosis.[25] The GAP report pointed out that individuals may engage in sexually inappropriate behavior for a number of reasons, some relating to illness and others not, and concludes that using sexual psychopathy as a common denominator to prescribe treatment is fatally flawed.[26] The recognition that sex offenders do not constitute a homogeneous group and that the treatment techniques which have been tried, have not had the followup studies which could demonstrate their success, lead to constitutional challenges to these laws based on a lack of treatment.

The lack of treatment challenges are based on equal protection grounds. The notion is that if someone is to be treated differently than other civilly committed individuals or differently than other convicted prisoners, there must be a rationale for that difference in treatment, in terms of the conditions and length of confinement. Thus, treatment became the rationale, and lack of treatment would render these laws subject to constitutional challenge based on the equal protection and due process clauses of the Constitution. As early as 1966, in *Millard v. Cameron*[27] the United States Court of Appeals for the District of Columbia held that indefinite confinement under MDSO laws was justified only upon a theory of therapeutic treatment and that the reality of "lack of treatment destroys any otherwise valid reason for differential consideration of the sexual psychopath."[28]

These differentials take on great importance when the individual is committed for an indefinite period as a sexual psychopath, when if he had been committed under the criminal laws he would possibly spend less time incarcerated. This was

---

23. Ohlinger v. Watson, 652 F.2d 775, 777 (9th Circ., 1980).
24. See Monahan & Davis, supra note 14 at 326.
25. See GAP Report, supra note 2 at 840, 935.
26. *Id.* at 858-860.
27. 373 F.2d 468 (D.C. Cir., 1966).
28. Id. at 473.

recognized by the United States Court of Appeals for the Ninth Circuit, reviewing a challenge to the Oregon sex offender statute, when it asserted in 1980:

> Adequate and effective treatment is constitutionally required because absent treatment, appeallants could be held indefinitely as a result of their mental illness, while those convicted and sentenced under statutes governing the state sodomy offense need only serve the fifteen year maximum term.[29]

The court went on to hold that "the rehabilitative rationale is not only desirable, but constitutionally required,"[30] and ordered petitioners transferred to a facility where they could receive treatment. The court said:

> Constitutionally adequate treatment is not that which must be provided to the general prison population, but that which must be provided to those committed for mental incapacity. At least due process requires that the nature and duration of the commitment bear some reasonable relation to the purpose for which the individual is committed.[31]

Thus, the practice of incarcerating a sex offender for a period longer than if they had been sentenced, with no meaningful treatment provided, probably cannot withstand constitutional attack. The lack of successful treatment methods or programs constitutes a basic condemnation of the MDSO laws, since the very justification for such legislation was that sex offenders should be treated in addition to being punished. Practically speaking, the lack of treatment, or the availability of unproven experimental treatment methods has led many prosecutors to conclude that it is preferable to seek conviction and sentence of sex offenders under the criminal law, rather than resort to the constitutionally suspect MDSO laws. These factors combined with the conviction that there is no specific illness that could explain the acts of all sex offenders has led to the calls for repeal of sex offender statutes,[32] and to their repeal in the majority of states.

TREATMENT OF SEX OFFENDERS WITHOUT SPECIFIC STATUTORY AUTHORITY

Although MDSO laws are fading from the criminal justice scene, there is still a great deal of interest in finding effective treatment techniques for sex offenders. Underlying these treatment approaches is the belief that certain types of sex offenders are likely to respond to specific types of treatment such as psychotherapy, behavior modification techniques, or treatment with psychopharmacologic agents, such as Depo Provera. The majority of treatment programs exist within prison

---

29. Ohlinger v. Watson, 652 F.2d 775, 778 (9th Cir., 1980).
30. *Id.* at 778.
31. *Id.* also citing Jackson v. Indiana, 406 U.S. 715, 738 (1972).
32. See GAP Report, note 2 supra at 843; the American Bar Association Committee on Mental Health Criminal Justice Standards, Standard 7.8-1.

BEHAVIORAL SCIENCES & THE LAW

systems and consist of the use of behavioral techniques.[33] There are now a few isolated programs in the United States which provide outpatient treatment to sex offenders with either behavioral techniques or the use of Depo Provera, or a combination of both.[34] In addition to formal programs there are individual mental health professionals who attempt to treat sex offenders as part of their private practice. In each of these situations there are numerous legal issues which arise both in terms of the ability of the offender to agree to participate in treatment, and in terms of the potential liability of the mental health professional.

Rights of the Sex Offender

When someone agrees to undergo treatment as a result of being labeled a ''sex offender'' numerous legal issues arise. If the treatment is received while the person is incarcerated, then the legal issues are more complex and the courts will more carefully scrutinize the defendant's rights, since he is being held in a captive situation. Even when the treatment is provided in an outpatient setting, when it is part of a probation or parole condition, the courts will carefully review the situation.

There are four primary rights which need to be addressed when examining the treatment of sex offenders. These are (1) his ability to give an informed consent to treatment, (2) the voluntariness of that consent, (3) his right to treatment, and (4) his right to refuse treatment. This section will examine these rights.

1. Informed Consent

The concept of informed consent is based on the premise that a person has a right to self-determination as to what is done to his body. First espoused judicially in 1914,[35] the concept did not gain wide attention and acceptance until the disposition of two medical cases in 1972.[36] Informed consent requires that the offender understand what he is being asked to consent to, what his participation will involve, and the potential risks and benefits to him. In obtaining an informed consent, the first issue which arises is whether the party has the capacity to consent. Is he legally competent? If he is a minor, he is not competent. If incompetent, his guardian must provide a substituted consent for him. If he is legally competent, meaning he has not been declared legally incompetent, and he is an adult, then the second issue is whether he is clinically competent. Since the offender must understand what he is being asked to consent to, he must have the intelligence and mental status to comprehend what is being requested. Thus, a severely or profoundly retarded person cannot provide an informed consent, nor can an actively

---

33. F.H. Knopt, Retraining Adult Sex Offenders, Methods and Models (Safer Society Press, Syracuse, N.Y. 1984).
34. Berlin & Meinecke, Treatment of Sex Offenders with Antiandrogenic Medication: Conceptualization, Review of Treatment Modalities and Preliminary Findings, 138 Am J of Psychiatry, 601 (1981).
35. Schloendorff v. New York Hospital, 105 N.E. 92 (N.Y., 1914).
36. Canterbury v. Spence, 464 F.2d 772 (D.C. Cir., 1972); Cobbs v. Grant, 502 P.2d I (Ca. 1972).

psychotic one. Obtaining an ''informed consent'' has become a routine procedure in both medical practice and research. This process serves to not only protect the patient from unwanted treatment, but also to protect the provider from potential legal liability.

When reviewing the issue of the ability of a sex offender to give an informed consent, one must be concerned with the treatment method used. The more intrusive the method, and also the more experimental, the more important it is that the consent given be one that truly reflects an understanding of the treatment process. In terms of traditional treatment techniques used for sex offenders, if aversive therapy is to be used or Depo Provera, the treatment provider should be sure that the offender fully understands and consents to the treatment approaches. In contrast, when behavioral approaches are used, these are less intrusive, and thus the level of understanding needed to consent to treatment is less.

2. Voluntariness

Perhaps the most critical issue when determining whether a sex offender has given a valid consent for treatment is whether the consent was given voluntarily. When the consent is given while the person is imprisoned the question of whether it is truly voluntary has great meaning. Can one who is incarcerated give a voluntary consent when those asking for the consent may have control over all aspects of his life, from the conditions under which he is confined to the date when he is to be released? Thus, treatment programs of sex offenders within the prison system must be carefully reviewed to determine if the offender entered the program voluntarily. The confined person may be motivated to act in a certain way because of a desire to secure freedom, to please the persons in charge, or to gain acceptance in his group. As the treatment becomes more intrusive, such as with Depo Provera, the issue of voluntariness takes on greater importance.

In perhaps the leading case on whether an involuntarily confined person can give consent for an experimental treatment, a Michigan state court in *Kaimowitz v. Department of Mental Health*[37] ruled that a detained mental patient could not give an informed consent for experimental psychosurgery. This case arose when ''John Doe,'' who had been committed as a sexual psychopath in 1955 for the murder and rape of a student nurse who was working in a state mental hospital where he was a patient, was asked to consent to experimental psychosurgery to determine if surgery on the amygdaloid portion of the limbic system of his brain would help control his aggression in the institution. Doe gave his ''informed consent.'' His parents consented, and there were two separate internal review committees that agreed that the procedure could take place. The proposed procedure became publicly known, and Kaimowitz, a legal aid attorney, challenged the proposed surgery.

---

37. No. 73-19434-AW, I MDLR 147 (Cir. Ct. of Wayne County, Mich., July 10, 1973). Although not reported in official legal reporters, the Kaimowitz case is widely known in both the mental health and the prison rights areas. It is reported in part in Miller, Dawson, Dix, & Parnas, The Mental Health Process at 567, (1976) and reprinted in A.D. Brooks, Law, Psychiatry and the Mental Health System 902 (1974).

The court held:

> Although an involuntarily detained mental patient may have a sufficient IQ to
> intellectually comprehend his circumstances . . . the very nature of his in-
> carceration diminishes the capacity to consent to psychosurgery. He is par-
> ticularly vulnerable as a result of his mental condition, the deprivation
> stemming from involuntary confinement, and the effects of the phenomenon
> of "institutionalization."[38]

The court went on to say:

> the involuntarily detained mental patient is in an inherently coercive atmo-
> sphere even though no direct pressures may be placed upon him. He finds
> himself stripped of customary amenities and defenses. Free movement is re-
> stricted. He becomes part of communal living subject to the control of insti-
> tutional authorities . . . The inherently coercive atmosphere to which the
> involuntarily detained mental patient is subjected has a bearing upon the vol-
> untariness of his consent.[39]

Although John Doe was a mental patient and not a prisoner, and the proposed
"treatment" was experimental psychosurgery which seemed to carry great risks,
with minimal benefits, the analogy to the prison situation is appropriate. Clearly,
the ability of a prisoner to make a free choice is greatly limited either directly or
implicitly by the fact of his incarceration. When this is combined with a treatment
process which may be considered to be risky and/or experimental it is almost impossible to obtain a truly informed consent. Although the *Kaimowitz* case has no
precedential value, it was widely discussed in the legal literature. As a result of
this case, and a few other incidents, there was more attention paid to the rights of
prisoners and mental patients to participate in research. In terms of sex offenders,
the concern about their voluntary participation in treatment has been reflected in
changes in some MDSO laws which mandate that the treatment be voluntary.[40]

The obviously coercive nature of being incarcerated makes clear why obtaining
a truly voluntary informed consent from a prisoner is difficult. Yet to a lesser extent
the same issues arise when the person is to be treated as an outpatient as a condition
of probation or parole. For in this circumstance the implied or stated assumption
is that without the offender's voluntary cooperation with the treatment modality,
he will violate the conditions of his release, and be subjected to incarceration.
Thus, one must question how willingly the offender is participating in the treatment. However, it must be borne in mind that the offender does have a choice, he
can decide to forego treatment and thus be imprisoned for the crime he has been
convicted of. In this circumstance, the issues are not clear-cut. The outpatient
treatment seems to be a humane and cost effective alternative to incarceration. It

---

38. Kaimowitz in the Mental Health process, note 37 supra, at 573.
39. *Id.* at 575.
40. See notes 5 and 6 and the text portion referring to these notes.

is providing the offender the opportunity to live in the community, while obtaining help. Although it would appear that anyone with common sense would choose almost any type of outpatient treatment over imprisonment, since imprisonment was the reality, there is truly a choice. Yet clearly, as the outpatient treatment is viewed as more experimental or intrusive, the true ability of the offender to enter treatment ''voluntarily'' remains a question.

For example, in Michigan, outpatient treatment with Depo Provera was ordered as a condition of probation for a man who molested his stepchildren.[41] In over-turning the lower court's order, the Court of Appeals of Michigan ruled that there was no statutory authority for ordering such a treatment, and this treatment had not gained widespread acceptance within the medical community.[42] The Appeals Court made clear that it felt the trial court's decision was improper, not only be-cause of the use of Depo Provera as a treatment method with its attendant risks as stated in the Physicians Desk Reference, but because the court felt the sentence was not severe enough and a longer period of incarceration was warranted under the statute given the facts of the case.

Yet the broader societal issues remain, at what point can the needs of society outweigh the needs of the individual? In the case of treating sex offenders with Depo Provera, for example, which is still viewed as experimental, yet has proven effective with certain types of sex offenders,[43] the issue arises at what point society should bear the costs of incarceration when there may be a more effective and less restrictive alternative? The additional societal issue arises when the incarceration has been completed, and the known sex offender who has committed multiple offenses, is to be released or whether society has a right to mandate treatment for the protection of the community. These types of cases would be similar to the state using its police power to override refusal of vaccinations or quarantines to protect the public health.[44] One could envision a day in the future when a particular type of treatment for certain categories of sex offenders was proven highly effective. At that point, the issue of voluntariness of treatment may become subsidiary to the protection of the community.[45] Clearly, before the courts would be prepared to override an individual's assertion of a right of privacy and mandate treatment, there would have to be proof that the treatment was likely to be effective and was not physically detrimental to the individual forced to undergo it. Of course, in the final analysis, the one way society can protect the community is to keep the convicted sex offender incarcerated. This seems like a costly and cruel alternative should effective treatment approaches be developed.

---

41. People v. Gauntlett, 353 N.W.2d 310 (Mich., 1984).
42. *Id.* at 315, 316.
43. See Berlin, Sex Offenders: A Biomedical Perspective and a Status Report on Biomedical Treat-ment, The Sexual Aggressor: Current Perspectives on Treatment 83 (1983); see Berlin & Mei-necke, note 34 supra.
44. For a more thorough discussion of this argument and an article which argues that Depo Provera can be ordered by the courts, see Rainear, Comments, The Use of Depo-Provera for Treating Male Sex Offenders: A Review of the Constitutional and Medical Issues, 16 Toledo L.R. 181 (1984).
45. *Id.* at 199-207.

3. The Right to Treatment

The concept that an institutionalized mentally disabled person is entitled to treatment is now widely accepted within the United States. Although not specifically recognized by the United States Supreme Court, the vast majority of state legislatures have mandated treatment for those who are involuntarily institutionalized.[46] This right was developed after a line of cases held that the only constitutional justification for institutionalizing someone who had not committed a crime, was to provide them with treatment.[47] Thus, the *quid pro quo* for deprivation of their liberty became a right to treatment.[48]

One might conclude that by analogy the convicted prisoner is in the same situation as the committed mental patient. Yet this is not the case. Although all prisoners are entitled to necessary medical care[49] and even mental health services when these are deemed crucial to their health,[50] the prisoner is incarcerated for punishment, not for treatment. Except for prisoners convicted under MDSO laws, where the notion that treatment can occur is part of the underlying rationale for imprisonment, prisoners are not entitled to treatment to alleviate them of their inappropriate sexual behaviors. Thus, a right to treatment has no meaning within the prison setting.

An Arizona case raised the issue of whether a sex offender who was ordered to undergo treatment as a condition of probation was entitled to be effectively treated and rehabilitated.[51] The sex offender violated his probation by committing numerous child molestations. The testimony revealed that at the time he was placed on probation, behavior modification and/or chemical castration was suggested as the most likely approach to help the offender.[52] Instead, he received psychotherapy, which seemingly had no effect on his behavior, thus resulting in the further molesting of children. He was convicted of these offenses and violation of his probation. In appealing his sentence he argued that the state's failure to afford him effective treatment and rehabilitation precluded his receiving a long prison sentence under the Eighth and Fourteenth Amendments to the Constitution. The court denied that the offender had any constitutional right to treatment. The court noted that "no society should be forced to guarantee effective rehabilitation to all offenders and ignore the other purposes of punishment"[53] which included retribution, restraint, and deterrence. Thus, a sex offender who is not committed under a MDSO law has no right to treatment for his inappropriate sexual behaviors.

---

46. For an extensive discussion of the right to treatment, see B. Weiner, Treatment Rights, Ch. 6 in S. Brakel, J. Parry & B. Weiner, The Mentally Disabled and the Law, 3rd Ed., (1985).
47. See, e.g., Rouse v. Cameron, 373 F.2d 451 (D.C. Cir., 1966) Wyatt v Stickney, 325 F. Supp. 781 (M.D. Ala, 1971); Donaldson v. O'Connor, 493 F.2d 507 (5th Cir. 1974).
48. In Donaldson v. O'Connor, note 47 supra the Fifth Circuit Court of Appeals first espoused the quid pro quo theory of commitment.
49. Estelle v. Gamble, 429 U.S. 97 (1976).
50. Bowring v. Godwin, 551 F.2d 44 (4th Cir. 1977).
51. State v. Christopher, 652 P.2d 1031 (Ar., 1982).
52. *Id.* at 1032.
53. *Id.* at 1033.

4. Right to Refuse Treatment

Like the right to treatment, the right of the civilly committed mental patient to refuse treatment, specifically medication, has become widely accepted during the past decade. Based on a constitutional right of privacy, the refusal of medication will be permitted in the nonemergency situation.[54] When the involuntarily committed mental patient refuses treatment, the courts have recognized a set of procedures to be followed before the patient's decision can be overridden.[55] Similarly, the issue has arisen of the rights of prisoners to refuse to participate in "treatment" programs within the correctional setting. The sex offender who has not been incarcerated under an MDSO law is different, however, than the involuntarily committed mental patient. The mental patient has been deemed "ill" and is being deprived of his liberty for the purposes of treatment. The prisoner in contrast, is deemed a "criminal" and is being incarcerated for the purposes of punishment. This distinction gives the prisoner more rights than the mentally disabled person to refuse to participate in a treatment program.

In a nonemergency situation the prisoner cannot be forced to undergo any type of intrusive or experimental treatment. If the prisoner has "voluntarily" agreed to participate in a treatment program, his continued participation must remain voluntary. If behavior modification is part of the treatment program, it must be designed in a way that if aversive techniques are used they appear reasonable.[56] Thus, he must have the option of withdrawing from treatment when he wishes.

The more complicated issue of refusal of treatment by the sex offender arises when the treatment is a condition of probation or parole. Without agreeing to treatment, the offender would not be released into the community. Yet the question becomes what type of treatment can the courts mandate? Clearly traditional treatment techniques which do not permanently alter the offender and are not deemed experimental or risky would be acceptable. Yet what about treatment with various types of medication, which may have powerful potential side effects? In the context of treating sex offenders this issue is most likely to arise when the suggestion has been made that he be treated with Depo Provera. Although recognized as effective in treating a particular group of sex offenders[57] this drug has not gained widespread acceptance within the medical community for this purpose, in part, because few physicians are willing to treat sex offenders. Thus, it is arguable that a court could at this time (without further research on the drug and more general acceptance by

---

54. For a broad discussion of the right to refuse medication see Weiner, note 46 supra.
55. See, e.g., Rennie v. Klein, 720 F.2d 266, (3rd Cir., 1983); Rogers v. Commissioner of Dept. of Mental Health, 458 N.E.2D 308 (Mass., 1983); Guardianship of Richard Roe III, 421 N.E.2d 40 (Mass., 1981); Jamison v. Farabee, 7 MDLR 436 (N.D. Cal., April 26, 1983).
56. In Knecht v. Gillman, 488 F.2d 1136 (8th Cir., 1973) the court held that the use of apomorphine, which induced vomiting, as a type of behavior modification technique constituted cruel and unusual punishment in violation of the Eighth Amendment. This occurred in a case where the patient supposedly agreed to participate in the treatment program.
57. Spodak, Falck, & Rappeport, The Hormonal Treatment of Paraphilias with Depo Provera, 5 Criminal Justice and Behavior 304, 1978.

the medical community) order this as part of a treatment program.[58] However, the courts do have the option of referring an offender to a program for an evaluation, and the program can determine if the offender is acceptable for treatment and under what conditions, including taking medication, or being prohibited from living or working with children. At that point the offender must voluntarily decide if he wishes to participate in the treatment. Should he decide to participate, he always has the option of withdrawing his consent, but this could result in his rejection from the program, and thus a violation of the conditions of his release, and subject him to incarceration. Although this appears to be a harsh alternative, the reality is that his release is based only on the belief that some efforts will be undertaken to change his criminal sexual behaviors for the purposes of protecting the community. It should always be borne in mind that the court's involvement and the requirement of treatment are only arising because of the individual's criminal sexual behavior, often involving a child or many children. Thus, being maintained in the community rather than being incarcerated is a privilege which can be granted under very specific conditions which are designed to prevent further criminal behavior. This means that the courts in balancing the rights of the individual against the rights of the community, will have an obligation to give greater weight to protecting the community.

LEGAL ISSUES FACING THE TREATMENT PROVIDER

Treating sex offenders in an outpatient or private practice setting raises the same legal issues which are presented when treating mentally ill persons—informed consent, confidentiality and the duty to warn, following child abuse reporting statutes, and liability for inappropriate treatment. Yet because of their sexual proclivities, the treatment provider must have a heightened sensitivity to these issues, as contrasted with treating other people. This section will discuss these issues in light of the particular problems which may be raised in attempting to treat the sex offender.

1. Informed Consent
Informed consent consists of three elements: the legal and clinical competency to make a decision, sufficient information to make a knowing decision, and the ability to make the decision voluntarily. These issues were discussed earlier. Yet when treating sex offenders particular concern must be paid to their competency. There is now a recognition that there are both adolescent and mentally retarded sex offenders. Their competency to consent to treatment poses special problems. For the adolescent, the treatment provider would be well advised to get the teenager's consent as well as the consent of one of his parents. This is particularly true

---

58. See People v. Gauntlett, note 41 supra, where the court held that the trial court had no authority to order the use of Depo Provera, in part because it had not gained acceptance within the medical community and had many serious potential side effects.

if some type of medication will be given. In assessing a mentally retarded person, the issue becomes how retarded is he, and what is his ability to understand what he is being asked to consent to. The fact of some level of retardation does not automatically mean an inability to consent. Each case must be evaluated on its own and a determination made. If it is concluded that the retarded offender does not have the capacity to consent then a guardian should be appointed who will provide a substituted consent for him. If the retarded offender is unable to consent to treatment for his sexually inappropriate behavior, he would not have the capacity to make decisions regarding other types of medical treatment, and, therefore, a guardian would be needed under any circumstance.

The second issue arises of what information is provided to the offender about the risks and benefits of the treatment. This is much more of a concern where Depo Provera is to be used, or other medications. A written consent for treatment should be obtained which explains the potential risks and benefits, including the fact that its carcogenic effects are still not known. Having the offender sign a consent form is not sufficient. Everything should be explained to him, and the treatment provider should be sure that the offender understands the form in addition to signing the consent. Periodically, I would suggest yearly, when medication is used, the provider should reconfirm the risks and benefits with the patient and this discussion can be noted in his record.

2. Confidentiality and the Duty to Warn

More than any other group of health care providers, mental health professionals are cognizant of the importance of confidentiality to their treatment relationship.[59] The notion that one should be able to seek mental health services without fear that his innermost feelings will be revealed has been translated into a public policy of privilege statutes which limit the circumstances under which a therapist can be forced to reveal something learned during the therapeutic relationship.[60] Yet confidentiality is not absolute and there are circumstances in which a therapist is required to violate confidentiality for the protection of the public or some specific individual. Beginning with the California Supreme Court's decision in *Tarasoff v. Regents of the University of California*[61] which held

> When a therapist determines, or pursuant to the standards of his profession should determine, that his patient presents a serious danger of violence to another, he incurs an obligation to use reasonable care to protect the intended victim against such danger. The discharge of this duty may require the therapist to take one or more of various steps, depending upon the nature of the

59. See Group for the Advancement of Psychiatry, Confidentiality and Privileged Communications in the Practice of Psychiatry, Report #45 (1960); Beigler, Psychiatric Confidentiality and the American Legal System: An Ethical Conflict, Chap 12 in S. Bloch & P. Chodoff (ed.), *Psychiatric Ethics,* (1981).
60. See Weiner, Provider-Patient Relations: Confidentiality and Liability, Ch. 10 in Brakel, Parry, & Weiner, note 46 supra.
61. Tarasoff v. Regents of University of California, 529 P.2d 553 (Ca., 1974) and Tarasoff II, 551 P.2d-334 (1976).

case. Thus, it may call for him to warn the intended victim of the danger, to notify the police, or to take whatever other steps are reasonably necessary under the circumstances.[62]

Therapists have become aware of an increased legal obligation to take some actions to protect third parties from their patients. In the decade since the *Tarasoff* decision, there has been a group of "duty to warn" cases decided.[63] Although most states have not yet addressed the issue, and some have rejected the notion of a duty to warn, the trend in the law appears to be that when a therapist is in a situation where he is aware that his patient is planning to harm another person, who is unlikely to be aware of that harm, he must take some type of action to protect the third person. This could consist of civil commitment, notifying the police, or notifying the third person.

Given the fact that sex offenders have usually been involved in repeated harmful acts they are at much higher risk to pose a danger to the general public, usually children, than others who seek mental health services. However, the cases are clear that the therapist must be aware of a specific intended victim or class of victims before he can be expected to give a warning.[64] Obviously, there is no point in trying to warn everyone in a city or even a neighborhood that a sex offender lives within their midsts, since the warning will have no relevance, and without a criminal act, can probably not result in any action which will remove the offender from their neighborhood. However, if the therapist becomes aware that the offender is planning on molesting a particular victim, or members of a particular family it would be wise for him to take some action. This would also be true if the offender is for example a coach, teacher, scout leader, or counselor, where he would have access to children and is actively planning or engaged in illegal sexual activity.

The concept of violating confidentiality and knowing when there is an obligation to undertake to warn a victim or class of victims will probably pose the most complicated legal issue for the treatment provider. This also may pose the greatest risk of legal liability. From the outset of undertaking any treatment, the therapist should make clear to the patient the limits of confidentiality placed upon him. This may result in the patient not being completely forthright, but a balance must be struck between the rights of the offender and the protection of the community, particularly when the victims are children who will not be able to protect themselves.

3. Child Abuse Reporting Statutes

Every state has some type of child abuse reporting statute. The statutes vary as to who is under an obligation to report. Yet in most states physicians have an obligation to report known or suspected cases of child abuse or neglect. Any sexual molesting of children would fall into the child abuse category. Therefore, a treat-

---

62. 551 P.2d 334, at 345.
63. See 2 Behavioral Sciences & Law (3) (1984) which is devoted to all aspects of the duty to warn area; also see Weiner, note 60 supra.
64. *Id.*, see also Thompson v. County of Alameda 614 P.3d 728 (1980) Leedy v. Hartnett, 510 F. Supp. (M.D. Pa, 1981); Lipari v. Sears Roebuck, 497 F. Supp. 185 (D. Neb., 1980).

ment provider must carefully review his state's child abuse reporting act. The Act may provide that only health care professionals or teachers who see the child have an obligation to report. Whatever the statute provides, the provider should be familiar with it, and keep up with any legislative changes in this area. It should however, be noted that the author was unable to find any reported cases where a therapist was held liable or prosecuted under such an act for failure to make a report.

4. Malpractice

As in any other type of treatment situation, the treatment provider must be sure that he is providing generally accepted treatments in a manner that conforms to what is accepted within a similarly situated group of treatment providers. In the event that the quality of care is substandard and negligence has occurred resulting in measureable damages, the provider may be liable for malpractice.[65] Since there has been so little treatment done with sex offenders, and very little research to support the efficacy of any specific approach over the long term, the provider must be concerned that his approach appears sound and is supported by the literature. If he is using medications or other approaches which can have permanent phyical effects on the patient, then he must carefully monitor the patient's response. Taking a careful clinical approach will assure that the provider will be successful should a suit be brought against him by the offender.

CONCLUSION

Undertaking the treatment of known sex offenders requires the treatment provider to have a specific knowledge of any mentally disordered sex offender statutes and child abuse reporting acts in the state in which he works. In addition the provider must be more sensitive to the legal issues which can arise with this population, such as the ability to give an informed consent and the increased likelihood that circumstances will arise where confidentiality may need to be breached. Although increased attention must be paid to legal issues, this does not mean that there is a greater likelihood of legal liability. In many instances the offender will be treated pursuant to a court order. This, to some extent, in the absence of malpractice, will provide a broad range of protection for the treatment provider. Finally, the fact that the patient is a sex offender will not make him a very appealing plaintiff in a lawsuit, and thus decreases dramatically, the likelihood of either a suit being brought or of its being successful.

---

65. See 1 Behavioral Sciences & Law (1) (1983) for many excellent articles on malpractice as it relates to mental health professionals.

Journal of Consulting and Clinical Psychology
1986, Vol. 54, No. 2, 176–182

Theory and Treatment in Child Molestation

Richard I. Lanyon
Arizona State University

This paper reviews the state of current knowledge on child molestation, as distinguished from child rape. The traditional view that deviant sexual behavior is based in a character disorder is contrasted with the functional view, which makes no assumptions about etiology. Descriptive characteristics of child molesters are presented; in particular, preference molesters or pedophiles, who prefer children, are distinguished from situational molesters, whose basic preference is for adult partners, but who choose children as a function of circumstances. Structured assessment devices are needed for making this distinction and also for assessing molesters' potential for violence. From a clinical perspective, the family-systems approach is widely considered to be the treatment of choice for incestuous families. For eliminating the deviant behavior and impulses of offenders themselves, the empirical treatment literature shows that behavioral methods using covert sensitization have considerable promise, at least for situational molesters.

Child molesters tend to be defined as older persons whose conscious sexual desires and responses are directed, at least in part, toward dependent, developmentally immature children and adolescents who do not fully comprehend these actions and are unable to give informed consent (Groth, Hobson, & Gary, 1982; Mrazek, 1984; Schechter & Roberge, 1976). Because such behavior is widely believed to constitute a serious risk for the children's well-being and further development (psychological, moral, and/or physical), such behavior is prohibited in our culture, and there are strong social sanctions against it.

Despite these sanctions, child molestation occurs with alarming frequency. Because of the traditional taboos surrounding the discussion and study of sexual matters, especially deviant behavior, the scientific investigation of this topic is a relatively recent enterprise. To gain a broader understanding of the current state of knowledge, it is helpful to examine briefly the topic of sexual deviations in general.

There are two major views in the literature as to how sexually deviant behavior is best conceptualized. The traditional view has its roots in the classical literature of Krafft-Ebing (1886/1965), Freud (1905/1953), and Ellis (1942), and has two basic premises: (a) that all sexually deviant behaviors are theoretically and etiologically similar, and (b) that they represent a single type of psychopathology, specifically, a form of character disorder. Two results have stemmed from this perspective. First, there have been a number of attempts to delineate a single theory of sexual psychopathology, usually involving psychoanalytic concepts and difficulties in psychosexual development. No specific theory has been agreed upon, however. Second, because sexual psychopathology is viewed as a character disorder, the behaviors have been regarded as highly resistant to change, so that treatment is lengthy and is based on restructuring of the character. This view is re-

flected in the writings and recommendations of Burgess, Groth, Holmstrom, and Sgroi (1978), Rada (1978), and others. It also tends to be the view held by the judicial system, by the social service agencies, and by the general public.

The second major view of sexual deviations is a more recent development and has its roots in the relatively atheoretical, elemental behavioral approaches to human disorders. Those who hold this view make no assumptions about etiology, and treatability is a purely empirical question. In particular, it is not assumed that a particular form of psychopathology (or any psychopathology) underlies the disorder and must be treated in order for the sexual behavior to change. Recommended interventions involve behavior therapy procedures for bringing about symptomatic changes and focus primarily on developing (or improving) adaptive sexual functioning and eliminating specific deviant behaviors, thoughts, and feelings. Proponents of this view include Abel, Blanchard, and Becker (1978) and Barlow (1974).

The behavioral or functional view does not imply that all or even most sexually deviant men or women are treatable in a practical sense, or that they are usually free of character disorder or other psychopathology. However, it is argued that such intrapsychic difficulties have not been shown to play a causal role in the development and maintenance of the deviant sexual behavior and that although they may hamper treatment, they are not the root of the disorder and do not necessarily require treatment for the sexual problem to be alleviated.

The empirical literature on sexual deviations is of three kinds: descriptive studies, laboratory studies in an experimental vein, and treatment studies. Although some of this work has been guided by theoretical notions, most of it has been undertaken with a minimum of assumptions about the nature of the phenomena.

The impetus for embarking on descriptive surveys came from the work of Kinsey and his colleagues (Kinsey, Pomeroy, & Martin, 1948; Kinsey, Pomeroy, Martin, & Gebhard, 1953) on normative sexual behaviors, which led to at least three surveys on deviant sexuality (Gebhard, Gagnon, Pomeroy, & Christianson, 1965; Karpman, 1954; Mohr, Turner, & Jerry, 1964). An inter-

The author is grateful to Paul Karoly for his thoughtful review of an earlier draft of this article.

Correspondence concerning this article should be addressed to Richard I. Lanyon, Department of Psychology, Arizona State University, Tempe, Arizona 85287.

126

esting result of these and other works, in addition to their function of demonstrating that deviant sexuality could be studied empirically, was that most sex offenders were found to be not remarkably different from other troubled people except in the deviant sexual behavior itself and in the failure of some types of offenders to establish satisfactory emotional and sexual relationships with their opposite sex peers.

These conclusions are consistent with the view that the differences are deep-seated and, therefore, difficult to approach therapeutically. They are also consistent with the view that sex offenders may not be very different from other troubled persons and that the sexual behavior can and should be studied in its own right. The latter view has given rise to a growing experimental literature that has attempted to map the differences in physiological arousal patterns among different types of sex offenders, as compared with nonoffenders. This literature is reviewed in detail by Langevin (1983).

The empirical development of behaviorally based treatments for sexual deviations occurred as an integral part of the behavior therapy movement. Early developments involved the use of aversive procedures alone and shared in the negative publicity received by early aversive behavior modification techniques. More recently, comprehensive behavioral models have been proposed (e.g., Abel et al., 1978; Barlow, 1974), and there is now a growing literature of behavioral treatment outcome studies. Reviews of particular aspects of this literature have tended to be optimistic in their conclusions (e.g., Adams & Sturgis, 1977; Blair & Lanyon, 1981; Kelly, 1982). All these empirical developments can be viewed as indicating the coming-of-age of deviant sexuality as a scientifically reputable topic that is potentially capable of being mapped, understood, and approached with viable treatment modalities.

Description and Classification

We now review the descriptive literature on child molestation. Because of space limitations, the review is necessarily selective, but it attempts to be representative. More focused reviews have been recently published by Howells (1981), Langevin (1983), and Kelly (1982). Excluded here are discussions of female offenders, a topic on which almost no data exist; characteristics of victims, the problems created for them, and their treatment; assessment issues; and questions of morals and values, as to how such men should be regarded by society.

Myths

A number of widely held beliefs about child sexual abusers have been shown to have no substance. Most prominent is the stereotype that child molesters are socially marginal persons or "dirty old men." Indeed, the molester is most commonly a respectable, otherwise law-abiding person, who may escape detection for exactly that reason. Furthermore, the median age of first offense is reported to be as young as 16 (Groth et al., 1982). Second, most molestation is done by men who are not strangers, but who are known to the victim, and in fact are often related to the victim (Conte & Berliner, 1981). Third, data and experienced clinical opinion suggest that children do not fabricate accounts of being molested except in rare instances, presumably when there are clear motivations to do so (Meiselman, 1978; Summit, 1983).

Violence

This review is limited to a consideration of child sexual abuse in which there is no direct physical coercion or violence. Cases including violence constitute about 10% to 15% of child sexual abuse cases (DeFrancis, 1969; Mrazek, Lynch, & Bentovim, 1981), but they receive disproportionate publicity and lead the public to believe that they are typical of child sexual abuse cases in general. Groth et al. (1982) have termed these men *child rapists* and believe that they are etiologically and motivationally more similar to rape than to child molestation. These authors have suggested that the term *child molestation* be used only when the pressures used are psychological ones and the harm done to the child is psychological rather than physical.

The question of potential for violence is obviously important in determining the appropriate disposition and treatment of sex offenders. Avery-Clark and Laws (1984) showed that physiological measures of sexual arousal could discriminate less dangerous from more dangerous sex offenders, and the work of Abel, Becker, Murphy, and Flanagan (1981) represents an empirical start toward developing procedures for distinguishing child molesters from child rapists. Particularly useful would be valid assessment devices that did not rely on physiological measurement and therefore could be used on a broad basis.

Frequency

As might be expected in view of the definitional problems and the secrecy surrounding this disorder, estimates of frequency from direct reports are generally believed to be serious underestimates. No data could be found on the incidence of child molestation as a disorder among adults. Following Mrazek's (1984) review of victimization among children, it would appear that perhaps 10% to 15% of children and adolescents suffer at least one incident of sexual victimization from an adult, and approximately twice as many girls as boys. Abusive behavior ranges from genital fondling to attempted or actual oral–genital contact and intercourse. In regard to sex of victim, available data appear to indicate that close to three-quarters of male abusers choose female victims exclusively (Frisbie, 1969; Langevin, 1983), about one-quarter choose male victims, and a small minority choose both sexes (Frisbie & Dondis, 1965; Groth & Birnbaum, 1978).

Sexual history

It is here that a distinction of considerable importance has been made. It appears to have originated with Karpman (1954), who distinguished molesters who have a stable erotic *preference* for children from those who utilize children as *surrogates* for adult sexual partners. Groth more recently made this distinction a cornerstone of his theoretical position on the development of child molestation and offered a list of characteristics that are said to differentiate the two types (Groth et al., 1982). These authors proposed the terms *fixated*, referring to arrested psychosexual development, and *regressed*, referring to psychopathologically regressive behavior under stress after more-or-less normal psychosexual development.

Howells (1981) likewise supported the distinction, preferring the atheoretical terms *preference* and *situational* molesters. Preference molesters are described by the sources just cited as having a primary sexual orientation to children and as being relatively disinterested in adult partners for the fulfillment of both sexual and emotional needs. They are usually unmarried, and any marriage or other apparent heterosexual relationship is usually either for convenience, as a cover, or for access to desired children. Victims are usually male children, whose role tends to be that of a substitute for an adult female partner. Preference molesters usually do not view their behavior as inappropriate and believe that society should stop harassing them and permit them to meet their needs. Offenses are usually preplanned, are an ongoing and persistent part of the offender's life, have a compulsive quality to them, and do not appear to be precipitated by stress.

Situational molesters, on the other hand, generally have a more-or-less normal history of heterosocial and heterosexual development and skills, although often with some deficits in these skills, particularly in intimate relationships. Their primary sexual and emotional interests are unequivocally toward adult partners, and they view their child-related urges as abnormal and as a problem. Significant life stresses are usually present, and episodes of molestation or urges to do so can often be tied to these stresses. The behavior is often impulsive, is generally not premeditated to any extent, and is episodic rather than persistent.

Empirical data to support this classification system was reported by Groth and Birnbaum (1978), who showed that 175 convicted child sexual abusers could be classified either as preference (83) or situational (92) and found significant differences on many of these factors. There is a question as to whether the classification was done independently of the results, however. It would seem reasonable to assume that the preference versus situational distinction might more profitably be approached as a dimension rather than as a dichotomy, and the development of a scale to quantify such a dimension is currently being undertaken by the present author.

It should be clear that if there are indeed three broad categories of child sexual abusers (including child rape), then the results of most of the existing research in this area, which has treated child sexual abusers as a single group, are of uncertain meaning. At the very least, future studies should be designed so as to take these categories into consideration.

Other Classifications

One traditional classification is that of incestuous versus non-incestuous situations. Some reviewers now believe that except insofar as incest additionally involves complex family dynamics, this is not a useful distinction in understanding the offender. For example, there is empirical evidence to suggest that both groups are similar in sexual preference patterns (Abel et al., 1981). A second classification is homosexual versus heterosexual molesters (e.g., Howells, 1981; Langevin, 1983), with its implication that male molesters of male victims are basically homosexual in orientation (and perhaps should be encouraged toward that goal in treatment). However, most molesters of boys state that they do not have adult homosexual preferences, and laboratory studies of sexual arousal suggest that this is indeed the case (e.g., Freund & Langevin, 1976). The preference versus situational distinction correlates positively with the homosexual versus heterosexual classification.

A third type of classification involves the use of the word pedophile. The *Diagnostic and Statistical Manual of Mental Dis-*

orders (DSM-III, American Psychiatric Association, 1980) restricts its use to refer to men for whom children provide the "repeatedly preferred or exclusive method of achieving sexual excitement" (p. 271) and excludes those men who are sexually drawn to children but who would readily choose an adult female peer if circumstances permitted. Once again, the preference versus situational distinction seems to capture the difference between pedophiles and nonpedophilic molesters as described in DSM-III.

A fourth aspect of classification has to do with the role of physiological sexual arousal in the definition of a child molester. On the one hand, the DSM-III definition requires such arousal, at least for its category of pedophile. Similarly, the experimental laboratory literature (Langevin, 1983) and certain treatment procedures are based on the use of physical arousal measures as the most central dependent variable and, in some cases, as the only criterion of deviancy. On the other hand, Groth et al. (1982) and others have argued persuasively that child molestation and other sex offenses are best characterized as sexual behavior in the service of primarily nonsexual needs, such as affection and love (and in the case of rapists, power or anger). Also, it is the writer's clinical observation that some molesters (and rapists and exhibitionists) achieve physical arousal with difficulty or not at all, so that for these men it is not a meaningful part of their deviant behavior pattern. Thus, it is perhaps safer to avoid the use of arousal as the sole criterion for deviancy and to await further research on this question.

Personality and Psychopathology

There is an extensive clinical psychoanalytic literature that offers a wide variety of ideas about the etiology of child molestation and the nature of molesters (e.g., Howells, 1981; Kraemer, 1976; Rosen, 1979). These ideas are perhaps best regarded as sources of hypotheses for further research. Consistencies among them include the significance of nonsexual (e.g., affectional or mastery) components of the molester's motivation, the idealization of childhood that is said to be a central aspect of the preference molester's motivation, and the context of anxiety-laden adult heterosexuality.

A number of studies have utilized objective test procedures, such as the Minnesota Multiphasic Personality Inventory (e.g., Atwood & Howell, 1971; McCreary, 1975; Toobert, Bartelme, & Jones, 1959), the Edwards Personal Preference Schedule (Fisher, 1969; Fisher & Howell, 1970), the Kelly Repertory Grid (Howells, 1978), and the semantic differential (Frisbie, Vanasek, & Dingman, 1967). No consistent findings emerge from these and similar studies except to support the view that molesters' sexual identification is not significantly feminine and that they tend to be somewhat more shy, passive, and unassertive than average (Langevin, 1983). Studies focusing exclusively on incestuous men have shown somewhat different trends (e.g., Meiselman, 1978), portraying them as often domineering and controlling, at least within the family itself.

Questions to do with psychological and psychosexual development and maturity have been inadequately addressed empirically. It is in this area in particular that preference and situational molesters should be separated for independent study. Overall, it is a frequent finding that molesters have some degree of social difficulty; however, it has been suggested that because the molesters studied are those who have been caught, the more socially skillful ones go undetected (Howells, 1981).

The studies in this section have addressed adult molesters. From the viewpoint of early intervention, primary attention should be given to adolescent offenders, the younger the better. Unfortunately, few data exist on adolescents, who as a group have interpersonal needs and characteristics that differ obviously from those of adults. Also relevant is the common belief that most or even all molesters are themselves victims of childhood molestation and that this is an important developmental component of their problem and must be addressed in treatment. This question appears not to have been studied systematically, although clinically it would appear that at the least, molesters report having been victimized with a frequency that is much greater than average.

Physico-Chemical Studies

There are few studies in this area, and results tend to be unremarkable. Rada, Laws, and Kellner (1976) found that plasma testosterone levels were within normal limits. Mental retardation and senility (Mohr et al., 1964) and other brain pathology (Regestein & Reich, 1978) have not been shown to be relevant factors in child sexual abuse.

Cognitive Studies

An area of potential relevance, though virtually unstudied, is the nature of molesters' cognitions about children. An interesting study by Howells (1978) using the Kelly Repertory Grid showed that for child sexual abusers, the differences between cognitions of adults and children were not the same as for normals. Because molesters (and preference molesters, in particular) report atypical cognitions about children, it would seem important to document systematically these differences in cognitions, both sexual and nonsexual, and to investigate possible causal relations.

Effects of Alcohol

Alcohol has at times been reported to be a causal factor in child molestation (e.g., Rada, 1978). However, other writers (e.g., Howells, 1981) believe that the association is overemphasized and that molesters are overeager to blame alcohol (and other factors such as job or marital stress) because it provides a more socially acceptable explanation than a personal deficiency. More research is needed in this area.

Treatment

Four different treatment approaches to child molestation have been reported: physiological, psychoanalytic, family systems, and behavioral.

Physiological Approaches

Castration. The surgical removal of the testicles is considered barbaric in this country but has been utilized in Europe on a voluntary basis for treatment of sex offenders, including child molesters. A review of several outcome studies on the long-term effects of castration (Heim & Hursch, 1979) showed a reported dramatic reduction in sex offenses, but the studies involved methodological difficulties such as sole reliance on self-report and lack of control data for recidivism rates. There are other data to indicate that sex drive is by no means reliably reduced by this method (Langevin, 1983). In addition, a wide variety of undesirable physical side effects and psychological side effects were reported. It is concluded that castration remains an undemonstrated method for the treatment of any type of sex offender.

Chemotherapy. The use of chemotherapy involving antiandrogens for sex offenders has considerable appeal for many segments of the public but is a highly controversial topic (e.g., Fisher, 1984). On the one hand, clinical reports (e.g., Spodak, Falck, & Rappeport, 1978) have shown mixed outcomes, and side effects are reported as problematic (Langevin, 1983). Also, the changes (reduction in the strength of arousal) are temporary, and sexual arousal to inappropriate stimuli is reported to return when the drug is terminated.

On the other hand, researchers employing drug treatments remain enthusiastic about their potential (e.g., Berlin & Meinecke, 1981), and there is the belief that new and more sophisticated drugs such as cyproterone hold particular promise for reducing deviant but not normal arousal. A middle-of-the-road position might be that at the present time, drug treatment should perhaps be considered for a small minority of offenders for whom other treatments have consistently failed or are unsuitable.

Psychoanalytic Approaches

Individual psychoanalytic therapy was virtually the sole treatment method for child molestation prior to the 1960s. Early accounts have been reviewed by Karpman (1954) and by Lorand and Balint (1956). Such treatments were typically addressed to the interplay of personality dynamics, which were said to account for both the etiology of the problem and its change during treatment. Later writers reported essentially the same approach to treatment (e.g., Kopp, 1962). Group psychoanalytic therapy has also been reported as an approach for child molestation (Hartman, 1965; Quinsey, 1977; Resnik & Peters, 1967). There are no systematic outcome data for these approaches. The opinions of Groth et al. (1982), after treating many child sex offenders from a general psychoanalytic perspective, were that "it would be misleading to suggest that we have reached a state of clinical knowledge that insures successful rehabilitation of adults who sexually molest children" (p. 140) and that the problem "is something the offender will need to work with every day of his life" (p. 143).

Family-Systems Approaches

With the development of systems approaches to the conceptualization and treatment of family problems in general, there has been a rapid increase of interest in using such an approach to incestuous child molestation. Indeed, a survey of recent writings on incest shows this to be the most widely recommended and utilized method (Burgess et al., 1978; Mrazek & Kempe, 1981; Sgroi, 1982). The major assumptions are that the psychodynamic interplay among family members is of prime importance and should be a basic focus of treatment, that the father needs to accept responsibility for his acts, that the mother also needs to accept her share of the responsibility, that peer support and self-awareness in the sense of the Alcoholics Anonymous model of alcoholism is needed, and that the process of change is an insight-oriented one. Treatment is accomplished by a combination of individual therapy for each family member, followed by therapy for each dyad and then family therapy, plus group therapy and self-help support groups.

One well-known family-systems program is the Child Abuse Treatment Program of Santa Clara County (Giarretto, 1982), where out of more than 4,000 cases, mostly father–daughter incest, 90% of the children were reportedly returned to the families with less than 1% recidivism. An independent analysis of this program by Kroth (1979) showed a slightly lower but meaningful percentage of success by subjective criteria: Fathers were returned to the home after a median period of 90 days, and 92% of fathers did eventually return to their homes. Mrazek (1984) offered the caution that the outcomes in other programs appeared to be less positive.

It is emphasized that the present article addresses men who molest children, whereas family-systems treatment is concerned with the functioning of all family members and of the family as a whole. It is clear that in an incestuous family situation, the victim, the offender, the wife, and possibly other family members have significant difficulties requiring treatment and that the family functioning also requires attention. For these purposes, the family-systems approach is the current state-of-the-art. However, systematic research is needed to identify its effective components because it is usually very costly in terms of therapeutic time. Another empirical need is to document the extent of its success in eliminating the man's deviant sexual behaviors, thoughts, and feelings.

Behavioral Approaches

The application of behavior therapy approaches to child sexual abusers has also developed actively in the last 20 years. Because this work has been recently reviewed systematically by Kelly (1982), such a review is not necessary here. Kelly identified 32 behavioral studies since 1960, 14 of which involved sufficient control procedures, quantification, and methodological sophistication to enable meaningful conclusions to be drawn from the findings. Most of these studies utilized some form of aversion procedure, the most frequent of which was aversive imagery (covert sensitization), either alone or in combination with other procedures.

For example, Maletzky (1980) treated 38 molesters of male children with covert sensitization in which aversive odors were paired with deviant sexual fantasies. Homework included aversive imaginal procedures, changes in masturbation fantasies, and manipulation of the environment. Of the 38 subjects, a nationwide search showed only four legal charges in a 3-year follow-up period. Other outcome data showed major reductions in frequency of self-reported deviant urges and masturbation fantasies and positive changes in penile plethysmograph records. Case-by-case data were not reported. In a different type of controlled study, Brownell, Hayes, and Barlow (1977) used covert sensitization to eliminate child-related sexual behavior and urges, plus an orgasmic reconditioning procedure to increase heterosexual

responsiveness. Positive changes as measured by self-report and plethysmography were stable over a 6-month follow-up period.

Kelly's (1982) conclusion was that the therapeutic behavioral reorientation of child molesters has now been clearly demonstrated. This conclusion appears warranted despite a number of problems and cautions with the outcome literature, such as the adequacy and objectivity of measurement procedures, bias in publication (positive studies are more likely to be accepted), and the fact that data as to which subjects respond most successfully are not available. In particular, no distinction was made in this literature between situational and preference molesters (or pedophiles as defined by DSM-III). Because the number of deviant aspects and also their nature are more extensive for preference than situational molesters, it is likely that the successful treatment outcomes have tended to be with situational, rather than preference, molesters.

The behavior therapy outcome literature has suffered from a consistent underemphasis on the development of adaptive ways of meeting sexual and affectional drives and on the need to deal with interpersonal and systems issues within the marital or family unit. In many cases that present for treatment in a typical practical setting, the family-systems and related problems (financial, alcohol-related, multiple crisis, police involvement, etc.) are so severe that they are beyond the capacity of the treatment setting to resolve. In these cases, the fact that aversive imagery can be successful in eliminating deviant characteristics is essentially irrelevant because the clinician is unable to set the stage for its successful use.

Clinical Suggestions

The following paragraphs state the author's tentative suggestions for a systematic treatment program for child molesters. They are based on an integration of the research and clinical literature on child molestation with 10 years of personal experience in treating such clients. Although the steps are presented in a particular order, there will necessarily be substantial overlap in practice as a number of aspects of treatment proceed simultaneously. This material is intended simply as a basis for discussion and hypotheses, and not as a set of proven procedures.

1. Any crises or immediate life problems are dealt with or stabilized. This may at times include a psychiatric evaluation for the possibility of medication to provide temporary relief from strong anxiety or depression. It may also include the therapist's involvement in family or legal matters. It is at this step that many cases, particularly those presenting at low-cost or public treatment facilities, cannot be processed further because adequate treatment resources are not available.

2. Sex education is provided as required.

3. If there is an existing adult sexual relationship that will continue, direct counseling and sex therapy are employed with the couple to alleviate any difficulties in the relationship and to ensure that the sexual and emotional aspects of the relationship are satisfying for both partners. If the offense is incestuous, then the full involvement of the family system in treatment is usually needed. These interventions are ongoing throughout the entire period of therapy.

4. If there is no ongoing adult sexual relationship, the client is encouraged to develop one. If he does not have the skills, or if

he experiences disabling anxiety in this area, these problems should be approached first. This is often a long and difficult aspect of treatment because many clients still have the complex anxieties and attitudes, often unrecognized, that prevented them from developing these skills during the usual period in their lives, namely, adolescence.

5. The behavior therapy procedure of aversive imagery is employed to eliminate the deviant behaviors and also thoughts and impulses about them. Included are permanent self-management skills and follow-up at gradually increasing intervals.

The following factors would appear to be related to good prognosis: (a) manageability of life crises and financial needs; (b) good heterosocial and heterosexual skills and experiences, plus a cooperative and committed adult sexual partner, or the willingness and motivation to learn such skills and find such a partner; (c) motivation and willingness to persist in treatment and follow therapeutic instructions; (d) relative freedom from other disorders such as alcoholism or drug addiction, psychosis, or substantial neurosis or character disorder; and (e) relative freedom from constrictive religious or moral beliefs about normal adult sexuality.

Conclusions

The literature on child molestation has yielded some tentative conclusions and hypotheses. The conclusions may be summarized as follows:

1. There are alternatives to the view that child molestation is necessarily based in a character disorder and must be treated accordingly.

2. There is a substantial research literature, mostly of an atheoretical nature, on descriptive aspects and on treatment.

3. An important distinction is made between preference molesters, or pedophiles, whose basic preference is for children, and situational molesters, whose basic preference is for adults.

4. It is also important to distinguish molesters, who control their victims by psychological means, from child rapists, who employ physical coercion and violence. Valid assessment devices are needed to identify those offenders who have the potential for violence.

5. There is little to suggest that analytic psychotherapy is a successful treatment procedure. For incestuous situations, the family-systems approach is widely used and is generally considered clinically to be the most useful, although adequate empirical data are not yet available.

6. For eliminating the offender's deviant behaviors, thoughts, and feelings, behavior therapy procedures involving aversive procedures (and covert sensitization, in particular) have shown a relatively high success rate. These data should be considered to apply as yet only to the most readily treated group, situational molesters.

7. Family-systems approaches have tended to underemphasize the need to address directly the offender's deviant behaviors and impulses; behavioral approaches have tended to underemphasize the necessity for attending to the offender's interpersonal context.

8. Future research should attend to the situational/preference dimension and also to the role of cognitive factors in the etiology and maintenance of child molestation.

References

Abel, G. G., Becker, J. V., Murphy, W. D., & Flanagan, B. (1981). Identifying dangerous child molesters. In R. B. Stuart (Ed.), *Violent behavior: Social learning approaches to prediction, management, and treatment* (pp. 116–137). New York: Brunner/Mazel.

Abel, G. G., Blanchard, E. B., & Becker, J V. (1978). An integrated treatment program for rapists. In R. T. Rada (Ed.), *Clinical aspects of the rapist* (pp. 161–214). New York: Grune & Stratton.

Adams, H. E., & Sturgis, E. T. (1977). Status of behavioral reorientation techniques in the modification of homosexuality: A review. *Psychological Bulletin, 84,* 1171–1188.

American Psychiatric Association. (1980). *Diagnostic and statistical manual of mental disorders* (3rd ed.). Washington, DC: Author.

Atwood, R., & Howell, R. (1971). Pupillometric and personality test scores of female aggressing pedophiliacs and normals. *Psychonomic Science, 22,* 115–116.

Avery-Clark, C. A., & Laws, D. R. (1984). Differential erection response patterns of sexual child abusers to stimuli describing activities with children. *Behavior Therapy, 15,* 71–83.

Barlow, D. H. (1974). The treatment of sexual deviation: Toward a comprehensive behavioral approach. In K. S. Calhoun, H. E. Adams, & K. M. Mitchell (Eds.), *Innovative treatment methods in psychopathology* (pp. 121–147). New York: Wiley.

Berlin, F. S., & Meinecke, C. F. (1981). Treatment of sex offenders with antiandrogenic medication: Conceptualization, review of treatment modalities, and preliminary findings. *American Journal of Psychiatry, 138,* 601–607.

Blair, C. D., & Lanyon, R. I. (1981). Exhibitionism: Etiology and treatment. *Psychological Bulletin, 89,* 439–463.

Brownell, K. D., Hayes, S. C., & Barlow, D. H. (1977). Patterns of appropriate and deviant sexual arousal: The behavioral treatment of multiple sexual deviations. *Journal of Consulting and Clinical Psychology, 45,* 1144–1155.

Burgess, A. W., Groth, A. N., Holstrom, L. L. & Sgroi, S. S. (1978). *Sexual assault of children and adolescents.* Lexington, MA: Heath.

Conte, J. R., & Berliner, L. (1981). Sexual abuse of children: Implications for practice. *Social Casework, 62,* 601–606.

DeFrancis, V. (1969). *Protecting the child victims of sex crimes committed by adults.* Denver, CO: American Humane Association.

Ellis, H. (1942). *Studies in the psychology of sex* (2 vols.). New York: Random House.

Fisher, G. (1969). Psychological needs of heterosexual pedophilics. *Diseases of the Nervous System, 30,* 419–421.

Fisher, G., & Howell, L. (1970). Psychological needs of homosexual pedophiliacs. *Diseases of the Nervous System, 31,* 623–625.

Fisher, K. (1984, May). Old attitudes slow treatment gains for sex offenders. *APA Monitor,* pp. 23–24.

Freud, S. (1953). Three essays on the theory of sexuality. In S. Freud, *The complete psychological works of Sigmund Freud.* (standard ed., Vol. 7, pp. 123–243). London: Hogarth Press. (Original work published 1905).

Freund, K., & Langevin, R. (1976). Bisexuality in homosexual pedophilia. *Archives of Sexual Behavior, 5,* 415–423.

Frisbie, L. (1969). *Another look at sex offenders in California* (Research Monograph No. 12). Sacramento: California Department of Mental Hygiene.

Frisbie, L. V., & Dondis, E. H. (1965). *Recidivism among treated sex offenders* (Research Monograph No. 5). Sacramento: California Department of Mental Hygiene.

Frisbie, L. V., Vanasek, F. J. & Dingman, H. F. (1967). The self and the ideal self: Methodological study of pedophiles. *Psychological Reports, 20,* 699–706.

Gebhard, P. H., Gagnon, J. H., Pomeroy, W. B., & Christianson, C. V. (1965). *Sex offenders: An analysis of types.* New York: Harper & Row.

Giarretto, H. (1982). A comprehensive child sexual abuse treatment program. *Child Abuse and Neglect, 6,* 263–278.

Groth, A. N., & Birnbaum, H. J. (1978). Adult sexual orientation and attraction to underage persons. *Archives of Sexual Behavior, 7,* 175–181.

Groth, A. N., Hobson, W. F., & Gary, T. S. (1982). The child molester: Clinical observations. In J. Conte & D. A. Shore (Eds.), *Social work and child sexual abuse* (pp. 129–144). New York: Haworth.

Hartman, V. (1965). Notes on group psychotherapy with pedophiles. *Canadian Psychiatric Association Journal, 10,* 283–288.

Heim, N., & Hursch, C. J. (1979). Castration for sex offenders: A review and critique of recent European literature. *Archives of Sexual Behavior, 8,* 281–304.

Howells, K. (1978). Some meanings of children for pedophiles. In M. Cook & G. Wilson (Eds.), *Love and attraction* (pp. 57–82). London: Pergamon Press.

Howells, K. (1981). Adult sexual interest in children: Considerations relevant to theories of etiology. In M. Cook & K. Howells (Eds.), *Adult sexual interest in children* (pp. 55–94). London: Academic Press.

Karpman, B. (1954). *The sexual offender and his offenses.* New York: Julian Press.

Kelly, R. J. (1982). Behavioral reorientation of pedophiliacs: Can it be done? *Clinical Psychology Review, 2,* 387–408.

Kinsey, A. C., Pomeroy, W. B., & Martin, C. E. (1948). *Sexual behavior in the human male.* Philadelphia: Saunders.

Kinsey, A. C., Pomeroy, W. B., Martin, C. E., & Gebhard, P. H. (1953). *Sexual behavior in the human female.* Philadelphia: Saunders.

Kopp, S. B. (1962). The character structure of sex offenders. *American Journal of Psychotherapy, 16,* 64–70.

Kraemer, W. (1976). *The normal and abnormal love of children.* London: Sheldon Press.

Krafft-Ebing, R., von. (1965). *Psychopathia sexualis.* New York: Putnam. (Original work published 1886).

Kroth, J. A. (1979). Family therapy impact on intra-familial child sexual abuse. *Child Abuse and Neglect, 3,* 297–302.

Langevin, R. (1983). *Sexual strands.* Hillsdale, NJ: Erlbaum.

Lorand, A. S., & Balint, M. (Eds.). (1956). *Perversions: Psychodynamics and therapy.* New York: Random House.

Maletzky, B. (1980). Self-referred versus court-referred sexually deviant patients: Success with assisted covert sensitization. *Behavior Therapy, 11,* 306–314.

McCreary, C. P. (1975). Personality differences among child molesters. *Journal of Personality Assessment, 39,* 591–593.

Meiselman, K. (1978). *Incest: A psychological study of causes and effects with treatment recommendations.* San Francisco: Jossey-Bass.

Mohr, J. W., Turner, R. W., & Jerry, M. B. (1964). *Pedophilia and exhibitionism.* Toronto: University of Toronto Press.

Mrazek, F. J. (1984). Sexual abuse of children. In B. Lahey & A. E. Kazdin (Eds.), *Advances in child clinical psychology* (Vol. 6, pp. 199–215). New York: Plenum Press.

Mrazek, P. B., & Kempe, C. H. (Eds.). (1981). *Sexually abused children and their families.* New York: Pergamon Press.

Mrazek, P. B., Lynch, M., & Bentovim, A. (1981). Recognition of child sexual abuse in the United Kingdom. In P. B. Mrazek & C. H. Kempe (Eds.), *Sexually abused children and their families* (pp. 35–49). Oxford: Pergamon Press.

Quinsey, V. L. (1977). The assessment and treatment of child molesters: A review. *Canadian Psychological Review, 18,* 204–220.

Rada, R. T. (1978). Sexual psychopathology: Historical survey and basic concepts. In R. T. Rada (Ed.), *Clinical aspects of the rapist* (pp. 1–19). New York: Grune & Stratton.

Rada, R., Laws, D., & Kellner, R. (1976). Plasma testosterone levels in the rapist. *Psychosomatic Medicine, 38,* 257–268.

Regestein, Q. R., & Reich, P. (1978). Pedophilia occurring after the onset of cognitive impairment. *Journal of Nervous and Mental Disease, 166,* 794–798.

Resnik, H. L. P., & Peters, J. J. (1967). Outpatient group therapy with convicted pedophiles. *International Journal of Group Psychotherapy, 17,* 151–158.

Rosen, I. (1979). *Sexual deviation* (2nd ed.). Oxford: Oxford University Press.

Schechter, M. D., & Roberge, L. (1976). Sexual exploitation. In R. E. Helfer & C. H. Kempe (Eds.), *Child abuse and neglect: The family and the community* (pp. 127–142). Cambridge: Ballinger.

Sgroi, S. M. (1982). *Handbook of clinical intervention in child sexual abuse.* Lexington, MA: Heath.

Spodak, M. K., Falck, Z. A., & Rappeport, J. R. (1978). The hormonal treatment of paraphilias with depo-provera. *Criminal Justice and Behavior, 5,* 304–311.

Summit, R. C. (1983). The child sexual abuse accommodation syndrome. *Child Abuse and Neglect, 7,* 177–193.

Toobert, S., Bartelme, K. F., & Jones, E. S. (1959). Some factors related to pedophilia. *International Journal of Psychiatry, 4,* 272–279.

Received November 14, 1984
Revision received April 23, 1985 ■

Child Abuse & Neglect. Vol. 11. pp. 433-442. 1987
Printed in the U.S.A. All rights reserved.

IS TREATMENT TOO LATE: WHAT TEN YEARS OF EVALUATIVE RESEARCH TELL US

ANNE HARRIS COHN, D.P.H. AND DEBORAH DARO, D.S.W.

National Committee for Prevention of Child Abuse, Chicago, IL

Abstract—Since 1974, the U.S. federal government has funded four major multiyear evaluation studies to determine the relative effectiveness of different approaches to the treatment of child abuse and neglect. A total of 89 different demonstration treatment programs were studied, and data on 3,253 families experiencing difficulties with abuse and neglect were gathered. Collectively, the studies document treatment approaches which improve clients' functioning (notably lay counseling and various group services including Parents Anonymous, group therapy, and parent evaluation) and suggest greater success with clients experiencing difficulty with sexual abuse than other forms of maltreatment. However, overall the studies show that one-third or more of the parents served by these intensive demonstration efforts maltreated their children while in treatment, and over one-half of the families served continued to be judged likely to mistreat their children following termination.

Résumé—Depuis 1974, le Gouvernement des Etats-Unis a financé 4 études majeures, comprenant plusieurs années, destinées à déterminer l'efficacité de diverses tactiques thérapeutiques employées dans la maltraitance-négligence à l'égard d'enfants. Ces 4 études ont englobé 89 programmes thérapeutiques pilotes; des données concernant 3,253 familles maltraitantes ou négligentes ou les deux ont été récoltées. Ce collectif d'études comprend un certain nombre d'approches thérapeutiques qui ont amélioré le fonctionnement de ces familles (entre autres la guidance par des non-professionnels, le système des "parents anonymes," la thérapie de groupe et l'évaluation familiale). On semble avoir plus de succès par ces approches avec des cas de sévices sexuels qu'avec des cas impliquant d'autres sortes de mauvais traitements. Malgré tout dans l'ensemble ces études ont montré que le tiers au moins des parents ayant bénéficié de ces formes de thérapie ont recommencé à maltraiter leurs enfants pendant la thérapie elle-même et que la moitié des parents ont été jugés capables de récidiver après la fin du traitement. Conclusion: les traitements surviennent trop tard, la prévention serait préférable.

INTRODUCTION

AS EARLY AS 1961, Dr. Brandt Steele and his colleagues noted that the abuse of children "is not confined to people with a psychopathic personality or borderline socioeconomic status. It also occurs among people with good education and stable financial and social background." And, they suggested that a professional's duty and responsibility to the child "requires a full evaluation of the problem and a guarantee that the expected repetition of trauma will not be permitted to occur" [1]. Therein began an ever growing battle to identify families from across all population groups in the U.S.A. who may be experiencing difficulties with abuse, to use investigative and diagnostic skills to determine if and why the maltreatment occurred, and to offer treatment services so the abuse would not recur.

In those early times, before reports of serious child abuse topped one million nationwide and before treatment workers carried caseloads of 50 to 60 with little or no supportive services to offer their clients, there appeared to be reason for optimism. Initially, treatment efforts looked promising with abuse families.

Reprint requests to Anne H. Cohn, D.P.H., Executive Director, National Committee for Prevention of Child Abuse, 332 S. Michigan Ave., Suite 950, Chicago, IL 60604-4357.

133

In discussing activities at what has come to be known as the C. Henry Kempe National Center for the Prevention and Treatment of Child Abuse and Neglect, Dr. Steele reported:

For the great majority of patients treatment was successful, highly so in some, moderately so in others. Criteria of success were multiple. Of primary importance was a change in the style of parent-child interaction to a degree which eliminated the danger of physical harm to the child and lessened the chance of serious emotional damage. . . . Of this treated group well over three-fourths showed significant improvement [2:138, 145].

Even for those not experiencing positive outcomes, Dr. Steele offered some thoughts on why it might appear that clients were regressing as treatment comes to a close and some clues on what to do about it:

Termination of treatment can arouse once more the feelings of being deserted and rejected, and not rarely these will be a mild transient recurrence of tendencies to demand too much and be too aggressive toward the infant. In response, "we let patients know we would be glad to hear from them again, after therapy had been tapered off and technically terminated" [2:141].

If only greater care had been taken to heed Dr. Steele's thoughtful remarks and to look upon treatment, not as a time-limited interaction between provider and client but as a longstanding relationship, perhaps the development and testing of treatment approaches since 1981 would have proved more successful. The expanding scope of maltreatment and the diversity of behaviors and service needs among high-risk or abusive populations have tested the limits of interventions once thought to be productive. This paper takes a look at large scale formal attempts undertaken in the last decade to improve our knowledge about effective treatment.

BACKGROUND

In the early 1970s, prior to the passage of the federal Child Abuse and Neglect Treatment Act, there were limited empirical research or program evaluations on how best to treat families experiencing child abuse. Ethnographic research, such as that of Dr. Steele [2], and clinical studies with small, nonrepresentative samples, undefined outcome variables, and a very narrow range of intervention strategies were all that was available. During the past ten years, in large part because of the establishment of the federal child abuse program, a number of evaluative and longitudinal studies have been conducted on approaches to treatment, creating a rich base of empirical data. One particularly large effort has been the multiple site program evaluations funded by the federal government since 1974 which included four major studies

- Study I: Berkeley Planning Associates' evaluation of the 11 joint OCD/SRS demonstration programs in child abuse and neglect conducted between 1974 and 1977 with a client impact sample of over 1,600 families;
- Study II: Abt Associates' evaluation of 20 demonstration and innovative treatment projects funded by the National Center on Child Abuse and Neglect (NCCAN) between 1977 and 1981 with a client impact sample of 488 families;
- Study III: E. H. White's evaluation of 29 service improvement grants funded by NCCAN between 1978 and 1981 with a client impact of 165 families; and
- Study IV: Berkeley Planning Associates' evaluation of 19 clinical demonstration

projects funded by NCCAN between 1978 and 1982 with a client impact of 1,000 families.

Collectively, these four studies represent over a $4 million federal investment in child abuse and neglect program research over a 10-year period. A total of 89 different demonstration treatment programs, on which the government spent approximately $40 million, were studied; data on 3,253 families experiencing difficulties with abuse and neglect were gathered. Detailed findings and descriptions of the evaluations can be obtained from the U.S. National Child Abuse and Neglect Clearinghouse and the National Technical Information Service [3-6]. While each of these studies explored some unique questions about the child maltreatment spectrum [7], each addressed common questions regarding the relative efficacy of different treatment strategies.

METHODOLOGY

A variety of methodological techniques was utilized by the four evaluations although sufficient similarity existed to allow for comparison of findings. Qualitative or descriptive approaches, such as case studies and in-depth interviews, were used both to explain the organizational and service structures of the individual demonstration projects [8, 9], as well as to highlight the key clinical issues raised in addressing the needs of multiproblem families and individuals [10]. These descriptive data provided a picture of what the projects did and how they did it. Quantitative approaches, primarily focusing on impact and outcome data, were used as well. These data were used to assess the most effective organizational and staffing patterns in working with maltreating families [11]; to determine the relative costs of providing various services to maltreating families [12, 13]; to determine the critical elements of a well-functioning community systems' response to maltreatment [14, 15]; and to assess the attributes of quality case management [16, 17]. Specific studies also identified the key issues in addressing child neglect [18] and in providing therapeutic interventions to young children [19, 20].

Three of the evaluations employed multivariate statistical techniques to identify the specific service and client characteristics which accounted for positive client outcomes [21-23]. The dependent variables used in the evaluations included clinician judgments regarding continued abuse or neglect during treatment, future likelihood for maltreatment following termination, progress in overall functioning, and progress in resolving a number of specific behavioral or psychosocial problems exhibited at intake. Utilizing data collection instruments developed by the evaluators, individual project staff provided detailed assessment of their clients at both intake and termination. Each of the evaluations used a multiple comparison group design in which the performance of clients receiving one set of services was compared to the performance of clients receiving a different service package. Multiple regression was utilized in the analyses, with covariates entered to control for differences in client characteristics and in the types and severity of maltreatment [24].

The variety of interventions provided families with similar presenting problems and the utilization of a common data collection system and uniform outcome measures created a natural experiment for assessing the relative merits of different treatment strategies. While true causal relationships between services and outcomes are best determined through experimental research designs with random assignment to treatment and control groups, the multiple comparison group design offers a pragmatic alternative to the ethical and logistical problems inherent in experimental research. The breadth of interventions

135

represented by the federal demonstration programs provided a program and client pool sufficiently diverse to effectively and appropriately use this research design to inform practice and policy development.

An additional methodological constraint is that the measures were limited to clinical judgment rather than direct behavior measures. The study design limited the researchers' ability to gather data directly from clients, and thus the reliance on professional observations was necessary.

Nature of the Study Population

The clients served by these 89 federally funded demonstration projects represented a broad spectrum of families. Wide variation in the types of maltreatment, household income, household composition, race, and presenting problems were noted in all four evaluation efforts. As summarized in Table 1, the four client impact samples represented a wide range of maltreatment [25]. The most notable differences among the four studies were the variations in the number of high-risk families included in each sample and in the recorded incidence of sexual abuse. While approximately one-quarter of the clients included in Studies II and III were identified as high risk, this classification applied to only 5% of the Study IV sample. Of the substantiated cases served by the projects, the percentage of families who had previously been reported for child maltreatment was 29% in the Study I sample and over 40% in Studies II and IV samples. Variations in the percentage of sexual abuse cases were partially reflected in the selection criteria NCCAN employed in establishing each demonstration effort [26].

Despite this diversity in family characteristics and type of maltreatment, the major presenting problems identified in these families are remarkably similar across the four studies and mirror the array of difficulties frequently cited in the literature for this population. As summarized in Table 2, contextual problems (such as financial difficulties or unemployment) and interpersonal problems (such as marital conflict, social isolation, substance abuse, and spouse abuse) were identified by sizable percentages of clients in each study population. As might be expected, since Studies III and IV included more severe cases, the frequency of all of these problems was also greater. For example, financial difficulties were noted for 46% of the client population in Study I, and over 80% in the client population in Study IV. Similarly, employment problems were identified in 18% and 36% of the respective clients samples.

STUDY FINDINGS

Study findings from three areas suggest the following: (1) the relative effectiveness of different services with abusers and neglecters; (2) the success rates in treatment for

Table 1. Type of Maltreatment

	Study 1 (1977)	Study 2 (1981)	Study 3 (1981)	Study 4 (1982)
High risk	28%	25%	42%	5%
Emotional maltreatment	14%			23%
Physical neglect	20%	26%	32%	27%
Physical abuse	31%	28%	21%	17%
Sexual maltreatment	4%	5%		28%
Emotional or sexual maltreatment			7%	
Neglect & physical abuse	3%	13%		
Sexual maltreatment, neglect and/or physical abuse		2%		
	(n = 1686)	(n = 488)	(n = 164)	(n = 895)

Table 2. Major Presenting Problems of Maltreating Families

	Study 1 (1977)	Study 2 (1981)	Study 3 (1981)	Study 4 (1982)
Financial difficulties	46%	44%	62%	80%
Employment problems	18%	30%	n.a.	36%
Marital conflict	40%	36%	40%	74%
Social isolation	29%	23%	n.a.	67%
Substance abuse	19%	24%	25%	54%
Spouse abuse	11%	13%	n.a.	42%
	(n = 1686)	(n = 488)	(n = 164)	(n = 903)

abusers and neglecters; and (3) the effectiveness of services for the abused and neglected children.

Service Effectiveness for Adults

While Study II found no notable correlation between a given set of services and positive client outcomes, both Studies I and IV identified specific services as enhancing client outcomes. Study I concluded that, relative to any other discrete services or combination of services, the receipt of lay services—lay counseling and Parents Anonymous—as part of a treatment package resulted in more positive treatment outcomes. The study also noted that group services, such as group therapy and parent education classes, as supplemental services also produced significant effects, particularly for the physical abuser. Although Study I cautioned that the lay services provided by the projects participating in that study required intensive on-the-job training and ongoing professional back-up and supervision for the lay therapist, the study clearly indicated that expansion beyond a strictly therapeutic or counseling service model was both beneficial to the client as well as cost-effective for the project [27, 28].

Similar findings were noted in Study IV. Again, the provision of group counseling and educational and skill development classes showed a significant relationship to a client's achievement of both overall progress and the elimination of a propensity toward future maltreatment. After considering the possible impacts of initial severity and client characteristics on outcomes, adults who received group counseling were 27% less likely than those who did not receive this particular service to demonstrate a continued propensity for future maltreatment. Similarly, those clients who received educational or skill development classes, such as household management, health care, and vocational skills development, were 16% less likely than the clients who did not receive this service to demonstrate a continued propensity for future maltreatment. Clients receiving group counseling and educational or skill development classes were also significantly more likely than clients not receiving these services to demonstrate overall progress during treatment [29-32]. Similar findings regarding the efficacy of group therapy and parenting education classes have also been noted in other program evaluations.

Studies I and IV both noted that clients engaged in treatment for less than six months were less likely to make overall progress in treatment or to demonstrate a reduced propensity toward future maltreatment. In addition, Study IV found that clients remaining in treatment over 18 months also performed less well on these indicators, suggesting that an optimal treatment period may be between 7 and 18 months. The Study IV findings corroborates Study II findings.

On balance, the findings summarized above suggest that successful intervention with maltreating families requires a comprehensive package of services which address both the interpersonal and concrete needs of all family members. Strategies which continue to rely solely upon costly professional therapy, without augmenting their service strategies with group counseling efforts and other supportive or remedial services to children and families, will offer less opportunity for maximizing client gains. Also, projects should be aware of the diminishing rate of return on services over time and invest the most intensive resources during the initial months of treatment, as close to the point of initial referral as possible, in order to successfully engage the family and begin altering behavior.

Success Rates in Treatment for Adults

In three of the studies, client outcome was measured. Overall, the data suggest that federally funded demonstration projects have had their problems in achieving client success, both in terms of initially stopping the abuse and in reducing the likelihood for further maltreatment. As summarized in Table 2, continued abuse while in treatment occurred in 30% to 47% of the cases evaluated. While the definition of this outcome measure varied among the three samples (e.g., Study II noted only cases involving severe neglect or physical abuse during treatment while Study II recorded all instances of maltreatment occurring while the family received services), the collective impression of these findings suggests that, in the short run, existing treatment efforts have not been very successful in protecting children from further harm.

On the other hand, repeated maltreatment while receiving services is not, in and of itself, a sufficient predictor of eventual progress in treatment or long standing propensity for future maltreatment. All three studies reported a relatively weak correlation between abusive behavior during treatment and other client outcome measures such as propensity for future maltreatment and overall progress in resolving a range of personal and family functioning problems. In every respect, the projects most successful in immediately eliminating abusive behavior were projects which generally separated the child from the abusive parent, either by placing the child in temporary foster care or requiring the maltreating parent to move out of the home [33].

Reduced propensity toward future maltreatment was also measured. In Study 1, 42% of the clients demonstrated a reduced propensity for future maltreatment compared to 80% of the clients included in Study II. While these clients were found less likely to maltreat their children in the future than they had been prior to services, the likelihood for future maltreatment continued to exist among many of the clients. Study IV identified 46% of the clients served as being unlikely to maltreat their children in the future.

Study IV also noted a dramatic difference in the performance of clients involved in different types of maltreatment on this indicator. For example, 70% of the clients served by the sexual abuse treatment projects were viewed as being unlikely to further maltreat their children, but only 40% of the adults served by the child neglect projects were viewed in this manner. This suggests that greater gains have been made in achieving success with incestuous families than have been made in the more intractable area of child neglect [34-36]. Similar findings have been noted by others evaluating sexual abuse interventions.

Measures of improved adult client functioning in behavior and attitudes associated with abuse were also used in three of the evaluation efforts. As summarized in Table 3, the projects in Study IV fared better than the other demonstration efforts in resolving the key functioning problems of their adult clients. While roughly two-thirds of the adults served by the 11 joint OCD/SRS demonstration projects (Study I) experienced improvement in only one-third or less of their functioning problems, 51% of the clients served by the most recent NCCAN-funded demonstration effort (Study IV) realized improvement on at least half of their problems, with 30% of these clients realizing gains on all of their presenting problems. Similarly, while Study II noted that 34% of its client sample achieved overall

138

progress during treatment, over 60% of the adults included in Study IV were identified at termination as having made progress.

The latest child abuse and neglect demonstration projects made more progress in reducing the propensity for future maltreatment and in improving client functioning than those funded a decade ago. The caseloads of these projects have included percentages of families experiencing severe maltreatment and multiple problems [37]. Expansions in the service package and the better targeting of services to specific child maltreatment subpopulations are among the factors which have most likely contributed to these successes [38].

Service Effectiveness for Children

In the earliest rounds of demonstration projects (Studies I and II) very few children received direct services, making the assessment of the impacts of such efforts on remediating the physical and emotional effects of maltreatment difficult. For example, only 70 children received direct services during the first federal demonstration effort (Study I). Of the 70 children who did receive some form of therapy, over 50% demonstrated improvements in those developmental, emotional, or socialization areas noted to be serious problems at the time treatment began. In contrast to the relatively few number of children provided direct services by these early demonstration efforts, over 1,600 children and adolescents served by the demonstration projects assessed in Study IV were provided a wide variety of direct services including individual therapy, group counseling, therapeutic day care, speech and physical therapy, and medical care. Over 70% of the young children and adolescents in Study IV demonstrated gains across all functional areas during treatment.

IMPLICATIONS

The collective results of the federally funded research and demonstration efforts certainly provide useful and positive program guidelines. In addition to descriptive data, which provide greater clarity on how to differentiate among families experiencing various

Table 3. Success Rates

Outcome Measures	Study 1	Study 2	Study 4
Reincidence	30% of all cases severe reincidence	44% reincidence for all cases	47% reincidence for all cases
Future likelihood to maltreat	42% reduced propensity	80% reduced propensity	46% unlikely to abuse in future
Improvement on functional problems adult clients exhibited at intake:			
Percentage showing any progress during treatment	—	33%	60%
Percentage of problems showing improvement:			
33%–0%	62%		
34%–66%	18%		
67%–100%	21%		
Less than 50%			49%
50%–74%			14%
75%–99%			7%
100%			30%

types of maltreatment when providing treatment and a better understanding of how to provide expanded intervention models which include direct services to both adults and children, the studies document

- approaches to improved client outcomes, especially in the areas of individual and family functioning with increasingly more severe forms of maltreatment; and
- methods for success in eliminating initial reabuse and future propensity among families involved in sexual abuse.

The studies also provide some cause for concern: Treatment efforts in general are not very successful. Child abuse and neglect continue despite early, thoughtful, and often costly intervention. Treatment programs have been relatively ineffective in initially halting abusive and neglectful behavior or in reducing the future likelihood of maltreatment in the most severe cases of physical abuse, chronic neglect, and emotional maltreatment. One-third or more of the parents served by these intensive demonstration efforts maltreated their children while in treatment, and over one-half of the families served continued to be judged by staff as likely to mistreat their children following termination. Whether one views this level of success as notable or disappointing is largely a function of personal perspective and professional choice.

Assessing the overall success rate one can hope to achieve in working with abusive and neglectful families, Kempe and Kempe in their earlier work estimated that, regardless of the interventions used, 20% of the parents will be treatment failures such that the child will not be returned home; 40% of the parents will grow and develop and eventually permanently change their parenting behaviors; and 40% of the parents will no longer physically abuse or neglect their children but will continue to be emotional maltreators [39]. More recent research experiences are less positive. While the combination of therapeutic and supportive services such as group and family therapy, educational and skill development classes, in-home lay therapist, and self-help groups, have enhanced overall performance with families agreeable to intervention, a sizable core of parents now appear to remain unchanged, and their children remain at risk. In addition to suggesting clear treatment paths, therefore, the collective findings of these national program evaluations identify clear limitations on strategies which serve families only after abusive and neglectful patterns have surfaced.

If research findings are to be of any use in setting policies, the results of a decade of evaluative research on treatment programs suggest that putting all resources into intervention after the fact does not make sense. Perhaps intervention much earlier with families would produce better results. Dr. Brandt Steele said it best:

We want to prevent not only the immediate, painful misery of children who are subjected to maltreatment, but also to prevent those lifelong disastrous consequences that are more and more difficult to treat as the person grows older. To work toward the prevention of all these unhappy lasting effects of maltreatment is one of the most valuable things we can do to benefit our fellow human beings [40].

NOTES AND REFERENCES

1. KEMPE, C. H., SILVERMAN, F. N. and STEELE, B. F., DROEGEMUELLER, W. and SILVER, H. K.,. The battered child syndrome. *Journal of the American Medical Association* 181:17-24 (1962).
2. STEELE, B. F. and POLLOCK, C. B. A psychiatric study of parents who abuse infants and small children. *The Battered Child*, R. E. HELFER and C. H. KEMPE (Eds.). University of Chicago Press, Chicago (1968).
3. BERKELEY PLANNING ASSOCIATES. *Evaluation of the Joint OCD/SRS Demonstration Projects in Child Abuse and Neglect* (Vols. 1-12). National Center for Health Services Research, Office of Assistant

Secretary for Health, DHEW, under Contracts HRA 106-74-120 and HRA 230-76-076, Washington DC (1977).

4. ABT ASSOCIATES. *Impact Evaluation of Twenty Demonstration and Innovative Child Abuse and Neglect Treatment Projects* (Vols. 1-2). National Center for Child Abuse and Neglect, Office of Human Development Services, DHHS under Contract 105-77-1047, Washington DC. (1981).

5. WHITE, E. H. *Evaluation of Service Improvements Grants: Analysis of Client Case Reports.* National Center for Child Abuse and Neglect, Office of Human Development Services, DHHS. under Contract HEW 105-78-1107, Washington DC (1981).

6. BERKELEY PLANNING ASSOCIATES. *Evaluation of the Clinical Demonstrations of the Treatment of Child Abuse and Neglect* (Vols. 1-9). National Center for Child Abuse and Neglect, Office of Human Development Services, DHHS, under Contract HEW 105-78-1108, Washington DC (1983).

7. Over the time period spanned by the four evaluations, fewer of the demonstration projects were housed in public protective service agencies; the client population became more dominated by substantiated rather than "high risk" families; the number and range of services provided by the projects to the children and adolescents in these maltreating families increased; and projects targeted their services to a more limited range of maltreatment behavior.

8. BERKELEY PLANNING ASSOCIATES. *Historical Case Studies: Eleven Child Abuse and Neglect Projects,* (Vol. 12). Berkeley Planning Associates, Berkeley, CA (1974-1977).

9. BERKELEY PLANNING ASSOCIATES. *Historical Case Studies.* (Vol. 9). Berkeley Planning Associates, Berkeley, CA (1983).

10. BERKELEY PLANNING ASSOCIATES. *A Qualitative Study of Most Successful and Least Successful Cases,* (Vol. 3). Berkeley Planning Associates, Berkeley, CA (1983).

11. BERKELEY PLANNING ASSOCIATES. *Project Management and Worker Burnout* (Vol. 9). Berkeley Planning Associates, Berkeley, CA (1977).

12. BERKELEY PLANNING ASSOCIATES. *Cost Report* (Vol. 7). Berkeley Planning Associates, Berkeley. CA (1977).

13. BERKELEY PLANNING ASSOCIATES. *Resource Allocation Study* (Vol 7). Berkeley Planning Associates, Berkeley, CA (1983).

14. BERKELEY PLANNING ASSOCIATES. *Community Systems Impact* (Vol. 5). Berkeley Planning Associates, Berkeley, CA (1977).

15. BERKELEY PLANNING ASSOCIATES. *Guide for Planning and Implementing Child Abuse and Neglect Programs* (Vol. 10). Berkeley Planning Associates, Berkeley, CA (1977).

16. BERKELEY PLANNING ASSOCIATES. *Quality of the Case Management Process* (Vol. 6). Berkeley Planning Associates, Berkeley, CA (1977).

17. COHN, A. and DEGRAAF, B. Assessing case management in the field of child abuse. *Journal of Social Service Research* 5:29-43 (1982).

18. BERKELEY PLANNING ASSOCIATES. *Child Neglect* (Vol. 4). Berkeley Planning Associates, Berkeley, CA (1983).

19. BERKELEY PLANNING ASSOCIATES. *Child Impact* (Vol. 11). Berkeley Planning Associates, Berkeley, CA (1977).

20. BERKELEY PLANNING ASSOCIATES. *Therapeutic Child Care: Approaches to Remediating the Effects of Child Abuse and Neglect* (Vol. 5). Berkeley Planning Associates, Berkeley, CA (1983).

21. BERKELEY PLANNING ASSOCIATES. *Methodology for Evaluating Child Abuse and Neglect Service Program* (Vol. 8). Berkeley Planning Associates, Berkeley, CA (1977).

22. ABT ASSOCIATES. *Detailed Account of Study Findings, Methods and Conclusion* (Vol. 2). Abt Associates, National Center for Child Abuse and Neglect, Office of Human Development Services, Washington DC (1981).

23. BERKELEY PLANNING ASSOCIATES. *Final Analysis Plan and Methodology for the Exploration of Client Characteristics, Services and Outcome* (Vol. 8). Berkeley Planning Associates, Berkeley, CA (1981).

24. This analytic method controls for all variation in the dependent variables explained by nonservice-related factors before considering the impact of the interventions. This method, while representing a very conservative approach to identifying significant service impacts, is one of the few analytic methods which can be used to determine service impact in the absence of a formal control or comparison group. To compensate for the lack of a true experimental research design, the method assumes services were randomly assigned to clients (i.e., no consistent relationship existed between client characteristics and the provision of services). Client characteristics and other nonservice variables are entered into the model first under this method as a means of controlling for their specific contribution to differential outcomes. Service impact is then determined to be the additional variance in the dependent variable of interest explained by the introduction of specific service variables.

25. Reviewing the demographic descriptions of these families, one would be hard-pressed to isolate patterns of maltreatment to a single socioeconomic class. For example, over 15% of the families in Study 1 had household incomes in excess of $12,00 while over 22% of the families in Study 4 had incomes in excess of $15,000. In addition, income was found in Study 4 to be highly correlated with the family's primary type of maltreatment.

26. Each project funded under this effort targeted services to one of five subpopulations including sexual abuse, adolescent maltreatment, substance abuse, remedial services for children, and child neglect.

27. BERKELEY PLANNING ASSOCIATES. *Adult Client Impact Reports* (Vol. 3). Berkeley Planning Associates, Berkeley, CA (1977).

28. COHN, A. Effective treatment of child abuse and neglect. *Social Work* 24:513-519 (1979).
29. BERKELEY PLANNING ASSOCIATES. *The Exploration of Client Characteristics, Services and Outcomes: Final Report and Summary of Findings* (Vol 2). Berkeley Planning Associates, Berkeley, CA (1983).
30. BEAN, S. L. A multiservice approach to the prevention of child abuse. *Child Welfare* 50:277-282 (1971).
31. MCNEIL, J. S. and MCBRIDE, M. L. Group therapy with abusive parents. *Social Casework* 60:36-42 (1979).
32. MOORE, J. B. Project Thrive: A supportive treatment approach to parents of children with nonorganic failure to thrive. *Child Welfare* 61:389-398 (1982).
33. For treatment projects committed to working with the entire family and in maintaining the family unit throughout the treatment process, this intervention strategy is less viable. Breaking the cycle of maltreatment is a difficult treatment issue that involves not only breaking the abusive or neglectful patterns but also cultivating different, more appropriate patterns of interaction and discipline. Prior to the completion of this process, families will likely fall back into those patterns that are familiar and comfortable. As each of these evaluations has pointed out, reincidence in this context is not solely an outcome indicator, but rather a continuum along which a family's progress may be monitored.
34. ANDERSON, L. M. and SHAFER, G. The character-disorder family: A community treatment model for family sexual abuse. *American Journal of Orthopsychiatry* 49:436-445 [1979].
35. GIARRETTO, H. The treatment of father-daughter incest: A psychosocial approach. *Children Today* 5:34-35 (1976).
36. GIARRETTO, H. Humanistic treatment of father-daughter incest. *Journal of Humanistic Psychology* 18:59-76 (1978).
37. The increased percentage of severe maltreatment cases being served by the demonstration projects has both positive and negative aspects. To see that solid success can be achieved with multiproblem families is certainly encouraging. On the other hand, the focus on the more severe cases places child abuse and neglect treatment projects in the difficult position of working with families which have fewer and fewer material and personal resources.
38. Hypotheses regarding subpopulations of maltreatment were supported by all four evaluations. Each identified significant differences in demographic characteristics, presenting problems, and service needs among families and perpetrators involved in different types of maltreatment. Segmenting the population for service purposes along this dimension, however, is problematic. The continued funding of projects to serve only one segment of the maltreatment population may be difficult to justify in light of rising fiscal constraints and service demands. For years, one of the keys to a successful community response to child maltreatment has been establishing a coordination system which includes all professional and voluntary agencies concerned with child health and well-being.
39. KEMPE, R. S. and KEMPE, C. H. *Child Abuse*. Harvard University Press, Cambridge, MA (1978).
40. STEELE, B. F. Notes on the lasting effects of early child abuse. *Child Abuse & Neglect* 10:283-291 (1986).

How Perpetrators View Child Sexual Abuse

Jane F. Gilgun and Teresa M. Connor

Effective work with clients requires understanding each client's point of view. Among the most difficult clients for social workers to understand may be perpetrators of child sexual abuse. Why do adults engage in sexual behaviors with children? One way to answer this question is to ask perpetrators. The current study was conducted to understand child sexual abuse from the point of view of perpetrators. In open-ended interviews, perpetrators gave accounts of their experience during the act of sexually abusing a child. Perpetrators' accounts suggest that sexual abuse of children feels good to them and that, during the sexual act, perpetrators view the child victim as an object.

Previous research and theory throw little light on perpetrators' perceptions. The perpetrators' subjective experience of child sexual abuse virtually was overlooked; when authors did note that children serve as objects of sexual gratification, they did not present empirical data to support the statements (Finkelhor, 1986; Groth & Birnbaum, 1978; Langevin, 1983, 1985). What sexual gratification might mean to perpetrators remained abstract and undefined. Morneau and Rockwell (1980), in discussing sexual crimes in general, did illuminate some aspects of sexual crimes: the "good feeling" is "the one thing all [sexual] acts have in common" (p. 18). They cited a quote from an exhibitionist. Immediately before he would expose himself, he said, "I began to feel bad, and I wanted to feel good" (Janov, 1970, p. 293). After he exhibited himself and had an orgasm, he reported:

> I would feel tremendously relieved like some great weight had been lifted. I would drive away feeling free and go to work trying to help other people, just like nothing happened. (Janov, 1970, p. 294)

The experience of an exhibitionist, however, is not necessarily the same as that of child sexual abusers.

Feminist writers have elaborated on the concept of children as objects, but they relied on historical records and not on the accounts of perpetrators (Armstrong, 1978; Gager & Schurr, 1976; Rush, 1980; Sanford, 1982). Brownmiller (1975), for example, said that although women historically were the property of men, children "were and are a wholly owned subsidiary" (p. 21).

The current study adds to the literature on sexual gratification and children as objects by presenting empirical data that support and develop these ideas to increase understanding of them. The data are the perceptions of perpetrators themselves.

Method

The study consisted of life history interviews with 14 male perpetrators of child sexual abuse. They ranged in age from 21 to 54, with a mean age of 30. Nine subjects were married at the time of the interview, two were divorced, and three had never married. The victims included their daughters, stepdaughters, sons, stepsons, and unrelated children and adolescents of both sexes. The victims ranged in age from 4 months to 14 years. Ten of the 14 subjects perpetrated sexual abuse with one to four victims and four of the perpetrators had from 10 to 100 victims. Some of the children were known to the perpetrators and some were not.

Subjects were recruited from maximum security prisons and community-based treatment programs. Eleven had served either prison or jail time. Two subjects had never been charged although the abuse had been reported to law enforcement officials and child pro-

tection agencies and a third was placed on probation and ordered into treatment. This was a volunteer sample that was not randomly selected. Researchers widely acknowledge that random samples cannot be obtained in perpetrator research because most sexual abuse is undetected. The sample, therefore, is skewed toward known perpetrators, who could be quite different from perpetrators whose abuse is not detected. Data from such skewed samples, however, can provide insight into how some abusers think about sexual abuse.

An interview guide provided structure to the interviews. The questions were open ended to minimize the imposition of the researcher's frame of reference on subjects. The average number of interviews was six, with a range of five to 10. Interviews averaged 12 hours total. Questions included those such as "Could you talk to me about the first time you thought of having sex with your daughter?" and "Did you have any feelings while you were being sexual with your daughter?"

Interviews were tape recorded and transcribed. Transcripts were content analyzed using the computer program *Ethnograph* (Seidel, Kjolseth, & Clark, 1985). Consistent with the social work commitment to self-determination, the interviews were designed to be noncoercive, and subjects had "freedom of choice" (Gilgun, 1987). Self-determination appears particularly important to emphasize when interviewing on sensitive topics such as child sexual abuse. The interviewer encouraged subjects not to talk about anything they did not want to talk about and to stop talking about a topic if they began to feel uncomfortable. Sometimes the researcher directly asked subjects if they wished to stop when subjects appeared uncomfortable. Not only is this an ethical approach but it also appeared to encourage disclosure. Subjects reported that they felt much freer to share when they knew they had a choice. Subjects signed a detailed informed-consent form.

CCC Code: 0037-8046/89 $1.00 © 1989, National Association of Social Workers, Inc.

249

Results

Subjects reported that their sexual interactions with the child victims felt good. The good feelings they experienced during the abuse were the reasons they gave for the abuse. Sometimes the good feeling came from orgasm; sometimes from genital touching; and sometimes from the entire process, from planning the abusive incident to orgasm. Perpetrators were so focused on their own needs that they were unable to see their victims as anything other than sources of pleasure.

Sources of Pleasure

Focus on Orgasm. Six of the men interviewed said that orgasm was the good feeling that motivated the abuse. They focused on achieving orgasm above all other aspects of their sexual relationships to their victims. Five of the six men had relatively few victims; these five were incest perpetrators. The sixth man in this category molested about 10 boys under age 4. As one man said, "To me, it was the good feeling I was after." The good feeling they sought was a "high" that helped them "fix" how they were feeling. A father who molested four of his five children said,

I remember that high, and, boy, I wanted it. I wanted it. The high came when I ejaculated. That's the high I was after. I didn't get a high out of fondling her.

Touching and Looking. Two men did not focus on orgasm. Each of these men had many more victims than other men in the sample. The first man, who abused about 100 children, said he would have an orgasm every few weeks when he was abusing children, but he wanted fellatio daily. He did not seek orgasm through fellatio. He discussed his experience of being fellated by children:

It would feel like being on top of the world. Up until now there's no greater feeling that I can experience than having somebody perform oral sex on me. That is my ultimate feeling.

The second man, who abused about 40 children, called himself a molester and a fondler. He was interested in touching children's sexual organs and wanted

children to look at his genitals. He described an incident with a 7-year-old girl during which they played the game "I'll show you mine and you show me yours." He knew this game was typical of young children. He said he fondled her first and then asked her, "Do you want to see me?"

Touching genitals, then, was a source of pleasure to two subjects. For one of them, displaying and looking at genitals also were sources of pleasure.

Multiple Sources of Pleasure. Six of the men studied sought orgasms with their child victims, but other aspects of the sexual act gave as much or more pleasure to them. Setting up the abusive situation, touching sexual organs and other parts of a child's body, and having fun were as important as orgasm. One man said,

The planning was almost more exciting than actually having sex with her, setting everything up, just to get her alone. It took a lot of my time, a lot of energy to do that. There was a lot of preoccupation, a lot of planning involved.

Controlling the interaction also was part of his excitement because "being in control of her life completely was a thrill for me." This man's experience was similar to that of the other five men in that each of them had multiple sources of pleasure in the abusive acts. One of the men saw his sexual behavior with his daughter as fun, "like playing doctor kind of thing." These men also believed that they had deep and loving relationships with their victims. As one man said, "We had a relationship. Right or wrong, it was a relationship."

Victim as Object

Ten of the 14 interviewed men said they did not see the children and adolescents as people during the sexual acts. Four men did not state that they saw the victims as objects; however, their words suggested that they were focused on their own pleasure and satisfaction and were unable to connect with the child's experience of the sexual acts. The specifics of how each of the men experienced their victims varied, but children as objects emerged in each life history.

One man, who abused 40 children, thought everyone knew he saw his victims as objects. He expressed astonishment that a woman asked him how he could do those things to babies. He asked, "Didn't she know those children were objects to me?" He said he was working hard to understand how "straight" people—meaning nonabusers of children—viewed his sexual behavior with children.

A second man used his younger sister and four of his children as sources of sexual stimulation. He used children to achieve an erection so he could masturbate and have an orgasm. He said he never thought that the children might have feelings about the sexual abuse. A third man, who had 100 victims, was indiscriminate about who his victims were. He said it did not matter whether he liked his victims or not, and their gender was not significant. He said that the more he enjoyed fellatio the less he cared who was doing it.

Three men denied that they saw their victims as objects only. Their words, however, suggested that they did. One man said he looked at his stepdaughter as

other than just an object, also, but as a pretty girl. I had it in my head that she's not just a girl, but she's mine and always will be mine.

Thus he perceived the child both as an object and as property. The second of these men called his 13-year-old victim a person, but he described her as "a conquest" and someone "who's going to satisfy me sexually." He said he did not love her but wanted her to love him so that she would be available to him whenever he wanted sex.

The third perpetrator provided an example of how the personhood of the victim can disappear during the sexually abusive act. He said he never looked at his victim's face when he was forcing her to manipulate his genitals. When the interviewer asked him what would happen if he did look at her face, he answered, "I probably would have lost my erection and left." While she masturbated him he looked at her hand on his penis and her breasts.

How the children functioned as objects varied for each man. The common theme across their accounts, however, is their focus on their own needs. What they felt they needed varied: control, sexual release, or fun. Focus on themselves was combined with an apparent inability or refusal to perceive or acknowledge what might be happening for the victims.

Discussion

The subjects interviewed stated that they achieved a great deal of pleasure in sexual acts with children and adolescents. They experienced the children not as persons but as objects during the sexual act. The victims, however, were not necessarily objects to the perpetrators outside of the content of the sexual acts; this research focused only on how perpetrators saw victims during periods of sexual excitement.

The findings may be helpful to social workers who work with sexual abuse survivors, who often struggle with the question of why they were sexually abused. A clear answer is that the perpetrator experienced pleasure while abusing them. The findings suggest that abuse is related to the wishes and desires of the perpetrators and that the children or adolescents did not exist as persons during the sexually abusive acts. Their best interest, their developmental level, and their needs and wants were not considered.

Practitioners may want to explore whether the perpetrator loved the victim outside of the abuse itself in their work with individual survivors of abuse. Children who were incest victims may have felt like objects, but they also may have believed that the perpetrator had some regard for them. Practitioners who work with children or adults who have been sexually abused should encourage them to share their experience and should avoid imposing a preconceived set of ideas on clients.

The findings can guide practitioners in assessment of and intervention with perpetrators. Perpetrators can experience a great deal of shame in discussing their sexually abusive behavior. A practitioner who understands that sexual abuse can be pleasurable can help perpetrators come to terms with this fact. For a perpetrator to make such an admission and still be accepted by the practitioner may be therapeutic and central to the perpetrator's recovery. Helping perpetrators come to terms with treating children as sexual objects also may serve a central therapeutic function. This type of facilitation is impossible, however, unless the practitioner has accepted that such factors are possible components of sexually abusive acts.

The findings of the current research are intended to be a source of hypotheses that may increase understanding of why adults sexually abuse children. The findings can be applied most effectively to direct practice if practitioners take a pattern-matching approach. In pattern matching, the practitioner regards research findings as hypotheses to be tested on the practitioner's own cases. The practitioner thus can assess whether the patterns found in individual cases fit the patterns described in this article. These findings, then, provide some guidance to practitioners and may help them discover new ways to think about and deal with child sexual abuse.

References

Armstrong, L. (1978). *Kiss Daddy goodnight.* New York: Hawthorn.
Brownmiller, S. (1975). *Against our will.* New York: Simon & Schuster.
Finkelhor, D. (1986). *A sourcebook on child sexual abuse.* Beverly Hills, CA: Sage.
Gager, N., & Schurr, C. (1976). *Sexual assault: Confronting rape in America.* New York: Grosset & Dunlap.
Gilgun, J. F. (1987, July). *Research interviewing in child sexual abuse.* Paper presented at the Third National Family Violence Research Conference, Durham, NH.
Groth, A. N., & Birnbaum, H. J. (1978). Adult sexual orientation and attraction to underage persons. *Archives of Sexual Behavior, 7,* 175–181.
Janov, A. (1970). *The primal scream.* New York: Dell.
Langevin, R. (1983). *Sexual strands: Understanding and treating sexual anomalies in men.* Hillsdale, NJ: Lawrence Erlbaum.
Langevin, R. (Ed.). (1985). *Erotic preference, gender identity, and aggression in men: New research studies.* Hillsdale, NJ: Lawrence Erlbaum.
Morneau, R. H., Jr., & Rockwell, R. R. (1980). *Sex, motivation, and the criminal offender.* Springfield, IL: Charles C Thomas.
Rush, F. (1980). *The best kept secret: Sexual abuse of children.* Englewood Cliffs, NJ: Prentice-Hall.
Sanford, L. T. (1982). *The silent children.* New York: McGraw-Hill.
Seidel, J. V., Kjolseth, R., & Clark, J. A. (1985). *The ethnograph.* Littleton, CO: Qualis Research Associates.

Jane F. Gilgun, PhD, is Assistant Professor, School of Social Work, University of Minnesota, 224 Church Street, SE, Minneapolis, MN 55455. Teresa M. Connor, MSW, is Social Worker, Program for Healthy Adolescent Sexual Expression, East Communities Family Center, Maplewood, Minnesota.

Accepted January 13, 1989

Briefly Stated

Child Molestation and Pedophilia

An Overview for the Physician

A. Kenneth Fuller, MD

Child sexual abuse is a serious, pervasive problem with clinical, social, moral, and legal implications. Between 100 000 and 500 000 children in the United States are thought to be sexually molested annually. Physicians in all specialties may detect sexual exploitation of youngsters and are mandated to report such cases. Failure to diagnose child molestation and pedophilia and to treat their cause can have serious, long-lasting consequences for innocent victims and continued distress for the perpetrator and for the professional who missed the diagnosis. A single child molester may commit hundreds of sexual acts on hundreds of children. The etiology of paraphilic syndromes is multifactorial. There are substantial differences among sexual abusers of children in their personalities and psychopathologies. Although available interventions are symptomatically palliative rather than curative, many pedophiles can benefit from appropriate treatment. Primary prevention may be the key to reducing the frequency of child sexual abuse.

(*JAMA* 1989;261:602-606)

EACH YEAR in the United States between 100 000 and 500 000 children suffer abuse in the form of sexual molestation.[1-3] A larger number of youngsters are sexually abused, but they do not report this exploitation for fear of retaliation, embarrassment, or unknown consequences. Child molestation and pedophilia are common and often overlooked

---
See also p 577.
---

syndromes that risk the child victim's well-being and further psychosocial development and adaptive functioning. The consequences of child sexual abuse are a major source of distress to the victim and, at times, the perpetrator, and are a source of concern to their respective families and communities.[2-4]

From Archbold Mental Health Center, Thomasville, Ga, and the Department of Psychiatry, University of Florida, Gainesville.

Reprint requests to 1811 Wimbledon Dr, Thomasville, GA 31792 (Dr Fuller).

Numerous books and articles have been published over the years positing opinions and often conflicting theories of the psychopathology of child molestation and pedophilia.[2-21] The literature on this subject is well developed. The current article attempts to acquaint physicians with the serious problem of child sexual abuse and to provide a concise general review that will help the physician deal with perpetrators of these crimes. The reader is urged to consult appropriate literature for elaboration of details in problem cases.

DEFINITIONS

The Diagnostic and Statistical Manual of Mental Disorders (edition 3, revised)[22] includes pedophilia among a group of sexual disorders, the paraphilias, characterized by recurrent intense sexual urges and fantasies in response to sexual objects or situations that are not part of normative arousal patterns. Pedophilia, which translates literally as

"love of children," requires a six-month period of recurrent, intense sexual urges and sexually arousing fantasies that involve sexual activity with prepubescent children (generally age 13 years or younger). In addition, the pedophile, or person with pedophilia, either must have acted on these urges or must be markedly distressed by them. Pedophilia, like child molestation, can be limited to incestuous, same sex, opposite sex, or both sex victims. Some patients with pedophilia are exclusively attracted to children; others are aroused by adults as well as children.[22]

Child sexual abuse is the sexual exploitation of a child for the gratification or gain of an adult that may be manifest by sexual intercourse, physical force, rape, exhibitionism, voyeurism, fondling, digital penetration, pornography, or the like.[21] Most perpetrators of child sexual abuse are classified as *child molesters*, herein defined as "older persons whose conscious sexual desires or responses are directed, at least in part, toward dependent, developmentally immature children and adolescents who do not fully comprehend these actions and are unable to give informed consent."[6]

Sexual abuse by women occurs in approximately 5% to 20% of reported cases; however, child molestation and pedophilia are primarily perpetrated by men.[1,2,4] Therefore, throughout this communication, the pronoun "he" is used to designate both genders. The term "patient" refers to a person undergoing medical treatment; its use does not imply that the child molester or pedophile meet legal or other nonmedical standards for exculpation, disability, incompetency, or lack of criminal responsibility.

146

FREQUENCY AND IMPORTANCE OF CHILD MOLESTATION

Recent studies of adults found that between 5% and 60% had at least one experience of being sexually victimized before reaching the age of majority.[23-28] Research also indicates that perhaps less than 6% of child molestations are ever reported.[26]

This complex social, ethical, and clinical issue constitutes an important matter of public health. Child molestation is important clinically not merely because it is common. Child molesters and pedophiles often are distressed by their obsession to use children as sexual objects.[22] Sexual abuse can have serious, long-lasting consequences for innocent victims and continued distress for the patient.

Research[26,29] documents a high morbidity from the trauma of child sexual abuse. Posttraumatic stress disorder may develop in victims immediately after the sexual abuse; however, symptoms commonly develop or redevelop in the victim months or years after the molestation. The victim's impairment may be mild or it may severely affect nearly all aspects of their life.

Pedophiles and child molesters do not, contrary to common opinion, limit themselves to a single victim or paraphilia.[30,31] Abusive acts are seldom a one-time occurrence. Sexual abusers of children commonly engage in exhibitionism, frotteurism, rape, sexual masochism, sexual sadism, and voyeurism. An individual child molester or pedophile may commit hundreds of sexual acts on a staggering number of children. The severity, number and type of victims, and permanence of the features vary from one child molester to the next and also vary with the passage of time in the same abuser.

PREDISPOSITION AND PSYCHOPHYSIOLOGY

The motivation for child molestation is complex and consists of both sexual and nonsexual factors.[1,2,4,14] Individuality with regard to etiology of paraphilias is the rule. So far, there is little evidence that race, religion, intelligence, education, occupation, or social class can differentiate a child molester or pedophile from the general population.[22] Many people with pedophilia and child molestation were themselves victims of child sexual abuse. Other predisposing and maintaining factors of pedophilia and child molestation include stress, dysfunctional home situations, familial violence, substance abuse, interpersonal deficits, failure of the incest taboo, antisocial mores, and distorted beliefs.[1,2,30,31]

Child molesters tend to differ from others in their cognitions.[30,31] These distorted beliefs may include the following: (1) a child who does not physically resist really wants to have sex, (2) having sex with a child is a good way to introduce him to sexual education; and (3) the adult-child relationship is enhanced by having sex with youngsters. Individuals who perceive the world in this deviant and distorted manner have built-in justification and rationalizations for their deviant sexual acting out that allow them to avoid negative intrapsychic aspects of their offensive behavior.

The physiological characteristics of child molesters and pedophiles have been subject to scientific investigation.[33-46] Studies that delineate sexual arousal patterns using penile plethysmography, a device for measuring penile tumescence, have begun to produce useful information. Research indicates that it is possible to identify rapists and child molesters, to determine age and gender preference, and to document propensity for violence of sexual offenders by tracking their penile arousal patterns to audio and visual stimuli.

Just as the normal sexual response cycle is a true psychophysiological experience influenced by a large number of incompletely understood factors, deviant sexual arousal is multifactorial.[2] Our understanding of the neuronal mechanisms for sexual preference is sparse, limited to case reports, and largely based on animal research that might not be applicable to humans.[46] Child molesting behavior has been associated with hypothalamic lesions, alterations in neurotransmitters, seizure disorders, postencephalitic parkinsonism, and other organic mental syndromes.[46,47]

Since testosterone regulates normal male sexual arousal, researchers have investigated whether endocrine differences are associated with child molestation and pedophilia.[15,18,48-52] There is little direct evidence to support that plasma testosterone levels are consistently altered in the perpetrators of sexual abuse. Early results involving a luteinizing hormone–releasing hormone stimulation test indicate that a hypothalamic-pituitary-gonadal dysfunction may exist in some pedophiles.[48]

Findings from case reports suggest that genetic factors may be involved in child molestation.[15,18,52] There may be an inherited tendency toward pedophilia[49]; however, presently there is inadequate evidence to draw conclusions on genetic factors in the development of child molesters and pedophiles.

Each psychiatric approach has its own theories to explain the development of sexual attraction to children.

Psychodynamic psychiatrists see it as a manifestation of unresolved conflicts, arrested development, mastery of trauma through repetition, identification with the aggressor, or unresolved oedipal dynamics.[11,14,19,20,32,53,54] Behaviorists interpret sexual abuse as the result of maladaptive learning, modeling, or conditioning from early childhood experience.[4,14,55] Sociological clinicians blame, in part, socialization through child pornography or advertising, cultural tolerance, male socialization to dominance, patriarchal norms, and other repressive attitudes toward sexual behavior.[4,14,56-58]

DIAGNOSTIC ISSUES

No specific diagnostic test for pedophilia or child molestation exists; therefore, diagnosis is made on the basis of the essential clinical features.[59-62] The diagnosis is a challenging one to make. The most common reason for missing the diagnosis of pedophilia or child molestation is the physician's failure to inquire about deviant sexual thoughts, urges, and behaviors when suspicion arises.[63,64] Most pedophiles and child molesters misrepresent, minimize, deny, or lie about their deviant sexuality. Therefore, the physician might be misled and not suspect that children are being victimized. Most pedophiles and molesters do not seek treatment because they fear legal consequences, they do not regard their behavior as aberrant, or they feel entitled to repeat their own child-adult experiences (ie, "I survived child abuse, therefore, I am entitled to abuse").

In the physician's office or the hospital setting, child molesters and pedophiles present as ordinary patients. Unless attention has been brought to the issue by social or legal forces, the physician generally has no way of knowing that paraphilic activity has been occurring. Since there are few clues to diagnose undisclosed paraphilias, a standard question during the urogenital portion of the systematic review should be: "Have you had any upsetting sexual thoughts, acts, or experiences?" The patient's facial and verbal response will allow for further explicit sexual questions.

A general psychiatric evaluation with a complete psychosexual history is essential. Detailed information about the patient's sexual offenses, sexual thoughts, sexual urges, sexual activities, and sexual education as well as his current social situation, impulse control, and violence history are required. The clinician should avoid relying solely on the self-report of the patient, which may have self-serving purposes. If lying is suspected, the patient's family should be interviewed. When suspicion remains, information from sources such as legal entities, social agencies, mental health centers, and other physicians should be used. Measurement of sexual arousal patterns often provides important information. Evaluation may include a sex hormone profile that measures levels of total plasma testosterone, free testosterone, luteinizing hormone, follicle-stimulating hormone, prolactin, and progesterone.[65]

Several psychiatric disorders, such as mental retardation, organic personality syndrome, alcohol intoxication, or drug abuse, may lower impulse control, judgment, and adaptive skills, leading to isolated sexual acts with children. In such cases, distinction between a primary psychiatric disorder with secondary child molestation and primary pedophilia can be difficult to make on incomplete evaluation. In addition to probing, challenging, and confronting the patient to get the essential information, often it is necessary to observe the patient over time.

COURSE

Although the sexual misuse of children has been described since antiquity, it has been largely ignored by researchers until recent times. As a result, knowledge of the pathogenesis of pedophilia is scanty. Clinical experience suggests that the most common age of onset is adolescence.[22] This is the time when individuals generally become sexually active and establish their sexual identities. As sexuality consolidates and hormones surge, child molesting behaviors may develop. However, child molestation may occur for the first time at any age.

There are a tremendous number of patterns of child molestation.[66] Some people repeatedly try to give up child sexual exploitation without success. Others have a brief course; they experience a concern or disgust about their molesting behavior and make a prompt and successful effort to stop.[17,21] Some of the varieties of interactions between perpetrator and child are (1) regular daily contact with many victims, (2) regular heavy interaction limited to a single victim, and (3) long periods of abstinence interspersed with episodic child molestation. An individual child molester may remain neat, well-groomed, and cooperative and otherwise behave in a socially appropriate way while continuing to molest children.

TREATMENT

Personalities, attitudes, deviant arousal, and clinical features of individuals who abuse children differ substantially. As a result of this variability the same treatment is unlikely to be equally suitable for all. There is, additionally, substantial disagreement on the best treatment. The aim of therapy is to stop sexual abuse of children, to prevent its recurrence, and to help the patient control his deviant behavior, impulses, and preoccupations. Most physicians are in no way equipped to treat perpetrators of child sexual abuse and should refer the patient to a psychiatrist or psychologist with a special interest in the treatment of sexual offenders. *Reporting actual or suspected abuse cases to child protection authorities is a statutory requirement, not a substitute for referring the victim and abuser for psychiatric or psychological assessment and treatment.*

Although currently available treatment modalities are symptomatically palliative rather than curative, many child molesters stand to benefit from appropriate intervention.[1,2,67-93] The therapeutic approaches summarized next can be regarded only as guidelines:

1. Effort should be made to prevent child sexual abuse before it occurs and to interrupt the abusive pattern in established molestations.[93,94]

2. Physicians must remember that the problem will not go away by itself and they must beware of promises to stop.[31,77] Even if sexual abuse has stopped for a time, it often returns.

3. The establishment of a therapeutic relationship and provision of information clearly are important.[16,21] The physician will need to educate the patient on the nature of his deviant behavior and on the course of treatment. Appropriate suggestions include to avoid situations wherein he is alone with a child for an extended period of time; to avoid drugs, alcohol, or medications that have disinhibiting effects; and to reduce contact with children, pornography, and sexually explicit materials.[17]

4. The physician must emphasize that he regards the patient's deviant sexual urges as serious and that he will report suspected cases of abuse to child protection authorities.[16,21] Every state has mandatory reporting of suspected cases of child sexual victimization. The mandate is to report suspected cases of child abuse, not someone who is suspected of abusing unidentified children.[95] The patient should understand by informed consent that some types of information he reveals to the physician might be transmitted to others to protect specific identified victims.

5. In the patient who believes cognitive distortions, eg, "child molesting is acceptable," it is crucial to the patient's progress to devise methods to convince him that his distorted thinking is wrong.[30,31]

6. The physician can employ or recommend drug treatment, psychotherapy, behavior therapy, or other specific intervention modalities.[1,2,6] Because these are complicated treatment techniques, the reader is directed to appropriate literature for elaboration.

Drugs

Medications have been used to suppress paraphilic symptoms. Child molesters may benefit from the use of antiandrogenic compounds (eg, oral cyproterone acetate and depot medroxyprogesterone acetate) that inhibit the action of testosterone.[15,18,66,67-75] Antiandrogens provide a reversible means for lowering testosterone levels and therefore sexual drive and aggression. Thus far, cyproterone is not available in the United States, and medroxyprogesterone acetate has not been approved by the Food and Drug Administration for use in people with paraphilias. However, clinicians can prescribe medroxyprogesterone acetate without any special government approval as long as they share the basis for their recommendations with and gain informed consent from the patient.[76] Medications should not be used alone; concomitant psychotherapy, behavior therapy, or psychosocial rehabilitation is indicated.[1,2]

Psychotherapy

Psychotherapy and other supportive measures can help the patient and his victim adjust more effectively to the consequences of paraphilic activity. Psychotherapy is useful in the treatment of some child molesters but probably not all, although the literature on individual psychotherapy for child molesters is sparse and preponderantly consists of case reports.[6,19,20,67,77-83]

Group psychotherapy is probably the most common method for treating sex offenders and often is considered to be more cost- and time-effective than individual therapy.[1,2] Group therapy has been evaluated poorly in general.[81,82] Outcome studies are mixed and ambivalent. Most discussions of the efficacy of group treatment for child molestation are scattered among studies of small, highly mixed samples usually drawn from prisons and hospitals.[1,2,81-82]

A variety of other kinds of psychotherapy, including family therapy, conjoint therapy, marital counseling, and cognitive therapy, have been used in treating child molesters and pedophiles.[6,77,84-87] None has emerged as clearly superior. Supportive psychotherapy combined with sexual education, asser-

tiveness training, anger modulation, social skills improvement, or other psychosocial intervention may be helpful in the rehabilitation of sexual abusers.[1,2,32]

Behavioral Treatment

Behavior therapy is a psychiatric treatment that emphasizes self-observation and monitoring to increase the patients' awareness of their current activity level associated with a symptom such as cruising for victims, deviant sexual arousal, or fondling youngsters. Such self-monitoring of behavior helps define the problem, provides feedback of information regarding progress, and reinforces behavior change.

Behavioral treatment is employed to decrease deviant sexual arousal and to enhance nondeviant sexual preference. There are few adequately controlled studies of behavior therapy in pedophilia and child molestation.[87-92] The studies that do exist are single or group case reports and do not permit evaluation of the effects of the multifactorial treatments.

Many behavioral interventions for child molesters are based on a method known as aversion therapy, which is designed to reduce unwanted or dangerous behaviors.[88,89] Studies that investigate the use of behavior therapy suggest that aversion therapy can change sexually deviant behavior.[89] A common form of aversion now in use is covert sensitization, in which the patient's imagined noxious scenes are paired with the deviant sexual fantasy.[2,63,87-90] A related technique, masturbatory satiation, requires the patient to masturbate through orgasm for a prolonged "aversive" refractory period while verbalizing deviant sexual fantasies.[83,87,90]

PREVENTION

Primary prevention may be the key to reducing sexual abuse. This complex problem requires a comprehensive, multifactorial prevention strategy such as the one outlined by the National Committee for the Prevention of Child Abuse.[93,94] This plan emphasizes education, including teaching youngsters to protect themselves; enlightening the general public about the nature of the problem, its chronicity, and the availability of treatment; sensitizing the medical community to identify abused children and to detect molesters before they offend; and establishing guidelines to regulate the screening, training, and monitoring of people working with children.

CONCLUSION

Our knowledge of child sexual abuse and its perpetrators is imperfect; however, since it is such an enormous social problem, physicians need to be familiar with current information regarding this challenging issue. It is an odd paradox that, despite its apparent increase in frequency and importance, child molestation constitutes a neglected area in clinical medicine. Every health care professional should learn to diagnose pedophilia and child molestation early in an attempt to prevent abuse to children, disruption of their lives, and complications of this trauma.

References

1. Barnard GW, Fuller AK, Robbins L: Child molesters, in Howells JG (ed): *Modern Perspectives in Psychosocial Pathology.* New York, Brunner/Mazel Inc, 1988, pp 23-42.
2. Barnard GW, Fuller AK, Robbins L, et al: *The Child Molester: An Integrated Approach to Evaluation and Treatment.* New York, Brunner/Mazel Inc, 1989.
3. Moore DS: A literature review on sexual abuse research. *J Nurse Midwifery* 1984;29:395-398.
4. Finkelhor D: *Child Sexual Abuse: New Theory and Research.* New York, Free Press, 1984.
5. Finkel KC: Sexual abuse of children: An update. *Can Med Assoc J* 1987;136:245-252.
6. Lanyon RI: Theory and treatment in child molestation. *J Consult Clin Psychol* 1986;54:176-182.
7. Brown N: Historical perspective on child abuse, in Downer A (ed): *Prevention of Child Sexual Abuse: A Trainer's Manual.* Seattle Institute for Child Advocacy Committee for Children, 1985, pp 22-28.
8. Ellis H: *Psychology of Sex.* London, Pan Books Ltd, 1933.
9. Finkelhor D: The sexual abuse of children: Current research reviewed. *Psychiatr Annals* 1987; 17:233-241.
10. Hartwich A: *Aberrations of Sexual Life After the 'Psychopathia Sexualis' of Dr. RV Krafft-Ebing,* Burbury AV (trans). London, Staples Press, 1959.
11. Karpman B: *The Sexual Offender and His Offences: Aetiology, Pathology, Psychodynamics and Treatment.* New York, Julian Press, 1954.
12. Krafft-Ebing RV: *Psychopathia Sexualis . . . Eine Medicinisch-Gerichtüche Studie.* Stuttgart, Ferdinand Enke, 1901.
13. Rada RT: Sexual psychopathology: Historical survey and basic concepts, in Rada RT (ed): *Clinical Aspects of the Rapist.* New York, Grune & Stratton, 1978, pp 1-19.
14. Araji S, Finkelhor D: Explanations of pedophilia: Review of empirical research. *Bull Am Acad Psychiatry Law* 1985;13:17-37.
15. Berlin FS: Sex offenders: A biomedical perspective and a status report on biomedical treatment, in Greer JG, Stuart IR (eds): *The Sexual Aggressor: Current Perspectives on Treatment.*

New York, Van Nostrand Reinhold Co, 1983, pp 83-123.
16. Kelly RJ: Limited confidentiality and the pedophile. *Hosp Community Psychiatry* 1987;38:1046-1048.
17. Smith TA: *You Don't Have to Molest That Child.* Chicago, National Committee for the Prevention of Child Abuse, 1987.
18. Bradford JMW: Organic treatments for the male sexual offender. *Behav Sci Law* 1985;3:355-375.
19. Gillespie WH: The general theory of sexual perversion. *Int J Psychoanal* 1956;37:396-403.
20. Socarides CW: Meaning and content of pedophilic perversions. *J Am Psychoanal Assoc* 1959;7:84-94.
21. Council on Scientific Affairs: AMA diagnostic and treatment guidelines concerning child abuse and neglect. *JAMA* 1985;254:796-800.
22. *Diagnostic and Statistical Manual of Mental Disorders,* ed 3, revised. Washington, DC, American Psychiatric Association, 1987.
23. Baker AW, Duncan SP: Child sexual abuse: A study of prevalence in Great Britain. *Child Abuse Negl* 1985;9:457-467.
24. Mrazek PJ, Lynch MA, Bentovim A: Sexual abuse of children in the United Kingdom. *Child Abuse Negl* 1983;7:147-153.
25. Russell DEH: The incidence and prevalence of intrafamilial and extrafamilial sexual abuse of female children. *Child Abuse Negl* 1983;7:133-146.
26. Russell DEH: *The Secret Trauma: Incest in the Lives of Girls and Women.* New York, Basic Books Inc Publishers, 1986.
27. Wyatt GE: The sexual abuse of Afro-American and White-American women in childhood. *Child Abuse Negl* 1985;9:507-519.
28. Wyatt GE, Peters SD: Issues in the definition of child sexual abuse in prevalence research. *Child Abuse Negl* 1986;10:231-240.
29. Herman J, Russell D, Trocki K: Long-term effects of incestuous abuse in childhood. *Am J Psychiatry* 1986;143:1293-1296.
30. Abel GG, Becker JV, Cunningham-Rathner J: Complications, consent and cognitions in sex between children and adults. *Int J Law Psychiatry* 1984;7:89-103.

31. Abel GG, Becker JV, Mittelman M, et al: Self-reported sex crimes of nonincarcerated paraphiliacs. *J Interpersonal Violence* 1987;2:3-25.
32. Groth AN, Hobson WF, Gary TS: The child molester: Clinical observations, in Conte J, Shore DA (eds): *Social Work and Child Sexual Abuse.* New York, Haworth Press Inc, 1982, pp 129-144.
33. Freund K: Diagnosing homo or heterosexuality and erotic age-preference by means of a psychophysiological test. *Behav Res Ther* 1967;5:209-228.
34. Abel GG, Barlow DH, Blanchard EB, et al: Measurement of sexual arousal in male heterosexuals: Effects of instructions and stimulus modality. *Arch Sex Behav* 1975;4:623-629.
35. Avery-Clark CA, Laws DR: Differential erection response patterns of sexual arousal of sexual abusers to stimuli describing activities with children. *Behav Ther* 1984;15:71-83.
36. Earls CM, Quinsey VL: What is to be done? Future research on the assessment and behavioral treatment of sex offenders. *Behav Sci Law* 1985;3:377-390.
37. Freund K, Chan S, Coulthard R: Phallometric diagnosis with 'nonadmittors.' *Behav Res Ther* 1979;17:451-457.
38. Fuller AK, Barnard GW, Robbins L, et al: Sexual maturity as a criterion for classification of phallametric stimulus slides. *Arch Sex Behav* 1988;17:271-276.
39. Grossman LS: Research directions in the evaluation and treatment of sex offenders: An analysis. *Behav Sci Law* 1985;3:421-440.
40. Laws DR, Holmen ML: Sexual response faking by pedophiles. *Criminal Justice Behav* 1978;5:343-357.
41. Laws DR, Osborn CA: How to build and operate a behavioral laboratory to evaluate and treat sexual deviance, in Greer JG, Stuart IR (eds): *The Sexual Aggressor: Current Perspectives on Treatment.* New York, Van Nostrand Reinhold Co, 1983, pp 293-335.
42. Laws DR, Rubin HB: Instructional controls of an autonomic sexual response. *J Appl Behav Anal* 1969;2:93-99.
43. Quinsey VL, Chaplin TC, Carrigan WF: Sexual preferences among incestuous and nonincestuous child molesters. *Behav Ther* 1979;10:562-565.

149

44. Quinsey VL, Steinman CM, Bergersen SG, et al: Penile circumference, skin conductance, and ranking responses of child molesters and 'normals' to sexual and nonsexual visual stimuli. *Behav Ther* 1975;6:213-219.
45. Rosen RC, Keefe FJ: The measurement of human penile tumescence. *Psychophysiology* 1978;15:366-376.
46. Miller BL, Cummings JL, McIntyre H, et al: Hypersexuality or altered sexual preference following brain injury. *J Neurol Neurosurg Psychiatry* 1986;49:867-873.
47. Lilly R, Cummings JL, Benson DF, et al: The human Kluver-Bucy syndrome. *Neurology* 1983;33:1141-1145.
48. Gaffney GR, Berlin FS: Is there hypothalamic-pituitary-gonadal dysfunction in pedophilia? *Br J Psychiatry* 1984;145:657-660.
49. Gaffney GR, Shelly FL, Berlin FS: Is there a familial transmission of pedophilia? *J Nerv Ment Dis* 1984;172:546-548.
50. Gurnani PD, Dwyer M: Serum testosterone levels in sex offenders. *J Offender Counsel Serv Rehabil* 1986;11:39-45.
51. Rada RT, Laws DR, Kellner R: Plasma testosterone levels in the rapist. *Psychosom Med* 1976;38:257-268.
52. Schiavi RC, Theilgaard A, Owen DR, et al: Sex chromosome anomalies, hormones and aggressivity. *Arch Gen Psychiatry* 1984;41:93-99.
53. Groth AN: Patterns of sexual assault against children and adolescents, in Burgess AW, Groth AN, Holmstrom LL, et al (eds): *Sexual Assault of Children and Adolescents.* Lexington, Mass, Lexington Books, 1978, pp 3-24.
54. Groth AN, Birnbaum HJ: Adult sexual orientation and attraction to underage persons. *Arch Sex Behav* 1979;7:175-181.
55. McGuire RJ, Carlisle JM, Young BG: Sexual deviations as conditioned behavior: A hypothesis. *Behav Res Ther* 1965;2:185-190.
56. Goldstein MJ, Kant HS: *Pornography and Sexual Deviance.* Berkeley, University of California Press, 1973.
57. Plummer K: Pedophilia: Constructing a sociological baseline, in Cook M, Howells K (eds): *Adult Sexual Interest in Children.* Academic Press Inc, 1981, pp 221-250.
58. Rothblum ED, Solomon LJ, Albee GW: A sociopolitical perspective of *DSM-III*, in Millon T, Klerman GL (eds): *Contemporary Directions in Psychopathology: Toward the DSM-III.* New York, Guilford Press, 1986, pp 167-189.
59. Tingle D, Barnard GW, Robbins L, et al: Childhood and adolescent characteristics of pedophiles and rapists. *Int J Law Psychiatry* 1986;9:108-122.
60. Conte JR: Clinical dimensions of adult sexual abuse of children. *Behav Sci Law* 1985;3:341-354.

61. Vermont Department of Health: Adolescent sex offenders—Vermont, 1984. *JAMA* 1985;255:181-182.
62. Hall GCN, Maiuro RD, Vitaliano PP, et al: The utility of the MMPI with men who have sexually assaulted children. *J Consult Clin Psychol* 1986;54:493-496.
63. Fuller AK, Barnard GW, Robbins L: Screening for child-molesting behavior. *Am J Psychiatry* 1988;145:274.
64. Fuller AK, Bartucci RJ: HIV transmission and childhood sexual abuse. *JAMA* 1988;259:2235-2236.
65. Bloom JD, Bradford J McD, Kofoed L: An overview of psychiatric treatment approaches to three offender groups. *Hosp Community Psychiatry* 1988;39:151-158.
66. Sgroi SM, Blick LC, Porter FS: A conceptual framework for child sexual abuse, in Sgroi SM (ed): *Handbook of Clinical Intervention in Child Sexual Abuse.* Lexington, Mass, Lexington Books, 1982, pp 1-38.
67. Reid WH: Treating sex offenders. *Harvard Med School Mental Health Letter* 1987;3:4.
68. Bancroft J, Tennent TG, Loucas K, et al: The control of deviant sexual behavior by drugs: I. Behavioral changes following oestrogens and anti-androgens. *Br J Psychiatry* 1974;125:310-315.
69. Bancroft J: Hormones and sexual behavior. *Psychol Med* 1977;7:553-556.
70. Freund K: Therapeutic sex drive reduction. *Acta Psychiatr Scand Suppl* 1980;287:5-38.
71. Gagne P: Treatment of sex offenders with medroxyprogesterone acetate. *Am J Psychiatry* 1981;138:644-646.
72. Hucker SJ: Management of anomalous sexual behavior with drugs. *Mod Med Can* 1985;40:150-153.
73. Laschet U: Antiandrogen in the treatment of sex offenders: Mode of action and therapeutic outcome, in Zubin J, Money J (eds): *Contemporary Sexual Behavior: Critical Issues in the 1970s.* Baltimore, The Johns Hopkins University Press, 1973, pp 311-319.
74. Laschet U, Laschet L: Three years' clinical results with cyproterone-acetate in the inhibiting regulation of male sexuality. *Acta Endocrinol Suppl* 1969;138:103.
75. Wincze JP, Bansal S, Malamud M: Effects of medroxy progesterone acetate on subjective arousal, arousal to erotic stimulation, and nocturnal penile tumescence in male sex offenders. *Arch Sex Behav* 1986;15:293-305.
76. Wettstein RM: Legal aspects of neuropsychiatry, in Hales RE, Yudofsky SC: *The American Psychiatric Press Textbook of Neuropsychiatry.* Washington, DC, American Psychiatric Press, 1987, pp 451-463.

77. Langevin R, Lang RA: Psychological treatment of pedophiles. *Behav Sci Law* 1985;3:403-419.
78. Cassity JH: Psychological considerations of pedophilia. *Psychoanal Rev* 1927;14:189-209.
79. Conn JH: Brief psychotherapy of the sex offender. *J Clin Psychopathol* 1949;10:347-372.
80. Crown S: Psychotherapy of sexual deviation. *Br J Psychiatry* 1983;143:242-247.
81. Langevin R: Sexual strands, in: *Understanding and Treating Sexual Anomalies in Men.* Hillsdale, NJ, Lawrence Erlbaum Associates Inc Publishers, 1983.
82. Hartman V: Notes on group psychotherapy with pedophiles. *Can Psychiatr Assoc J* 1965;10:283-289.
83. Travin S, Bluestone H, Coleman E, et al: Pedophilia: An update on theory and practice. *Psychiatr Q* 1985;57:89-103.
84. Giarretto H: A comprehensive child sexual abuse treatment program. *Child Abuse Negl* 1982;6:263-278.
85. Giarretto H: *Integrated Treatment of Child Sexual Abuse: A Treatment and Training Manual.* Palo Alto, Calif, Science and Behavior Books, 1982.
86. Knopp FH: *Retraining Adult Sex Offenders: Methods and Models.* Syracuse, NY, Safer Society Press, 1984.
87. Abel GG, Becker JV, Cunningham-Rathner J, et al: *The Treatment of Child Molesters.* Atlanta, Emory University, 1984.
88. Kelly RJ: Behavioral reorientation of pedophiliacs: Can it be done? *Clin Psychol Rev* 1982;2:387-408.
89. Council on Scientific Affairs: Aversion therapy. *JAMA* 1987;258:2562-2566.
90. Abel GG: MD: Sex offenders need treatment, not punishment. *Am Med News* 1986;Oct 10:21-23.
91. Quinsey VL: The assessment and treatment of child molesters: A review. *Can Psychol Rev* 1977;18:204-222.
92. Quinsey VL, Marshall WL: Procedures for reducing inappropriate sexual arousal: An evaluation review, in Greer JG, Stuart IR (eds): *The Sexual Aggressor: Current Perspectives on Treatment.* New York, Van Nostrand Reinhold Co, 1983, pp 267-289.
93. Cohn A, Finkelhor D, Holmes C: *Preventing Adults From Becoming Child Sexual Molesters,* working paper 25. Chicago, National Committee for the Prevention of Child Abuse, 1985.
94. Cohn AH: Preventing adults from becoming sexual molesters. *Child Abuse Negl* 1986;10:559-562.
95. Berlin FS: Laws on mandatory reporting of suspected child sexual abuse. *Am J Psychiatry* 1988;145:1039.

150

FUTURE DIRECTIONS IN THE TREATMENT OF PHYSICAL CHILD ABUSE

KEITH L. KAUFMAN

Ohio State University
Children's Hospital, Columbus

LESLIE RUDY

Ohio State University

The incidence of physical child abuse has continued to increase over the past 15 years. During this time, studies have identified a myriad of serious acute and long-term consequences for its victims. Early approaches to treatment varied on a number of dimensions but failed to consistently demonstrate their effectiveness with perpetrators of physical abuse. Despite an obvious and pressing need, intensive efforts to identify the most efficacious treatment approaches appear to have been abandoned in favor of prevention, early intervention initiatives and in general, the area of child sexual abuse. This article examines the shift in priorities, selectively examines treatment approaches, discusses key research and programmatic issues, and offers suggestions for future directions.

A s a clinical and research area physical child abuse predates other forms of maltreatment by a good many years (Kempe, Silverman, Steele, Droegemuller, & Silver, 1962). Early interest in this area has fostered the development of a considerable literature on the assessment (Wolfe, 1988) and treatment (Azar & Wolfe, 1989; Isaacs, 1982) of physical abuse. Despite the breadth of the existing

AUTHORS' NOTE: *An expanded version of this article containing additional detail regarding treatemnt approaches is available from the first author. For a copy of this article or the expanded version please write: Keith L. Kaufman, Ph.D., Children's Hospital, CHPB —4th Floor, 700 Children's Drive, Columbus, OH 43205.*

CRIMINAL JUSTICE AND BEHAVIOR, Vol. 18 No. 1, March 1991 82-97

TABLE 1: Frequency of Articles Published on Physical and Sexual Abuse in *Child Abuse & Neglect* From 1979 to the Present

Years of Publication	Number of Issues Reviewed	Physical Abuse Articles	Sexual Abuse Articles
1979 - 1982	13	28	19
1983 - 1986	16	34	40
1987 - 1990	14	17	83

NOTE: Reflects articles with content purely in one area or the other.

literature, there remains a lack of consensus regarding the most efficacious treatment approaches for physically abusive parents (Azar &
Wolfe, 1989; Isaacs, 1982).

This lack of consensus may be due, in part, to an apparent shift away
from the investigation of physical abuse treatment in the early to mid-
1980s. At the same time, interest increased in prevention/early intervention approaches and the area of child sexual abuse. Greater emphasis on early intervention/prevention approaches may be linked to:
the ineffective nature of federally funded physical abuse programs
between 1974 and 1982 (Cohn & Daro, 1987; Daro, 1988); the publication of major prevention review articles (Helfer, 1982; Rosenberg &
Reppucci, 1985); successful early intervention efforts reported by
Wolfe and Manion (1984); a legislative mandate to make funds
available specifically for prevention efforts (Amendment to Child
Abuse Prevention and Treatment Act, 1984) and the availability of
prevention-oriented grant funds.

The progression from a focus on the investigation of physical abuse
to an emphasis on the area of sexual abuse is apparent in the content
of articles published in *Child Abuse & Neglect* from 1979 to the
present. Table 1 reflects a review of study titles, abstracts and methodology sections intended to characterize these articles as primarily
physical-abuse related or sexual-abuse related (articles related to other
child abuse topics were excluded from the table). Results revealed the
publication of approximately 30% more physical abuse than sexual
abuse articles from 1979 to 1982, 15% more sexual abuse articles in
the following 4 years and more than four times as many sexual abuse
as opposed to physical abuse articles between 1987 and 1990. If

153

findings from *Child Abuse & Neglect* can be considered a barometer for publications in other journals, the distribution of articles underscore the aforementioned shift in priorities. An attempt to identify similar patterns in federal demonstration/research grant funding was not successful due to the lack of aggregate data kept by the National Center on Child Abuse and Neglect (NCCAN; Bates, personal communication, July 12, 1990).

Despite the need to fund, conduct, and evaluate early intervention and prevention efforts in the area of abuse, a number of compelling reasons remain to concurrently examine and refine the treatment of physical abuse: (a) the continued increase in the rate of physical child abuse (NCCAN, 1988); (b) well-documented acute and long-term consequences for children experiencing physical abuse (see Wolfe, 1987, for review) and (c) the goal of prevention (i.e., ameliorate abuse) cannot be achieved when ineffective treatment programs perpetuate the development of future generations of abusive parents.

This article will briefly review selected perpetrator treatment strategies reflecting the existing physical abuse data base. A critical evaluation of this literature will provide support for the suggestion of future directions in key areas (e.g., model development, treatment design, client motivation).

Historically, the treatment of physical child abuse reflects a variety of theoretical formulations. An initial focus on intrapsychic and individually focused models gave way to the sociological, interactional and social learning perspectives (see Walker, Bonner, & Kaufman, 1989, for review). Recent efforts have attempted to integrate previous conceptualizations into more comprehensive models (e.g., Walker et al., 1989; Wolfe, 1988).

Despite the myriad of theoretical formulations, the majority of literature reflects an emphasis on a limited number of treatment approaches. Although other types of treatment continue to be used (e.g., psychodynamic, lay therapy) the behavioral (Isaacs, 1982; Wolfe, 1988), eco-behavioral (Lutzker, 1984), family-centered, home-based (Amundson, 1989; Frankel, 1988), and multisystemic (Brunk, Henggeler, & Whelan, 1987) approaches appear to offer the greatest future promise in the treatment of child physical abuse. The brief review which follows is intended to highlight these approaches.

SOCIAL LEARNING

Behavioral or social learning initiatives appear with considerable frequency in the treatment literature. The involvement of behavioral scientists in this area can be related to: mandated efforts to maintain the family unit and reduce children's out-of-home placement (Adoption Assistance and Child Welfare Act of 1980); indications that more traditional approaches (e.g., lay counseling, parent education) were only minimally effective; and the fact that in many cases abuse continued during the treatment process (Cohn, 1979). Further, behavioral approaches were appealing due to their demonstrated success with other populations experiencing similar difficulties (Graziano, 1977), the ability to effectively use such techniques with clients of varying cognitive capabilities (Foxx, McMorrow, & Schloss, 1983), and the excellent fit between the pragmatic nature of the behavioral approach and the treatment expectations of lower socioeconomic status (SES) clients (Lorion, 1978).

Behaviorally oriented approaches typically reflect a number of programmatic commonalties. Treatment is closely tied to assessment findings and may include: self-report data from multiple family members (e.g., child, parent); more objective reports from nonfamily members (e.g., teacher reports); and behavioral observation results of clinic or in-home sessions (Wolfe, 1988). Parent-training techniques represent the core of most behaviorally oriented programs and treatment frequently focuses on reducing parents' reliance on physical discipline by offering alternative means of shaping more positive child behaviors (Azar & Wolfe, 1989; Isaacs, 1982; Walker et al., 1989; Wolfe, Kaufman, Aragona, & Sandler, 1981). With few exceptions, parents have been the exclusive focus of behavioral treatment programs (see Wolfe, 1987, for victim treatment information).

Treatment approaches described in the literature have varied both in their clinical content and in their methodological sophistication. Clinically, programs have offered multiple-treatment components which have included anger management, stress management, cognitive self-control, problem solving and realistic developmental expectations (e.g., Wolfe, Kaufman, Aragona, & Sandler, 1981) or have focused more exlusively on training in child management skills

155

(e.g., Golub, Espinosa, Damon, & Card, 1987). Treatment has also varied based on the treatment format (i.e., group vs. individual) and the setting (clinic vs. home vs. combination). Limited findings suggest that group treatment may offer the advantages of enhancing parents' ability to develop social networks (Azar, 1984) and making more efficient use of staff time. Although more costly, it is likely that the combination of treatment settings offers the greatest potential for generalization (Embry & Baer, 1979) as well as affording the opportunity for group-based treatment.

ECOBEHAVIORAL

In the ecobehavioral perspective problems are viewed as occurring within a multifaceted context that is broader than simply the parent-child relationship or an examination of antecedents and consequences (Lutzker, 1984). Behaviors are examined in the settings in which they occur (e.g., schools, homes, playgrounds) and a focus is placed on the reciprocal influence of the child's behavior (and changes in his/her behavior) on those in the environment and the environment itself (Lutzker, 1984). Lutzker's "Project 12-Ways," an ecobehavioral program, served a clientele characterized as predominantly unemployed, young single parents from low SES backgrounds who were often unwed mothers (Lutzker, Frame, & Rice, 1982). The program was university affiliated and utilized graduate student therapists as well as paid counselors. Clients received some combination of the following services based on a thorough assessment: parent-child training; stress reduction; assertiveness training; self-control (e.g., anger management); basic skills (e.g., conversational skills); leisure skills; marital therapy; alcohol referral/treatment; social support; job-finding skills; money management; prevention (e.g., services to pregnant teenagers); health maintenance and nutrition; home safety; and multiple-setting behavior management (e.g., behavior management consultation in schools, day care settings; Lutzker, 1984; Lutzker et al., 1982). Fitting with the ecobehavioral model and the tailored nature of this approach, treatment was provided in the family's home or in the setting where difficulties arise (e.g., the day care center). The integration of program evaluation and research methodologies into clients' ongoing treatment insured that services were not terminated prematurely.

Outcome studies for Project 12-Ways were suggestive of the approach's efficacy. Single subject design investigations provided some support for interventions with a host of specific deficits (e.g., headaches, personal hygiene; see Lutzker, 1984, for description of intervention target areas). Clinical data also suggested the attainment of parent-specified goals in the majority of cases (Lutzker, 1984). Program evaluation data indicated significantly lower recidivism rates, across a 5 year period of time (i.e., 1981-1985), for Project 12-Ways participants when compared to controls (Lutzker & Rice, 1987). The authors of this investigation did, however, note that treatment effects did decay over time. As a result, the need for ongoing monitoring and booster sessions were suggested. Although potential difficulties related to client attrition were mentioned (Lutzker, 1984; Lutzker & Rice, 1987), overall rates were not specified.

FAMILY-CENTERED, HOME-BASED TREATMENT (FCHBT)

FCHBT reflects aspects of traditional social work practice and recently developed technologies from a variety of fields (e.g., mental health, family services, child welfare). Such services have been based on an ecological model, with the family and the larger social contexts considered appropriate targets for intervention (Amundson, 1989; Bryce & Lloyd, 1980). FCHBT was developed as a specific response to requirements for states to demonstrate sufficient efforts to prevent out-of-home placement in order to secure continued funding under the Adoption Assistance Act of 1980 (Frankel, 1988). Since their inception, FCHBT programs have included a variety of components including: supportive counseling and behavioral parent training (Nicol et al., 1988); parent education, behavior modification, assertiveness, problem solving, and Rational Emotional Therapy crisis intervention strategies (Haapala, 1983); and traditional case management services and counseling (see Lyle and Nelson's 1983 study of the home-based services demonstration project in the Ramsey County Community Human Services Department, cited in Frankel, 1988).

Many FCHBT have excluded abuse cases from their caseload, however, Amundson (1989) has described an application of the FCHBT model design specifically for abusive and neglectful families. The program is based on the homebuilders model (Haapala, 1983) and is divided into three phases. The intensive "crisis intervention" phase (6 weeks) involves an extensive assessment, goal setting, and networking with other community agencies offering services to program clientele. The second phase, "stabilization" (2-6 weeks), focuses on maintaining progress achieved during the first phase and continuing to provide support, needed services, and linkages with community agencies. The "follow-up" period offers ongoing services from therapists who are on call 24 hours a day. Family-community linkages are also monitored to ensure that clients follow through with referrals to community agencies. A cotherapy team works throughout the process to create a network of formal (i.e., community agency) and informal (i.e., extended family, friends) supports to reduce the family's social isolation. Interventions are tailored to the family's needs (e.g., parenting education, stress reduction) and may be provided in a variety of settings (e.g., home, school, day care). Follow-up evaluations were provided at termination, 3-months and 6-months posttreatment. In general, FCHBT programs have shown promise in meeting their mandate to prevent the need for out-of-home placement in at-risk families (Frankel, 1988). However, many programs do not include "at-risk" or abused children due to competing demands to ensure a safe environment for the child (Meddin & Hansen, 1985). Further, programs that do serve this population only do so as a small portion of their overall caseload. Amundson's (1989) focus on this population is a notable exception. Her findings indicated that families participating in the program: remained intact (90% at 6 month follow-up); displayed significant problem solving and communication improvements (80%); reported reductions in problem behaviors and their reliance on physical punishment (95%); and used suggested community resources (85%). The lack of a comparison group in the study design makes it difficult to draw conclusions regarding the actual effectiveness of the approach.

In fact, only one study in this area has used a design which incorporates a comparison group to evaluate the effectiveness of their intervention. Lyle and Nelson (cited in Frankel, 1988) randomly assigned clients to either a traditional child protection unit or to FCHBT (i.e., counseling and concrete services). Their findings indicated that 3 months after treatment, 67% of the FCHBT clients' families remained intact as compared to 45% of the protective services unit group.

Finally, two other issues merit mentioning in regard to the viability of FCHBT. First, these approaches are staff intensive (i.e. smaller caseloads), raising issues related to the cost-effectiveness (Frankel, 1988; Nicol et al., 1988). This concern may, however, be offset by reductions in placement costs. Second, client attrition rates are difficult to assess since drop-outs in FCHBT programs are likely to be counted as treatment failures and subsumed into the percentage of families who go on to have a child placed outside of their home. An exception has been Nicol and associates' (1988) report of a 45% drop out rate in their investigation. If their experience is at all representative, there is substantial reason for concern.

MULTISYSTEMIC THERAPY

The multisystemic model embraces the family therapy notion that behavior must be examined within applicable larger system contexts and acknowledges the ecological nature of individual's actions. The assertion, based on this model, that cognitive and extrafamilial variables maintain problem behaviors represents something of a divergence from other family systems conceptualizations. The treatment approach is described as utilizing "joining, reframing and prescribed tasks designed to change interaction patterns" as well as family restructuring (Brunk et al. 1987, p. 173).

Brunk and her associates (1987) report the effective use of this approach with a group of abusive parents. Findings indicated pretreatment-posttreatment differences on self-report as well as observational measures and suggested that multisystemic therapy offered certain advantages over a behavioral group parent training approach also examined in this study. However, the study's small sample size, moderate drop-out rate (23%), lack of follow-up data, and lack of control group indicate the need for additional investigations prior to drawing firm conclusions regarding the efficacy of the multisystemic approach.

SUMMARY, CRITIQUE, AND FUTURE DIRECTIONS

Recognition that the findings of this review would be only minimally different if it had been undertaken in 1985 is quite disturbing. It is of particular concern given the increasing incidence of physical abuse (NCCAN, 1988) and the devastating consequences of abuse for child victims (e.g., Wolfe, 1987). The lack of continued interest by many investigators may be due, in part, to the interplay of factors both specific to the area of physical abuse (e.g., inadequate model development, client resistance) and related to the larger working context (e.g., legislative impact, funding priorities). Despite the almost overwhelming complexity of this area, there are a number of specific issues that could be addressed. We will present and discuss some of these issues in the final section of this article.

Further development of basic models. Treatment assumes an adequate foundation in both the areas of model formulation and empirical testing to support the efficacy of a particular explanatory model. As evident from our review, a substantial number of models currently exist. A considerable amount of empirical information is also available regarding physical abuse perpetrators' characteristics (Wolfe, 1985), those of their victims (e.g., Wolfe, 1987), and the impact on the abused child (e.g., Lamphear, 1985). It is difficult to conclude, however, that the available models incorporate the existing knowledge base in such a way as to guide the development of treatment programs or offer insights regarding what would be effective with particular populations or presenting problems. Clearly, the introduction of the ecological model (Belsky, 1980) greatly broadened the fields' perspective and offered enhanced opportunities to intervene. It also presented a means of integrating previously divergent models (Rosenberg & Reppucci, 1985). Yet the direction that the ecological model provides (i.e., intervene at individual, familial, community, and societal level) may outstrip our current ability to develop treatment packages which respond effectively at each level. Further development appears necessary to create theoretical models which better utilize existing empirical data and offer more specific direction regarding the development of effective treatment components. Such models should focus on a more micro level (e.g., individual or family or community) and should be sensitive to the nuances of differing client populations, family constellations, and community characteristics. A blend of these models and the larger ecological model would offer greater promise for the development of truly successful interventions.

Including victim intervention components in treatment. Although treatment packages have varied considerably in their content, focus, and approach to treatment, a number of consistent limitations continue to exist and should be addressed in future clinical and research endeavors. For many child victims developmental delays, speech and language difficulties, and handicaps may have facilitated their selection as the target of abusive acts (Walker et al., 1989). For other children interpersonal, emotional, and cognitive difficulties may be a consequence of physical abuse (Wolfe, 1987). Despite the prevalence of these developmental, behavioral, and emotional problems, the majority of treatment programs have either not included or not evaluated child-focused intervention components (Azar & Wolfe, 1989). Parent-child interaction training (e.g., Wolfe, Edwards, Manion, & Koverola, 1988) represents one exception. However, abuse victims' needs are broad based and necessitate comprehensive services and well-designed programs. Such programs should be developmentally appropriate, with the flexibility to meet each child's particular needs.

Methodological implications. A detailed discussion of methodological difficulties present in the child abuse treatment literature is beyond the scope of this article. However, it is important to acknowledge that methodological limitations have represented a significant barrier to the development of this area. Reliance on single subject designs, the use of small samples, studies without control/comparison groups or those where assignment is not necessarily random in nature, poorly defined intervention protocols, unreliable or unidimensional outcome measures, abuse recidivism not included as an outcome measure, and inadequate follow-up duration have limited our ability to draw conclusions regarding the effectiveness of particular approaches and the generalizability of findings. (see Mash & Wolfe's methodological review in this issue).

The use of competency based clinical evaluation procedures. Few studies in the literature adequately describe the criteria that they use to make termination-related decisions. Without this information it is difficult to determine if "treatment failures" were related to ineffective intervention procedures or to a lack of generalization from classroom teaching or individual differences in parents' abilities to learn skills and approaches. Competency-based evaluations offer the ability to readily assess parents' competencies in a naturalistic environment. Data offer specific indications of areas in need of additional training or parents' successful mastery of requisite skills. Positive results have been reported by Wolfe and his associates in using competency-based evaluation procedures (Wolfe & Manion, 1984; Wolfe, Sandler, & Kaufman, 1981). Treatment programs should not only incorporate this technology, but should be sure to report the details of its use in resulting journal articles.

Ethnic, cultural, and economic specificity. Programs should be designed with consideration given to the ethnic, cultural, and economic character of the population that it serves. Cohn (1982) has suggested the tailoring of child abuse prevention programs based on these factors. Treatment programs would also benefit from attention to these factors. In fact, some evidence already exists regarding the benefits of tailoring programs (Lorion, 1978). The work of Szapocznik and his colleagues (Szapocznik et al., 1989) represents an excellent example of the successful tailoring of treatment approaches for Hispanic children with behavioral and emotional difficulties. This and similar studies could serve as models for the development of physical abuse intervention programs.

Integration of fathers into treatment. There is some evidence to suggest that males may be more likely to perpetrate physical abuse than females (American Humane Association, 1984). Despite this, mothers appear to be overrepresented in the treatment literature (Golub et al., 1987; Lutzker & Rice, 1984; Wolfe, Sandler, & Kaufman, 1981). Although it is possible that participants in research-based treatment initiatives are not representative of clinical treatment programs in general, it seems more likely that males are simply more reluctant to participate. If this is so, special efforts should be instituted to ensure that male perpetrators do not circumvent the treatment process.

Collaborative treatment endeavors. Historically, it seems that certain types of treatment approaches were more likely to be associated with particular service settings. More time and labor intensive approaches (e.g., behavioral parent training with in-home generalization component) were more likely to be affiliated with university graduate school programs. In contrast, state administered social service agencies used intensive case-work approaches or more family-centered techniques with greater frequency. Efforts should be undertaken to develop more collaborative treatment efforts. Programs such as Project 12-Ways, would offer the technological expertise and person power of university-based programs as well as the larger systems perspective of the case-work approach. This may allow for greater experimentation in the types of interventions that are combined in a particular program. For example, integrating skill-based parent training and child therapy with family therapy (e.g., multisystemic approach) may offer a treatment approach more consistent with an ecological treatment model.

Increasing client compliance with treatment. The shift away from research on the treatment of physical abuse may have partially reflected the resistant nature of many clients. High attrition rates have been associated with various treatment approaches, underscoring the resistant nature of the abusive parent (Irueste-Montes & Montes, 1988; Nicol et al., 1988; Rivara, 1985; Wolfe, Aragona, Kaufman, & Sandler, 1980). With few exceptions (e.g., Wolfe, Dumas, & Wahler, 1983), little information has been available regarding parents who do not complete treatment. Studies have suggested that parents who drop out of treatment may have younger children (Wolfe et al., 1988), may be lacking in external contingencies to motivate their participation

(Wolfe et al., 1980), and may live alone or with a parent and may have a previous history of abuse (Johnson, 1988). The generalizability of these findings, however, may be limited by the representativeness of the samples used in the studies.

Strategies have been suggested in the literature to deal with resistant clients. These have included "client salaries" for attendance and completing assignments (Fleischman, 1979) and gifts for parents who comply with treatment objectives (Wolfe & Manion, 1984). Although findings have been contradictory, there is some evidence to support the notion that a specific court order for treatment represents a relatively effective contingency for abusive parents attending treatment (e.g., type of treatment, for how long; Irueste-Montes & Montes, 1988; Wolfe et al., 1980). There is a pressing need to delineate differences between clients who complete treatment and those who do not. It is also important to acknowledge the multiproblem nature of this population and the effect of external pressors (e.g., unemployment, lack of child care) on individuals' ability to comply with treatment demands. Future research should strive to identify reliable offender subgroups as well as particular situations and stressors that represent treatment barriers and then examine the efficacy of various motivational approaches with subgroup/life-situation combinations.

Influencing the larger system. Although larger context issues are often difficult to affect, annual requests for comments on funding agencies' research priorities, grant submissions to "field initiated research" categories, and lobbying through local, state and national organizations offer opportunities to influence the system. A positive example is reflected in the influence that researchers had on NCCAN's funding priorities for fiscal year 1990-1991. Input at the 1989 "Research Symposium on Treatment Approaches to Child Maltreatment" suggested the need for outcome evaluation studies. NCCAN responded by offering nine demonstration grants ($200,000/grant) to investigate this area (Bates, personal communication, July 12, 1990). When the grant review process is completed, it is quite possible that some of these funds will be committed to physical abuse treatment evaluation.

CONCLUSION

Physical child abuse represents a devastating form of maltreatment which has continued to increase over the past 15 years (based on reported cases). Intensive efforts to identify the most effective treatment approaches appear to have been abandoned in favor of prevention and early intervention initiatives. Although prevention and early intervention services represent significant priorities, treatment goals must also be met. Clearly, it will be impossible to ameliorate this form of maltreatment unless identified abusers receive effective treatment that reduces their potential to reoffend and unless victims receive services which preclude them from becoming part of the intergenerational "cycle of abuse."

REFERENCES

Adoption Assistance and Child Welfare Act of 1980. P. L. 96-272, H. R. 3434, 94 Stat. 500. (1980).

Amendment to Child Abuse Prevention and Treatment Act. P. L. 98-457. (1984).

American Humane Association. (1984). *Highlights of official child abuse and neglect reporting —1982.* Denver, CO: Author.

Amundson, M. J. (1989). Family crisis care: A home-based intervention program for child abuse. *Issues in Mental Health Nursing, 10*, 285-296.

Azar, S. T. (1984). *An evaluation of the effectiveness of cognitive behavioral versus insight oriented mothers groups with child maltreaters.* Unpublished doctoral dissertation, University of Rochester, NY.

Azar, S. T., & Wolfe, D. A. (1989). Child abuse & neglect. In E. J. Mash & R. A. Barkely (Eds.), *Treatment of childhood disorders* (pp. 451-493). New York: Guilford.

Belsky, J. (1980). Child maltreatment: An ecological integration. *American Psychologist, 35*, 320-335.

Brunk, M., Henggeler, S., & Whelan, J. (1987). Comparison of multisystemic therapy and parent training in the brief treatment of child abuse and neglect. *Journal of Consulting and Clinical Psychology, 55*, 171-178.

Bryce, M., & Lloyd, J. (1980). Placement prevention and family unification. In M. Bryce & J. Lloyd (Eds.), *Planning and supervising the home-based family-centered program* (pp. 62-83). Oakdale: University of Iowa, School of Social Work, National Clearinghouse for Home-Based Services.

Cohn, A. (1979). Effective treatment of child abuse and neglect. *Social Work, 24*, 513-519.

Cohn, A. H. (1982). Stopping abuse before it occurs: Different solutions for different population groups. *Child Abuse & Neglect, 6*, 473-483.

Cohn, A. H., & Daro, D. (1987). Is treatment too late: What ten years of evaluative research tell us. *Child Abuse & Neglect, 11*, 433-442.

Daro, D. (1988). *Confronting child abuse: Research for effective program design.* New York: Free Press.

Embry, L. H., & Baer, D. M. (1979). *Group parent training: An analysis of generalization from classroom to home.* Unpublished doctoral dissertation, University of Kansas.

Fleischman, M. J. (1979). Using parent salaries to control attrition and cooperation in therapy. *Behavior Therapy, 10,* 111-116.

Foxx, R. M., McMorrow, M. J., & Schloss, C. (1983). Stacking the deck: Teaching social skills to retarded adults with a modified table game. *Journal of Applied Behavior Analysis, 16,* 157-170.

Frankel, H. (1988). Family-centered, home-based services in child protection: A review of the research. *Social Service Review, 62,* 137-157.

Golub, J. S., Espinosa, M., Damon, L., & Card, J. (1987). A video-tape parent education program for abusive parents. *Child Abuse & Neglect, 11,* 255-265.

Graziano, A. M. (1977). Parents as behavior therapists. In M. Hersen, R. M. Eisler, & P. M. Miller (Eds.), *Progress in behavior modification.* (Vol. 9, pp. 251-298). New York: Academic Press.

Haapala, D. (1983). *Perceived helpfulness, attributed critical incident responsibility, and a discrimination of home-based family therapy treatment outcome: Homebuilders model.* Unpublished final report to U.S. Department of Health and Human Services, Adminstration for Children, Youth and Families. Federal Way, WA: Behavioral Sciences Institute.

Helfer, R. E. (1982). A review of the literature on the prevention of child abuse and neglect. *Child Abuse & Neglect, 6,* 251-261.

Irueste-Montes, A. M., & Montes, F. (1988). Court-ordered vs. voluntary treatment of abusive and neglectful parents. *Child Abuse & Neglect, 12,* 33-39.

Isaacs, C. D. (1982). Treatment of child abuse: A review of the behavioral interventions. *Journal of Applied Behavior Analysis, 15,* 273-294.

Johnson, W. B. (1988). Child-abusing parents: Factors associated with successful completion of treatment. *Psychological Reports, 63,* 434.

Kempe, C. H., Silverman, F. N., Steele, B. F., Droegemueller, W., & Silver, H. K. (1962). The battered child syndrome. *Journal of the American Medical Association, 191,* 17-24.

Lamphear, V. S. (1985). The impact of maltreatment on children's psychosocial adjustment: A review of the research. *Child Abuse & Neglect, 9,* 251-263.

Lorion, R. P. (1978). Research on psychotherapy and behavior change with the disadvantaged. In S. L. Garfield & A. E. Bergin (Eds.), *Handbook of psychotherapy and behavior change: An empirical analysis* (2nd ed., pp. 903-938). New York: Wiley.

Lutzker, J. R. (1984). Project 12-Ways: Treating child abuse and neglect from an ecobehavioral perspective. In R. F. Dangel & R. A. Polster (Eds.), *Parent training: Foundations of research and practice* (pp. 260-291). New York: Guilford.

Lutzker, J. R., Frame, R., & Rice, J. (1982). Project 12-Ways: An ecobehavioral approach to the treatment and prevention of child abuse and neglect. *Education and Treatment of Children, 5,* 141-155.

Lutzker, J. R., & Rice, J. M. (1984). Project 12-Ways: Measuring outcome of a large-scale in-home service for the treatment and prevention of child abuse and neglect. *Child Abuse & Neglect, 8,* 519-524.

Lutzker, J. R., & Rice, J. M. (1987). Using recidivism data to evaluate Project 12-Ways: An ecobehavioral approach to the treatment and prevention of child abuse and neglect. *Journal of Family Violence, 2,* 283-290.

Meddin, B. J., & Hansen, I. (1985). The services provided during a child abuse and/or neglect investigation and the barriers that exist to service provision. *Child Abuse & Neglect, 9,* 175-182.

National Center on Child Abuse and Neglect (1988). *Study findings: Study of national incidence and prevalence of child abuse and neglect.* U.S. Department of Health and Human Services.

Nicol, A. R., Smith, J., Kay, B., Hall, D., Barlow, J., & Williams, B. (1988). A focused casework approach to the treatment of child abuse: A controlled comparison. *Journal of Child Psychology & Psychiatry, 29,* 703-711.

Rivara, F. P. (1985). Physical abuse in children under two: A study of therapeutic outcomes. *Child Abuse & Neglect, 9,* 81-87.

Rosenberg, M. S., & Reppucci, N. D. (1985). Primary prevention of child abuse. *Journal of Consulting and Clinical Psychology, 5,* 576-585.

Szapocznik, J., Rio, A., Murray, E., Cohen, R., Scopetta, M., Rivas-Vazquez, A., Hervis, O., Pasada, V., & Kurtines, W. (1989). Structural family versus psychodynamic child therapy for problematic hispanic boys. *Journal of Consulting and Clinical Psychology, 57,* 571-578.

Walker, C. E., Bonner, B. L., & Kaufman, K. L. (1989). *The physically and sexually abused child: Evaluation and treatment.* New York: Pergamon.

Wolfe, D. A. (1985). Child-abusive parents: An empirical review and analysis. *Psychological Bulletin, 97,* 462-482.

Wolfe, D. A. (1987). *Child abuse: Implications for child development and psychopathology.* Newbury Park, CA: Sage.

Wolfe, D. A. (1988). Child abuse and neglect. In E. J. Mash & L. G. Terdol (Eds.), *Behavioral assessment of childhood disorders* (2nd ed., pp. 627-669). New York: Guilford.

Wolfe, D. A., Aragona, J., Kaufman, K., & Sandler, J. (1980). The importance of adjudication in the treatment of child abuse: Some preliminary findings. *Child Abuse & Neglect, 4,* 127-135.

Wolfe, D. A., Dumas, J., & Wahler, R. G. (1983). *An analysis of drop-outs and families in the behavioral parent training literature.* Paper presented at the Special Interest Group on Social Learning and the Family, Association for Advancement of Behavior Therapy, Washington, DC.

Wolfe, D. A., Edwards, B., Manion, I., & Koverola, C. (1988). Early intervention for child abuse and neglect: A preliminary investigation. *Journal of Consulting and Clinical Psychology, 56,* 40-47.

Wolfe, D. A., Kaufman, K., Aragona, J., & Sandler, J. (1981). *A child management program for abusive parents: Procedures for developing a child abuse intervention program.* Orlando, FL: Anna.

Wolfe, D. A., & Manion, I. G. (1984). Impediments to child abuse prevention: Issues and directions. *Advances in Behavior Research and Therapy, 6,* 47-62.

Wolfe, D. A., Sandler, J., & Kaufman, K. (1981). A competency-based parent training program for abusive parents. *Journal of Consulting and Clinical Psychology, 49,* 633-640.

Sex-Offender Risk Assessment and Disposition Planning: A Review of Empirical and Clinical Findings

Robert J. McGrath

Abstract: *The p mary goal of intervention with sex offenders is to protect the community from further sexual aggression. As the availability of jail beds decreases, it is imperative that professionals discriminate between those offenders who must be incarcerated to protect the public and those offenders who can be supervised with reasonable safety in community settings. This article will review the research on variables related to sex offender recidivism which is a critical factor to consider in making these decisions. In addition, criteria for determining an offender's amenability to treatment will be examined and guidelines for formulating disposition plans will be outlined.*

INTRODUCTION

During the last decade, there has been a dramatic increase in the number of sex offenders who have come to the attention of the courts, correctional agencies, social service organizations, and mental health professionals. What to do with these offenders has become a vitally important societal question. The availability of ever-expensive jail beds continues to decrease while public demands for community safety may be at an all-time high. Those who find themselves faced with the responsibility of making risk-assessment and disposition-planning decisions about sex offenders indeed confront a challenging task. A number of researchers have provided assistance by detailing the information that should be elicited from offenders and collaterals (Barnard, Fuller, Robbins, & Shaw, 1989; Groth & Birnbaum, 1979; O'Connell, Leberg, & Donaldson, 1990) and recommending specialized interview techniques (McGrath, 1990). To date, however, specific guidance on risk assessment and disposition planning with this population has generally been limited to summaries of clinical impressions (e.g., Groth, Hobson, & Gary, 1982; Knopp, 1984) or empirical studies of circumscribed populations. A review and integration of these findings can be of benefit to both researchers and practitioners.

The goal of this article is to provide professionals who are responsible for managing sex offenders with information that can enhance their

The author would like to thank Carolyn Carey, Stephen Hoke, and Susan Keniston for their comments on an earlier draft of this manuscript.

International Journal of Offender Therapy and Comparative Criminology, 35(4), 1991 risk-assessment and disposition-planning skills. The article is divided into three sections. The first two, on rehabilitation and risk factors, provide the reader with background information necessary for disposition planning, which is covered in the final section. Since most risk-management and disposition-planning research with this population has been conducted with males convicted of rape, child molestation, and exhibitionism, discussion is limited to these populations.

REHABILITATION: AMENABILITY TO TREATMENT

Specialized sex-offender treatment is a common disposition option and can reduce and offender's risk to reoffend. Disposition plans that incorporate rehabilitation components must take several factors into consideration. Treatment programs vary in their effectiveness, and no rehabilitation program can expect to be 100% effective. In addition, some individuals who suffer from psychological disturbances are not amenable to psychological intervention. Those who make decisions concerning rehabilitation should have at least a rudimentary knowledge of sex-offender treatment efficacy, accepted intervention components, and standard admission criteria.

While some would argue that sex offenders do not deserve treatment services, Prentky and Burgess (1990) underscore the fact that the primary goal of sex-offender treatment is actually reduction of victimization rates. Their recent research also suggests that rehabilitation efforts are cost effective even when treatment reduces recidivism rates by only a small degree.

Although the knowledgeable skeptic would be justified in questioning the ability of mental health professionals to rehabilitate sex offenders (Furby, Weinrott, & Blackshaw, 1989), several recent outcome studies of specialized sex-offender treatment have offered encouraging results. Estimates by the United States Department of Justice (1988a) suggest that the recidivism rate of untreated sex offenders is about 60% within 3 years of release from incarcerated settings, while recidivism among those who have completed specialized treatment within these institutions is about 15% to 20%. The efficacy of some specialized community based treatment programs for sex offenders has likewise shown very promising results (Maletsky, 1990; Marshall & Barbaree, 1988; Pithers & Cumming, 1989).

A variety of components commonly comprise effective sex-offender treatment programs. It is worth nothing that there is little to suggest that analytic or other insight-oriented psychotherapies alone are effective with this population (Lanyon, 1986; Quinsey, 1990; Salter, 1988). Rather, the vast majority of specialized programs employ a combination of psychoeducational, cognitive-behavioral, and family-system intervention strategies (Knopp & Stevenson, 1988). Psychoeducational interventions assist offenders in acquiring knowledge in areas such as sex education, sexual assault cycles, and victimology. Cognitive-behavioral interventions incorporate treatment components designed to alter deviant arousal patterns, improve appropriate sexual functioning, increase social competence, and correct distorted thinking (Marshall & Barbaree, 1990). Family therapy seems to be an especially critical treatment component in incest cases (Giarretto, 1982; Trepper & Barrett, 1989). Recent applications of relapse prevention strategies designed to assist clients in maintaining treatment benefits over time have also proved to be promising (Marques, Day, Nelson, & Miner, 1989; Pithers & Cumming, 1989). Intensive probation supervision of sex offenders, coupled with these above psychological interventions, makes good intuitive sense and may further reduce recidivism rates (Romero & Williams, 1985).

With respect to decisions about which sex offenders can be considered amenable to treatment, at least three factors seem important. (It should be noted that "amenability" refers to the offender's ability to engage in treatment, but is neither a judgment about the setting in which treatment should take place nor a prediction about the effectiveness of treatment.) First, the offender must acknowledge that he committed a sexual offense and accept responsibility for his behavior. Such acknowledgment is critical since treatment interventions rely fundamentally on the offender's ability to identify and later modify the types of feelings, thoughts, situations, and behaviors that were proximal to his sexually aggressive act. An offender obviously cannot identify the precursors to an offense that he states he did not commit.

Second, he must consider his sexual offending to be a problem behavior that he wants to stop. Ideally, the offender would wish to stop offending for the sake of future victims; however, at least initially, motivation based on reasons that are more self-serving can open the door to treatment.

Last, the offender must be willing to enter into and fully participate in treatment. This willingness can be formalized through a written treatment contract that describes the components of treatment and alerts the offender to any risks that may be involved. The offender's informed consent is essential for purposes of clarity and is in keeping with good ethical practice.

Risk assessments and disposition plans must take into consideration the fact that amenability to treatment is not a static variable. Offenders who initially deny committing their offense may later accept responsibility and desire treatment. Conversely, offenders who are initially found amenable and begin treatment may later decide that rehabilitation is too demanding and drop out.

RISK ASSESSMENT: SAFETY OF THE COMMUNITY

After a determination has been made as to whether or not an offender is amenable to treatment, several other variables must be examined to ascertain the degree of risk that the offender poses to the community. This risk assessment will help identify the types of controls that must be established to protect the community from the offender.

Predicting risk to commit violence in general and sexual aggression in particular is an extremely difficult task (Hall, 1990; Monahan, 1981; Quinsey, 1983). Although explication of the complexities of predicting risk per se is not the purpose of this article, the following brief caveats are warranted. Due to the low base rates of some types of sexual aggression, and also to political pressure to avoid making false-positive decision errors, clinicians must guard against a tendency to overpredict violence (Melton, Petrila, Poythress, & Slobogin, 1987). In addition, predictions of dangerousness are only as good as the data upon which they are based. The tendency of offenders to lie about, deny, and minimize their sexual deviancy requires evaluators to be thorough and gather data from a variety of collateral sources. Last, professionals often overestimate their clinical decision-making ability (Turk & Salovey, 1988) and must remember that actuarial methods of prediction generally outperform clinical ones (Sawyer, 1966).

Despite the difficulties inherent in predicting risk, those who work with sex offenders are forced to assess dangerousness on a regular basis. It is imperative that decisions that can affect the liberty of offenders and the safety of the community are based not only on clinical experience but on empirical findings as well.

Since 1980, there have been a large number of studies investigating factors associated with risk to recidivate among known sex offenders. Table 1 summarizes the essential findings from a number of these recent studies. The consistency with which various risk factors emerge in this literature is particularly noteworthy in light of the many differences among the studies reviewed. In addition, it is important to consider a number of other risk factors that are based on clinical impression and have not as yet been adequately researched.

LEVEL OF DENIAL

Given that an offender's acceptance of at least some responsibility for his offenses is a prerequisite for acceptance into virtually all specialized sex-offender treatment programs, and given that adequately treated sex offenders are less likely to recidivate, those offenders who deny their offenses and remain untreated can be viewed as a higher risk for recidivism. Researchers have found that low levels of denial are positively correlated

TABLE 1
FACTORS COMMONLY ASSOCIATED WITH SEXUAL OFFENSE RECIDIVISM

Study	Sample	Follow-Up	Recidivism Criteria	Risk Factors[1]								
				UEMP	UREL	PARA	CRIM	SEXC	MALE	FORC	UMAR	DEVI
Abel, Mittleman, Becker, Rathner, & Rouleau (1988)	98 treated outpatient child molesters	12 mos	self-report of sex offense	o	+						+	
Barbaree & Marshall (1988)	35 untreated outpatient child molesters	12-117 mos	reconviction or unofficial record for sex offense	+					o			+
Hanson, Steffy, & Gauthier (1990)	106 treated incarcerated child molesters	10-23 yrs	reconviction for sex offense		+		+		+		+	
Maletsky (1990)	3,995 treated outpatient sex offenders	1-17 yrs	reconviction sex offense or failed treatment goals	+	+	+			+	+	+	+
Rice, Harris, & Quinsey (1989a)	136 treated incarcerated nonfamilial child molesters	6.3 yrs mean	reconviction for sex offense				+	+	+	+	+	+

Study	Sample	Follow-up	Outcome							
Rice, Harris, & Qunisey (1989b)	54 treated incarcerated rapists	44 mos mean	any criminal reconviction		+	+	+	+	o	+
Romero & Williams (1985)	231 treated outpatients sex offenders	10 yrs	arrest for sex offense	+	+	o	+	+		o
Sturgon & Taylor (1990)	260 treated incarcerated rapists & child molesters	49-72 mos	arrest for any crime		+	+	+	+	+	+
Tracy, Donnelly, Morgenbesser, & MacDonald (1983)	83 untreated incarcerated sex offenders	5 yrs	return to jail for sex offense		+	+	+			

1. UNEP = unemployed or low socioeconomic status; UREL = unrelated to victim; PARA = multiple paraphilias; CRIM = prior nonsexual criminal offense convictions; SEXC = prior sexual offense convictions; MALE = male victims; FORC = used force or violence during past offenses; UMAR = unmarried; DEVI = deviant arousal pattern on plethysmographic assessment; + = positive association found in the study; o = no association found in the study; blank space = factor not examined or reported in the study.

with favorable treatment progress (Simkins, Ward, Bowman, & Rinck, 1989). Interestingly enough however, among those offenders who remain untreated, it appears that there may be no difference in reoffense rates between deniers and admitters (Marshall & Barbaree, 1988).

TYPE OF OFFENSE

The type of sexual offense is related to the probability of recidivism. I found only two studies that compared three or more offense types in a single sample (Frisbie & Dondis, 1965, cited in Quinsey, 1977; Romero & Williams, 1985). These studies allow a comparison of the relative reoffense rates among various offenders by type of offense, in a single geographic area during a prescribed period. This is an improvement over studies that compare offender recidivism among different studies conducted in different locales and at different time periods where, for example, variability of reporting, arrest, and clearance rates may affect subject comparability.

Romero and Williams (1985) conducted a 10-year follow-up on a sample of 231 convicted sex offenders who were randomly assigned either to group psychotherapy and probation or to probation only, in Philadelphia between 1966 and 1969. Twenty-six men (11.3%) had been rearrested for a sex offense at follow-up. Only 6.2% of the 39 convicted of pedophilia reoffended, whereas 10.4% of the 144 convicted of sexual assault reoffended. The highest reoffense rate, 20.5%, was found among the 48 convicted of exhibitionism.

Frisbie and Dondis (1965, cited in Quinsey, 1977) found similar reoffense relationships when examining the type of offense. They studied a sample of 1,760 "sexual psychopaths" who were treated and released from Atascadero State Hospital in California between 1954 and 1960. Over the 1 to 6-year follow-up period, those convicted of exhibitionism had the highest reoffense rate, at 40.7%. The rate of reoffense for those convicted of sexual aggression was 35.6%. The child molesters in this study were grouped according to the sex and relatedness of their victims. Of father-daughter and father-stepdaughter incest offenders, 10.2% recidivated, whereas 21.5% of men who molested minor nonrelated females reoffended. Those who molested underage males had the highest reoffense rate, 34.5%.

The findings suggested by these two studies are generally supported by others. Untreated exhibitionists are consistently reported to have the highest recidivism rates (20%-41%) among all sex offenders (Blair & Lanyon, 1981; Cox, 1980). The recidivism rates of rapists range between a low of 7.7% (U.S. Department of Justice, 1989) to a high of 35.6% as reported in Frisbie and Dondis (1965, cited in Quinsey, 1977). Among nonfamilial child molesters, the reoffense rates of those who molest boys (13%-40%) tend to be much higher than of those who molest girls (10%-29%) (Fitch, 1962;

Radzinowicz, 1957). Incest offenders display the lowest untreated recidivism, generally 10% or less (Gibbins, Soothill, & Way, 1979, 1981).

While these studies may provide helpful comparative information about the differential risk of recidivism according to the type of offense, the true reoffense rates for the subjects in each of the previous studies are likely to be much higher. In general, the skill with which most offenders avoid detection seriously compromises our ability to assess actual recidivism rates (Abel, Becker, Cunningham-Rathner, Rouleau, & Murphy, 1987; Groth, Longo, & McFadin, 1982; Marshall & Barbaree, 1988).

MULTIPLE PARAPHILIAS

The foregoing discussion of recidivism based on the type of offense could be taken to suggest that offenders limit themselves to a single class of deviant behavior. In reality, however, many offenders have multiple paraphilias, and those who do so are at increased risk to reoffend.

Longo and Groth (1983) found that as many as 35% of their sample of incarcerated rapists and child molesters actually began their deviant sexual histories committing hands-off sex offenses such as exhibitionism and voyeurism, before progressing to hands-on offenses. In another study (Abel, Becker, Cunningham-Rathner, Mittleman, & Rouleau, 1988), researchers who assured confidentality to 561 nonincarcerated paraphiliacs found that the child molesters, rapists, and exhibitionists averaged between 3.3 and 4.2 paraphilias each.

One hundred and ninety-two of these child molesters later volunteered to enroll in a structured treatment program with Abel and his colleagues (Abel, Mittleman, Becker, Rathner, & Rouleau, 1988). The researchers found that the number of age and gender categories into which the subject's victims fell were powerful predictors of recidivism. For instance, the overall reoffense rate for the 98 subjects who were followed up 1 year after treatment was 12.2% ($n = 12$). Of those offenders who targeted both males and females and both children and adolescents, 75% recidivated ($n = 9$). This variable alone correctly classified 83.7% of both recidivists and nonrecidivists in the study. In addition, offenders whose pretreatment sexual offense history included hands-off offenses, reoffended at a higher rate than offenders without such a history.

Romero and Williams' (1985) analysis of recidivism among their sample of 231 assaulters, pedophiles, and exhibitionists supports this association between a history of hands-off offenses and subsequent recidivism for a sexual offense. Of 26 recidivists in their study, 16 reported a prior history of indecent exposure, and of this group 30.4% were rearrested. Only 9.1% of the entire sample who reported no such history of indecent exposure reoffended. More recently, Maletsky (1990) found that those offenders with histories of multiple paraphilias were over five times more likely to be treatment failures or recidivate than those who did not have multiple paraphilias.

CRIMINALITY

A prior criminal record, both for sexual and nonsexual crimes, has consistently proven to be one of the best predictors of future sexual criminal behavior. For example, Danish researcher Christiansen (1965, cited in Tracy, Donnelly, Morgenbesser, & Macdonald, 1983) conducted a 12 to 24-year follow-up of 2,934 sex offenders from 1929 to 1939. Those offenders with criminal records recidivated at a rate of 38.6%, compared to 18.6% for first offenders. Romero and Williams (1985) found that the prior sex offense arrest rate was the single best predictor of sexual recidivism in their 10-year follow-up study of 231 sex offenders. Specifically, of offenders whose prior adult sex-offense rate was low (zero to one arrest every 3 years), only 7.9% reoffended sexually. Conversely, for offenders whose prior arrest rate was higher (greater than one arrest every 3 years), the sex offense recidivism rate was 26.2%.

Criminal personality traits have also been associated with recidivism, as well as with treatment failure. Rapists appear to have more deeply ingrained sociopathy than do child molesters. In a study of 411 outpatient sex offenders conducted by Abel, Mittelman, and Becker (1985), 29.2% of the rapists were given a diagnosis of antisocial personality disorder, whereas only 11.6% of the child molesters were so diagnosed. Abel and his colleagues (Abel, Mittelman, Becker, Rathner, & Rouleau, 1988) later treated 192 of the child molesters on a voluntary basis. A diagnosis of antisocial personality was predictive of eventual drop out: Of the 19 child molesters so diagnosed, over half (10) dropped out during treatment and an additional 5 dropped out during follow-up. A DSM III–R diagnosis of antisocial personality disorder was not, however, predictive of sexual recidivism during the 1 year of follow-up.

Using longer follow-up periods and a more restrictive definition of antisocial character traits, Rice, Harris, and Quinsey (1989b) found that high scores on the Psychopathy Checklist (Hare, 1980) were powerful predictors of both sexual recidivism and violence recidivism among a group of 54 incarcerated rapists.

SEXUAL AROUSAL PATTERNS

The assessment of sexual arousal patterns by phallometric measurements has become an accepted and common element in a significant proportion of sex-offender treatment programs (Knopp, 1984; Knopp & Stevenson, 1990). The results of such assessment procedures are generally predictive of subsequent reoffense among identified sex offenders. Given the controversy that often surrounds this assessment procedure, each of the seven studies located for this review will be briefly examined.

Quinsey, Chaplin, and Carrigan (1980) provided behavioral treatment to a group of 30 child molesters in a psychiatric institution. At follow-up (average of 29 months), posttreatment penile response data proved to be a small but significant predictor of recidivism, in that it differentiated the 6 recidivists from nonrecidivists. Subsequently the sample size was increased to 132 offenders and the length of follow-up period extended to an average of 34 months. Under these conditions, there was no relationship between posttreatment arousal measures and recidivism (Quinsey & Marshall, 1983). Interestingly enough, however, the initial arousal data from the first 100 treated and untreated child molesters did prove to be significantly related to recidivism.

In a community-based study, Barbaree and Marshall (1988) followed 35 extrafamilial child molesters for an average of almost 4 years after their assessment and, using penile response data correctly predicted the treatment outcome of just over 75% of the sample with respect to recidivism. From among a large number of variables, inappropriate age preference ratios as measured by plethysmography were the strongest predictors of treatment failure. When they increased their sample size to 126 and the follow-up period up to as long as 11 years, neither pretreatment, posttreatment, nor pre/post changes in pedophile indexes predicted outcome (Marshall & Barbaree, 1988).

Rice, Quinsey, and Harris (1989a) determined the recidivism rates of 136 extrafamilial child molesters in a maximum security psychiatric institution over an average 6.3-year follow-up period. Deviant pedophile indexes at intake were positively correlated with reconviction for a sexual offense. Given the propensity of sex offenders to deny the extent of their deviant sexual interests, however, it is not surprising that subjects' self-report of their arousal preferences were not predictive of reconviction. Studies conducted at the same facility on a group of 54 rapists found that sexual recidivism and violent recidivism were predicted by phallometric measures of sexual interest in nonsexual violence, to an even greater extent than arousal to rape per se (Rice, Harris, & Quinsey, 1989b).

Most recently, Maletsky (1990) reported on his 1 to 17 year follow-up of almost 4,000 outpatient sex offenders. Almost three-fifths (57.8%) of his sample who evidenced pretreatment deviant arousal greater than 80% became treatment failures, whereas only 18.9% of the treatment successes evidenced such an arousal pattern. His definition of treatment success was an individual who completed all treatment sessions, did not evidence deviant arousal at the end of treatment, and had not been arrested for a sexual offense at follow-up. Unfortunately, Maletsky did not break his sample down by offense type or report the actual number of arrests or convictions.

Of the seven studies located for this review, six show positive correlations between deviant sexual arousal and reoffense. Although phallometric measures should never stand alone as predictors of sexual recidivism, in combination with other variables they provide an important data source.

IMPULSIVITY

Impulsivity has long been known to be a stable and robust predictor of reoffending among the general criminal population (Pritchard, 1979). Only recently has this variable been carefully examined in a sex-offender population. Prentky (1990) determined the recidivism rates of 106 rapists over a period of 25 years following their discharge from a maximum security treatment facility. His subjects were assessed as having either high and low lifestyle impulsivity. Decision criteria for impulsivity have been described in detail elsewhere (Prentky, Cohen, & Seghorn, 1985; Prentky & Knight, 1986); briefly, however, high impulsivity includes hyperactivity and behavior management problems beginning in late childhood, and instability in relationships, jobs, and living situations. Rapists in the high-impulsivity group were almost three times more likely to be convicted of new sexual offenses than those who were judged to be in the low-impulsivity group. The ability of this variable to have differentiated between recidivists and nonrecidivists is even more striking when one considers that the sample consisted of a fairly homogeneous group of highly repetitive rapists.

ALCOHOL ABUSE

Sexual aggression and alcohol are closely associated. Studies suggest that about half of all of sex offenses are committed by offenders who consumed alcohol at the time of their offense, and that about half of all sex offenders are alcoholic (e.g., Rada, 1976 Rada, Kellner, Laws, & Winslow, 1979). According to these studies, incest offenders tend to have the highest rate of drinking at the time of offense (63%). While male-oriented pedophiles drink alcohol less often than other sex offenders prior to committing offenses (38%), there seems to be little difference in the rates of offense-related drinking among extrafamilial female-target child molesters, rapists, and exhibitionists (57%, 57%, and 55%, respectively).

Alcohol can reduce inhibitions and social controls, as well as increase sexual arousal. Abel and colleagues (1985) found that 30% of the child molesters they studied reported that alcohol use increased their sexual arousal to children, and 45% of rapists reported a connection between alcohol use and increased urges to rape. These connections notwithstanding, in a recent thorough review of the literature on alcohol and human sexuality, Crowe and George (1989) conclude, "There is no suggestion that alcohol causes sexual aggression; rather, alcohol can facilitate a preexisting inclination to sexual aggression" (p. 384). Of course, many offenders do blame their deviant sexual behavior on alcohol, partly in an effort to avoid legal and other external consequences but also in an attempt to define themselves as "normal" people (McCaghy, 1968). Understandably, most individuals would rather be viewed as alcoholics than as sexual deviants.

PSYCHOPATHOLOGY

Besides sociopathy and substance abuse, sex offenders occasionally suffer from other forms of mental disorder. Knopp's (1984) review suggests that 5% to 8% percent of sex offenders have psychotic illnesses. Few studies examine recidivism rates for these offenders; however, Tracy and colleagues (1983) contend that recidivist sex offenders are generally not found to be psychotic.

Of course, common sense would suggest that a convicted dually diagnosed schizophrenic sex offender who is again hearing auditory hallucinations from the devil commanding him to rape women is at high risk to reoffend. Likewise, individuals with a history of sexually aggressive behavior who experience hypersexuality as a symptom of their manic-depressive illness are also at high risk to reoffend during the active manic phase of their illness. Appropriate psychotropic medication may greatly reduce the risk of reoffense for both of these types of conditions.

USE OF FORCE

There is ample evidence that offenders who use force in committing their offenses recidivate at a higher rate than those offenders who do not use force (Barbaree & Marshall, 1988; Gebhard, Gagnon, Pomeroy, & Christenson, 1965; Maletsky, 1990). Particularly prone to recidiviate may be those offenders whose sexual arousal is fused with aggression or sadism (Groth & Birnbaum, 1979; Hazelwood, Reboussin, & Warren, 1989; Rice et al., 1989b). Plethysmographic data may help identify offenders with these predispositions (Rice et al., 1989a).

An exception to these generalizations are the high rates of recidivism found among individuals who commit hands-off offenses such as exhibitionism, who, as mentioned earlier, are more likely to reoffend than other types of sex offenders. Nevertheless, from a practical point of view, society clearly seems much more willing to risk allowing a compulsive exhibitionist to remain in the community under supervision than to take a similar gamble with an offender whose first conviction has been for a violent sexual offense.

SOCIAL SUPPORTS

Especially in incest cases, the reactions of the offender's family and support network to the abuse can have a profound influence on his recovery process. If, for example, the offender's spouse sides with him in blaming the victim, denies his need for treatment and supervision, or believes that the abuse did not occur, it will be more difficult for the offender to take responsibility for his behavior, follow probation or parole conditions, and actively engage in treatment. Family and friends who continue to value their relationship with the offender, but at the same time hold him accountable for avoiding high-risk behaviors, can be a stabilizing and beneficial resource.

Offenders who do not, either through choice or circumstance, have a stable, supportive social network may be at a higher risk to reoffend. There are a number of studies that have found that convicted child molesters who are unmarried reoffend at a slight higher rate than offenders who are married (Abel, Mittleman, & Becker, 1985; Fitch, 1962; Maletsky, 1990).

EMPLOYMENT STATUS

Employment can be another stabilizing and positive influence on offenders. For example, Maletsky (1990) followed almost 4,000 outpatient sex offenders for between 1 and 17 years. Men who had worked at three or more jobs during the 3 years preceding their offense or were unemployed at the time of their offense were almost four times more likely to be treatment failures than men with more stable employment patterns. Maletsky defined treatment failure as not completing treatment, maintaining a deviant arousal pattern throughout treatment, or being arrested for a sexual offense.

OFFENDER AGE

Analysis of the Uniform Crime Reports for the United States (U.S. Department of Justice, 1988c) clearly reveals that rape is generally committed by young adult males. Men in the 20 to 29-year-old age bracket accounted for a larger proportion of arrests for rape (41.5%) than those in any other similar age span. Overall, men under the age of 40 accounted for 88.2% of all rape arrests. Unfortunately, other types of sexual offenses are not broken down by category in the Uniform Crime Reports, and one must rely on analysis of geographically limited studies. Studies reviewed by Blair and Lanyon (1981) suggest that exhibitionism, like rape, tends to be perpetrated by males in their late teens or twenties, and there seem to be relatively few males over age 40 who publicly expose themselves. The age at which incest offenders typically commit their offenses is not surprising; it seems to coincide with their parenting years, between the ages of 30 and 45 (Williams & Finkelhor, 1990).

These age ranges found to be typical of rapists and incest offenders are supported by the findings of Frisbie (1969), who in addition studied nonfamilial child molesters. In her sample of 91 men who had molested nonrelated minor females, she found that 42% were under the age of 30, whereas only 35% percent of the 55 men who had molested nonrelated minor males were under the age of 30. Further analysis of her findings suggests that molestation of nonrelated children of both sexes, but especially of male children, is perpetrated by offenders across the age span.

The courts customarily look askance at basing sentencing decisions on an offender's age, reasoning that this variable, like race, is outside the offender's control and is inherently prejudicial. Nevertheless, offender age appears to be related to the likelihood of recommitting an offense, so it should apply at least to decisions concerning intensity of supervision.

GROOMING OR ATTACK BEHAVIOR

The method that an offender uses to gain access to his victims may be related to risk of reoffense and is clearly related to the supervisability of the offender. Those offenders who develop lengthy preoffense relationships with their victims, as in the case of many child molesters, may provide a protracted window of opportunity for probation or parole officers and others to identify precursive offense behaviors and intervene with the offender prior to the commission of an actual offense. On the other hand, offenders whose prodromal phase is relatively brief, as is the case with many rapists, may give those that supervise them few observable warning signs.

Pithers, Buell, Kashima, Cumming, and Beal (1987) have identified a variety of emotional states that typically precede relapse among sex offenders. Child molesters commonly report feeling anxiety and depression prior to relapse, whereas rapists almost universally report feeling angry. Anger tends to be a relatively intense emotion that can be aroused quite quickly, so it may be comparatively more difficult for offenders to control than feelings of anxiety and depression, which tend to be less intense and often have a more gradual onset.

Studies by Barbaree and Marshall (1988) found that offenders whose sexual abuse of children had proceeded through the grooming process to the point of genital-to-genital contact had higher recidivism rates than those offenders who limited their sexual abuse to less intrusive behaviors.

VICTIM CHARACTERISTICS

Sexual abuse and assault is by definition the taking advantage of a weaker, more vulnerable person. Unfortunately, some offenders choose victims who are at such an extreme disadvantage that they cannot effectively fight back, even after being attacked. Offenders who assault very young children, or persons with mental illness or mental retardation or others with compromised intellectual and communication abilities are assaulting victims who cannot effectively report their abuse or provide credible testimony in court. Whether offenders who select these disadvantaged victims present an increased risk for reoffense remains an unanswered empirical question. At any rate, such offenders can be considered more dangerous in that their reoffenses may be more difficult to detect and certainly more difficult to prosecute.

LENGTH OF TIME AT RISK

Although recidivism rates continue to climb the longer sex offenders remain at risk in the community, the pace of recidivism seems to vary by offender type. For example, Frisbie (1969) found that, among her sample of formerly incarcerated rapists, reoffenses were more likely to occur during the first year following release and that the yearly rate of reoffense continued to decrease each year thereafter. The U.S. Department of Justice (1989) statistics indicate that slightly over half of all rapists released in 1983 were rearrested within three years and that they were 10.5 times more likely than other released felons to be rearrested for rape. Studies conducted on child molesters suggest that their reoffense curves are more gradual than those of rapists (Frisbie, 1969; Hanson et al., 1990).

ENVIRONMENTAL FACTORS

The preceding risk factors have all pertained directly to the offender himself, yet some environmental factors also appear to influence sexual aggression. Like the previous discussion of the length of time at risk, information from the following studies can be useful in directing supervision practices of sex offenders, but would not be germane to sentencing decisions.

Michael and Zumpe (1983) and the Uniform Crime Reports (U.S. Department of Justice, 1988c) have found large and statistically significant seasonal variations in the commission of rapes, with the maxima occurring in the summer months, even in states with consistently moderate climates. Cox (1980) has noted similar findings among exhibitionists. Time of day also seems to be an important factor among rapists: U.S. Department of Justice (1985) studies highlight that two-thirds of all rapes and rape attempts occur at night.

SUPERVISION AND TREATMENT RESOURCES

Another variable that may be outside an offender's control, but must also be considered a risk factor, is the availability of quality treatment and supervision resources. A relatively high-risk offender who is convicted in a jurisdiction in which there is a comprehensive outpatient sex-offender treatment program and a highly trained and well-equipped probation department may be considered appropriate for community probation. Yet a similarly high-risk offender who is convicted in a jurisdiction without these resources may not be able to be managed safely in the community.

MULTIPLE VARIABLES

Professionals who assess offender risk can benefit from examination of each of the forementioned individual variables. Unfortunately, generating a comprehensive risk-assessment tool by assigning the proper weight to each of these variables is a difficult task, as only a few researchers have undertaken the study of multivariate models of risk prediction with sex offenders.

Hall (1988) found that the combination of the factors of age, offense history, IQ, and MMPI scores resulted in improved accuracy in identifying sex offenders most likely to reoffend. Researchers in Canada (Rice et al., 1989a, 1989b) identified the combination of deviant arousal patterns and scores on the Psychopathy Checklist (Hare, 1980) as powerful predictors of recidivism among both rapists and child molesters. Factor analytic studies conducted by Barbaree and Marshall (1988) determined that a group of variables labeled "sexual deviance" correctly classified approximately 70% of successes and failures in their outpatient treatment program for child molesters. This cluster was comprised of deviant sexual arousal, amount of force, whether or not the offender had intercourse with the victim(s), and the number of previous victims. A number of ongoing research projects are attempting to identify the predictive ability of combinations of variables relative to sex offender recidivism (Bemus & Smith, 1988; Doke, 1989; Prentky, 1989).

DISPOSITION PLANNING: COMMUNITY OR INCARCERATED PLACEMENT

The two central issues that must be examined in order to formulate a sex-offender disposition plan — amenability to treatment and risk factors — have been described in the first two sections of this article. Based on this information, evaluators typically have four general disposition options: incarceration without treatment, incarceration with treatment, community supervision with treatment, and community supervision without treatment.

Whether or not an offender is amenable to treatment is a relatively clear-cut issue and has been discussed. Whether to place a convicted sex offender initially in a secure setting, such as a jail, hospital, or halfway house, or in a community setting under the supervision of probation or parole, is a more difficult decision. Placement decisions are by necessity subjective determinations as to the relative risk that different offenders present to the community. The degree of risk tolerated in different locales varies considerably. For example, according to United States Department of Justice (1988b) statistics, during 1984 in both Vermont and Minnesota, for each offender who was in a jail or prison, approximately eight offenders lived in the community under the supervision of probation or parole. This one-to-eight ratio contrasts significantly with the approximately one-to-two ratio found in states such as Arizona and Alabama. The latter states appear to rely more frequently on incarceration for community protection, as well as perhaps for reasons of punishment and deterrence. These examples are offered to highlight the fact that guidelines for disposition are profoundly influenced by local laws, mores, and conventions.

Since empirically validated multivariate risk-assessment instruments have yet to be developed, disposition decisions can be facilitated by consideration of the empirical and clinical variables outlined in the preceding sections of this paper. In addition, the following suggestions and the decision tree in Figure 1 incorporate and are in concert with clinically and intuitively based guidelines formulated by others (Groth, Hobson, & Gary, 1982; Knopp, 1984).

Offenders who are not considered amenable to treatment are generally recommended for incarceration. Certainly this is well justified for high-risk offenders, but decisions to incarcerate nonamenable offenders who are low recidivism risks pose a more difficult challenge. Nevertheless, it is important to consider that low-risk offenders who are ambivalent about rehabilitation efforts may become motivated to enroll in treatment if they are aware that failure to do so will result in more severe punishments.

Other offender variables that are considered contraindications for community placement include history of using extensive violence, force, or weapons in the commission of offenses. Offenders whose sexual interests are fixated on illegal behaviors, such as sex with children and other nonconsensual sexual activity, and who have no history of consensual adult sexual functioning, may also be considered poor risks for community placement. Likewise, offenders who commit ritualistic or bizarre offenses should be placed in a secure setting. Extensive criminality and predatoriness are other poor risk factors.

Evaluators who assess dually diagnosed sex offenders should investigate carefully the primacy of each disorder. Sex offenders who suffer from a psychotic illness may require psychiatric hospitalization and psychotropic medication, but may not need specialized sex offender treatment. Intervention with alcoholic sex offenders may consist of either inpatient alcohol treatment or outpatient alcohol services. In any case, abstinence from

Disposition Planning with Sex Offenders[1]

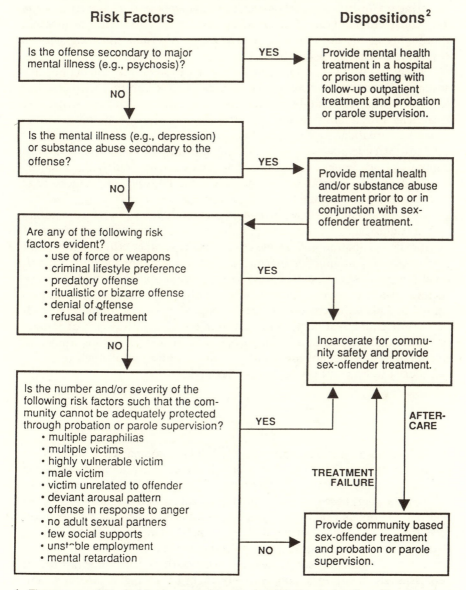

Risk Factors

Dispositions[2]

Is the offense secondary to major mental illness (e.g., psychosis)? — **YES** → Provide mental health treatment in a hospital or prison setting with follow-up outpatient treatment and probation or parole supervision.

NO ↓

Is the mental illness (e.g., depression) or substance abuse secondary to the offense? — **YES** → Provide mental health and/or substance abuse treatment prior to or in conjunction with sex-offender treatment.

NO ↓

Are any of the following risk factors evident?
- use of force or weapons
- criminal lifestyle preference
- predatory offense
- ritualistic or bizarre offense
- denial of offense
- refusal of treatment

YES → Incarcerate for community safety and provide sex-offender treatment.

NO ↓

Is the number and/or severity of the following risk factors such that the community cannot be adequately protected through probation or parole supervision? — **YES**
- multiple paraphilias
- multiple victims
- highly vulnerable victim
- male victim
- victim unrelated to offender
- deviant arousal pattern
- offense in response to anger
- no adult sexual partners
- few social supports
- unstable employment
- mental retardation

NO → Provide community based sex-offender treatment and probation or parole supervision.

AFTER-CARE

TREATMENT FAILURE

1. The purpose of this decision tree is to aid professionals in developing disposition plans that address the sentencing goals of community safety and rehabilitation. The decision tree does not address the sentencing goals of punishment or deterrence.
2. If the offender is not amenable to treatment or fails to make adequate progress in treatment, he should be incapacitated by incarceration or community supervision measures to reduce his opportunity to reoffend.

Figure 1

185

alcohol must be mandatory with this population and should occur prior to initiating treatment of sexual deviancy. Individuals with mental retardation vary considerably in their functional ability and therefore must be assessed thoroughly at the beginning of treatment, to determine their capacity to control their deviant sexual behavior in the community.

Clearly, offenders who have a history of multiple convictions for sexual and nonsexual offenses need incarceration to control their behavior. Offenders who reoffend despite having completed specialized sex offender treatment presumably require incarceration or, at a minimum, more intensive outpatient treatment and supervision.

Sex offenders whose lives are chaotic and unstable may be poor community placement risks. These individuals are often difficult to supervise and require assistance with employment, housing, and other social supports prior to treatment for their sexual deviancy.

Almost all convicted sex offenders eventually return to the community and a significant number never serve any jail time. The crafting of appropriate probation and parole conditions is another critical component of disposition planning for offenders. Model conditions have been developed (Oregon Department of Corrections, 1988) and should address risk factors specific to each offender (Pithers et al., 1987). Generally conditions should include requirements to enroll in and successfully complete specialized sex offender treatment, to refrain from establishing any type of contact with potential victims, to avoid high-risk behaviors (e.g., pornography use, hitchhiking, and alcohol use), and to allow monitoring of one's behavior (e.g., drug testing and property searches).

CONCLUSION

Disposition planning with sex offenders encompasses a number of important decisions that can profoundly influence the rehabilitation of the offender and the safety of the community. Effective decision making with this population is based on a thorough evaluation of an offender's strengths and risk factors and on an analysis of available treatment and supervision resources. Since the expertise that is required in making these types of decisions rarely rests within any one individual or discipline, the courts, correctional agencies, social service organizations, and mental health professionals must work cooperatively in order to make informed and professional judgments. Disposition plans should not be influenced by misinformation, politics, or fear, but should be solidly grounded in clinical experience, empirical knowledge, and availability of specialized resources. Rehabilitation of offenders who show potential for change is imperative, while protection of the community must remain a continual priority.

REFERENCES

Abel, G., Becker, J., Cunningham-Rathner, J., Mittleman, M., & Rouleau, J. (1988). Multiple paraphilic diagnoses among sex offenders. *Bulletin of the American Academy of Psychiatry and the Law, 16,* 153-168.

Abel, G., Becker, J., Cunningham-Rathner, J., Rouleau, J., & Murphy, W. (1987). Self-reported sex crimes of nonincarcerated paraphiliacs. *Journal of Interpersonal Violence, 2,* 3-35.

Abel, G., Mittleman, M., & Becker, J. (1985). Sexual offenders: Results of assessment and recommendations for treatment. In M. H. Ben-Aron, S. J. Hucker, & C. D. Webster (Eds.), *Clinical criminology: Current concepts* (pp. 191-205). Toronto: M&M Graphics.

Abel, G., Mittleman, M., Becker, J., Rathner, J., & Rouleau, J. (1988). Predicting child molesters' response to treatment. In R. A. Prentky & V. L. Quinsey (Eds.), *Human sexual aggression: Current perspectives* (pp. 223-234). New York: New York Academy of Sciences.

Barbaree, H., & Marshall, W. (1988). Deviant sexual arousal, offense history, and demographic variables as predictors of reoffense among child molesters. *Behavioral Sciences and the Law, 6,* 267-280.

Barnard, G., Fuller, A., Robbins, L., & Shaw, T. (1989). *The child molester: An integrated approach to evaluation and treatment.* New York: Brunner/Mazel.

Beck, A., & Shipley, B. (1989). *Recidivism of prisoners released in 1983.* Washington, DC: U.S. Department of Justice.

Bemus, B., & Smith, R. (1988). Assessment of sex offender risk. *Perspectives, Fall,* 16-18.

Blair, C., & Lanyon, R. (1981). Exhibitionism: Etiology and Treatment. *Psychological Bulletin, 89,* 439-463.

Cox, D. (1980). Exhibitionism: An overview. In D. J. Cox & R. J. Daitzman (Eds.), *Exhibitionism: Description, assessment, and treatment* (pp. 3-10). New York: Garland.

Crowe, L., & George, W. (1989). Alcohol and human sexuality: Review and Integration. *Psychological Bulletin, 105,* 374-386.

Doke, J. (1989). *Standardized risk assessment scales for incarcerated sex offenders.* Paper presented at the Association for the Behavioral Treatment of Sex Abusers 8th Annual Research and Data Conference, Seattle, WA.

Fitch, J. (1962). Men convicted of sexual offenses against children: A descriptive follow-up study. *British Journal of Criminology, 3,* 18-37.

Frisbie, L. (1969). *Another look at sex offenders in California. Mental Health Research Monograph (No. 12).* Sacramento: State of California, Department of Mental Hygiene.

Furby, L., Weinrott, M., & Blackshaw, L. (1989). Sex offender recidivism: A review. *Psychological Bulletin, 105,* 3-30.

Gebhard, P., Gagnon, J., Pomeroy, W., & Christenson, C. (1965). *Sex offenders: An analysis of types.* New York: Harper and Row.

Gibbins, T., Soothill, K., & Way, C. (1978). Sibling and parent-child incest offenders. *British Journal of Criminology, 18,* 40-52.

Gibbins, T., Soothill, K., & Way, C. (1981). Sex offenses against young girls: A long-term record study. *Psychological Medicine, 11,* 351-357.

Giarretto, H. (1982). A comprehensive child sexual abuse treatment program. *Child Abuse and Neglect, 6,* 363-278.

Groth, A., & Birnbaum, H. (1979). *Men who rape: The psychology of the offender.* New York: Plenum.

Groth, A., Hobson, W., & Gary, T. (1982). The child molester: Clinical observations. In J. Conte & D. Shore (Eds.), *Social work and child sexual abuse* (pp. 129-144). New York: Haworth.

Groth, A., Longo, R., & McFadin, J. (1982). Undetected recidivism among rapists and child molesters. *Crime and Delinquency, 28,* 450-458.

Hall, G. (1988). Criminal behavior as a function of clinical and actuarial variables in a sex offender population. *Journal of Consulting and Clinical Psychology, 56,* 773-775.

Hall, G. (1990). Prediction of sexual aggression. *Clinical Psychology Review, 10,* 229-245.

Hanson, R., Steffy, R., & Gauthier, R. (1990). *Long-term follow-up of treated child molesters in Canada.* Paper presented at the Ninth Annual Clinical and Research Conference on the Assessment and Treatment of Sexual Abusers, Their Families, and Victims, Toronto, Canada.

Hare, R. (1980). A research scale for the assessment of psychopathy in criminal populations. *Personality and Individual Differences, 1,* 111-119.

Hazelwood, R., Reboussin, R., & Warren, J. (1989). Serial rape: Correlates of increased aggression and the relationship of offender pleasure to victim resistance. *Journal of Interpersonal Violence, 4,* 65-78.

Knopp, F. (1984). *Retraining adult sex offenders: Methods and models.* Syracuse, NY: Safer Society Press.

Knopp, F., & Stevenson, W. F. (1989). *Nationwide survey of juvenile and adult sex-offender treatment programs and models: 1988.* Orwell, VT: The Safer Society Program.

Knopp, F., & Stevenson, W. F. (1990). *Nationwide survey of juvenile and adult sex-offender treatment programs: 1990.* Orwell, VT: The Safer Society Program.

Laynon, R. (1986). Theory and treatment in child molestation. *Journal of Consulting and Clinical Psychology, 54,* 176-182.

Longo, R., & Groth, A. (1983). Juvenile sexual offenses in the histories of adult rapists and child molesters. *International Journal of Offender Therapy and Comparative Criminology, 27,* 150-155.

Maletsky, B. (1990). *Treating the sexual offender.* Newbury Park, CA: Sage.

Marshall, W., & Barbaree, H. (1988). The long-term evaluation of a behavioral treatment program for child molesters. *Behavior Research and Therapy, 26,* 499-511.

Marshall, W., & Barbaree, H. (1990). Outcome of comprehensive cognitive-behavioral treatment programs. In W. L. Marshall, D. R. Laws, & H. E. Barbaree (Eds.), *Handbook of sexual assault: Issues, theories, and treatment of offenders* (pp. 363-385). New York: Plenum.

Marques, J., Day, D., Nelson, C., & Miner, M. (1989). *The sex offender treatment and evaluation project: Third report to the Legislature in response to PC 1365.* Sacramento, CA: California Department of Mental Health.

McCaghy, C. (1968). Drinking and deviance disavowel: The case of child molesters. *Social Problems, 16,* 43-49.

McGrath, R. (1990). Assessment of sexual aggressors: Practical clinical interviewing strategies. *Journal of Interpersonal Violence, 5,* 507-519.

Melton, G., Petrila, J., Poythress, N., & Slobogin, C. (1987). *Psychological evaluation for the courts: A handbook for mental health professionals and lawyers.* New York: Guilford.

Michael, R., & Zumpe, D. (1983). Sexual violence in the United States and the role of season. *American Journal of Psychiatry, 140,* 883-886.

Monahan, J. (1981). *Predicting violent behavior: An assessment of clinical techniques.* Beverly Hills, CA: Sage Publications.

O'Connell, M., Leberg, E., & Donaldson, C. (1990). *Working with sex offenders: Guidelines for therapist selection.* Newbury Park, CA: Sage.

Oregon Department of Corrections (1988). Suggested parole conditions. In B. K. Schwartz (Ed.), *A practitioner's guide to treating the incarcerated male sex offender* (pp. 213-214). Washington, DC: U.S. Department of Justice.

Pithers, W., Buell, M., Kashima, K., Cumming, G., & Beal, L. (1987). *Precursors to relapse of sexual offenders.* Paper presented at the first meeting of the Association for the Advancement of Behavior Therapy for Sexual Abusers, Newport, OR.

Pithers, W., & Cumming, G. (1989). Can relapses be prevented? Initial outcome data from the Vermont Treatment Program for Sexual Aggressors. In D. R. Laws (Ed.), *Relapse prevention with sex offenders* (313–325). New York: Guilford Press.

Prentky, R. (1989). *Development of a risk assessment scale for child molesters.* Paper presented at the Association for the Behavioral Treatment of Sex Abusers 8th Annual Research and Data Conference, Seattle, WA.

Prentky, R. (1990). *Sexual violence: A review.* Paper presented at the Ninth Annual Clinical and Research Conference on the Assessment and Treatment of Sexual Abusers, Their Families and Victims, Toronto, Canada.

Prentky, R., & Burgess, A. (1990). Rehabilitation of child molesters: A cost benefit analysis. *American Journal of Orthopsychiatry, 60,* 108–117.

Prentky, R., Cohen, M., & Seghorn, T. (1985). Development of a rational taxonomy for the classification of sexual offenders: Rapists. *Bulletin of the American Academy of Psychiatry and the Law, 13,* 39–70.

Prentky, R., & Knight, R. (1986). Impulsivity in the lifestyle and criminal behavior of sexual offenders. *Criminal Justice and Behavior, 13,* 141–164.

Pritchard, D. (1979). Stable predictors of recidivism: A summary. *Criminology, 17,* 15–21.

Quinsey, V. (1983). Prediction of recidivism and the evaluation of treatment programs for sex offenders. In S. N. Verdun-Jones & A. A. Keltner (Eds.), *Sexual aggression and the law* (pp. 27–40). Burnaby, BC: Criminology Research Centre Press.

Quinsey, V. (1977). The assessment and treatment of child molesters: A review. *Canadian Psychological Review, 18,* 204–220.

Quinsey, V. (1990). *Strategies for assessment, treatment, and management of sexual offenders.* Paper presented at the Ninth Annual Clinical and Research Conference on the Assessment and Treatment of Sexual Abusers, Their Families, and Victims, Toronto, Canada.

Quinsey, V., Chaplin, T., & Carrigan, W. (1980). Biofeedback and signaled punishment in the modification of sexual age preferences. *Behavior Therapy, 11,* 567–576.

Quinsey, V., & Marshall, W. (1983). Procedures for reducing inappropriate sexual arousal: An evaluation review. In J. G. Greer & I. R. Stuart (Eds.), *The sexual aggressor: Current perspectives on treatment* (pp. 267–289). New York: Van Nostrand Reinhold.

Rada, R. (1976). Alcoholism and the child molester. *Annals of New York Academy of Sciences, 273,* 492–496.

Rada, R., Kellner, R., Laws, D., & Winslow, W. (1979). Drinking, alcoholism, and the mentally disordered sex offender. *Bulletin of the American Academy of Psychiatry and Law, 6,* 296–300.

Radzinowicz, L. (Ed.). (1957). *Sexual offenses: A report of the Cambridge Department of Criminal Science.* London: Macmillan.

Rice, M., Harris, G., & Quinsey, V. (1989a). *Sexual recidivism among child molesters.* (Research Report, Volume VI, No. 3). Penetanguishene, Ontario: Penetanguishene Mental Health Centre.

Rice, M., Harris, G., & Quinsey, V. (1989b). *A followup of rapists assessed in a maximum security facility.* (Research Report, Volume VI, No. 4). Penetanguishene, Ontario: Penetanguishene Mental Health Centre.

Romero, J., & Williams, L. (1985). Recidivism among convicted sex offenders: A 10-year followup study. *Federal Probation, 49,* 58–64.

Salter, A. (1988). *Treating child sex offenders and their victims: A practical guide.* Newbury Park, CA: Sage Publications.

Sawyer, J. (1966). Measurement and prediction: Clinical and statistical. *Psychological Bulletin, 66,* 178–200.

Simkins, L., Ward, W., Bowman, S., & Rinck, C. (1989). The Multiphasic Sex Inventory: Diagnosis and prediction of treatment response in child sexual abusers. *Annals of Sex Research, 2,* 205–226.

Sturgeon, V., & Taylor, J. (1980). Report of a five-year follow-up study of mentally disordered sex offenders released from Atascadero State Hospital in 1973. *Criminal Justice Journal, 4,* 31–63.

Trepper, T., & Barrett, M. (1989). *Systemic treatment of incest: A therapeutic handbook.* New York: Brunner/Mazel.

Tracy, F., Donnelly, H., Morgenbesser, L., & MacDonald, D. (1983). Program Evaluation: Recidivism research involving sex offenders. In J. G. Greer & I. R. Stuart (Eds.), *The sexual aggressor: Current perspectives on treatment* (pp. 198–213). New York: Van Nostrand Reinhold.

Turk, D., & Salovey, P. (Eds.). (1988). *Reasoning, inference, and judgment in clinical psychology.* New York: Free Press.

United States Department of Justice. (1985). *The crime of rape.* (Report No. NCJ-96777) Washington, DC: Author.

United States Department of Justice. (1988a). *An administrator's overview: Questions and answers on issues related to the incarcerated male sex offender.* Washington, DC: Author.

United States Department of Justice. (1988b). *Report to the nation on crime and justice: Second edition.* (Report No. NCJ-105506) Washington, DC: Author.

United States Department of Justice. (1988c). *Uniform crime reports for the United States: 1987.* Washington, DC: U.S. Government Printing Office.

United States Department of Justice. (1989). *Recidivism of prisoners released in 1983.* (Report No. NCJ-116261) Washington, DC: Author.

Williams, L., & Finkelhor, D. (1990). The characteristics of incestuous fathers: A review of recent studies. In W. L. Marshall, D. R. Laws, & H. E. Barbaree (Eds.), *The handbook of sexual assault: Issues, theories, and treatment of the offender* (pp. 231–255). New York: Plenum Press.

Robert J. McGrath, M.A.
Director, Sex Offender Treatment
Counseling Service of Addison County
89 Main Street
Middlebury, Vermont 05753
USA

EVALUATION OF TREATMENT OUTCOME FOR ADULT PERPETRATORS OF CHILD SEXUAL ABUSE

JUDITH V. BECKER
University of Arizona
JOHN A. HUNTER, JR.
The Pines Residential Treatment Center

This article reviews therapy outcome studies on adult sexual perpetrators of child victims. The majority of studies reviewed indicate relatively low recidivism rates for treated child molesters. Future research issues are discussed.

C hildren in our society continue to fall prey to individuals who use them to meet their own emotional and sexual needs. A considerable body of literature has begun to amass on the prevalence of sexual abuse (Badgley et al., 1984; Finkelhor, 1984; Russell, 1983; Wyatt, 1985), the impact abuse has on children and on the victim during the lifespan (Browne & Finkelhor, 1986), and the treatment of sexual abuse. Within the past 30 years case reports and clinical research studies also have been published on the perpetrators of child sexual abuse. These studies have described typologies, discussed the

AUTHORS' NOTE: *The authors wish to thank Maryruth Farrell and Kevin Russell for their assistance. Correspondence may be addressed to Judith V. Becker, Department of Psychiatry, College of Medicine, Health Sciences Center, University of Arizona, Tucson, AZ 85724.*

CRIMINAL JUSTICE AND BEHAVIOR, Vol. 19 No. 1, March 1992 74-92

assessment of child sexual abusers, and described treatment for this population.

The purpose of this article is to review those studies that have described and/or evaluated treatment outcome for adult perpetrators of child sexual abuse. Although both men and women have committed sexual offenses against children, the majority of reported cases of child sexual abuse involve a male perpetrator. Because no therapy outcome studies with female perpetrators were found in the literature, this review will focus on male perpetrators. Both adolescent and adult males have committed sexual offenses against children. Clinical researchers are beginning to evaluate treatment strategies with adolescent sexual offenders, but in general controlled therapy outcome studies are lacking. Consequently, this review will focus on the treatment of adult males who perpetrate sexual offenses against children.

DEFINITIONS

The term child molester is frequently used to describe a person who has engaged in sexual activity with a child. The term, however, does not in and of itself provide us with specific behavioral characteristics of the perpetrator or typography of the offense. The person so labeled may have engaged in sexual activity with a child on one occasion and not have a paraphilia per se. A paraphilia as described in the *Diagnostic and Statistical Manual of Mental Disorders—Revised (DSM-III-R*; American Psychiatric Association, 1987) is defined as behavior characterized by repetitive sexual acts that involve nonconsenting partners, or a preference for the use of a nonhuman object for sexual arousal. The term pedophile applies to adults who have urges and fantasies involving sexual activity with prepubescent children and have either acted on these urges or are distressed by them. The child might be a relative, acquaintance, or a perfect stranger; male or female in gender, and the sexual activity might consist of fondling or vaginal, anal, or oral penetration.

ETIOLOGICAL THEORIES

Various theories have been put forth to explain why some adults engage in sexual activity with children. Treatment usually follows from these theoretical models. Psychoanalytic theory relates the cause to conflicts or trauma experienced in early childhood and espouses the premise that the molester is "fixated" at an infantile level and therefore chooses an immature sexual object. Such theorists view paraphilia as an expression of unresolved problems in childhood development (Bell & Hall, 1976; Cook & Howells, 1981; Storr, 1964).

Finkelhor and his colleagues (1986) have proposed a 4-factor theory to explain why adults commit sex offenses against children. These factors are (a) emotional congruence (why offenders need to relate to children emotionally); (b) sexual arousal (why adults are sexually aroused to children); (c) blockage (why offenders do not have alternative sources of gratification); and (d) disinhibition (why normal prohibitions do not stop the offenses).

Numerous researchers cite social learning theory approaches as important contributing factors to the development and maintenance of pedophilia. They emphasize the importance of modeling and conditioning experiences. It has been suggested that early sexual behavior with immature peers may play a role in the conditioning of deviant arousal. McGuire, Carlisle, and Young (1965) have postulated that learning is established by the process of fantasizing the initial deviant experience. They theorize that the sexual perpetrator frequently recalls his first sexual experience. The repeated pairing of these fantasies with orgasm results in their acquiring sexually arousing properties, which are continually reinforced.

Several researchers have investigated the role of androgens, principally testosterone, the hormone most responsible for male sexual behavior (Bancroft, 1983; Bradford & McLean, 1984).

TREATMENT

Several authors have reviewed treatment studies conducted with child molesters (Furby, Weinrott, & Blackshaw, 1989; Kelly, 1982;

Quinsey, 1986). Marshall, Ward, Jones, Johnston, and Barbaree (1991), in their article entitled "An Optimistic Evaluation of Treatment Outcome With Sex Offenders," note that previous reviews have taken one of two methodological stances in the evaluation of treatment outcome studies with sex offenders. They note that Furby et al. (1989) took a "methodologically ideal approach." According to Marshall et al. (1991), this approach tends to be used by those individuals who are not actively involved in clinical service and for whom tight experimental designs and statistical significance are of paramount importance. On the other hand, the authors note that clinicians who are not researchers might take a "methodologically indifferent" perspective in which methodology does not appear to be of primary importance. This review will focus on treatment outcome recognizing the importance of good methodology as well as some of the limitations in research design given the clinical population being served.

BIOLOGICAL/ORGANIC TREATMENTS

Three forms of organic treatments for sex offenders have been reported in the literature: antiandrogens and other hormonal treatments, surgical castration, and stereotaxic neurosurgery. As noted by Bradford (1988), the latter two forms of treatment are only of theoretical and academic interest in that it is highly unlikely that these treatments would be employed in North America.

In Europe, castration was mostly used in cases of rape and homosexual pedophilia. Heim and Hursch (1979) provide an extensive review and critique of the literature on the surgical castration of sex offenders. Although low recidivism rates have been reported, these authors conclude that there is no scientific (based on methodological problems with studies conducted to date) or ethical basis for the use of surgical castration in the treatment of sex offenders.

The most extensively used antiandrogenic medications include Medroxyprogesterone Acetate (MPA) and Cyproterone Acetate (CPA). These medications represent a pharmacological method of reducing the sexual drive and thereby affecting the sexual behavior of offenders. Berlin and Meinecke (1981) report on the treatment of 20 chronic paraphiliac male patients treated with MPA. These included 10 cases of homosexual pedophilia, 1 case of homosexual incest, 1 case of bisexual pedophilia, and 1 case of heterosexual pedophilia. The remaining cases were exhibitionism or voyeurism. These authors report that only 3 of the 20 patients showed recurrence of sexually deviant behavior while taking medication. Of those 3 cases, two involved homosexual pedophilia. The recidivism rate, however, increased dramatically when the patients discontinued their medication. Eleven of the 20 patients discontinued MPA against medical advice. Of those 11, 10 relapsed: 5 were cases of homosexual pedophilia, 1 of bisexual pedophilia, and 1 person was an individual whose behavior was diagnosed as both heterosexual pedophilia and voyeurism. These authors do not report if relapse was measured by self-report of the patients or whether these patients were arrested. Also, objective measures of arousal such as penile plethysmography were not used in this study. The authors concluded that their data indicate that men appear to do well in response to antiandrogenic medications as long as they continue taking it.

Cordoba and Chapel (1983) report on the treatment of a heterosexual pedophile with MPA. Serum testosterone levels were taken over a period of 500 days while he remained on the medication. The patient reported decreased libido and/or significant decrease in sexual fantasies, although the orientation of his fantasies did not change. Two weeks after the onset of MPA treatment a decrease in serum testosterone, FSH and LH were measured. The authors note, however, that serum testosterone level was not an absolute indicator of decreased sex drive. No follow-up data were presented.

More recently, Kiersch (1990) reported on the use of MPA in the treatment of eight court-committed sexual offenders. Six of the men were pedophiles (two were bisexual pedophiles and in the other four cases the gender of the victims was not specified). The patients served as their own controls and received alternating MPA injections for 16 weeks followed by saline injections for a corresponding 16 weeks (alternating for a period of 64 weeks). The effectiveness of MPA was evaluated by patient's self-reports, serum testosterone levels, and penile plethysmography. Only four of the eight patients completed the entire protocol. These authors reported that although the patients self-reported desirable changes in sex drive, the majority did not experience the expected results from MPA versus saline injections. Additionally, penile plethysmography measures were too variable and inconsistent to evaluate the necessary MPA dosage to reduce penile responding. Although a follow-up period was not specified, the authors do note that four of the patients were returned to court for sentencing. Three remained in the hospital and one was released on an outpatient treatment status and re-offended 1 year later and subsequently was returned to prison. The Kiersch (1990) study is noteworthy in that it did use a quasi-experimental design and three categories of dependent measures were also used: self-report, serum testosterone levels, and sexual arousal assessment. Future research on the use of MPA should focus on and specify the following: the gender of the victims (the Kiersch 1990 study did not indicate for four of the cases what the victim gender was); measures other than self-report and serum testosterone levels should be used, such as penile plethysmography (only the Kiersch study used penile plethysmography); factors related to noncompliance should be assessed; and a placebo condition such as that used by Kiersch should be included.

Data to date appear to indicate that MPA may be of use to some paraphiliac individuals in reducing their sexual drive and fantasies; however, it does not affect sexual orientation. Consequently, controlled therapy outcome studies should investigate the use of MPA along with an active therapeutic intervention which specifically targets the inappropriate sexual fantasies and behaviors.

Bradford and Pawlak (1987) report on the use of Cyproterone Acetate in the treatment of a 23-year-old sadistic homosexual pedophile. Prior to treatment with CPA, the patient had received a variety of behavioral treatment techniques over a 5-year period in an attempt to alter his deviant sexual arousal pattern. This case report is of particular interest in that it is the first published report in which erection measurement was used to assess the impact of CPA on penile responding. Results indicated that CPA reduced the deviant pedophiliac arousal and increased the ability to suppress this arousal. The patient's ability to control his sexual arousal was noted by the authors to be considerably improved; however, they stated that this improvement appeared to be due to the cognitive components of sexual arousal.

197

The patient also maintained the improvement at a 22-week follow up. The authors hypothesize that during the 3-month suppression of deviant sexual fantasy, the cognitive antecedents to it may have been disrupted. They also suggest that it is possible that the androgen receptor sensitivity continues to be suppressed for as long as 22 weeks post-CPA administration. The authors propose that a further explanation might be related to the possibility that the reduction of deviant sexual behavior in relation to the CPA treatment interrupted the conditioned behavioral response. This case is of particular importance given that a differential effect of CPA on sexual arousal pattern was reported.

Bradford (1988) reports on a double blind placebo crossover study with 12 sexual offenders using CPA. The specific type of paraphilias of those sex offenders was not mentioned. He reports that CPA reduced testosterone, LH, and FSH during the active treatment as compared to placebo and baseline phases. Sexual arousal as measured by penile tumescence measures was also decreased by CPA as compared to placebo. Follow-up information regarding recidivism on those treated individuals was not provided.

CPA appears to be effective in reducing sexual drive, increasing the ability to suppress deviant arousal, and in the case report by Bradford and Pawlak (1987), differentially effecting the sexual arousal pattern. Future research should focus on whether or not there is a differential impact of CPA on those individuals with homosexual versus heterosexual versus bisexual pedophilia, and on the long-term outcome of CPA treated perpetrators. Future studies should also focus on elucidating the exact manner in which this treatment affects the cognitive components of sexual arousal.

Perilstein, Lipper, and Friedman (1991) used Fluoxetine in the treatment of three cases of paraphilias. One patient was a 26-year-old male who was preoccupied with male pedophiliac fantasies which he had not acted on. After 1 year of psychotherapy with no reduction of symptoms, he was placed on Fluoxetine. After 5 weeks of medication he self-reported a dramatic reduction in pedophiliac fantasies and frequency of masturbation. It is important to note that the patient also experienced retarded ejaculation and loss of interest in sex with his wife. No measures other than self-report data were collected and long-term follow-up data was not reported. Controlled outcome studies with sufficient sample sizes should be conducted. As with MPA, the potential side effects may provide difficulty in compliance with some patients.

TRADITIONAL THERAPIES

Psychoanalysis and psychodynamic therapy have been used in treating people with paraphilias. Identification and resolution of early conflicts, trauma, and humiliation are thought to remove the individual's anxiety toward appropriate partners and enable the patient to give up the paraphiliac fantasies. Unfortunately, evaluating results is extremely complicated because there are no common standards of measurement. Moreover, several investigators have reported disappointment with the results of psychoanalysis or psychotherapy as the sole form of treatment in cases of deviant sexual behavior (Cook & Howells, 1981). An exception is the study published by Stava (1984). A bisexual male pedophile in his early 20s was treated with hypnotic uncovering techniques of induced dreams. Dependent measures included a number of projective techniques (human figure drawings and Rorschach) as well as penile tumescent measurement. Although the author indicated that the patient had molested 20 male and female children, only female stimuli were presented during the plethysmograph evaluation. There was a significant pre-post therapy decrease in erectile response to pictures of female children. The patient also self-reported a decrease in sexual arousal to children. Long term follow-up results were not reported. It is important to note that the patient was committed and was a patient at a state mental hospital during the course of the treatment. Although the patient had off-grounds, self-escorted activities which brought him into contact with children, he had 6 years left to serve on his commitment.

GROUP THERAPIES

Romero and Williams (1983) report on a 10-year follow-up study of 231 male sex offenders (48 pedophiles) who were randomly assigned to either group therapy and probation or probation only. Results indicated that 13.6% of the men in group therapy recidivated as compared to 7.2% of the men who received probation only. Recidivism was measured by re-arrest. Exhibitionists had the highest sex offense recidivism rate among the sex offenders. No significant differences in sex offense recidivism was found for the other subgroups. The authors found that the best predictor of re-arrest was rate of arrest for sex offenses per year prior to intervention. The authors acknowledge that a problem exists in only using arrest data. Specifically, that undetected crime is quite extensive among sex offenders and that official data may reveal only a small percentage of the total sexual offenses committed. The authors also point out that although the probation-only group did not participate in group psychotherapy, this did not mean that they were excluded from potential "treatment" by contact with their probation officers who were experienced in assisting the probationers in numerous ways.

In essence, these results indicate that probation and the supervision that it affords the perpetrator appear to be effective in the majority of cases in assisting them in not acting out on their atypical sexual urges during probation. Future research might consist of random assignment to three groups: probation only, probation plus therapy, and therapy only. Dependent measures should include self-report data (the person interviewed by someone not in the probation department and not connected with the study), and the subject interviewed under a condition of confidentiality), plethysmography, and reviewing arrest records. Also, whether or not an individual on his own or at the recommendation of the probation officer receives therapy should be recorded and controlled for in data analysis. Further, it would be important to conduct a follow-up of these men after they have been discharged from their probationary status.

Lang, Pugh, and Langevin (1988) describe a multimodal treatment for incest offenders ($n = 29$) and heterosexual pedophiles ($n = 27$). All subjects had acknowledged their sexual offenses and had volunteered to participate in the treatment. Treatment was on an inpatient basis and consisted of group psychotherapy (non-Freudian, daily community meetings, social skills training, anger management, human sexuality, psychodrama, films discussing victims, and stress inoculation). Phallometric monitoring of sexual arousal patterns was conducted. Adjunctive therapies including family, marital, and relationship enhancement were also used when indicated.

Both groups showed improvement on 16 of 19 dependent measures. Incest offenders as compared to pedophiles showed marked treatment improvement on five factors: trait anxiety, fear of negative evaluation, social-skills deficits, indirect hostility, and irritability. The authors hypothesize these findings to be a function of marital status (married subjects showed more improvement). Pedophiles on the whole appeared to be more treatment resistant. By the end of a 3-year follow-up, 7% of the incest offenders and 18% of the pedophiles had reoffended. Reoffense data was obtained from information provided by the Royal Canadian Offender Profiles, parole and probation reports, and community or outpatient clinical contacts. As with the previous study, it was recommended that an individual not connected with the project interview participants under a certificate of confidentiality and anonymously to determine whether or not any further sex offenses had been committed and self-reported by the participants.

FAMILY THERAPY

Giarretto, Giarretto, and Sgroi (1978) described a community-based treatment program for families in which incest has occurred. Based on his experience with more than 600 of these families, Giarretto (1978) stated that the primary emphasis of the program should be to maintain family integrity. In addition, he feels that the authority of the criminal justice system is essential in treating incest cases. Program drop outs have largely been those men who were not under criminal justice system supervision. The treatment program combines individual therapy with group therapy and self-help groups. Giarretto (1982) reported that no recidivism had been reported in the more than 600 families who received a minimum of 10 hours of treatment and whose cases had been formally terminated. Unfortunately, data regarding length of follow-up recidivism rates are not reported.

BEHAVIORAL TREATMENTS

A variety of behavioral techniques have been used in the treatment of men who sexually molest children. These techniques have included covert sensitization, cognitive restructuring, biofeedback, biofeedback plus signaled punishment aversion therapy, aversive behavioral rehearsal, social-skills training, and masturbatory satiation and arousal conditioning. Kelly (1982) provides an extensive and critical review of 32 (26 case and 6 group studies) that have been conducted since 1960. Kelly noted that over 20 different therapeutic techniques were used either singly or in combination. The most widely used treatment included some form of aversion therapy (78% of the studies). Treatment in these studies ranged anywhere from 1 day to 18 months. Kelly noted that unfortunately only 44% of the studies employed adequate control factors. Sixty-three percent of the studies employed self-report measures, 63% included physiological indices (penile tumescence or heart rate measures), and 78% of the studies included self-monitoring data.

Regarding the successful attainment of target behaviors, Kelly (1982) reports that for 79% of those subjects for whom there was an attempt to decrease pedophilic urges and behaviors, a significant decrease occurred. For 66% of the subjects for whom there was an attempt to increase adult heterosexual urges and behavior, increases occurred. He notes that only 20% of the subjects from a total of five studies showed no significant change in any target behavior. The majority of the studies (81%) did report that follow-up had been conducted. The average time of follow-up was 17 months. Kelly (1982) states that a statistical summary of the studies that he reviewed would indicate that reorientation of pedophiles can be therapeutically induced. He notes, however, that none of the therapeutic strategies are without weaknesses. He also states that it is difficult to interpret the results because 56% of the studies lacked control techniques.

Studies published since Kelly's (1982) review will now be examined. Enright (1989) describes a case report of the successful treatment of a 48-year-old bisexual pedophile with a 13-year history of molesting young children of both sexes. Treatment consisted of covert sensitization and orgasmic reconditioning, sex education and therapy, cognitive reappraisal, and mixed group assertiveness training and behavioral target setting exercises. The patient was seen weekly over a 6-month period and 4-year follow-up data were reported. No measures other than the subject's self-report were used. Results indicated that the client reported no reoccurrence of offenses against children and only rare and fleeting deviant fantasies over a 4-year period.

Alford, Morin, Atkins, and Schoen (1987) present results from a controlled case study of a 27-year-old male heterosexual who engaged in pedophiliac behavior and also reported fantasies and strong sexual attraction to adolescent females. A multiple baseline design was used and dependent measures included patient self-report as well as penile plethysmography. Treatment consisted of masturbatory extinction. The patient showed a decrease in arousal to deviant stimuli. However, during the target phase of pedophiliac arousal, a drop also occurred in arousal to adolescent female stimuli. This could have been due to generalization from pedophiliac to adolescent stimuli or to the subject's expectancy of treatment efficacy. A 1-year follow-up of the subject revealed low arousal to deviant stimuli, indicating lasting effects of either the intervention or the patient's expectancy. The authors note that this design problem could have been avoided by including a reversal-spontaneous recovery phase immediately after decrements in percentage erection began to be obtained. Although this study is much more rigorous than the case presented by Enright (1989) in terms of using objective assessment and a multiple baseline design, as the authors have noted, they are unable to conclude that their results are unequivocally due to the extinction procedure per se.

Earls and Castonguay (1989) assessed the impact of olfactory aversion in the treatment of a 17-year-old bisexual pedophile. A single-case multiple-baseline design was used. This treatment procedure was effective in reducing deviant sexual arousal. This study, as opposed to the Alford et al. (1987) study, was able to demonstrate that arousal decreased only when the specific gender was targeted. Treatment effects were maintained at 1-year follow-up.

Several studies have focused on the behavioral treatment of child molesters using large sample sizes. Maletzky (1980) evaluated the effectiveness of assisted covert sensitization (aversive odor paired with deviant imagery) in the treatment of 100 male paraphiliacs (38 were homosexual pedophiles and 62 were exhibitionists). Groups were subdivided as to source of referral: court or self-referral. Treatment occurred weekly over a period of 24 weeks, followed by "booster sessions" every 3 months for 3 years. Follow-up was conducted at 6-, 12-, 18-, 24-, and 30-month intervals. Assessment consisted of self-report, penile plethysmography, observer reports, attendance at treatment session, and legal records. Results indicated that all four groups significantly decreased self-reported deviant behaviors and urges and this was also noted by penile plethysmograph measures. Self-referred patients missed appointments at a slightly higher rate than court referred. Eight of the 100 patients recidivated (11 legal charges) over the 36-month follow-up. There were no significant differences between the subgroups.

Abel, Mittelman, Becker, Rathner, and Rouleau (1988) evaluated the effectiveness of a multicomponent cognitive-behavioral treatment program for 192 nonincarcerated pedophiles. A unique aspect of this study is that extensive steps were taken to predict the confidentiality of the participants. All participants were interviewed under a certificate of confidentiality. Treatment consisted of thirty 90-minute sessions given in a group format. Sessions were held weekly. The three components of treatment were (a) decreasing deviant arousal (masturbatory satiation and covert sensitization); (b) sex education/sex dysfunction and cognitive restructuring; and (c) social and assertiveness skills training. Recidivism was evaluated using structured clinical interviews at 6 and 12 months.

Of the 192 pedophiles entering treatment, 34.9% dropped out. Factors associated with treatment dropout included the amount of pressure the pedophile was under to participate, diagnosis of antisocial personality disorder, and lack of discrimination in choice of the sex of the victim and paraphiliac act. Of the 98 pedophiles evaluated 1 year after treatment ended, 12 had recidivated. Factors associated with recidivism included marital status (married were less likely to recidivate). Recidivists were also less likely to endorse the goals of the behavioral treatment program, and recidivists were more likely to have more varied pedophiliac behavior and targets than nonrecidivists.

Marshall and Barbaree (1988) provide recidivism data on treated child molesters (n = 68) and untreated molesters (n = 58) for a follow-up period of from 1 to 11 years. None of the patients were hospitalized or incarcerated at the time of initial assessment and none of the patients were institutionalized during the treatment. The men were categorized as to whether they were incest offenders, molesters of nonfamilial female children, or molesters of nonfamilial male children. Treatment consisted of electrical aversion, masturbatory reconditioning, self-administration of smelling salts contingent on deviant thoughts or urges, and skills training. Conflict resolution and techniques on how to use leisure time constructively were also provided. Sexual arousal was measured by penile plethysmography.

Recidivism was measured by official reports, unofficial records held by police and Children's Aide Society and self-report. Because patients were not randomly assigned, the authors evaluated whether the treatment and untreated groups differed on any relevant factors. They differed on one factor: The treated incest offenders targeted older victims than did the untreated incest offenders. The recidivism rate for the treated patients was 13.2% compared to a rate of 34.5% for the untreated. Eight percent of the incest offenders recidivated as compared to 17.9% of the molesters of nonfamilial female children and 13.9% of the molesters of nonfamilial male children. Two factors predicted higher recidivism: younger age (less than 40) and genital to genital contact between molester and victim. Although the treatment goals of reducing deviant sexual arousal was achieved for all of their treated patient groups, this change was not related to treatment outcome. Increases in recidivism was associated with longer follow-up periods. Recidivism data showed an advantage for treated patients only after a 4-year follow up. These authors note that official recidivism figures were underestimates of actual reoffending.

The three above cited studies showed favorable treatment outcome as compared to a study on recidivism conducted by Rice, Quinsey, and Harris (1991). These authors examined the long-term recidivism of extrafamilial (n = 136) molesters referred for assessment or treatment to a maximum security institution and compared the outcome of patients who had received behavioral treatment with those who had not. Treatment consisted of a laboratory-based aversion therapy designed to alter sexual age preferences. Penile plethysmography was used pre- and posttreatment. Recidivism was defined as "sexual conviction," "violent failure" (arrest for a violent offense), and "failure" (arrest or conviction for an offense). Thirty-one percent of the subjects were convicted of a new sex offense, 43% committed a violent offense, and 56% were arrested for any offense. Factors associated with recidivism included number of previous sexual offenses and selection of male victims. The authors note that neither laboratory treatment nor judged success of treatment was related to recidivism. Recidivists had shown more inappropriate sexual preferences in initial telemetric assessment. Other factors associated with recidivism include diagnosis of a personality disorder and marital status (not being married).

The authors note the major limitation to the study as being lack of random assignment. The treated and untreated patients were not comparable on a number of variables. They note that perhaps the reason for the higher recidivism rate may be related to the subjects being very serious offenders who were in a maximum security psychiatric facility.

CONCLUSION

We are in agreement with Marshall et al. (1991) in their optimistic evaluation of treatment outcome with sex offenders. Those authors state that "the picture is not at all as gloomy as Furby et al.'s (1989) review would have us believe. Sex offenders can be treated and demonstrably effective programs are available." The studies reviewed in this article with the exception of the Rice et al. (1991) study indicate relatively low recidivism rates for child molesters. The studies, however, are not without some methodological problems. Future research evaluating the outcome of treatment programs for child molesters and pedophiles should specify the victim gender as well as nature of the paraphiliac act engaged in. Prior criminal history (both sexual and nonsexual) should also be evaluated and taken into consideration. Soothill and Gibbens (1978), as cited in Marshall et al. (1991), found that reoffense rates were higher for those sex offenders who had more than one prior conviction than for those for whom this was a first offense. The legal status of the individual at the time he is entered into treatment and his degree of motivation to participate is also a variable to be considered. Because two studies have found a relationship between personality disorder and treatment outcome, future studies should indicate whether or not there is the presence of an Axis II diagnosis.

Although ethically the clinical researcher cannot randomly assign an admitted sex offender to a no-treatment control group, different forms of therapeutic intervention can be evaluated. Because the data indicate that the longer the follow-up period the more likely the offender is to reoffend, any therapy outcome study conducted should use long-term follow-up (Marshall et al., 1991). Researchers should also focus on standardization of assessment procedures, including self-report methods as well as psychometrics and penile plethysmography. Both Marshall et al. (1991) and Prentky and Burgess (1990) have commented on the cost to society to not treat a sexual offender. Marshall et al. (1991) states that the cost to society to investigate, prosecute and incarcerate a single offender, as well as to assess and treat his victim, has been shown to be close to $200,000 (Canadian). Prentky and Burgess (1990) present a cost-benefit analysis in rehabilitating child molesters. These authors found that the total projected cost to society is $67,989 less for a treated than an untreated child molester.

We are beyond the point of asking whether treatment for child molesters works. Data indicate that it works for some in the short-run and for others in the long-run. The questions that require further empirical inquiry pertain to determining which therapeutic approaches are most efficacious given various client characteristics and conditions of treatment. These data would be of value in refining treatment protocols and helping determine which child molesters can be treated in the community on an outpatient basis, and which are too dangerous and need treatment in a correctional or residential setting. As noted by Marshall et al. (1991), "At the moment, there is insufficient data to identify in advance those patients who will profit least (except of course for rapists), and this topic urgently needs research. However, such research should be directed at identifying what it is current programs are missing rather than identifying who should or should not be treated" (p. 681). A continuum of care is needed, including follow-up services to already treated clients, and long-term legal monitoring to ensure their compliance with therapeutic directives. Children in our society will be best served if those individuals who have a proclivity to molest children are identified and treated. Data are now available and should be presented to legislators to inform them that not only is it efficacious to provide treatment to men who molest children, but it is also cost effective.

REFERENCES

Abel, G. G., Mittelman, M., Becker, J. V., Rathner, J., & Rouleau, J. L. (1988). Predicting child molesters' response to treatment. In R. A. Prentky & V. L. Quinsey (Eds.), *Annals of the New York Academy of Science* (pp. 223-235). New York: New York Academy of Science.

American Psychiatric Association. (1987). *Diagnostic and statistical manual of mental disorders* (3rd ed.). Washington, DC: Author.

Alford, G., Morin, C., Atkins, M., & Schoen, L. (1987). Masturbatory extinction of deviant sexual arousal: A case study. *Behavior Therapy, 18*, 265-271.

Badgley, R., Allard, H., McCormick, N., Proudfoot, P., Fortin, D., Ogilvie, D., RaeGrant, Q., Gelinas, P., Pepin, L., & Sutherland, S. (Committee on Sexual Offences Against Children and Youth). (1984). *Sexual offences against children* (Vol. 1). Ottawa: Canadian Government Publishing Centre.

Bancroft, J. (1983). The hormonal and biochemical basis of human sexuality. In J. Bancroft (Ed.), *Human sexuality and its problems* (pp. 64-107). New York: Churchhill Livingstone, Longman Group.

Bell, A., & Hall, C. (1976). The personality of a child molester. In M. Weinberg (Ed.), *Sex research: Studies from the Kinsey Institute*. Oxford: Oxford University Press.

Berlin, F., & Meinecke, C. (1981). Treatment of sex offenders with antiandrogen medication: Conceptualization, review of treatment modalities and preliminary findings. *American Journal of Psychiatry, 138*, 601-607.

Bradford, J. M. (1988). Organic treatment for the male sexual offender. In R. A. Prentky & V. L. Quinsey (Eds.), *Human sexual aggression: Current perspectives* (Vol. 528) *Annals of the New York Academy of Sciences* (pp. 193-202). New York: New York Academy of Sciences.

Bradford, J., & McLean, D. (1984). Sexual offenders, violence, and testosterone: A clinical study. *Canadian Journal of Psychiatry, 29*, 343-355.

Bradford, J., & Pawlak, A. (1987). Sadistic homosexual pedophilia: Treatment with cyproterone acetate: A single case study. *Canadian Journal of Psychiatry, 32*, 22-30.

Browne, A., & Finkelhor, D. (1986). Initial and long-term effects: A review of the research. In D. Finkelhor (Ed.), *Sourcebook on child sexual abuse* (pp. 143-179). Beverly Hills, CA: Sage.

Cook, M., & Howells, K. (Eds.). (1981). *Adult sexual interest in children*. New York: Academic Press.

Cordoba, O., & Chapel, J. (1983). Medroxyprogesterone acetate antiandrogen treatment of hypersexuality in a pedophiliac sex offender. *American Journal of Psychiatry, 140*, 1036-1039.

Earls, C., & Castonguay, L. (1989). The evaluation of olfactory aversion for a bisexual pedophile with a single-case multiple baseline design. *Behavior Therapy, 20*, 137-146.

Enright, S. (1989). Paedophilia: A cognitive/behavioural treatment approach in a single case. *British Journal of Psychiatry, 155*, 399-401.

Finkelhor, D. (1984). *Child sexual abuse: New theory and research*. New York: Free Press.

Finkelhor, D., Araji, S., Baron, L., Browne, A., Peters, S. D., & Wyatt, G. E. (1986). *A sourcebook on child sexual abuse*. Beverly Hills, CA: Sage.

Furby, L., Weinrott, M., & Blackshaw, L. (1989). Sex offender recidivism: A review. *Psychological Bulletin, 105*, 3-30.

Giarretto, H. (1978). Humanistic treatment of father-daughter incest. *Journal of Humanistic Psychology, 32*, 20-25.

Giarretto, H. (1982). A comprehensive child sexual abuse treatment program. *Child Abuse & Neglect, 6*, 263-278.

Giarretto, H., Giarretto, A., & Sgroi, S. (1978). Coordinated community treatment of incest. In A. Burgess, A. Groth, L. Holmstrom, & S. Sgroi (Eds.), *Sexual assault of children and adolescents*. Lexington, MA: Lexington Books.

Heim, N., & Hursch, C. (1979). Castration for sex offenders: Treatment or punishment? *Archives of Sexual Behavior, 8*, 281-304.

Kelly, R. (1982). Behavioral reorientation of pedophiliacs: Can it be done? *Clinical Psychology Review, 2*, 387-408.

Kiersch, T. (1990). Treatment of sex offenders with Depo-Provera. *Bulletin of the American Academy of Psychiatry and the Law, 18*, 179-187.

Lang, R., Pugh, G., & Langevin, R. (1988). Treatment of incest and pedophilic offenders: A pilot study. *Behavioral Sciences and the Law, 6*, 239-255.

Maletzky, B. (1980). Self-referred vs. court-referred sexually deviant patients: Success with assisted covert sensitization. *Behavior Therapy, 11*, 306-314.

Marshall, W., & Barbaree, H. (1988). The long-term evaluation of a behavioral treatment program for child molesters. *Behavior Research and Therapy, 26*, 499-511.

Marshall, W., Ward, T., Jones, R., Johnston, P., & Barbaree, H. (1991). An optimistic evaluation of treatment outcome with sex offenders. In *Violence Update, 1*(7), 1, 9.

McGuire, R., Carlisle, J., & Young, B. (1965). Sexual deviations as conditioned behavior: A hypothesis. *Behavior Research and Therapy, 2*, 185-190.

Perilstein, R. D., Lipper, S., & Friedman, L. J. (1991). Three cases of paraphilias responsive to fluoxetine treatment. *Journal of Clinical Psychiatry, 52*, 169-170.

Prentky, R., & Burgess, A. (1990). Rehabilitation of child molesters: A cost-benefit analysis. *American Journal of Orthopsychiatry, 60*, 108-117.

Quinsey, V. (1986). Men who have sex with children. In D. Weistub (Ed.), *Law and mental health: International perspectives* (Vol. 2, pp. 140-172). New York: Pergamon.

Rice, M. E., Quinsey, V. L., & Harris, G. T. (1991). Sexual recidivism among child molesters released from a maximum security psychiatric institution. *Journal of Consulting and Clinical Psychology, 59*(3), 381-386.

Romero, J., & Williams, L. (1983). Group psychotherapy and intensive probation supervision with sex offenders: A comparative study. *Federal Probation, 47*(4), 36-42.

Russell, D. (1983). The incidence and prevalence of intrafamilial and extrafamilial sexual abuse of female children. *Child Abuse & Neglect, 7,* 133-146.

Soothill, K. L., & Gibbens, T. C. (1978). Recidivism of sexual offenders: A re-appraisal. *British Journal of Criminology, 18,* 267-276.

Stava, L. (1984). The use of hypnotic uncovering techniques in the treatment of pedophilia. *International Journal of Clinical and Experimental Hypnosis, 32,* 350-355.

Storr, A. (1964). *Sexual deviation.* Baltimore, MD: Penguin.

Wyatt, G. (1985). The sexual abuse of Afro-American and White American women in childhood. *Child Abuse & Neglect, 9,* 507-519.

Counseling Adult Sex Offenders: Unique Challenges and Treatment Paradigms

Ronnie Priest and Annalee Smith

Current definitions and research literature related to characteristics of adults who sexually victimize children are reviewed. Treatment issues that may confront counselors engaged in treating adults who sexually victimize children are examined, and implications for practitioners are discussed.

There are few more reprehensible situations than an adult becoming sexually active with a child. Compounding the disturbing reality of sexual victimization is the recognition that the number of reported cases of child sexual victimization is increasing (Courtois, 1988; Haugaard & Reppucci, 1988; Herman, 1981; Hunter, 1990; Russell, 1986; Wyatt, 1985). Traditionally, the major emphasis and concern of counselors have been on the psychological and emotional well-being of the victim (Courtois, 1988; Finkelhor, 1979; Russell, 1986; Sgroi, 1985). It is difficult to dispute the logic inherent in this position; yet logic also dictates that offenders should receive therapeutic attention if the incidence of child sexual victimization is to be reduced. The purposes of this article are to present a discussion of pedophilia as a sexual deviation, counseling issues that may pose unique dilemmas for counselors engaging in therapy with pedophiles, and possible treatment modalities that may be effective in treating pedophiles.

DEFINITION OF PEDOPHILE

Berlin and Meineche (1981) listed a wide array of paraphilia under the classification of sexual deviation disorders. They identified voyeurism, exhibitionism, erotic sadism, and pedophilia as sexual deviations. The American Psychiatric Association (1987) considers paraphilias components of a psychiatric syndromes and lists them under atypical gender identity disorders. The term *paraphilia* seems preferable because it emphasizes deviation (*para*) while (*philia*) underscoring that to which the individual is attracted. The essential features of the disorder are unusual or bizarre imagery and acts that facilitate sexual arousal.

Finkelhor and Williams (1988) have noted, "Pedophilia, although a controversial and often misused concept, is generally taken to mean a strong sexual preference for children" (p. 53). Kaplan and Sadock (1981) stated that "pedophilia involves preferential sexual activity with children either in fantasy or in actuality" (p. 558). Campbell (1981) defined *pedophile* as a "love of children." Inherent in Campbell's definition of pedophilia is a love of prepubertal children by an adult for sexual purposes. For an offender to be classified as an adult, he or she must be at least 5 years older than the victim.

The American Psychiatric Association (1987) furnished additional specificity to this definition in the *Diagnostic and Statistical Manual of Mental Disorders–Revised (DSM-III-R)*:

> People with pedophilia generally report an attraction to children of a particular age range, which may be as specific as within a range of only one or two years. Those attracted to girls usually prefer eight-to-ten-year-olds . . . whereas, those attracted to boys usually prefer slightly older children. (p. 284)

ETIOLOGY AND DESCRIPTION OF PEDOPHILIA

The specific etiology of pedophilia is unknown. Current research suggests, however, that pedophiles have certain characteristics in common (Abel et al., 1987; Abel, Becker, Murphy, & Flanagan, 1981; Alford, Kasper, & Baumann, 1984; Groth, Hobson, & Gary, (1982). A significant number of offenders have experienced or observed deviant sexual behavior at an early age, usually prior to puberty (Groth et al., 1982). Bernard (1975) found that most of the participants in his study became conscious of their sexual attraction to children prior to adolescence.

In reviewing the literature, the reader becomes acutely aware of the reference to male sex offenders. Pacht and Cowden (1974) conducted a study of 500 sex offenders, all of whom were male. Finkelhor (1984) cited research that indicates "as many as 95% of adults who victimize female children and 80% of adults who victimize male children may be male" (p. 12). In reported cases of child sexual victimization, the literature suggests that women do not sexually interact with children on a level comparable to men (Finkelhor, 1979, 1984; Groth, 1979; Herman, 1981; Langevin, 1985). A new body of research (Faller, 1987; Fehrenbach & Monastersky, 1988; Scavo 1989), however, is accumulating, which suggests that women are sexually victimizing children at much higher rates than were earlier suspected.

In seeking possible explanations for the seeming disparity between the prevalence of men and women who sexually victimize children, Finkelhor (1984) theorized that "men are socialized to see as their appropriate sexual partners persons who are younger and smaller than themselves, while women are socialized to see as their appropriate sexual partners persons older and bigger" (p. 13). It may also be appropriate to note that men are generally socialized to be aggressive, whereas women are socialized to be nurturing. Consequently, men may translate this learned aggression into sexual conquest and exploitation (Herman, 1981).

Some researchers (Groth, 1979; Justice & Justice, 1979) have expressed the belief that a more accurate picture of the incidence of women who are sexually active with children may be elusive. These researchers observed that women are afforded a certain degree of latitude in terms of physical contact with children because of their role as primary caretaker. Consequently, some instances of child sexual victimization committed by women may go unreported. Knopp (1984) recommended that better research instruments should be created if the true incidence of child sexual victimization is to be ascertained.

Pedophiles frequently assert that their sexual attraction to children is not a source of self-imposed stress and that their source of concern relates to societal sanctions against sexual activity with children; other offenders acknowledge feelings of guilt, shame, depression, and a lack of self-esteem (Salter, 1988). In many instances, the pedophilic behavior becomes the central activity in the individual's life (APA, 1987).

211

Freeman-Longo and Wall (1986) suggested that the obsession with deviant sexual behavior can become so severe that it impairs the individual's ability to concentrate on any task that is not related to sexual activity.

Paraphilias involving a child and an adult present both legal and societal concerns. Pedophiles do not usually self-refer; consequently, counselors' first opportunity to interact therapeutically with these clients does not usually occur until the pedophile has encountered the legal system (Groth & Birnbaum, 1978).

CLASSIFICATION OF PEDOPHILIA

Groth et al. (1982) emphasized that sexual assault against children is a behavior. This behavior can be classified according to characteristics of offenders and their selection of victims.

Fixated Offenders

Groth and Birnbaum (1978) defined fixation as "a temporary or permanent arrest of psychological maturation resulting from unresolved formative issues which persist and underlie the organization of the subsequent phases of development" (p. 176). This may indicate that there are individuals who at the onset of their sexual maturation develop a primary or exclusive attraction to children. Children become the preferred subject of sexual interest and although these individuals may also engage in sexual activity with peers, these relationships are generally initiated by the other party and are the result of some form of societal pressure or constitute an additional means of gaining access to children. Groth (1979) also found in his study of 175 convicted male sexual offenders of children that a majority of the fixated offenders were known to their victims.

In general, fixated offenders are sexually attracted to children based on their identification with children and the desire to remain childlike. Pedophiles tend to adapt their behaviors and interests to the level of the child. The fixated offender is characterized as immature and possesses poor sociosexual skills. Groth (1979) observed that the primary targets of fixated offenders are male children.

Regressed Offenders

Groth and Birnbaum (1978) defined regressed offenders as "a temporary appearance of premature behavior after more mature forms of behavior have been attained regardless of whether the immature behavior was actually manifested earlier in the individual's development" (p. 177). Regressed offenders do not seem to display a predisposition to be sexually active with children. Regressed offenders, as compared to fixated offenders, seem to have a more conventional peer orientation and sociosexual development. When these adult relationships become conflicted or the offender experiences stress, he or she becomes motivated to interact sexually with a child. The findings suggest that, in general, regressed offenders select female victims as their primary targets and that these victims are frequently related to the offender.

ASSESSMENT OF THE PEDOPHILE

Groth (1979) suggested that when a pedophile is referred to a counselor for assessment, it is essential that certain information related to the

offense behavior be obtained. Groth suggested, for example, that counselors determine if the offender is fixated or regressed and the extent to which he or she poses a threat to the community. In attempting to discern the degree of risk offenders may pose to the community, counselors can consider whether the offenders have used force or the threat of force to access their victims. Offenders who have ritualized the sexual abuse of their victims by invoking spirits or chants or by having the victim engage in repetitive behaviors are not appropriate for counseling in outpatient settings. Similarly, offenders who sexually victimized children and then photographed the children for pornographic purposes may not be suitable candidates for nonresidential counseling.

Others have suggested that it is essential for counselors to also obtain a complete psychosocial and sexual history of the client (Becker & Kaplan, 1988; Knopp, 1984; Salter, 1988). In formulating a protocol for assessing pedophilic clients, Groth (1979) warned the counselor to ascertain the following:

> How the offender accessed the child, what sexual activities were involved, the length of time the offender was involved with the child, the frequency of the sexual involvement, the offender's developmental stage, the range of the offender's emotional experiences, and how frequently and under what conditions the offender thinks about becoming sexually active with a child. (p. 38)

The offender's developmental stage is assessed by conducting an extensive psychosocial evaluation of the client. Included in this evaluation are questions related to the client's abuse history. Berlin and Meineche (1981) identified three areas that are of primary importance when assessing the pedophilic client: (a) cognitive examination to reveal recurring and persistent fantasies about deviant sexual behavior, (b) examination of feeling state to ascertain the erotic cravings perceived as noxious when frustrated, and (c) behavior examination to discern the level of gratification realized by offenders and methods of modifying the behavior (p. 602).

TREATMENT OUTLOOK AND MANAGEMENT

Treatment issues related to pedophiles represent unique challenges for counselors. Roundy and Horton (1990) have determined that prior to engaging a pedophile in counseling, the counselor should examine (a) his or her willingness to treat the client, (b) personal biases and issues that might negatively affect treatment, and (c) belief that treatment is an appropriate response to the problem. An additional concern articulated by James and Nasjleti (1983) involves the lack of positive professional and community recognition received by counselors who work with pedophiles. It is not unusual for persons to disparagingly inquire of counselors "How can you work with those people?"

Groth (1979) suggested that it is not unusual for pedophilic clients to report a history of being sexually victimized as children. This may complicate counseling from the counselor's perspective. The client's disclosure of being sexually victimized as a child may dictate that the counselor consider addressing the client's victimization in addition to focusing on issues related to the client's pedophilic behavior (Vasington, 1989). Treatment issues related to the sexual victimization of children have been well documented elsewhere (Briere, 1989; Courtois, 1988; Long, 1986; Porter, Blick, & Sgroi, 1982; Waterman, 1986; Wheeler & Berliner, 1988) and are not discussed here.

Salter (1988) and Wolff (cited in Knopp [1984]) believed that the first priority for counselors who work with pedophiles is to ensure that their abusive behaviors are discontinued. The fact that the cessation of the abusive behavior may cause some clients emotional and psychological discomfort is secondary. Placing cessation of the abusive behavior over the client's emotional or psychological comfort may, initially, be disconcerting for some counselors. Counselors are traditionally taught that clients' emotional well-being is of primary concern.

One of the first things that counselors may want to consider is the removal of the client from any environment where he or she will have access to children (Finkelhor, 1984; Herman, 1979, Salter, 1988). In cases of intrafamilial sexual victimization, it is generally therapeutically more appropriate to remove the offender from the home than to remove the victim. By suggesting the pedophile locate a different residence, counselors avoid the possibility of giving an implicit message to the offender that he or she is not responsible for the victimization.

An additional consideration for counselors who engage pedophilic clients in therapy involves the very nature of counseling. In traditional counseling, a significant number of counselors acquire their information about their clients based on the clients' self-reports. Assessment of how well clients are progressing during counseling is likewise determined by clients' self-reports and counselors' clinical judgments. Unfortunately, many clients who are sexually active with children tend to be manipulative and deceptive in their interactions with their victims and counselors (O'Connell, Leberg, & Donaldson, 1990; Salter, 1988). It is not unusual for the clients who report a history of sexually abusive behaviors to minimize the severity of their behaviors, engage in rationalization, project responsibility for the sexual abuse onto their victims, or a combination of these (Knopp, 1984; Salter, 1988). Barnard, Fuller, Robbins, and Shaw (1989) have noted that pedophiles may also pronounce themselves cured after a minimal number of counseling appointments.

A significant number of researchers and practitioners (Groth, 1979; Knopp, 1984; O'Connell, Leberg, & Donaldson, 1990; Salter, 1988) avoided any discussion of the word *cure* when working with pedophiles. Knopp (1984) stated, "No one claims that treatment programs will end the problem, and most practitioners draw the parallel between sex offenders and persons involved in other long-term addictive patterns of behavior" (p. 19). The operative word seems to be *control* as opposed to *cure*.

In treating pedophilic clients, the issue of client confidentiality may arise. These clients will be aware that to disclose the magnitude of their behaviors may lead to legal entanglements and the dissolution of existing adult relationships. Confidentiality is one of the cornerstones of the counseling relationship (American Association for Counseling and Development, 1988). Consequently, counselors who have pedophilic clients may experience a sense of professional conflict related to the issue of reporting a client's sexually inappropriate behavior.

Limited confidentiality, wherein the client is informed during the initial counseling session that information related to the sexually abusive behavior may be furnished to the proper designated authorities, seems an appropriate solution to this dilemma (Groth, 1979; Knopp, 1984; Priest, 1987; Priest & Wilcoxon, 1988). Counselors must certainly avoid the situation of having clients disclose information they thought was confidential only to have the counselor state he or she has a duty to report the disclosure. As clients begin to assume responsibility for their prior inappropriate sexual behaviors and begin to feel more competent in relationship to counseling, they may increasingly disclose information about prior deviant sexual behavior. Counselors must be prepared for this. Counselors in all 50 states are legislatively mandated to report instances of child sexual victimization. Because of variations in state laws, however, we suggest that counselors become familiar with the duty to report laws in their respective states prior to engaging sex

offenders in counseling. We also recommend an additional source of information to clarify duty to report statutes, which involves contacting the local Human Resource Services/Child Protective Service Agency to determine their statute of limitation policy on prosecution of child sexual abuse cases.

It should also be noted that while in counseling, the client may relapse. We suggest that if the client discloses that he or she has relapsed, the counselor can consider affording the client the opportunity to report the deviant behavior to the appropriate authorities. If the client demonstrates reticence about making the report, it can be explained that the report must be made; the only issue is who will actually make it.

TOOLS

Two of the more controversial, but apparently effective tools at the disposal of counselors of pedophiles are the polygraph and the plethysmograph. Polygraph and plethysmograph tests have the benefit of furnishing to counselors additional information related to the efficacy of clients' counseling.

Polygraph testing can be used to measure both the extent of the client's abusive behavior and the level of compliance to treatment objectives. It has been our experience that individuals who have emphatically stated that they have been sexually active with children on only one or two occasions are dramatically able to recall additional sexually abusive episodes with children when confronted with the prospect of a polygraph examination.

The existing literature (Barnard, Fuller, Robbins, & Shaw, 1989; O'Connell, Leberg, & Donaldson, 1990) consistently and adamantly articulates the belief that pedophiles should be precluded from any employment that will allow them access to children (e.g., day-care center employees, school teachers, Boy Scout leaders). Thus, an additional possible situation when the polygraph examination may prove beneficial involves adherence to therapeutic guidelines and goals. For example, a client who is restricted from being employed where he or she has either indirect or direct responsibility for children may deceptively report adhering to that particular mandate. When confronted with the prospect of a polygraph test, that same client may either become more forthright in counseling or at least have his or her deception uncovered. O'Connell, Leberg, and Donaldson (1990) have identified another possible use for polygraph examinations related to evaluation of counseling outcomes. They suggested that "polygraph testing may also indicate changed beliefs and attitudes" (p. 100).

We are not suggesting that counselors administer polygraph examinations themselves. The administration of the polygraph examination and subsequent interpretation of the results should be conducted by trained professionals. Before a counselor recommends that a client submit to a polygraph examination, the counselor may be well advised to ascertain the polygraph examiner's level of expertise relevant to the context. An additional word of caution furnished by O'Connell et al. (1990) seems appropriate here: "The polygraph is effective in testing for what the subject thinks to be the truth or a lie at the time of the test, it is not an absolute test of the truth" (p. 89).

Plethysmograph assessment "measures the erection response to various stimuli" (Knopp, 1984, p. 30). Existing research (Marshall, Barbaree, & Butt, 1988; Quinsey, Steinman, Bergersen, & Holmes, 1975) indicates that a significant correspondence exists between adult males' sexual arousal and prior sexual interactions with children. Abel, Becker, Murphy, and Flanagan (1981) have used plethysmography to identify clients who have reoffended while in counseling. Plethysmo-

213

graph assessment has the added benefit of serving as a possible means of better monitoring the reduction of the client's deviant arousal pattern and response to treatment (Quinsey, Chaplin, & Carrigan, 1980). Thus, counselors are removed from having to rely solely on the client's self-reports and counselor judgment.

The polygraph and plethysmograph serve as objective means of validating the veracity of the client's self-reports and quantifying the client's progress while in counseling. These tools, however, pose at least two ethical considerations. The first involves the degree to which clients are informed about the types of assessment techniques that the counselor may use. We suggest that counselors inform prospective clients that they may be requested to take random polygraph and plethysmograph examinations. To minimize the possibility that the client may subsequently state that he or she did not render informed consent, the counselor can request that the client furnish a brief written statement attesting to his or her understanding and agreement to be tested.

The second consideration involves the adequacy of training counselors receive prior to administering a plethysmograph examination and the level of understanding a counselor has related to what determinations can be made based on plethysmograph results. For example, it is essential for counselors to understand that the client does not pass or fail a plethysmograph. When appropriately used, a plethysmograph may be of assistance in determining sexual activities that are stimulating to the client, thus facilitating the implementation of a counseling plan. It cannot be inferred, however, that because an individual is aroused by the thought of being sexually active with a child, that he or she has acted or will act on that arousal.

INTERVENTIONS

Behavioral counseling with pedophiles has as its primary goal a reduction of the client's deviant arousal patterns (Forgione, 1976; Knopp, 1984; Salter, 1988). Counselors may use an array of behavioral approaches that include covert sensitization, role playing, modified aversive behavioral rehearsal, and cognitive restructuring.

Covert Sensitization

Becker and Kaplan (1988) stated that "covert sensitization is utilized to disrupt the behaviors that are antecedent to the offender's actually coming in contact with the victim" (p. 144). Counselors who use covert sensitization when working with adult sex offenders should attempt to pair events that precipitate clients' becoming sexually active with a child to an aversive image that serves to dramatically reduce the inclination to offend. The goal of such a pairing is to create in the client a significant level of discomfort whenever the client experiences the urge to offend (Barnard, Fuller, Robbins, & Shaw, 1989; Knopp, 1984). In discussing the use of aversive imagery, Salter (1988) suggested that the "offender describe on tape some extremely aversive experience that is likely to elicit negative emotions such as repulsion, disgust, or fear" (p. 119).

Knopp (1984) and Salter (1988) advocated that during counseling sessions, the counselor should have the client extensively discuss experiences that were terrifying or painful. The counselor can then create audiotapes that extenuate experiences and situations that are aversive for the client. The counselor is then able to use the audiotapes in subsequent counseling sessions with the offender. Following is an audiotape used by one of the authors:

You have just had an argument with your wife. You go to bed because you have nothing more to say to her and she does not

understand you anyway. You wake up at 1 A.M. restless and still agitated. Your wife has already gone to her night job. As you sit on the edge of the bed, you think of your daughter who is asleep in the next room.

She always seems to understand you. And what is the harm if you just go in her room to check up on her. As you become aroused thinking about her, you begin to walk toward her bedroom. You begin to think about all the things you will do to her sexually. Your arousal increases with each step toward her bedroom. You undress as you stand outside the door to your daughter's bedroom.

When you open the door to her room, the police are there. They take you, undressed, downstairs to the waiting police car. Newspaper reporters are everywhere and your neighbors are pointing at you. Your mind is flooded with shame for now everyone knows what you have done.

The counselor may use audiotapes that have a playing time of between 30 to 40 minutes' duration. We suggest that multiple tapes be used, and different tapes be substituted on a weekly basis. Although the initial tape may be made by the counselor and given to the client, subsequent tapes can be made by the client. Becker and Kaplan (1988) have noted that "the effective implementation of covert sensitization is heavily dependent on . . . [clients'] ability to use self-control when they experience deviant fantasies or urges"(p. 144).

Role Playing

Counselors can use role playing to increase clients' level of victim empathy (Knopp, 1984). The following illustrates the possible benefits to be derived from having the client role play a child he or she has sexually victimized. The client is urged to assume the role of the victim and to experience and express the trauma the victim went through. In an effort to assist clients in assuming the role of victim, counselors may reconstruct the abusive situation from the victim's perspective. For example, the counselor could have the client remember what it was like to be 10 years old. The client is then requested to simulate being in a helpless physiologic state and being assaulted by someone much more physically dominating than himself or herself. In addition to gaining increased insight into the trauma the victim experienced, it is not unusual for the offender to acknowledge for the first time that he or she was victimized as a child.

Modified Aversive Behavior Rehearsal

The use of modified aversive behavior rehearsal involves the client reenacting his or her offense behavior with mannequins serving as the victim (Forgione, 1976). The counselor has the client re-create the victimization during counseling, and the re-creation is videorecorded and replayed to the client and his or her significant other. O'Connell, Leberg, and Donaldson (1990) stated, "This experience can dramatically strip away pleasurable illusions about the deviant fantasies" (p. 98).

Cognitive Restructuring

Counselors working with pedophiles will invariably have to confront clients' denial, rationalization, minimization, justification, and other faulty cognitions that permit clients to become sexually active with their victims. The clinical experience of one of the authors suggests that it is not unusual for some pedophiles to be unaware of their faulty cognitions.

An actual case example (with the client's name masked) may serve to illustrate this point:

> Jeremy was unaware of any psychological or emotional trauma his being sexually active with his 7-year-old granddaughter and two of her friends caused the children. After all, he reasoned, "He loved his granddaughter and he would never do anything to harm her." And as cute as her two little friends were, "He would never hurt those two little cute girls." Jeremy buttressed his assertions with the equally faulty cognition that "If he had hurt any of the girls, they would have told him."

The counselor, in this instance, was able to challenge the client's faulty cognitions in the context of a sex offender group. Salter (1988) stated, "Identifying and effectively challenging cognitive distortions in a neutral setting, as well as teaching the offender how to identify and challenge distortions while under the influence of deviant urges, is an aspect of treatment that cannot be ignored" (p. 125).

Group Counseling

Existing literature suggests that group counseling may represent the most efficacious treatment modality to eliminate client rationalization and minimization (Knopp, 1984; O'Connell, Leberg, & Donaldson, 1990; Salter, 1988). Alluding to the frequent futility encountered by counselors attempting to remove clients' denial and minimization behaviors during individual counseling, Salter (1988) stated, "It is rarely effective for an individual therapist to use arguments against cognitive distortions as a therapeutic technique, although it is entirely appropriate for the therapist to make it clear (s)he does not in any sense agree with them" (p. 125).

Group counseling seems to be a more appropriate treatment modality because the offender's faulty cognitions are challenged and confronted by persons who also once relied on distorted cognitions to avoid assuming responsibility for their actions. The reality that the client is challenged, in a supportive environment by other pedophiles, may eliminate the client's rejoinder of "You don't know what you are talking about; you have never been there." Group counseling in relationship to pedophiles also has the added benefit of affording the client an opportunity to see other group members modeling both responsibility for their behavior and responsible behavior.

SUMMARY

The purpose of this article was to present significant issues related to counseling pedophiles. We have addressed the need for counselors working with pedophiles to first engage in self-evaluation and careful assessment. The use of random plethysmograph and polygraph examinations may be considered as a means of ascertaining the level of adherence of pedophilic clients to the counseling guidelines. Behavioral counseling techniques that may be effective in working with pedophiles were also discussed. Counseling adults who have a history of sexual interaction with children requires specialized training (Groth, 1979; O'Connell, Leberg, & Donaldson, 1990; Salter, 1988). Such counselors are in short supply; it is essential that the ranks of qualified professionals willing to work with pedophiles be increased.

REFERENCES

Abel, G. G., Becker, J. V., Mittelman, M., Cunningham-Rathner, Rouleau, J. L., & Murphy, W. D. (1987). Self-reported sex crimes of nonincarcerated paraphiliacs. *Journal of Interpersonal Violence, 2,* 3–26.

Abel, G. G., Becker, J. V., Murphy, W. D., & Flanagan, B. (1981). Identifying dangerous child molesters. In R. B. Stuart (Ed.), *Violent behavior* (pp. 37–49). New York: Brunner/Mazel.

Alford, J. M., Kasper, C. J., & Baumann, R. C. (1984). Diagnostic classification of sexual child offenders. *Corrective and Social Psychiatry and Journal of Behavioral Technology Methods and Therapy, 30,* 40–46.

American Association for Counseling and Development. (1988). *Ethical standards* (rev. ed.). Alexandria, VA: Author.

American Psychiatric Association. (1987). *Diagnostic and statistical manual of mental disorders* (3rd ed., rev.). Washington, DC: American Psychiatric Association.

Barnard, G. W., Fuller, A. K., Robbins, L., & Shaw, T. (1989). *The child molester: An integrated approach to evaluation and treatment.* New York: Brunner/Mazel.

Becker, J. V., & Kaplan, M. S. (1988). Assessment and treatment of the male sex offender. In D. H. Schetky & A. H. Green (Eds.), *Child sexual abuse* (pp. 136–149). New York: Brunner/Mazel.

Berlin, F. S., & Meineche, C. F. (1981). Treatment of sex offenders with antiandrogenic medication: Conceptualization, review of treatment modalities, and preliminary findings. *American Journal of Psychiatry, 138,* 601–607.

Bernard, B. (1975). An inquiry among a group of pedophiles. *Journal of Sex Research, 11,* 242–255.

Briere, J. (1989). *Therapy for adults molested as children.* New York: Springer.

Campbell, R. J. (1981). *Psychiatric dictionary* (5th ed.). New York: Oxford University Press.

Courtois, C. A. (1988). *Healing the incest wound: Adult survivors in therapy.* New York: Norton.

Faller, K. (1987). Women who sexually abuse children. *Violence and Victims, 2,* 263–276.

Fehrenbach, P., & Monastersky, C. (1988). Characteristics of female adolescent sexual offenders. *American Journal of Orthopsychiatry, 58,* 148–151.

Finkelhor, D. (1979). *Sexually victimized children.* New York: The Free Press.

Finkelhor, D. (1984). *Child sexual abuse: New theory and research.* New York: The Free Press.

Finkelhor, D., & Williams, L. M. (1988). Perpetrators. In D. Finkelhor, L. M. Williams, & N. Burns (Eds.), *Nursery crimes* (pp. 27–69). Newbury Park, CA: Sage.

Forgione, A. G. (1976). The use of mannequins in the behavioral assessment of child molesters: Two case reports. *Behavior Therapy, 7,* 678–685.

Freeman-Longo, R. E., & Wall, R. V. (1986). Changing a lifetime of sexual crime. *Psychology Today, 20,* 58–63.

Groth, A. N. (1979). *Men who rape.* New York: Plenum Press.

Groth, A. N., & Birnbaum, R. C. (1978). Adult sexual orientation and attraction to underage persons. *Archives of Sexual Behavior, 7,* 175–181.

Groth, A. N., Hobson, W. F., & Gary, T. (1982). The child molester: Clinical observations. In J. Conte & D. Shores (Eds.), *Social work and sexual abuse* (pp. 129–142). New York: Haworth Press.

Haugaard, J. J., & Reppucci, N. D. (1988). *The sexual abuse of children.* San Francisco, CA: Jossey-Bass.

Herman, J. L. (1981). *Father-daughter incest.* Cambridge, MA: Harvard University Press.

Hunter, M. (1990). *Abused boys: The neglected victims of sexual abuse.* Lexington, MA: Lexington Books.

James, B., & Nasjleti, M. (1983). *Treating sexually abused children and their families.* Palo Alto, CA: Consulting Psychologists Press.

Justice, B., & Justice, R. (1979). *The broken taboo.* New York: Human Services.

Kaplan, H. I., & Sadock, B. J. (1981). *Modern synopsis of comprehensive textbook of psychiatry III.* Baltimore: Williams & Wilkins.

Knopp, F. H. (1984). *Retraining adult sex offenders: Methods and Models.* Syracuse: Safer Society Press.

Langevin, R. (Ed.). (1985). *Erotic preference, gender identity, and aggression in men: New research studies.* Hillsdale, NJ: Erlbaum.

Long, S. (1986). Guideline for treating young children. In K. MacFarlane, J. Waterman, S. Conerly, L. Damon, M. Durfee, & S. Long (Eds.), *Sexual abuse of young children* (pp. 220–243). New York: Guilford Press.

Marshall, W. L., Barbaree, H. E., & Butt, J. (1988). Sexual offenders against

215

male children: Sexual preferences. *Behavior Research and Therapy, 26,* 383–391.

O'Connell, M. A., Leberg, E., & Donaldson, C. R. (1990). *Working with sex offenders: Guidelines for therapist selection.* Newbury Park, CA: Sage.

Pacht, A. R., & Cowden, J. E. (1974). An exploratory study of five hundred sex offenders. *Criminal Justice and Behavior, 1,* 13–20.

Porter, F. S., Blick, L. C., & Sgroi, S. M. (1982). Treatment of the sexually abused child. In S. M. Sgroi (Ed.), *Handbook of clinical intervention in child sexual abuse.* Lexington, MA: Lexington Books.

Priest, R. (1987). Confidentiality: Should it apply to child sex offenders? *Alabama A. C. D. Journal, 14,* 42–48.

Priest, R., & Wilcoxon, S. A. (1988). Confidentiality and the child sexual offender: Unique challenges and dilemmas. Family Therapy, 15, 107–111.

Quinsey, V. L., Steinman, C. M., Bergersen, S. G., & Holmes, T. F. (1975). Penile circumference, skin conductance, and ranking responses of child molesters and normals to sexual and nonsexual visual stimuli. Behavior Therapy, 6, 213–219.

Quinsey, V. L., Chaplin, T. C., & Carrigan, W. F. (1980). Biofeedback and signaled punishment in the modification of inappropriate sexual age preferences. Behavioral Therapy, 11, 567–576.

Roundy, L. M., & Horton, A. L. (1990). Professional and treatment issues for clinicians who intervene with incest perpetrators. In A. L. Horton, B. L., Johnson, L. M. Roundy, & D. Williams (Eds.), *The incest perpetrator* (pp. 164–189). Newbury Park, CA: Sage.

Russell, D. E. H. (1986). *The secret trauma: Incest in the lives of young girls.* New York: Basic Books.

Salter, A. C. (1988). *Treating child sex offenders and victims.* Beverly Hills, CA: Sage.

Scavo, R. R. (1989). Female adolescent sex offenders: A neglected treatment group. *Social Casework, 70,* 114–117.

Sgroi, S. M. (1985). The state of the art in child sexual victimization. In S. M. Sgroi (Ed.), *Handbook of clinical intervention in child sexual abuse* (pp. 1–9). Lexington, MA: Lexington Books.

Vasington, M. C. (1989). Sexual offenders as victims: Implications for treatment and the therapeutic relationship. In S. M. Sgroi (Ed.), *Vulnerable populations* (Vol. 2, pp. 329–350). Lexington, MA: Lexington Books.

Waterman, J. (1986). Overview of treatment issues. In K. MacFarlane, J. Waterman, S. Conerly, L. Damon, M. Durfee, & S. Long (Eds.), *Sexual abuse of young children* (pp. 197–203). New York: Guilford Press.

Wheeler, J. R., & Berliner, L. (1988). Treating the effects of sexual abuse on children. In G. E. Wyatt & G. J. Powell (Eds.), *Lasting effects of child sexual abuse* (pp. 227–248). Newbury Park, CA: Sage.

Wyatt, G. E. (1985). The sexual abuse of Afro-American and White American women in childhood. *Child Abuse and Neglect, 9,* 231–240.

Ronnie Priest is an assistant professor of mental health counseling in the Department of Counseling and Professional Services at Memphis State University, Memphis, Tennessee. Annalee Smith is a registered nurse in the Emergency Department at University Hospital, Birmingham, Alabama. Correspondence regarding this article should be sent to Ronnie Priest, Memphis State University, Department of Counseling and Professional Services, 113 Patterson Building, Memphis, TN 38152.

216

EFFECTIVE INTERVENTION WITH NEGLECTFUL FAMILIES

JAMES M. GAUDIN, Jr.

University of Georgia

The limited research on approaches to intervention with neglectful families is reviewed and guidelines for intervening with neglect are suggested. Most outcome studies have not employed experimental designs with control groups. Definitions of neglect vary among studies and distinctions have not been made between subtypes of neglect treated. Intervention programs have been successful in remedying neglect with less than 50% of the families served. Group interventions with child and adolescent victims have been more successful. Behavioral techniques have be used to successfully teach home management, parent-child interaction, and meal preparation skills to neglectful parents. Multiservice interventions are necessary to remedy the multiple problems presented by neglectful families. Group approaches, family treatment, use of paraprofessionals, and social network interventions have been used successfully with neglectful families. Short-term interventions have not been successful.

C hild neglect is the most frequently reported type of child mal-treatment in the United States. Although the true rate of neglect is unknown, an update to the 1986 *Study of National Incidence and Prevalence of Child Abuse and Neglect* (Sedlak, 1990) indicates that the incidence rate for child neglect known to professionals is 14.6 per 1,000 children. The corresponding estimates for physical abuse are 4.9 per thousand and for sexual abuse 2.1 per thousand. In 1986 over 55% of all child maltreatment reported to child protective agencies was for child neglect (American Association for Protecting Children,

AUTHOR'S NOTE: *This research is partially supported by Grant Number 90-CA-1400 from the U.S. Department of Health and Human Services, National Center on Child Abuse and Neglect. Correspondence may be addressed to James M. Gaudin, School of Social Work, University of Georgia, Athens, GA 30602-7016.*

CRIMINAL JUSTICE AND BEHAVIOR, Vol. 20 No. 1, March 1993 66-89

1988). Yet child neglect has not received proportionate attention from researchers and practitioners (Wolock & Horowitz, 1984).

Most reports of interventions with maltreating families provide limited information about effective interventions with neglectful families, because they typically fail to differentiate between abusive and neglectful parents, much less between subtypes of neglect. Yet our current understanding of the etiology of child neglect indicates there are unique characteristics and contributing causes of neglect that require differential treatment of neglectful and abusive families. The purpose of this article is to review the existing studies of interventions with neglectful parents and their children and to identify interventions whose effectiveness is supported by the studies. Studies reviewed are limited to those reported over the past 12 years that clearly identify neglectful parents or children as at least part of the sample. Studies of neglect interventions that do not employ rigorous experimental designs with control groups have of necessity been included in this review, because they comprise the majority of existing studies.

Child neglect is a term that encompasses a broad range of conditions for which there is little consistency of definition among practitioners, policymakers, or researchers. Child neglect is the term used most often to encompass parents' or other caretakers' failure to provide basic physical health care, supervision, nutrition, personal hygiene, emotional nurturing, education, or safe housing. It also includes child abandonment or expulsion, and custody-related forms of inattention to the child's needs. There are serious dilemmas in operationally defining what constitutes basic or "minimally adequate" care of children in all of the above areas, and thus in defining child neglect. The issues involve the seriousness of the harm or threatened harm to the child and intention or culpability of the parent versus community or societal conditions for which parents can hardly be held responsible (Dubowitz, Black, Starr, & Zuravin, 1993 [this issue]). There is also a lack of consistency among researchers on conceptual and operational definitions for subtypes of neglect (Zuravin, 1991). Because the outcomes for children and the effects of interventions may be quite different for different types of neglect, this is a serious deficiency in the existing research on neglect (Zuravin, 1991).

This review of intervention efforts is constrained by the lack of clarity in definition of neglect in most studies. For the purposes of this review, the term child neglect will be used to mean failure of a child's or adolescent's parents or other primary care provider to provide one or more of their child's basic physical, emotional, or educational needs. This broad definition of neglect encompasses the deprived condition of children toward which the interventive efforts reviewed here are directed.

DIFFERENTIAL ASSESSMENT OF NEGLECT

Effective intervention to remedy child neglect must be based on a comprehensive assessment of the neglectful family, with attention to the type of neglect and to the contributing causes at the individual, family, neighborhood, and community level. Research into characteristics and causality of neglect identifies significant differences between chronically neglectful and nonchronic, "new neglect" families (Nelson, Saunders, & Landsman, 1990). Chronically neglectful families are typically multiproblem families with pervasive deficits in knowledge, skills, and tangible resources, whereas nonchronically neglectful families have experienced recent life crises that have overwhelmed normally sufficient coping strategies. The characteristics of chronically neglectful families suggest the need for a comprehensive array of tangible aid, supportive, and therapeutic interventions over a long period of time to increase home management, child care, and social skills. The more recent, nonchronic neglect suggests the need for shorter-term crisis intervention, stress management, support groups, and family counseling (Nelson et al., 1990).

Although emotional/psychological and physical neglect are often intertwined, they also exhibit important differences. The author's current study of family functioning in neglectful families indicates that families who are psychologically neglectful function less well than do those whose neglect is only physical (Gaudin, Polansky, & Kilpatrick, 1989).

To formulate appropriate interventions with neglectful families it is critical to distinguish between inadequate supervision that is related to the parent's impulsive behavior, depression, alcoholism or other dysfunctional behavior and that which is related to a parent's lack of knowledge and understanding of age appropriate expectations for a toddler (Azar, Robinson, Hekimian, & Twentyman, 1984; Herrenkohl, Herrenkohl, & Egolf, 1983). For example, neglect that is related to a parent's mental retardation requires intensive, in-home, behavioral instruction to remedy knowledge and skills deficits (Lutzker, 1990).

Much neglect is related to the dilapidated and hazardous housing occupied by many poor families. Leaded paint or rat-infested homes place children at great risk of serious harm, although the neglect may be more societal than parental. On the other hand, lack of money management, shopping, menu-planning, and cooking skills may be at the root of a parent's nutritional neglect. Effective intervention to remedy neglect in the former situation may call for advocacy with landlords and housing authorities, whereas the latter calls for structured, behavioral approaches to teaching home management, budgeting, and shopping skills (Lutzker, 1990).

Psychological immaturity, characterized as "infantile personality," "impulse ridden," or "apathy-futility syndrome" by Polansky, Chalmers, Williams, and Buttenwieser (1981) or lack of "psychological complexity" by Pianta, Egeland, and Erickson (1989), is a personality characteristic of many neglectful mothers that is often related to their failure to receive nurturing as children. This diagnosis indicates the need for skillful therapeutic interventions over an extended period that enable the parent to modify negative, dysfunctional self-images incorporated as a result of early experiences of neglect and abuse. Project STEEP is an example of an intensive, individual, in-home counseling and group intervention program that seeks to change these dysfunctional self-perceptions and break the intergenerational cycle of maltreatment (Egeland & Erickson, 1990). The effectiveness of this program has not yet been confirmed by published research.

A significant portion of neglectful families exhibit symptoms of depression, but most are not receiving treatment for depression (Zuravin, 1988). Differential diagnosis and treatment for depression should be a component of the interventions with many neglectful parents.

For the most part, intervention efforts with neglectful families have not made these critical distinctions between types and causes of neglect. Nevertheless, the relatively modest number of studies of interventions that do differentiate neglectful families from other types of maltreatment provide some direction for more effective interventions with neglectful families.

ASSUMPTIONS AND GENERAL
GUIDELINES FOR INTERVENTION

Because of the close association of neglect with poverty, progressive social policy that allocates significantly greater proportions of public funds for programs in the areas of housing, health care, education, and child care will be the most significant intervention to reduce the epidemic proportions of child neglect in the United States. The one fifth of all U.S. children who are currently living in poverty are at high risk for child neglect. The 1988 *National Incidence Study* indicated that the rate of known neglect among families with income less than $15,000 per year was *nine times* the rate for families with income more than $15,000 (U.S. Department of Health and Human Services, 1988). Significant increases in health, education, housing, and employment programs will be necessary to improve the economic resources of the families of these 13.4 million children, to raise them out of poverty, and to enable them to provide adequate care for their children.

Recognizing that poverty continues to be a major contributing cause of child neglect, from our current knowledge of the nature and causes of neglect we can formulate some general guidelines for intervention at the individual, parent-child dyad, and family systems levels to remedy or prevent child neglect. Effective interventions must be predicated on the following assumptions.

First, neglectful parents are typically poor and lack access to resources. Therefore, the intervention plan must include brokering and advocacy to mobilize concrete formal and informal helping resources. Case management of multiple services is necessary. Successful mobilization of outside resources to meet the parent's needs, as they identify them, helps to overcome the neglectful parent's sense of hopelessness, resistance, and distrust of professional helpers. A range of community services often must be mobilized to meet critical needs of neglectful families. Services may include the following: (a) emergency financial assistance, (b) low-cost housing, (c) emergency food and clothing, (d) free or low-cost medical care, (e) transportation, (f) homemaker/home management aides, (g) low-cost child care, (h) mental health assessment and treatment, (i) temporary foster care, (j) budget/credit counseling, (k) job training and placement, (l) parent support/skills training, and (m) recreation programs for children and parents.

Second, neglectful parents are typically lacking in psychological maturity, often as a result of their own deficient nurturing as children. They tend to be egocentric, impulsive, and lack the ability to arrange their lives to meet their needs and those of their children (Polansky et al., 1981). They require nurturing themselves to enable them to nurture their children adequately. They have negative perceptions of themselves as parents and lack confidence in their abilities to improve their parenting (Pianta, Egeland, & Erickson, 1989). Treatment goals must include building feelings of hope, self-esteem, and self-efficacy. Intervention with neglectful parents requires that the professional helper "parent the parent" before they are able to nurture successfully. They must realize that neglectful parents are often childlike in their self-centeredness and must "begin where the client is." It has been suggested that this kind of temporary parental role-taking by the family therapist is essential for successful family intervention with severely dysfunctional families (Wietzman, 1985). The professional helper must listen empathetically and validate the concerns and feelings of the neglectful parent, then support and encourage progressively more independent, responsible behavior. Fostering dysfunctional dependency is avoided by maintaining a balance between supportive counseling, enabling the parent to use supportive formal and informal services, and communicating clear expectations for improved functioning.

Third, most neglectful parents want to be good parents but lack the personal, financial, and/or supportive resources. Professional helpers must assume that parents want to improve the quality of care for their children. Interventions should be planned and delivered under that assumption.

Fourth, all parents have strengths that can be mobilized. The often hidden strengths of the neglectful parent must be identified during the assessment process, reinforced, and interventions planned to build on those strengths (Landsman, Nelson, Allen, & Tyler, 1992). Neglectful parents are empowered when the professional helper systematically reinforces the parent's limited, incremental achievements with tangible rewards and praise. It is helpful to reward a parent's efforts to wash the dishes, make a positive statement about herself or her child, play with her child, prepare a hot meal, make a friend, or keep an appointment.

Fifth, treatment goals must be relevant, realistic, clearly stated, and achievable. They must be mutually agreed on by the parents, children, and the professional helper. Goals should emerge from the problems identified by the parents and the professional helper and from the causes of, or obstacles to remedying, the problems. Goals should be clearly expressed in a written treatment plan that is developed with the family. An example of a limited goal might be for a chronically neglectful parent to secure hazardous materials in a cabinet out of children's reach or to keep a medical appointment. The treatment/service plan should be clearly outlined with responsibilities for parent and professional helpers clearly identified and expressed in the form of a written contract between the neglecting parent and the professional helper.

Sixth, the exercise of legal authority by the professional helper is sometimes necessary to overcome the initial denial and apathy of the neglectful parent. The use of a court order to obtain medical treatment for a child is an example of how legal action may be required in the interests of a medically neglected child (Hawes, 1982). The results of one study indicated that legally mandated participation of maltreating parents in parenting groups was found to produce comparably successful outcomes to those obtained from voluntary participants (Irueste-Montes & Montes, 1988). Confrontation with the reality of legal mandates and the possibility of legal intervention is sometimes necessary to disturb the dysfunctional family balance and mobilize the parent to change neglectful parenting practices. Threat of legal action should be used only as a last resort, after other efforts to obtain cooperation have failed.

Seventh, treatment of chronic neglect is not a short-term project. Successful intervention with neglectful parents should last for 12 to 18 months (Daro, 1988). When neglect is not a chronic pattern, shorter-term, intensive intervention may be successful, but this has not been established by empirical studies.

DIRECTIONS FROM RESEARCH

Evaluative research on the effectiveness of interventions with neglectful families is very limited. Most of the studies are based on small, nonrandom, clinical samples of parents who have been reported, investigated, and verified as neglectful according to operational definitions of neglect that are not consistent between studies. Controlled, experimental designs are rare. Subtypes of neglect are not identified nor are the unique contributions of discrete interventions evaluated in most of the studies. The most rigorously designed studies are those that involve behavioral approaches, evaluated using time series, single-case designs.

The overall results of the studies of interventions with neglect are not highly encouraging. Reviews of projects to remedy neglect indicate that, with few exceptions, even the best conceived and funded intervention programs with neglectful families have had limited success. Daro (1988) reviewed 19 demonstration programs, funded by the National Center on Child Abuse and Neglect over the period from 1978 to 1982, five of which specifically targeted neglectful families. The evaluations of these projects were based on ratings by project staff at case closing of improvements in client functioning on a 3-point scale and ratings of the likelihood of future neglect occurring. The programs evaluated did not include control groups. Daro's study revealed that in only 53% of the neglectful families was there improvement in the family's overall level of functioning, and 70% were judged likely to recidivate after case closing. In 66% of the neglectful families there were additional reports of neglect while intervention was in progress. She concluded that regardless of the type of intervention, the severity of the families' problems was the most powerful predictor of outcome. The presence of alcohol and drug problems consistently correlated with less successful outcomes. Nevertheless, some interventions proved more successful than others, and the reviews by Daro and others provide some helpful guidelines for more effective interventions with neglectful families (Cohn, 1979; Cohn & Daro, 1987; Daro, 1988; Videka-Sherman, 1988).

BEHAVIORAL APPROACHES/SOCIAL SKILLS TRAINING

Behavioral techniques appear to be very effective with neglectful families because they break problems down into manageable components, emphasize immediate positive reinforcement for limited improvements, include real-life application and practice to acquire skills, and provide for follow-up to maintain gains (Howing, Wodarski, Gaudin, & Kurtz, 1989). Because of the emphasis on skills acquisition and behavior change, the results appear to endure, whereas other efforts to provide supportive services indicate that improvements made by neglectful families are lost when intensive, supportive services are withdrawn at termination (Edgington & Hall, 1982).

Prior reviews of intervention projects with neglectful families suggest that structured intervention approaches that have clearly defined, short-range goals, and well-defined intervention activities and procedures are more successful than loosely defined "casework" or "counseling" interventions (Cohn, 1979; Daro, 1988; Videka-Sherman, 1988). Contracting with neglectful parents for specific activities and goals to be achieved has been found to be helpful (Rozansky & Chambers, 1982). The Nurturing Program and the Small Wonder infant stimulation exercises are two examples of structured programs that provide such clearly articulated sequential activities (American Guidance Services, 1982; Bavolek & Comstock, 1983).

Project 12-Ways is one of the most carefully documented and successful programs for neglectful parents reported in the research literature. The program uses in-home behavioral training to teach neglectful parents grocery-shopping and menu-planning skills, skills to remedy specific safety hazards and improve the cleanliness in the home, and identification of children's illness symptoms. Parents and children were taught specific skills using the behavioral techniques of modeling, coaching, and positive reinforcement to remedy specific skill deficits and environmental conditions. Evaluation of changes in home cleanliness, meal planning, and home safety using single-subject designs did reveal significant positive gains over time. Reviews for up to 42 weeks after termination of interventions revealed that improvement in specific skills was maintained (Barone, Greene, & Lutzker, 1986; Delgado & Lutzker, 1988; Lutzker, 1990; Watson-Percel, Lutzker, Greene, & McGimpsey, 1988).

Behavioral, skill-training approaches have been used successfully to enhance the typically impoverished parent-child interactions between neglectful mothers and their preschool children. Levenstein's (1975) Mother-Child Home Program is an in-home program that uses toys and behavioral techniques to teach mothers verbal and nonverbal interaction skills. This program was used by McLaren (1988) to increase the positive verbal interactions between neglectful mothers and their preschool children, who also improved on a measure of their socioemotional behavior. However, the absence of controls and undocumented reliability and validity of the measures used severely limit the confidence that can be placed in these results. Lutzker and colleagues (Lutzker, Lutzker, Braunling-McMorrow, & Eddleman, 1987) used modeling, coaching, and positive reinforcement to teach affective adult-child interaction skills to two neglectful mothers and infant stimulation skills to young mothers at high risk of neglect or abuse. The neglectful mothers continued to consistently display the desired behaviors at follow-up observations (Lutzker, 1990).

The use of printed material, books, charts, or other handouts as part of the intervention has also proved to be useful with neglectful families.

> Props such as these can enhance generalization and maintenance of treatment effects because they assist the use of intervention ideas in the home when the practitioner is not present. They may also enhance needed structure in the home environment and serve as visible reminders of concepts and techniques used in the treatment. (Videka-Sherman, 1988, p. D-59)

In Project 12-Ways, Sarber and colleagues used pictures, color-coded index cards, and charts for teaching nutrition, menu-planning, and grocery-shopping skills to a mentally retarded neglectful mother (Sarber, Halasz, Messmer, Bickett, & Lutzker, 1983; see also, Lutzker, 1990). On the other hand, the use of printed instructional materials alone to teach enhanced mother-child interaction skills to neglectful and abusive mothers resulted in less satisfactory mother-child interactions in one experimental study (Crittenden, 1991). In this trial of multiple methods for improving mother-child interactions, strategies that only passively involved the mothers (demonstration/modeling,

227

positive reinforcement of mothers' responsive behaviors, and use of printed materials) were ineffective and sometimes counterproductive. The successful strategies were those that involved direct work with each parent and active involvement of mothers in role playing, reviewing, and critiquing videotapes of their own interactions with their children and receiving specific feedback in a nonjudgmental context.

Neglectful parents typically have poor social/interactional skills, and behavioral interventions to teach social skills have proven to be an essential component of successful programs like the Homebuilders family preservation program (Kinney, Haapala, Booth, & Leavitt, 1991). Neglectful parents often lack basic verbal/social interaction skills necessary for group participation and for initiating and maintaining social relationships. Use of modeling, coaching, rehearsing, and feedback — individually, then in support groups — can significantly enhance neglectful parents' social skills and result in strengthened informal support networks (Gaudin, Wodarski, Arkinson, & Avery, 1991).

MULTISERVICE INTERVENTIONS

Because most chronically neglectful families are multiproblem families with many deficits, no one intervention technique or method will be successful (Cohn & Daro, 1987; Daro, 1988). Successful intervention requires the delivery of a broad range of concrete, supportive community services from multiple sources and a combination of individual, family, and group methods that include individual counseling, behavioral methods, individual and group parenting education, and family therapy.

Project 12-Ways, mentioned above, is an example of such a multiservice approach (Lutzker, Frame, & Rice, 1982). The 12 different services offered to neglectful families included emergency financial assistance, transportation, homemakers, recreational opportunities, weight loss program, and parent support groups, as well as behavioral techniques for teaching parenting and home management skills. Comparison of recidivism rates for recipients of these special services with a randomly selected group of families with similar histories of maltreatment who did not receive the services revealed significant differences in reduction of multiple incidents of maltreatment in the experimental group, but not significant differences in overall recidivism rates (Lutzker & Rice, 1984). However, as mentioned above, follow-up reviews revealed that improvement in specific home management and child management skills endured.

The Family Support Center in Ogden, Utah (Mugridge, 1991) is another intensive, in-home, family-centered intervention model with multiple services designed for chronically neglectful families. This program combines intensive, biweekly, in-home instruction in nutrition, home and money management, and child care skills from a trained parent aide, parent support groups, employment preparation, and facilitation of connections with community services. Outcome results of this project have not yet been published.

The National Center on Child Abuse and Neglect funded six 3-year demonstration projects targeting chronic child neglect. Reports from two of the six funded sites in this demonstration confirm that a combination of parenting groups, intensive individual in-home counseling, and supportive interventions by indigenous paraprofessional parent aides was necessary to bring about improvements in neglectful parenting practices (Landsman et al., 1992; Perez de Colon, 1992). Parenting practices were measured using Polansky et al.'s (1981) Childhood Level of Living Scale but the research designs did not include control groups.

FAMILY-FOCUSED INTERVENTIONS

Daro (1988) concluded from her review of demonstration projects that interventions that included all family members, rather than focusing only on the principal care provider, were more successful with neglectful families. Although not definitive about the type of family intervention, she concluded that interventions must target the dysfunctional family system, not just the parent. Traditional, in-office, one-to-one counseling by professionals has proven to be ineffective with neglect (Cohn & Daro, 1987). This conclusion is consistent with what we know from systems theory about the resistance of systems to change, even if the balance is dysfunctional. In their Philadelphia study, Polansky and colleagues advised that assertive, intrusive intervention is often necessary with neglectful families to disturb the dysfunctional family balance in the interest of achieving a more functional family system balance that does not sacrifice the needs of the children (Polansky et al., 1981). Some examples of such family interventions are those that seek to re-allocate family role tasks, establish clear intergenerational boundaries, clarify communication between family members, reframe parents' dysfunctional perceptions of themselves and their children, and enable parents to assume a responsible leadership role in the family.

Family empowerment was an emphasis in both the Family Support Center (Mugridge, 1991) and the Self-Sufficiency Project (Landsman et al., 1992). These intervention models emphasized mobilization of family strengths, active involvement in services by all family members, and active participation in decision making by neglectful parents about the services they received. A constructivist therapy approach (White & Epston, 1990) was used by the Self-Sufficiency Project. Families participating in weekly multifamily group sessions were encouraged to remember and talk about times when they had been effective in their lives, to reconstruct their life stories to show how inner strengths had allowed them to overcome adversities.

The Nurturing Program is a time-limited parent education program for abusive and neglectful families that insists on the importance of the active involvement of both parents and children (Bavolek & Comstock, 1983). The rationale is that to change established patterns of abusive and neglectful parenting all family members must learn new ways of interacting. This cannot be accomplished unless the children, as well as the adults, are taught new ways of thinking and responding.

Project TIME for Parents was one of the more successful demonstration programs reviewed by Daro (1988) that employed in-home family therapy along with contracting, behavioral interventions, and financial incentives to assist neglectful families (Rozansky & Chambers, 1982).

Intensive family preservation programs (IFP), developed over the past 15 years to prevent out-of-home placement of abused and neglected children, also offer promise for intervention with neglectful families. These short-term, intensive intervention programs offer families on the brink of disintegration an array of tangible, supportive, and family therapy services. Several variations of family preservation programs have been developed following the prototypic Homebuilders model (Nelson, Landsman, & Deutelbaum, 1990). Because most of these programs deliver a range of intensive in-home services to dysfunctional families, they offer some promise for neglectful families. However, two recent evaluations of the effectiveness of family preservation programs with neglectful families have indicated less satisfactory results than with abusive families or families of delinquents. In one study the out-of-home placement rate for children at risk due to neglect was almost 2.5 times greater than that for children at risk of placement for other types of maltreatment (Yuan & Struckman-Johnson, 1991). In the other study, families identified at intake as neglectful received IFP services longer, but fewer hours per week. The out-of-home placement rate for children served from neglectful families (24%) was twice the average placement rate of 12% for all children served (Berry, in press). Nevertheless, further study is needed to test the effectiveness of other IFP models with neglectful families. Mugridge's (1991) Family Support Center program in Utah is one such program for chronic neglect that is being evaluated. Such programs may prove to be more effective with nonchronic neglect, which has been found to be associated with recent life crises (Nelson et al., 1990).

GROUP APPROACHES

The reviews of child abuse and neglect demonstration projects by both Daro (1988) and Cohn (1979) concluded that projects that included group methods were more successful with abusing and neglecting families. Participation in Parents Anonymous groups was found to be particularly effective, regardless of what other services were received by parents (Cohn, 1979). Groups for neglectful parents that provide very basic child care information and skills, problem solving, home management, and social interaction skills were more successful with neglectful parents than those offering more general content on child development and needs of children (Daro, 1988).

Aderman and Russell (1990) reported improvements in abusive and neglectful parents' care and nurturing of their children after their participation in nine weeklong group meetings that used techniques derived from constructivist approaches to family treatment. The therapists used metalevel circular questioning to challenge the premises underlying the families' dysfunctional patterns of interaction and to shift parents' focus from their perceived need to defend themselves to the needs of their children. Unfortunately, the evaluation of this latter study was based on nonsystematic, qualitative judgments of the therapists with a small group of abusive and neglectful parents.

Groups were the primary method used in the Oregon Self-Sufficiency Project to improve the functioning of chronically neglecting families (Landsman et al., 1992). Separate groups for parents, children, and teens followed by combined multiple family groups ran simultaneously one evening a week for 24 weeks. Because of the project's emphasis on "family empowerment," the initial parent group was largely unstructured and encouraged parent involvement in setting group agendas and activities. Experience dictated that more direction and structure was needed, at least initially, to facilitate active involvement of neglectful parents. Rather than being parenting classes to provide information, the groups were designed to provide encouragement and support for families to develop their strengths, become involved in decisions about their lives, and provide mutual support. The group services were supplemented by a range of services that included in-home parent training, individual and family therapy, emergency assistance, crisis nursery, homemaker services, alcohol and drug treatment, public health and mental health services. Families attended, on average, only half of the 24 group sessions. Only 14 of 31 families served over a period of a year and a half showed significant improvements on self-report and observational measures. Measured improvements were positively correlated with number of group sessions attended and hours of in-house parent training from parent aides. Drug and alcohol problems were associated with negative outcomes.

INTENSIVE, PROBLEM-FOCUSED CASEWORK/COUNSELING TECHNIQUES

Daro's (1988) review indicated that intensive, weekly, in-home casework counseling focusing on concrete problem solving is effective with neglectful families. This conclusion was confirmed by the author's experience with the Social Network Intervention Project, by the earlier Bowen Center Project, and by the results of Lutzker and colleagues with Project 12-Ways (Gaudin et al., 1991; Lutzker et al., 1982; Sullivan, Spasser, & Penner, 1977).

Dawson, DeArmas, McGrath, and Kelly (1986) successfully taught problem-solving skills to three neglectful mothers through weekly in-home sessions over a 9-week period. Systematic assessments pre, post, and at 15-month follow-up documented improved abilities to apply acquired problem-solving skills. Mugridge's (1991) Family Support Center and the Self-Sufficiency Project (Landsman et al., 1992) also featured intensive, weekly, in-home instruction, plus counseling and support from a parent aide.

INTERVENTIONS TO STRENGTHEN INFORMAL SUPPORT NETWORKS

The informal social networks of neglectful parents are typically closed, unstable, and tend to be dominated by often critical, non-supportive relatives (Crittenden, 1988; Polansky, Gaudin, Ammons, & Davis, 1985). They do not provide the kind of tangible aid, advice and guidance, social and emotional support most helpful to parents. The members of their social networks typically share and reinforce neglectful parenting norms and behavior. Neglectful families often lack the social skills to maintain or to expand their social networks. Interventions to enhance network supports include the following (Gaudin et al., 1991):

1. Direct intervention by the professional into network linkages to mediate, facilitate communication, problem-solve, modify, and reframe network members' negative, dysfunctional perceptions of the neglectful parent and/or the parent's negative perceptions of network members.
2. Use of volunteers and paid parent aides to expand and enrich limited networks, provide new information, positive norms, and helpful suggestions about child care.
3. Social skills training to teach basic communication and social skills individually and in parent support groups through modeling, practice, rehearsal, and reinforcement. Teaching neglectful parents to make and maintain friendships, and to reciprocate aid received from social network members in order to maintain mutually supportive linkages.

4. Parent support groups that provide safe opportunities for development of social skills and for making new friends to expand support networks.
5. Identification, linking, consultation with indigenous "neighborhood natural helpers" (people in the area with recognized natural helping skills) to enhance the parent's informal helping network.
6. Linking neglectful parents with existing supportive groups in the community, for example, church, school, or neighborhood groups.

These network interventions, when employed with intensive casework, case management, and tangible aid, were successful in significantly strengthening informal supports and improving the adequacy of child care on objective measures completed by the caseworkers providing services over an average of 10 months of service. Nonsignificant gains were achieved over the same period of time by neglectful families who received routine casework/case management services. The conclusions of this study are limited by design flaws that allow for bias on outcome measures completed by the workers and lack of follow-up assessments.

USE OF PARAPROFESSIONAL PARENT-AIDES AND VOLUNTEERS

The use of paraprofessionals to support and supplement the interventions of professionals has proven to enhance the effectiveness of interventions with neglectful and abusive parents (Cohn, 1979; Cohn & Daro, 1987; Gaudin et al., 1991; Landsman et al., 1992; Mugridge, 1991). Paid or volunteer paraprofessionals provide emotional support, supplemental child care and nurturing, home management training, help with problem solving, and essential transportation to enable parents and children to obtain supportive community services (Landsman et al., 1992; Miller, Fein, Howe, Gaudio, & Bishop, 1985; Videka-Sherman, 1988). Paraprofessionals have also been trained to teach parent-child interaction skills to neglectful parents through structured interaction exercises. One successful program used paraprofessional parent educators to teach parents simple to more complex interaction skills using simple counting and color recognition games (Videka-Sherman, 1988).

The services provided by paraprofessionals cannot replace the essential intensive counseling by the trained professional helper, but in combination with such professional intervention have been found to be a cost-effective way to enhance the effectiveness of interventions (Cohn & Daro, 1987). It is essential that paraprofessionals be well-trained, have clearly defined roles and tasks, and have ongoing professional consultation and supervision.

TREATMENT OF NEGLECTED CHILDREN

Longitudinal studies indicate that child victims of neglect suffer serious developmental deficits (Erickson, Egeland, & Pianta, 1989; Wodarski, Kurtz, Gaudin, & Howing, 1990). Prevention of these consequences of neglect requires interventions to supplement the inadequate nurturing that children receive from their parents. The results of the existing treatment research indicate that much more of the intervention resources should be devoted to direct therapeutic efforts with the preschool, school-age, and teenage children and adolescents who are victims of neglect.

Most intervention programs with neglectful families focus services on the parents, and few offer direct therapeutic services to the children (Cohn & Daro, 1987). Removal of children and placement in foster care to assure the safety of the child is the most widely used direct intervention with children. But the results of demonstration projects that provided direct intervention to remedy the effects of neglect on the children have been much more promising than the outcomes of interventions with the parents.

Daro's (1988) review of 19 demonstration projects providing a wide range of direct services for over 1,600 abused and neglected children revealed improvements in all areas of functioning for more than 70% of the children served. Group counseling, temporary shelter, and personal skill development classes were effective interventions with adolescents. Therapeutic day care services for preschool children proved to be the most effective service for both the neglected and physically abused children served by the 19 projects reviewed. Removal and placement of children resulted in reduced rates of repeated maltreatment for children and adolescents. However, the lack of control groups and reliance on the judgments of the children's therapists for assessment of outcomes suggests the need for controlled replication studies to further evaluate these results.

Howing, Wodarski, Kurtz, and Gaudin (1990) have proposed a social skills training model for neglected and abused children to remedy developmental skills deficits. The model relies on learning theory and the effectiveness of social skills training with adults, and with socially withdrawn and aggressive children.

THERAPEUTIC INTERVENTIONS WITH YOUNG CHILDREN

Daro's (1988) review indicated that child care programs for children containing specially designed therapeutic activities to provide cognitive stimulation, cultural enrichment, and development of motor skills and social skills had a significant impact on the child's functioning and the prevention of repeated maltreatment by parents. She suggested that therapeutic child care requires thorough individual assessments to identify specific cognitive, physical, emotional, and behavioral problems and intensive, daily contact between the children and the child care staff to carry out the planned therapeutic activities. Child care staff must be well-trained to understand the negative developmental effects of neglect and provide therapeutic interactions with the children. Neglectful parents should also be involved in the program and be receiving simultaneous intervention to remedy deficits in parenting. The Berkeley Planning Associates (1982) evaluation of therapeutic child care projects for the National Council on Child Abuse and Neglect (NCCAN) provides guidelines for the development of these programs for preschoolers. Daro (1988) has briefly summarized these guidelines for therapeutic child care strategies specific to identified developmental problems of children.

Preschool children who are victims of neglect often have severe deficits in peer interaction skills. The use of peer-initiated social interactions has been used to enhance the peer interaction skills of socially withdrawn neglected preschool children (Fantuzzo, Stovall, Schacchtel, Goins, & Hall, 1987). The significant increases in social interactions by the maltreated children were maintained at follow-up, 2 weeks after treatment ended. Peer-mediated interactions were found to be more effective than adult-mediated interactions for increasing neglected children's social skills (Davis & Fantuzzo, 1989).

236

PROGRAMS FOR OLDER CHILDREN AND ADOLESCENTS

School-age children who are victims of neglect have serious deficits in cognitive, academic skills that require intervention to prevent school failure and dropout, and a continuing downward cycle of functioning (Wodarski et al., 1990). School-based and community programs are required to remedy social and learning deficits and thus to prevent a continued cycle of cognitive deprivation, failure, and possible subsequent neglect in the next generation of parents. Remedial and preventive programs and services for school age children and adolescents should include

1. Special education programs with low teacher-to-child ratios, structured learning-by-doing activities, positive reinforcement, and the best computer-assisted learning technology available are needed to remedy deficits in cognitive stimulation and motivation to learn.
2. School or community-based tutorial programs using professional teachers or volunteers can provide neglected children and adolescents with the necessary academic help, encouragement, and a relationship with a nurturing adult to help overcome academic deficits.
3. Group counseling and personal skills development classes for older children and adolescents provide opportunities for developing life skills appropriate to their age and developmental level. Such programs have been found to result in improved functioning and reduced likelihood of further maltreatment for maltreated adolescents (Daro, 1988).
4. Volunteer or paid paraprofessional parent aides can provide one-to-one assistance to parents with learning child care skills and also provide supplemental parenting to children while parents are learning to improve their own child-caring abilities.
5. Volunteer big brothers and big sisters can provide neglected children with emotional nurturing, tutoring, cultural enrichment and recreation activities, positive role modeling, and vocational and career counseling.

SUMMARY AND CONCLUSIONS

The conclusions that can be drawn from most of the outcome studies of interventions with neglectful families are limited by the lack of rigor in the research. The studies are limited by small, nonrandom sampling of reported neglect cases, inconsistent definitions of neglect across studies, failure to specify subtypes of neglect, absence of control groups, use of unreliable measures, and failure to evaluate outcomes of discrete components of interventions. A small number of outcome studies on behavioral interventions with very small, nonrandom samples of neglectful parents and children have used single-subject, time series designs to demonstrate the effectiveness of these interventions in remedying specific skill deficits in neglectful parents.

The empirical support for the effectiveness of specific interventions with neglectful parents and children is thus very limited. Research on interventions with neglectful families is needed that is characterized by (a) clear operational definitions of neglect, (b) specification of subtypes of neglect treated, (c) inclusion of control groups, (d) specification of outcomes for discrete interventions or elements of intervention within multiservice models, (e) random samples, (f) inclusion of male family members, and (g) controlled studies of interventions with pre-school, school-age, and adolescent victims of neglect to remedy cognitive and social skill deficits.

Existing studies indicate that most interventions to remedy child neglect have been effective less than 50% of the time. One review of demonstration projects offers evidence that therapeutic group child care for preschool victims of abuse and neglect and group interventions with adolescents are successful in improving the children's functioning 70% of the time. Multiservice models that use family counseling, parent groups, and trained paraprofessionals to supplement skilled professional problem-solving counseling offer the best chances of success. Behavioral, skills-training interventions have been successfully used to significantly improve the social-interactional, and home management skills of neglectful parents. Although some short-term, in-home behavioral interventions have been successful in remedying specific deficits of neglectful mothers, interventions with neglectful families that continue for at least one year are the most successful in many studies.

Finally, because child neglect is so highly associated with poverty, effective interventions to prevent or remedy child neglect in the United States must be supported by social and economic programs needed to remedy the poverty that places one out of five children at nine times the risk of neglect as children from families with higher, more adequate incomes.

REFERENCES

Aderman, J., & Russell, T. (1990). A constructivist approach to working with abusive and neglectful parents. *Family Systems Medicine, 8*, 241-250.

American Association for Protecting Children. (1988). *Highlights of official child abuse and neglect reporting: 1986.* Denver, CO: American Humane Association.

American Guidance Services. (1982). *Small wonder kit.* Circle Pines, MN: Author.

Azar, S. T., Robinson, D. R., Hekimian, E., & Twentyman, C. T. (1984). Unrealistic expectations and problem-solving ability in maltreating and comparison mothers. *Journal of Consulting and Clinical Psychology, 52*, 687-691.

Barone, V. J., Greene, B. F., & Lutzker, J. R. (1986). Home safety with families being treated for child abuse and neglect. *Behavioral Modification, 14*, 230-254.

Bavolek, S., & Comstock, C. M. (1983). *The nurturing program for parents and children.* Eau Claire, WI: Family Development Associates.

Berkeley Planning Associates. (1982, February). *Therapeutic child care: Approaches to remediating the effects of child abuse and neglect: Evaluation of the clinical demonstration prospects on child abuse and neglect* (Report prepared for the National Center on Child Abuse and Neglect). Washington, DC: National Clearinghouse on Child Abuse and Neglect.

Berry, M. (in press). The relative effectiveness of family preservation services with neglecting families. In E. S. Morton & R. K. Grigsby (Eds.), *Advancing family preservation practice.* Newbury Park, CA: Sage.

Cohn, A. H. (1979). Essential elements of successful child abuse and neglect treatment. *Child Abuse & Neglect, 3*, 491-496.

Cohn, A. H., & Daro, D. (1987). Is treatment too late: What ten years of evaluation research tell us. *Child Abuse & Neglect, 11*, 433-442.

Crittenden, P. M. (1988). Family and dyadic patterns of functioning in maltreating families. In K. Browne, C. Davis, & P. Stratton (Eds.), *Early prediction and prevention of child abuse* (pp. 161-189). New York: Wiley.

Crittenden, P. M. (1991). Strategies for changing parental behavior. *The Advocate, 4*(2), 9.

Daro, D. (1988). *Confronting child abuse.* New York: Free Press.

Davis, S., & Fantuzzo, J. W. (1989). The effects of adult and peer social initiations on social behavior of withdrawn and aggressive maltreated preschool children. *Journal of Family Violence, 4*, 227-248.

Dawson, B., DeArmas, A., McGrath, M. L., & Kelly, J. A. (1986). Cognitive problem-solving training to improve the child-care judgement of child neglectful parents. *Journal of Family Violence, 1*(3), 209-221.

Delgado, L., & Lutzker, J. R. (1988). Training young parents to identify and report their children's illnesses. *Journal of Applied Behavior Analysis, 21*, 311-319.

Dubowitz, H., Black, M., Starr, R. H., Jr., & Zuravin, S. (1993). A conceptual definition of child neglect. *Criminal Justice & Behavior, 20*, 8-26.

Edgington, A., & Hall, M. (1982). *Dallas Children and Youth Project Child Neglect Demonstration Grant* (NCCAN Grant No. 90-C-1688). Dallas: University of Texas Health Services Center.

Egeland, F., & Erickson, M. F. (1990). Rising above the past: Strategies for helping new mothers break the cycle of abuse and neglect. *Zero to Three, 10*, 29-35.

Erickson, M. F., Egeland, B., & Pianta, R. (1989). The effects of maltreatment on the development of young children. In D. Cicchetti & V. Carlson (Eds.), *Child maltreatment: Theory and research on the causes and consequences of child abuse and neglect* (pp. 647-684). New York: Cambridge University Press.

Fantuzzo, J. W., Stovall, A., Schacchtel, D., Goins, C., & Hall, R. (1987). The effects of peer social initiations on social behavior of withdrawn maltreated preschool children. *Journal of Behavior Therapy and Experiential Psychiatry, 18*, 357-363.

Gaudin, J. M., Polansky, N. A., & Kilpatrick, A. C. (1989). *Family structure and functioning in neglectful families* (Grant No. 90-CA-1400). Washington, DC: National Center on Child Abuse and Neglect.

Gaudin, J. M., Wodarski, J. S., Arkinson, M. K., & Avery, L. S. (1991). Remedying child neglect: Effectiveness of social network interventions. *Journal of Applied Social Sciences, 15*, 97-123.

Hawes, B. (1982). Relief for the neglected child: Court-ordered medical treatment in nonemergency situations. *Santa Clara Law Review, 22*, 471-490.

Herrenkohl, R. C., Herrenkohl, E. C., & Egolf, B. P. (1983). Circumstances surrounding the occurrence of child maltreatment. *Journal of Consulting and Clinical Psychology, 51*, 424-431.

Howing, P. T., Wodarski, J. S., Gaudin, J. M., & Kurtz, P. D. (1989). Effective interventions to ameliorate the incidence of child maltreatment: The empirical base. *Social Work, 34*, 330-338.

Howing, P. T., Wodarski, J. S., Kurtz, P. D., & Gaudin, J. M. (1990). The empirical base for the implementation of social skills training with maltreated children. *Social Work, 35*, 460-467.

Irueste-Montes, A. M., & Montes, F. (1988). Court-ordered vs. voluntary treatment of abusive and neglectful parents. *Child Abuse & Neglect, 12*, 33-39.

Kinney, J., Haapala, D. A., Booth, C., & Leavitt, S. (1991). The HOMEBUILDERS Model. In E. M. Tracy, D. A. Haapala, J. Kinney, & P. Pecora (Eds.), *Intensive family preservation services: An instructional source book* (pp. 15-49). Cleveland, OH: Mandel School of Applied Social Sciences.

Landsman, M. J., Nelson, K., Allen, M., & Tyler, M. (1992). *The self-sufficiency project: Final report*. Iowa City, IA: National Resource Center in Family Based Services.

Levenstein, P. (1975). The mother-child home program. In M. C. Day & R. K. Parker (Eds.), *The preschool in action*. Boston: Allyn & Bacon.

Lutzker, J. R. (1990). Behavioral treatment of child neglect. *Behavior Modification, 14*, 301-315.

Lutzker, J. R., Frame, R. E., & Rice, J. M. (1982). Project 12-Ways: An eco-behavioral approach to the treatment and prevention of child abuse and neglect. *Education and Treatment of Children, 5*, 141-156.

Lutzker, J. R., & Rice, J. M. (1984). Project 12-Ways: Measuring outcome of a large in-home service for treatment and prevention of child abuse and neglect. *Child Abuse & Neglect, 8*, 519-524.

Lutzker, S. Z., Lutzker, J. R., Braunling-McMorrow, D., & Eddleman, J. (1987). Prompting to increase mother-baby stimulation with single mothers. *Journal of Child and Adolescent Psychotherapy, 4*, 3-12.

McLaren, L. (1988). Fostering mother-child relationships. *Child Welfare, 67*, 353-365.

Miller, K., Fein, E., Howe, G., Gaudio, C., & Bishop, G. (1985). A parent-aide program: Record-keeping, outcomes and costs. *Child Welfare, 64*, 407-419.

Mugridge, G. B. (1991, September). *Reducing chronic neglect*. Paper presented at Ninth National Conference on Child Abuse and Neglect, Denver, CO.

Nelson, K. E., Landsman, J. J., & Deutelbaum, W. (1990). Three models of family-centered placement prevention services. *Child Welfare, 69*, 3-21.

240

Nelson, K. E., Saunders, E., & Landsman, J. J. (1990). *Chronic neglect in perspective; A study of chronically neglected families in a large metropolitan county: Final report.* Oakdale: University of Iowa, National Center on Family Based Services.

Perez de Colon, M. (1992). *Identification and treatment of chronically neglectful parents: Final report.* San Antonio, TX: Avance-San Antonio.

Pianta, R., Egeland, B., & Erickson, M. F. (1989). The antecedents of maltreatment: Results of the mother-child interaction research project. In D. Cicchetti & V. Carlson (Eds.), *Child maltreatment: Theory and research on the causes of child abuse and neglect* (pp. 203-253). New York: Cambridge University Press.

Polansky, N. A., Chalmers, M. A., Williams, D. P., & Buttenwieser, E. W. (1981). *Damaged parents: An anatomy of child neglect.* Chicago: University of Chicago Press.

Polansky, N. A., Gaudin, J. M., Ammons, P. W., & Davis, K. B. (1985). The psychological ecology of the neglectful mother. *Child Abuse & Neglect, 9*, 265-275.

Rozansky, P., & Chambers, P. M. (1982). *Final report: Project TIME for parents* (Grant No. 90-C-1967). Washington, DC: National Center on Child Abuse and Neglect.

Sarber, R. E., Halasz, M. M., Messmer, M. C., Bickett, A. D., & Lutzker, J. R. (1983). Teaching menu planning and grocery shopping to a mentally retarded mother. *Mental Retardation, 21*, 101-106.

Sedlak, A. J. (1990). *Technical amendment to the study findings: National incidence and prevalence of child abuse and neglect, 1988.* Rockville, MD: Westat.

Sullivan, M., Spasser, M., & Penner, G. L. (1977). *The Bowen Center project for abused and neglected children.* Washington, DC: Public Services Administration, Office of Human Development.

U.S. Department of Health and Human Services. (1988). *Study findings: Study of national incidence and prevalence of child abuse and neglect.* Washington, DC: U.S. Government Printing Office.

Videka-Sherman, L. (1988). Intervention in child neglect: The empirical knowledge base. In *Research symposium on child neglect* (pp. 49-77). Washington, DC: National Center on Child Abuse and Neglect.

Watson-Percel, M., Lutzker, J. R., Greene, B. F., & McGimpsey, B. J. (1988). Assessment and modification of home cleanliness among families adjudicated for child neglect. *Behavioral Modification, 132*, 57-81.

Wietzman, J. (1985). Engaging the severely dysfunctional family in treatment: Basic considerations. *Family Process, 24*, 473-485.

White, M., & Epston, D. (1990). *Narrative means to therapeutic ends.* New York: Norton.

Wodarski, J. S., Kurtz, P. D., Gaudin, J. M., & Howing, P. T. (1990). Maltreatment and the school-aged child: Major academic, socioemotional and adaptive outcomes. *Social Work, 35*, 460-467.

Wolock, I., & Horowitz, B. (1984). Child maltreatment as a social problem: The neglect of neglect. *American Journal of Orthopsychiatry, 54*, 530-543.

Yuan, Y. T., & Struckman-Johnson, D. L. (1991). Placement outcomes for neglected children with prior placements in Family Preservation Programs. In M. K. Wells & D. E. Bigel (Eds.), *Family preservation services: Research and evaluation* (pp. 92-118). Newbury Park, CA: Sage.

Zuravin, S. (1988). Child abuse, child neglect, and maternal depression: Is there a connection? In *Research symposium on child neglect* (pp. D-23-D-48). Washington, DC: National Center on Child Abuse and Neglect.

Zuravin, S. (1991). Research definitions of child abuse and neglect: Current problems. In R. H. Starr & D. Wolfe (Eds.), *The effects of child abuse and neglect: Issues and research* (pp. 100-128). New York: Guilford.

ACKNOWLEDGMENTS

Kempe, C. Henry. "A Practical Approach to the Protection of the Abused Child and Rehabilitation of the Abusing Parent." *Pediatrics* 51 (1973): 804–12. Reprinted by permission of *Pediatrics*.

Davoren, Elizabeth. "Working with Abusive Parents: A Social Worker's View" *Children Today* 4 (1975): 2, 38–43. Reprinted with the permission of the U.S. Department of Health and Human Services. Courtesy of *Children Today*.

Steele, Brandt F. "Working with Abusive Parents: A Psychiatrist's View." *Children Today* 4 (1975): 3–5, 44. Reprinted with the permission of the U.S. Department of Health and Human Services. Courtesy of *Children Today*.

Reed, Judith. "Working with Abusive Parents: A Parent's View: An Interview with Jolly K." *Children Today* 4 (1975): 6–9. Reprinted with the permission of the U.S. Department of Health and Human Services. Courtesy of *Children Today*.

Fontana, Vincent J., and Esther Robison. "A Multidisciplinary Approach to the Treatment of Child Abuse." *Pediatrics* 57 (1976): 760–64. Reprinted by permission of *Pediatrics*.

Green, Arthur H. "A Psychodynamic Approach to the Study and Treatment of Child-Abusing Parents." *Journal of the American Academy of Child Psychiatry* 15 (1976): 414–29. Reprinted with the permission of Williams & Wilkins.

Blumberg, Marvin L. "Treatment of the Abused Child and the Child Abuser." *American Journal of Psychotherapy* 31 (1977): 204–15. Reprinted with the permission of the Association for the Advancement of Psychotherapy.

Roberts, Jacqueline, Keith Beswick, Bridget Leverton, and Margaret A. Lynch. "Prevention of Child Abuse: Group Therapy for Mothers and Children." *Practitioner* 219 (1977): 111–15. Reprinted with the permission of Morgan-Grampian Ltd. Courtesy of the *Practitioner*.

Wodarski, John S. "Comprehensive Treatment of Parents Who Abuse Their Children." *Adolescence* 16 (1981): 959–72. Reprinted with permission of Libra Publishers, Inc.

Shelton, Patricia Ross. "Separation and Treatment of Child-Abusing Families." *Family Therapy* 9 (1982): 53–60. Reprinted with the permission of Libra Publishers, Inc.

Conger, Rand D., and Benjamin B. Lahey. "Behavioral Intervention for Child Abuse." *Behavior Therapist* 5 (1982): 49–53. Reprinted with the permission of the Association for the Advancement of Behavior Therapy. Courtesy of Temple University.

Martin, Judith A. "Neglected Fathers: Limitations in Diagnostic and Treatment Resources for Violent Men." *Child Abuse & Neglect* 8 (1984): 387–92. Reprinted with the permission of Elsevier Science Ltd. Courtesy of Yale University Law Library.

Russell, Caroline M. and Barbara Bowlus. "A Bird's Eye View of the Child Molester." *Journal of Evolutionary Psychology* 5 (1984): 87–89. Reprinted with the permission of the Institute for Evolutionary Psychology. Courtesy of the *Journal of Evolutionary Psychology*.

Weiner, Barbara A. "Legal Issues Raised in Treating Sex Offenders." *Behavioral Sciences & the Law* 3 (1985): 325–40. Reprinted with the permission of John Wiley & Sons Ltd. Courtesy of Yale University Law Library.

Lanyon, Richard I. "Theory and Treatment in Child Molestation." *Journal of Consulting and Clinical Psychology* 54 (1986): 176–82. Copyright (1986) by the American Psychological Association. Reprinted by permission.

Cohn, Anne Harris, and Deborah Daro. "Is Treatment Too Late: What Ten Years of Evaluative Research Tell Us." *Child Abuse & Neglect* 11 (1987): 433–42. Reprinted with the permission of Elsevier Science Ltd. Courtesy of Yale University Law Library.

Gilgun, Jane F., and Teresa M. Connor. "How Perpetrators View Child Sexual Abuse." *Social Work* 34 (1989): 249–51. Reprinted with the permission of the National Association of Social Workers.

Fuller, A. Kenneth. "Child Molestation and Pedophilia: An Overview for the Physician." *Journal of the American Medical*

Association 261 (1989): 602–6. Copyright 1989, The American Medical Association.

Kaufman, Keith L., and Leslie Rudy. "Future Directions in the Treatment of Physical Child Abuse" *Criminal Justice and Behavior* 18 (1991): 82–97. Reprinted with the permission of Sage Publications, Inc.

McGrath, Robert J. "Sex-Offender Risk Assessment and Disposition Planning: A Review of Empirical and Clinical Findings." *International Journal of Offender Therapy and Comparative Criminology* 35 (1991): 328–50. Reprinted with the permission of Guilford Publications, Inc.

Becker, Judith V., and John A. Hunter, Jr. "Evaluation of Treatment Outcome for Adult Perpetrators of Child Sexual Abuse." *Criminal Justice and Behavior* 19 (1992): 74–92. Reprinted with the permission of Sage Publications, Inc.

Priest, Ronnie, and Annalee Smith. "Counseling Adult Sex Offenders: Unique Challenges and Treatment Paradigms." *Journal of Counseling & Development* 71 (1992): 27–32. Reprinted with the permission of the American Association for Counseling and Development.

Gaudin, James M., Jr. "Effective Intervention with Neglectful Families" *Criminal Justice and Behavior* 20 (1993): 66–89. Reprinted with the permission of Sage Publications, Inc.

SERIES INDEX BY AUTHOR

Please Note: Numbers at the end of each entry refer to the volume in which the article appears.

Rights Termination for Abused and Neglected Children" (1981) 7

Bourne, R., et al., "'Family Autonomy' or 'Coercive Intervention'? Ambiguity and Conflict in the Proposed Standards for Child Abuse and Neglect" (1977) 10

Briere, J., et al., "Symptomatology in Men Who Were Molested As Children: A Comparison Study" (1988) 4

Britton, H.L., et al., "Use of Nonanatomical Dolls in the Sexual Abuse Interview" (1991) 9

Browne, A., et al., "Impact of Child Sexual Abuse: A Review of the Research" (1986) 4

Bryer, J.B., et al., "Childhood Sexual and Physical Abuse as Factors in Adult Psychiatric Illness" (1987) 4

Bulkley, J.A., "Evidentiary and Procedural Trends in State Legislation and Other Emerging Legal Issues in Child Sexual Abuse Cases" (1985) 8

Burgess, et al., "Abused to Abuser: Antecedents of Socially Deviant Behaviors" (1987) 4

Cahill, C., et al., "Treatment of Sexual Abuse which Occurred in Childhood: A Review" (1991) 5

Callanan, B., et al., "The Interstate Compact on the Placement of Children" (1975) 7

Campbell, E., "Birth Control as a Condition of Probation for Those Convicted of Child Abuse: A Psycholegal Discussion of Whether the Condition Prevents Future Child Abuse or Is a Violation of Liberty" (1992/3) 9

Campbell, G.E., "Criminal Law—

Sodomy—The Crime and the Penalty" (1954) 2

Catz, R.S., et al., "The Requirement of Appointment of Counsel for Indigent Parents in Neglect or Termination Proceedings: A Developing Area" (1973/4) 7

Cerkovnik, M., "The Sexual Abuse of Children: Myths, Research, and Policy Implications" (1985) 2

Claman, L., et al., "The Adolescent as a Witness in a Case of Incest: Assessment and Outcome" (1986) 8

Cohn, A.H., et al., "Is Treatment Too Late: What Ten Years of Evaluative Research Tell Us" (1987) 6

Conger, R.D., "Behavioral Intervention for Child Abuse" (1982) 6

Crouch, J., et al., "Effects of Child Neglect on Children" (1993) 4

Curriden, M., "Sterilization Ordered for Child Abuser" (1993) 9

Daugherty, M.K., "The Crime of Incest Against the Minor Child and the States' Statutory Responses" (1978) 2

Davidson, A.T., "Child Abuse: Causes and Prevention" (1977) 3

Davoren, E., "Working with Abusive Parents: A Social Worker's View" (1975) 6

DeFrancis, V., "Protecting the Child Victim of Sex Crimes Committed by Adults" (1971) 2

DeJong, A.R., et al., "Epidemiologic Factors in Sexual Abuse of Boys" (1982) 2
———, "Epidemiologic Variations in Childhood Sexual Abuse" (1983) 2

Derdeyn, A.P., et al., "Alterna-